STUDIES IN ECONOMICS AND POLITICAL SCIENCE

Edited by

THE DIRECTOR OF THE LONDON SCHOOL OF ECONOMICS AND POLITICAL SCIENCE

No. 67 in the series of Monographs by writers connected with the London School of Economics and Political Science

COMMERCIAL RELATIONS BETWEEN INDIA AND ENGLAND

OTHER WORKS BY THE AUTHOR

(In English)

1. THE INDUSTRIAL DECLINE IN INDIA
2. VEDIC PSALMS. (In press)
3. FROM THE COUNTER TO THE CROWN; OR, A STUDY OF THE CAUSES WHICH LED TO THE ROMANCE OF THE CONQUEST OF INDIA BY A COMMERCIAL CORPORATION. (In press)
4. THEORY OF THE STATE IN ANCIENT INDIA. (Under preparation)

(In Hindi)

1. THE PRINCIPLES OF ECONOMICS. VOL. I
2. HISTORY OF INDIA. 2 VOLS.
3. ANCIENT POLITY
4. MODERN CONSTITUTIONS
5. VEDA—THE WORD OF GOD
6. PHILOSOPHY OF YAGNA
7. SUKRANITI WITH NOTES AND EXPLANATIONS. (In press)

NATOLIAE PARS
ANADOLE
GEMECH
PEGIAN
AR:
MENIA
DIARBECH
Mesopotamia
Cyprus
MARIS MEDI TERRANEI PARS
SYRIA
ARDEN
MOAB
CALDEA
CHALDEA
ARABIA DESERTA
AE GYP TUS
Cabeca de maffamede
MARE RUBRUM
MAR ROXO
AYAM
HEAMA
GANFRILA
AFR
DAFRIL
BARNA
I GASSO
Æ
LACCA
ZIBIT
ADEM
Babelmandel
DANGALI
DOBAS
DOARA
BALLI
ANGO TE
PAR S
MAGADOXO
OLABI
FATIGAR

[front

Bāla-Kṛishṇa

Commercial Relations
between
India and England
(1601 to 1757)

BY

BAL KRISHNA, M.A., Ph.D.,

Fellow of the Royal Statistical Society, London; the Royal Economic Society, London; Professor of Economics, and Principal, Rajaram College, Kolhapur, India

WITH A MAP

London

GEORGE ROUTLEDGE & SONS, LTD.

BROADWAY HOUSE, 68–74 CARTER LANE, E.C.

1924

10-29-47

Printed in Great Britain by
Wm. Brendon & Son, Ltd., Plymouth

PREFACE

THE want of a comprehensive and systematic history of the rise and progress of the most extensive branch of commerce ever known in the annals of mankind and reared up with a marvellous tact and tenacity by a body of London merchants is to be deeply regretted. The romantic creation of an Empire greater than that of ancient Rome, the extraordinary magnitude of the Indo-British trade, the wonderful ramifications of British capital in India, the complete monopoly of the carrying and shipping trades of the major part of the Orient, the political domination of the British in the two continents of Asia and Africa—all demand a serious study of the beginnings of the English relations with the East. The phenomenal growth and gigantic dimensions of the Anglo-Oriental trade in the nineteenth century have led people to forget the long and bitter struggles made by the East India Company to build it up. The slow and sluggish course of the trickling rill of this trade which has swelled to a mighty stream in the present age, does not deserve oblivion.

The real volume and character of the East India Company's trade and navigation which have so long remained hidden from the public view, will form the theme of this work. In the greater part of it I have had no predecessor. The published works of Abbé Raynal, Anderson, Bruce, Charles D'Avenant, Mill, Milburn, Moreau, Macpherson and Wisset, supply only fragmentary evidence for the century and a half dealt with in this book. There is a large number of tracts of controversial character written by the apologists and opponents of the Company in the years 1615–25 and 1670–1710, when questions like the monopoly of the Indian trade by the

Company, the export of bullion and the effects of Indian imports on English manufactures, formed the storm centres of partisan controversy. The writers of the second period were so much occupied with the bullion and protection controversies in the abstract that there is almost nothing in their works on the export and import trade between India and England, and whatever little there is, has been very much marred by their exaggerations and understatements which are only too natural in a polemic literature. The period of fifty-five years from 1625 to 1679 is more or less a blank in all these works, and even before and after this dark period the reader looks in vain for any continuous narration of the extent and character of the commercial dealings of the English before their acquisition of political power in Bengal.

The work opens with a detailed description of the commercial, industrial and economic conditions of India at the beginning of the seventeenth century, and afterwards traces the changes wrought in them by the Anglo-Indian relation during the century and a half following. Then an attempt has been made to construct a consecutive history of the Indo-British trade in all its essential aspects. The structure has been built by collecting data bit by bit from the published and manuscript records at the India Office, the British Museum, the Public Record Office, and the Board of Customs Library.

For the detailed survey of the volume, character and mechanism of this trade, it has been necessary *for the first time* to

1. Fill up the blank from 1625 to 1680 regarding exports, imports and shipping, as far as it was possible to do from the existing records.

2. Compile the annual returns of English exports, separately both in money and merchandise, from 1654 to 1707, from the Letter Books of the Court of Directors of the East India Company and other records.

3. Make a complete list of all the ships that sailed out from England for the Indies from 1601 to 1707, and thus supple-

ment the rare work done by Charles Hardy in preparing "A Register of Ships employed in the service of the Hon. the United East India Company from the Union of the two Companies, in 1707, to the year 1760," published in 1800.

4. Compile a list of the ships which returned home from the East up to 1660.

5. Give the tonnage, destination and cargo of each of the outgoing ships.

6. Collect the annual quantities and values of each of the chief English commodities exported to the East and of those imported into England during the seventeenth century as far as it was possible to do ; and finally,

7. Extract figures for the quantities of Eastern goods imported in each year from 1698 to 1760 from the sixty-two manuscript volumes on imports and exports available in the Public Record Office and the Board of Customs Library.

I have also given a comparative view of the English and Dutch trades with the East, as well as of their shipping, stocks and dividends from the beginning up to 1760, with frequent references to the Portuguese and French activities. This study brings out the essential fact that the trade between England and the East *was not inferior* in value to that between Holland and the Indies, in spite of the much-vaunted monopolies, power and prosperity of the Dutch.

The chapter on the history of the East India Company's shipping with particular reference to the rates of freights paid for the various parts of Asia from the beginning of the practice of freighting ships up to 1760, the system of hiring ships, and the rules of measuring and rating tonnage, will, it is hoped, be of exceptional use and interest to the students of commercial history.

The last chapter presents a short but clear survey of the very intricate subject of the import duties imposed from time to time in England upon the East India goods. It elucidates their working and their consequences on the Indian trade before the foundation of the political sovereignty of the British in India.

The large mass of original information compiled from numerous sources after much investigation has been given in the form of appendices in Part II, with the necessary references in the text.

As all the chapters have been written from the study of original records, manuscript documents, and authentic contemporary accounts, it is to be hoped that the book will prove to be a lucid commentary on the romance of the genesis and rise of the British power and trade in the Indies.

In conclusion, it gives me much pleasure to acknowledge my indebtedness to Professor A. J. Sargent, Mr. W. H. Moreland, and Mr. W. Foster of the India Office for making many valuable suggestions for the improvement of the language and subject-matter of this book.

BAL KRISHNA.

BIBLIOGRAPHY

India Office Manuscript Records

Home Miscellaneous. Vols. 1, 4, 15, 39, 40, 44, 49, 68, 69.

Court Books (Minutes of the Proceedings of the Court of Directors). Vols. 1 to 50.

Dutch Records :

Hague Transcripts. Series I. Vols. 1 to 29 for the years 1600–1670.

Hague Transcripts. Series II. Vols. 1 and 2.

Letter Books (Copies of Despatches from the Court of Directors to the various factories in the East). Vols. 1–18.

Letters received from Bengal. Vols. 1–4.

Factory Records :

Surat. Vols. 1–42.
Patna. Vols. 1, 2.
Hugly. Vols. 1, 2.
Java. Vols. 1–10.
Miscellaneous. Vols. 1 12, 21, 26.

Marine Records, Miscellaneous. Vols. 1, 2, 4.

Marine Journals. Vols. 4, 6.

Miscellaneous. Vols. 1–12.

Mackenzie Collection. 20.1.

Portuguese Records :

Documents Remettidos da India. Vols. 1–4.
Conselho Ultramarinho. Vol. 1, part i.

Public Record Office

Customs 2. Vols. 1–10 for the years 1696–1702.

Customs 3. Vols. 1–60 for the years 1697–1760.

Customs 17. Vols. 12, 13.

Treasury 30. Vol. 1.

Treasury 49. Vol. 1 for 1702–1714:
Papers relating to Import and Export Duties.

Foreign State Papers Archives. Nos. 147–150. Court Books of the Levant Company.

C.O.=Original Correspondence. Vols. 1, 2, 14, 16.

BOARD OF CUSTOMS LIBRARY

(a) Circular Letters issued by the Board of Customs: London and Yarmouth. 1662–1722.

(b) Manuscript volumes of Imports and Exports to supplement the missing ones in the Public Record Office.

(c) Imports and Exports from 1680 to 1732.

(d) Gross and Net Duties on Exports and Imports.

BRITISH MUSEUM MANUSCRIPTS

Additional. 31,146; 34,123; 37,146.

Egerton. 2,123; 2,086.

Harleian. 7,013; 7,019; 7,310.

Jure Impt. 22,185; 15,898; 17,019.

Sloane. 2,902.

State Papers. 22,185; 22,854–56.

PUBLISHED RECORDS

English Factories. Vols. 1–10 for the years 1619–64.

Court Minutes. All the volumes for the years 1635–59.

Calendar of State Papers, East Indies. Five vols. for the years 1515–1634.

Journals of the House of Commons. Vols. 1–14.

Letters Received. Vols. 1–6.

Parliamentary Paper. No. 152 of 1812–13.

Statutes of the Realm. Vols. 5–9.

PUBLICATIONS OF THE HAKLUYT SOCIETY

First Series:

1. The Observations of Sir Richard Hawkins, Knt.
4. Sir Francis Drake his Voyage, 1595.
8. Memorials of the Empire of Japan.

16. John Jourdain's Journal of a Voyage to the East Indies, 1608–17.

18. East and West Indian Mirror.

19. The Voyage of Sir Henry Middleton to Bantam and the Maluca Islands.

22. India in the Fifteenth Century.

32. The Travels of Ludovico di Varthema.

35. A Description of the Coasts of East Africa and Malabar.

36–37. Cathay and the Way Thither.

70–71. The Voyage of John Huyghen van Linschoten to the East Indies.

74–75. The Diary of William Hedges, Esq.

76–77. The Voyage of François Pyrard, of Laval, to the East Indies.

84–85. The Travels of Pietro della Valle to India.

87. Early Voyages and Travels in the Levant.

89. The Philippine Islands, by Antonio de Morga.

Second Series:

1–2. The Embassy of Sir Thomas Roe to the Court of the Great Mogul, 1615–19.

5. The Voyage of Captain John Saris to Japan in 1613.

9. The Journey of Pedro Teixeira from India to Italy by land, 1604–05.

12. The Countries round the Bay of Bengal, by Th. Bowrey.

17, 35, 45. The Travels of Peter Mundy in Europe and Asia.

44, 49. The Book of Duarte Barbosa.

Extra Series:

Vols. 2, 3, 4, 5, 9, 10.

LIST OF BOOKS QUOTED

References in the brackets are to the location of the books in the British Museum Library.

I.O. = India Office. B.M. = British Museum.

A Treatise touching the East India Trade. I.O. Tracts. Vol. 268.

A Letter to a Friend concerning the E.I. Trade. 1696.

A True Relation of Strange and Admirable Accounts, etc. 1622. (582.e.37.)

A Reply to a Paper, etc. 1700. (816.m.13(138).)

A Brief State of the E.I. Trade. 1715. (16.m.11(64).)

A Memento to the E.I. Companies. 1700. (1029.a.31.)

Advantages of the E.I. Trade. 1720. (T.765(1).)

A Discourse concerning the E.I. Trade. (184.a.11.)

A Particular of Silks, etc. 1690. (1888.e.11(46).)

An Historical Account, etc. 1744. (455.g.i.)

Abul Fazl Allami. Ain-i-Akbari, tr. from the original Persian by H. Blochmann, M.A. Calcutta, 1873. Vol. I. Vols. II and III translated by Col. H. S. Jarrett. Calcutta, 1891–94.

Alton, H., and Holland, H. H. The King's Customs. Two vols. London, 1908.

Anderson, A. Annals of Commerce. Four vols.

Avenant, Charles D'. The Political and Commercial Works. (633.f.24–28.)

Baines, E. History of the Cotton Manufacture in Great Britain.

Baldaeus, Philippus. A True and Exact Description of the E.I. Coast of Malabar and Coromandel. 1732. (566.k.8.)

Barretto. Relation de la Province de Malabar. Paris, 1646.

Bartholomeo. Voyages. 1796.

Bernier, François. Travels in the Mogul Empire. 1656–58.

Birdwood, Sir George, and Foster, W. The First Letter Book of the E.I. Company. 1600–19. London, 1893.

Blackmore, E. The British Mercantile Marine. 1890–91. (2248.d.4.)

Book of Rates. { 1642. 1660. 1697. 1714. 1757. } Custom House Library.

Boothby, Richard. A Brief Description of Madagascar. London, 1644.

Bruce, John. Annals of the Honourable East India Company.

Bruton. News from the East Indies, 1632.

BURTON. Zanzibar.

,, Goa. 1890. (10068.aa.40.)

Calendar of the E.I. Company. 1700. (816.m.11.k.)

CANTILLON, P. The Analysis of Trade. 1759.

CAREY, W. H. The Good Old Days of the Honourable John Company. Two vols.

CARKESSE, CHARLES. Acts of Tonnage and Poundage. (288.b. 10 ; 509.h.7(1).)

CARTWRIGHT, JOHN. The Preacher's Travels. London, 1611.

CASTANEDA, F. L. DE. Historia do descobrimento e conquista da India.

Charters of the E.I. Company. India Office Library.

CHILD, SIR JOSIAH. A Treatise on the East Indies Trade. 1677.

,, ,, The Supplement. 1689.

Chronologist, East Indian. Anonymous and dateless. (1434-k-15.)

COKE, ROGER. Reflection upon the E.I. and Royal African Companies. 1696.

,, ,, A Treatise concerning the Regulation, etc. 1696.

Collection of Papers relating to the E.I. Trade. 1730. (1139.c.9 (1).)

Considerations upon the E.I. Trade. 1701. (1139.g.3.)

D'ACUNHA. History of Chaul and Bassein.

DANVERS. A Report on the Marine Records in the India Office.

Diary of Strensham Master. Three vols.

Dictionnaire du Commerce de L'Encyclopédia Méthodique. 1783–9. (12215.t.)

DIGGES, SIR DUDLEY. The Trade's Increase. 1615.

DUPLEIX. Mémoire.

EDGAR, WILLIAM. Customs Vectigalium Systema. 1714.

England. Proclamations II, 1631. (506.h.11(2).)

England's Almanack. 1700. (816.m.11.92.)

FONSECA, J. N. Goa. 1878.

FRYER, DR. JOHN. A New Account of East India and Persia, in Eight Letters. Being Nine Years' Travels. Begun 1672 and finished 1681. London, 1698.

HAMILTON, ALEX., CAPT. A New Account of the East Indies.

HARRIS. Collection of Voyages. Two vols. 1764.

HOBSON-JOBSON. By Yule and Burnell. 1903.

KAUTILAYA. Arthashastra. English tr. Mysore. 1915.

LANGHAM. Net Duties. 1713.

" " " 1757.

LAURISTAN, JEAN LAW DE. Mémoire. Sociétié de L'Histoire des Colonies Françaises.

LEDIARD, THOMAS. Naval History of England. Two vols. 1735.

LEWIS, ROBERTS. The Merchant's Map of Commerce. 1667. (1522.m.8.)

" " The Treasure of Trafficke. 1641. (08245.e.2 (2).)

LOCKYER, CHARLES. An Account of the Trade in India, etc. 1711.

MACCULLOCH, J. R. E. Considerations on the E.I. Trade. (08245.e.218.)

MACGREGOR. Commercial Statistics. 1844–50.

MACPHERSON, DAVID. Annals of Commerce. 1805.

MAHABHARATA. English tr. by M. M. Dass, Calcutta.

MALYNES, G. DE. The Centre of the Circle of Commerce. 1623. (1391.c.18.)

" " The Maintenance of Free Trade. 1622. (712.c.30.)

MANDELSLO. Voyages and Travels of, into the East Indies.

MARCO POLO. The Venetian, concerning the Kingdoms and Marvels of the East. Two vols. London. 1875.

MILBURN, WILLIAM. Oriental Commerce. Two vols. 1813.

MILL, JAMES. History of British India.

MISSELDON, EDW. The Circle of Commerce. 1623. (1029.b.2.)

" " Free Trade. 1622. (712.c.2(1).)

MOREAU, CÆSAR. E.I. Company's Records. 1825. (714.k.17(1).)

" " State of the Trade of Great Britain. (1231.1. (27).)

" " Rise and Progress of the Silk Trade. (714.k.17 (2).)

MOREAU, CÆSAR, Chronological Records of the Royal British Navy. (714.k.17(3).)

MORELAND, W. H. India at the Death of Akbar. London. 1920.

New Dialogues upon the Present Posture. 1710. (104.b.66.)

News from the East Indies. 1691. (816.m.11(77).)

OPPENHEIM, M. Administration of the Royal Navy. 1846. (2248.e.8.)

PETTY, SIR WILLIAM. Political Arithmetic.

POSTLETHWAYT, M. G. Great Britain's Commercial Interest. Two vols. 1759.

Proposals for Settling the E.I. Trade. 1696.

Purchas, his Pilgrims. Original Edition.

Rates of Custom. 1590. (c.40.b.29.)

RAYNAL, ABBÉ, W. F. East and West Indies. Ten vols.

Reasons for Constituting a New E.I. Co. Anonymous and dateless.

Reasons humbly offered, etc. 1697. (1029.a.30.)

Reasons for Restraining the Wearing of Wrought Silks. 1699. (816.m.13(135).)

Reasons against the Prohibiting, etc. 1700. (816.m.13(137).)

Remarks on the Accounts, etc. 1704. (1890.b.4(3).)

ROGERS, J. E. T. History of Prices.

SCOTT, W. R. The Constitution and Finance of English, Scottish and Irish Joint-Stock Companies to 1720. Cambridge. 1910.

SMITH, VINCENT. Akbar.

STAVORINUS, J. S. Voyages to the East Indies.

STEVENS, HY. The Dawn of British Trade to the East Indies as Recorded in the Court Minutes of the E.I. Company. 1599–1603. London. 1886.

TAVERNIER, E. T. Collection of Travels, etc. London. 1684.

TERRY, EDWARD. A Voyage to East India. Reprint from Edition of 1655. London. 1777.

The E.I. Trade. 1693. (816.m.11(81).)

The Pathway to Knowledge. 1596. (c.54.e.9.)

The Petition and Remonstrance of the Governor and Company, etc. 1641. (1029.c.31.)

The Profit and Loss of the E.I. Trade. (100.n.46.)

Valentijn, Frans. Oud en nieuw Oost-Indien. Five vols. Dordrecht. 1724–26.

Watson, Sir C. M. British Weights. 1910. (8548.ccc.13.)

Wheeler, John. A Treatise of Commerce. 1601. (1029.e.52.)

Whiteway. The Rise of the Portuguese Power.

Whitworth, Charles. State of the Trade of Great Britain. 1776. (188.f.10.)

Wilson, C. R. Early Annals of the English in Bengal.

Wisset, Robert. A Compendium of East Indian Affairs. Two vols. 1802.

Wood, William. A Survey of Trade. 1722. (1029.c.25.)

Wylde, Richard. Humble Petition and Remonstrance. 1654. (1029.g.21.)

CONTENTS

PART I.—HISTORY OF THE INDO-BRITISH TRADE

CHAPTER I

CHAPTER II

CHAPTER III

CHAPTER IV

CHAPTER V

CHAPTER VI

CHAPTER VII

CHAPTER VIII

CHAPTER IX

CHAPTER X

PART II.—APPENDICES

CHAPTER I

CHAPTER II

CHAPTER III

CHAPTER IV

CHAPTER V

CHAPTER IX

CHAPTER X

PART I

HISTORY OF THE INDO-BRITISH TRADE

COMMERCIAL RELATIONS BETWEEN INDIA & ENGLAND

CHAPTER I

AT THE DAWN OF THE SEVENTEENTH CENTURY

THE great changes wrought by the Dutch and English in the nature and volume of the internal and external trades of India cannot be intelligently followed until the commercial and industrial conditions and the whole mechanism of the maritime trade of the country at the time of the appearance of those two nations in the Orient be fully grasped. How the whole character of European, Asiatic, and American trades was profoundly modified, how the trade routes changed, how the Turkish, Egyptian, Arabian, and Italian centres decayed, how the Portuguese passed off the stage, how the Indians in particular and the Asiatics in general lost their carrying and foreign trades, can be understood only when we look at these questions before the modifying cause began to operate.

For a realistic comprehension of the mechanism, character, and extent of the maritime activity of India and the vital parts she played in the commerce of the world, it is necessary to study severally the sea-borne trade of the principal marts of Africa and Asia, some of which also served as connecting links between Asia and Europe. It is only then that a fair judgment can be formed of the commercial situation of the country and of its future changes. It is then alone that we can realise how all the streams of ocean-borne commerce converged on Indian soil during the seventeenth century.

Indo-African Trade

Starting from the Cape of Good Hope, we find that the Cape country had not yet been settled, nor its resources tapped by any European nation till then. On the eastern coast of that black continent the chief marts were Sofala, Mozambique, Malinda, Abyssinia, the Islands of Socotra and Madagascar. A summary view of the nature of their foreign trade clearly shows that practically they had commercial relations with no other country but India, and exclusively depended for all kinds of manufactured goods upon her. She, in turn, got her main supplies of gold from the mines of Africa.

Mozambique was a very great and safe haven for ships on the outward voyage from Portugal to India. It was very rich on account of the extensive trade done in the valuable articles found thereabout. Gold, gold dust, ambergris, ebony wood, the blackest and most excellent in the world, large quantities of ivory of the best sort, " vastly pretty " mats, many slaves, both male and female, to do the filthiest and hardest labour, were carried to India from this port. Very fine precious metal was obtained from mines at Manica (Sanskrit, gold), Monotapa, and Sofala. A number of ships laden with these goods sailed from Mozambique in the months of August and September for India, and left that country in April with a merchandise consisting largely of corn, rice, and other grains, calicoes of many sorts in large quantities, silks and beads from Gujerat, spices of Sumatra, earthenware of Pegu procurable at Goa, and some Portuguese goods. Both the outward and inward trade of Mozambique was the monopoly of its Governor and of the Viceroy of Goa. All other merchants were shut out from a share in this lucrative trade.[1]

Next to Mozambique and Sofala was Malinda or Ethiopia, with the chief fortress at Mombassa. Ambergris, myrrh and frankincense were the Ethiopian exports to India. The Island of Socotra furnished a marvellous quantity of dates, aloes Socotrina, very pretty mats of palm leaves, large amounts of gum for covering vessels in the place of tar and pitch, civet-cats, a few horses and some ambergris. The people of this island traded all along the coast of Arabia, and thence to Goa and elsewhere, with passports from the Portuguese like the Indians. They carried back the merchandise of India to Arabia and their own country.[2]

Abyssinia and the northern coast of Ethiopia were the resort of many merchants for the abundant supply of gold, ivory, wax, honey, and especially of slaves, who worked as domestic servants and sailors in many parts of India. Free Arabians and Abyssinian slaves were employed all over India as sailors and seafaring men with such merchants as sailed from Goa to China, Japan, Bengal, Malacca, Ormus, and all the Oriental coast. Even the Portuguese had no other sailors, because it was below their dignity to serve as sailors in India.[3] Each ship had a Portuguese captain, and some galleys had a Portuguese pilot also, while all the rest of the crew used to be Asiatics and mostly slaves.

Thus the whole eastern coast of Africa supplied gold, ivory, ebony and other very useful articles for India, and all

[1] The Account of Ethiopia, by Friar Joanuo Dos Sanctos, surpasses in detail and accuracy that of Barbosa, Linschoten, and Pyrard. Manica was the "land of much gold." Sanctos gives three ways of getting gold in Manica. Purchas, E. S., IX, pp. 200, 217, 234–7. Pyrard, II, pp. 223–37; Linschoten, I, pp. 24–36; Payton, Purchas, E. S., IV, pp. 306–9; Finch, Purchas, E. S., IV, pp. 16–17; Monfart, p. 36.

[2] Linschoten, I, pp. 267–8; Pliny, Bk. XXVII; Purchas, I, pp. 418–19.

[3] Pyrard says that all the Portuguese ships had Indian mariners and officers. The *Indian Christians* dressed in the Portuguese style were not deemed Indians, but Portuguese (II, p. 149). "The vast number of slaves taken thence every year, and carried to America and Portugal, is a marvellous thing indeed, without counting those that remain in the country to serve the Portuguese and the Kings of that coast" (Pyrard, II, p. 322).

these in exchange, mainly for Indian cloths, beads, and provisions. India alone supplied all the clothing required by the Moslem and Christian population of the vast coast of Africa and its adjacent islands.[1]

Indo-Arabian Trade

Passing on to Arabia, we find that *Mocha*, on the Red Sea, was very well situated for an extensive trade, and in general all the manufactures of Europe and India found there a very good market for exchange. It was the key of Egyptian, and through Egypt of the Indo-European trade. The produce of Abyssinia, Egypt, and Arabia and the merchandise of Europe found vent at this place. It supplied India with the best Arab horses, white and black frankincense,[2] "coffee by whole ships lading," the best myrrh, manna, red-dyeing stuffs, ambergris, gold, pearls, aloes, bezoar, raisins, Arabic gum, and many other precious articles.[3]

The ramifications and character of Mocha commerce have been vividly described by an eye-witness, William Rivett. This Englishman had the rare opportunity of visiting this great emporium. He avers in his queer English that this city "serveth the merchants of Constantinopell, Alleppo, Trippolie, Damasco, and Grand Cairo of turbandes, callicoes of all sorts, pyntadoes and divers other coullored stuffs, as also white of *great vallew*, with all sort of spyce, cotton wolle and in fyne indico, *which goeth by this passadge into most parts of the worlde.* They bring also and serveth this place out of India *much iron*, which they reape great benefytt by and are shewer of their sales."

Aden—once the key and capital of all Arabia Felix and an extremely beautiful, populous, ancient, and rich city—had lost its great importance. According to Lewis Barthema

[1] For the volume of trade with India see Appendix.

[2] Frankincense was exported to India, China, and other places in great abundance (Linschoten, II, p. 99; Purchas, E. S., IX, pp. 93, 107, 111).

[3] Alex. Sharpey, 1609; Purchas, E. S., III, p. 57; John Saris, *ibid.*; II, pp. 89–91.

(1503), it was the rendezvous for all the ships which came from India Major and Minor, from Ethiopia and Persia. Then all the ships which were bound to Mecca put in here. Twenty-five ships laden with madder or "Rubricke" alone (a certain red earth used to dye cloth) brought out of Arabia, departed yearly from the city of Aden for India. But much of its trade was during the sixteenth century transferred to Mocha and Ormus.[1] Jourdain found it ruinated and destroyed by the Turks.

This Red Sea trade was indirectly controlled by the Portuguese, since no ship could leave or enter the ports of India without their permits. Except for this restriction Indian and Arabian merchants fully enjoyed this lucrative branch of commerce. Mocha, being the port of Mecca, was greatly frequented by Moslem pilgrims from the whole of the Moslem world. A number of pilgrim and merchant ships used to go to Mocha every year before the monsoons from the various ports of India and Africa, and returned after the rains with the products of Arabia, Africa, and Europe, but particularly with gold and silver.

Purchas gives descriptions of two such fleets which sailed from India to Mocha in 1612 and 1613 (consisting of about fifteen ships each), the tonnage in one case being probably more than 7,500 tons. Captain Sharpeigh found many ships at Mocha "*whereof sixteen were of greatt burthens and of the Indies.*" This testimony is further corroborated by William Rivett, who says, "Wee founde many ships rydinge," while Jourdain on the basis of the information supplied to him by the Governor of Mocha mentions "forty sails of ships great and small."[2] The trade by this route can hence be taken approximately equal to that with Portugal by the sea route, i.e. 10,000 tons either way.

The Euro-Asiatic Centres. From Aden we come to the

[1] Purchas, E. S., IX, pp. 59, 85, 87–8; *cf.* Heynes' account in Purchas, I, pp. 622–3; Jourdain, pp. 74–8; the Adventure of Sir Edward Michelborne in Letter Book, I, p. 247.

[2] Marine Journals, VII; Capt. Sharpeigh's account and William Rivett's Narrative; Jourdain, pp. 100, 104.

main centre of Asiatic trade. The Island of Ormus was the best and the most profitable place of all the Indies. It was a common proverb that if the world were an egg, Ormus would be the yolk. Another proverb made the world a ring and Ormus the gem. It was the best commercial place in the world on account of its central situation for the traffic of all parts. It was really the greatest centre of the Indian, Persian, Arabian, Egyptian, Turkish, Armenian, Syrian, and European trade. There was always a great concourse of the merchants of all nations. The products of Europe, Asia, and Africa were carried there for distribution into various countries. Cotton and silk stuffs, precious stones, spices, pepper, copra, ginger, drugs, and numerous articles used to be carried thither from India. Persia supplied rich carpets, raw silk, silks, horses, rhubarb, pearls,[1] and larins[2] consisting of the finest silver in the world. From Turkey came blankets, turquoises, emeralds, and fine lapis lazuli. Arabia sent its drugs, as also aloes, raisins, manna, myrrh, frankincense, dates, jams, and horses. While quicksilver, vermilion, rose-water, glassware, brocade, silk stuffs, woollens, cutlery, swords, and many other European commodities found their way to Ormus.

In the words of Pyrard, "the merchandise and goods of all the world must pass there and pay tribute to the Portuguese,[3] who search all the ships to see if any merchandise is being carried that is contraband and is prohibited by their King. But that is the place where Governors fill their pockets in as much as they will for money let everything pass." The

[1] Ralph Fitch (A.D. 1583) in Pinkerton's Voyages, Vol. IX, p. 407; 'Abder-Razzak, pp. 5–6.

Pyrard has justly said that the *Persian pearls* are the finest, biggest, and cleanest of any in the E. Indies (II, p. 239; *cf.* Varthema, p. 95).

Four kinds of *manna* (Linschoten, II, p. 100). *Rhubarb* was brought from the Chinese Territory through Persia to Ormus, and thence to India, but the most part of it was carried overland. For European consumption it was mainly carried to Venice. The Portuguese also dealt in it to some extent (Linschoten, II, p. 101).

[2] One larin=1s. nearly.

[3] Monfart saw one ship willingly paying 100,000 franks=£10,000—for her customs (p. 14). This is probably an exaggeration, for the Viceroy Meneses informs us that the annual revenue from the customs of Ormus amounted to £31,875 only.

major portion of the trade was controlled by the Portuguese, who sent their ships to Goa, Chaul, Bengal, Muscat, and other places. No man could buy, sell, lade any commodity before the Portuguese captain had sold, shipped, freighted, and despatched his wares away. The trade in horses was completely reserved for the captain or his licencees. This monopoly gave them immense profits, for horses were very dear and in great demand in India. They were generally sold for four or five hundred pardaos, and some from seven to one thousand pardaos.[1]

So far as the European trade was concerned, *Aleppo* was the chief emporium. It can be called the Queen of the Orient. It was "one of the fairest and greatest mart-cities in the world."[2] All European nations, with the exception of the Spaniards, Portuguese, or other subjects of the King of Spain who were forbidden to trade with Aleppo, used to bring their wares to this centre, had their factors there and returned with Indian goods to Venice, Marseilles, London, Amsterdam, etc. Twice every year, in the months of April and September, two caravans used to come from Aleppo overland through Turkey to the town of Bassora, making a special stay for several days at Bagdad and other principal marts in coming and going. From Bassora the goods were conveyed to Ormus in small boats. Monsieur de Monfart

[1] Pyrard, Part II, pp. 238–45; Linschoten, I, pp. 46–57; Ralph Fitch (1583–91) in Purchas, E. S., X, p. 168; Barbosa, pp. 42–3, 89; Frederick in Purchas, E. S., X, p. 92.

In Yule's Hobson-Jobson the value of pardao or xeraphin at this time is stated from 4s. 2d. to 4s. 6d., or, say, 4s. 4d. The prices of horses would be £104 to £112 a piece, and the best as much as £224. They were imported into Goa free of duty, and even goods brought in ships carrying twenty horses (C. Frederick), and later on, ten (William Barret in Hak. Voy., I, p. 215), were allowed to enter Goa free of duty. But forty pagodas were charged a piece for export from Goa—a pagoda being worth 6s. 8d., the duty amounted to £14 (cf. Barbosa, p. 76). John Cartwright saw some of these horses sold for a thousand and even sixteen hundred ducats a piece (p. 65).

[2] Another caravan has been described by William Lithgow who accompanied it in 1614. It consisted of 1500 men and 100 soldiers. Trade was jeopardised by the naval wars of the Dutch, English, and Portuguese. Moreover, the sea-borne trade of these three nations was telling upon the prosperity of Aleppo, hence the number of men is far smaller this season. (Purchas, E. S., X, p. 481).

(1609) accompanied one such party which consisted of more than ten thousand men.[1] Such a vast number of merchants and other people is a sure index of the immensity of the Euro-Asiatic commerce of those days. *In one word, the European trade through Turkey was centred in Ormus, where the Portuguese held the monopoly of importing horses into India and had, moreover, the privilege of pre-emption in the purchase and disposal of general merchandise.*

Indo-Persian Relations. Before proceeding to witness the busy trade and prosperity of Indian ports, we should get a glimpse of the relation of Persia and India. They had an extensive trade both by land and water from time immemorial.

Persia purchased a great many Europe-manufactured articles, especially coarse woollen cloth of various colours, but a far greater quantity of cotton cloths, drugs, and all the usual exports of India were in constant demand. Spices and metals of the Southern Islands and many Far Eastern products were also carried thither from some entrepôt of the western coast. On the other hand, all kinds of luxury articles and a large quantity of its silver money were brought back to India. There was always a favourable balance for the latter in the Persian trade, paid in the form of larins, which were in request all over the country, because they were of very good silver, and "useful and handy for all occasions."[1]

The tonnage of the Indo-Ormus trade cannot be ascertained, as every traveller has attested the great number of ships in vague terms only. Yet on the evidence of Monfart and Pyrard, one could not place it at less than the Mocha-India trade. In other words, 10,000 tons of shipping either way will be a fair estimate of the Indo-Ormus trade.[2]

[1] Cf. Cartwright's description (1611), pp. 8–9; Varthema, p. 7.

[2] Monfart, pp. 8–13; Pyrard, II, pp. 128, 174, 239, 468; I, pp. 232–4; Varthema, pp. 101–2.

Salbank's Persian Travels by Land and Sea (Purchas, I, p. 237). The best report on the commodities obtainable and vendible is from the pen of John Cartwright (pp. 41, 50, 55). From the Georgian capital Arasse alone, 500 and sometimes 1000 mules laden with silk went to Aleppo (p. 41).

Tatta and Lauribunder

Passing on to the Indian coast, we find that the first city of supreme importance was Tatta. No city was of greater trade in the north of India than Tatta. Its chief harbour was Lauribunder,[1] three days' journey from it. In two months traders could go by water to Lahore, passing Multan on the way, and return in one month. Goods from Agra were carried on camels to Bucker in twenty days, and from that town to Lauribunder in fifteen or sixteen days in boats.

Thus the three most inland, but the most prosperous and greatest emporiums of Central and Northern India found a market for their merchandise in Tatta. The special commodities of local growth were foodstuffs and raw material, like rice, sugar, butter, and salt ; iron, pitch, and tar ; cotton and indigo, though not as good as the Biana kind. Divers sorts of excellent fine cotton-stuffs, baftas, and lawns were available in large quantities. The country was also well known for its horses and camels. Besides these, smoked fish was exported to other ports and cities, affording a considerable profit. Fish oil was also extracted and much used in boat building. "There were also large quantities of most excellent and faire Leather, which are most workmanlike, and cunningly wrought with silke of all colours, both flowers and personages, this leather is in India much esteemed, to lay upon beds and tables instead of carpets (and coverlets), they make also all sorts of desks, cupboards, coffers, boxes,

[1] Sir Thomas Roe's Embassy (Hakl.), pp. 331, 345, 468. As the port of Tatta, Lauribunder was in Roe's time a place of considerable trade ; but changes in the Indus Delta reduced it gradually to insignificance, and now even its site is doubtful (Foster in Embassy, p. 122 n.).

On looking at the maps of the sixteenth and seventeenth centuries preserved in the British Museum, I find that Diul was recognised as a separate port situated at the mouth of the River Indus, which is named R. de Diul Sinde by Linschoten, but he makes no mention of Tatta in his map (569, G. 10, and 10,025, f. 15). On the other hand, Tatta is shown far up the river and Diul on the sea coast in the map of Sir Thomas Roe (K. 115, 22), and that of D. Johanni Huyde Koper, dated 1619 and 1670 respectively. This situation of Diul as a separate port seems to have been based on tradition, because neither Abul Fazl nor Shirley and the English factors at Surat speak of Diul as a separate port.

and a thousand such-like devices all inlaid, and wrought with mother-of-pearl, which are carried throughout all India, especially to Goa and Cochin, against the time that the Portugals shippes came thither to take in their lading." It must have been a busy port, because 40,000 boats of many kinds, large and small, plied about in the River Indus.

The Sind goods were carried to Ormus, Diu, Cambay, Goa, Surat, and many of the Malabar ports. Numerous kinds of Indian commodities were imported into the province in return for them.[1]

Diu was the next important port. Even at the beginning of the *sixteenth* century, it was described by Barbosa as having a very good harbour, much trade in merchandise and much shipping from all parts of the Western world and Malabar. Varthema was a personal witness to the immense traffic of the city, which he calls "The Port of the Turks," probably because four hundred Turkish merchants resided there constantly.[2] It seems to have grown into a still more celebrated port by the occupation of the Portuguese. It has been described by Pyrard as passing fair, rich, and fertile; *innumerable vessels* touched there, and rendered it the most wealthy place in the Indies after Goa. *It was "the mart and staple for all the vessels coming from Cambaye, Surat, the Red Sea, the Persian Sea, Ormus, and other places in the Indies."* There was much traffic with Cambay; numerous barques of 15 to 20 tons burden each plied between the two ports. One could live cheaply and command "all the conveniences and luxuries imaginable." Its custom-house produced the large income of £38,500 for the Portuguese. The Malabar pirates, too, made a great profit by seizing as many boats of the Diu merchants as they liked. Pyrard himself saw them capturing at one swoop forty or fifty of them, and that was no

[1] Thevenot, V, p. 159; Purchas, E. S., IV, pp. 171, 201; Linschoten, I, pp. 55–9; Ain-i-Akbari, II, pp. 337–8; Purchas, E. S., IV, p. 297. Walter Payton's report (A.D. 1613) for the articles required for Sind mentions broadcloth, ivory, iron, tin, lead, steel, spices, and money (Purchas, IV, p. 207). Barbosa, p. 59; Pyrard, II, p. 255. His statement is fully confirmed by Linschoten, I, p. 58; Ralph Fitch, Purchas, X, p. 169; C. Frederick, *ibid.*, p. 89.

[2] Varthema, pp. 91–2.

uncommon occurrence. The coastal trade must have been extraordinarily profitable to meet all those losses on the sea.

Cambay[1] has been called the "Indian Cairo." In modern terminology it can appropriately be styled the "Indian Manchester," being the commercial centre of Gujerat, the Lancashire of India. From Ptolemy onward all travellers have attested its great wealth, magnificence, and flourishing trade. This port being one of the greatest and richest of all the coast towns of India, merchants resorted to it from all quarters of the world. It was the home and nursery of all that was best in India. The workmanship of its inhabitants in weaving and dyeing, in embroidery as well as curious works of art, made of wood, metal, ivory, amber, horns of sea-horses, and various kinds of stones was the wonder of the world. There were found all kinds of cotton and silk manufactures, perfumes, innumerable things of ivory, beautiful woodwork of all kinds, bedsteads of all colours, works of art made of coral, as well as agates, cornelians, onyxes, and other precious stones, delicate cushions, quilted cloths, canopies of delicate workmanship, beautiful paintings, shields made of tortoise-shells which were "wrought and inlaide very workmanlike," fair signets, rings, buttons, handles of knives, and beads of white-as-milk stone which were sold in all parts of the world.

Speaking of the excellence of cotton cloths, Linschoten says that "they make some so fine, that you cannot perceive the threads, so that for fineness it surpasseth any Holland cloth."

The enthusiastic evidence of Pyrard on the greatness and originality of Indian industries and the wonderful culture of the people is of permanent interest :—

In short, I could never make an end of telling such a variety

[1] Yule's Cathay, Vol. II, p. 355; Marco Polo, Vol. II, p. 389; Varthema, pp. 105–7; and Nikitin, II, p. 20; III, p. 19. Realistic description of Cambay by Valle, I, p. 67 *et seq.* Cf. Polo's description of Gujerat, p. 383, and of Monfart, pp. 16–20. Cf. Barbosa—"Thus from Mecca and Aden alone they bring hither coral, copper, quicksilver, vermillion, lead, alum, madder, rose-water, saffron, gold, silver (coined and uncoined), in such abundance that it cannot be reckoned." Conti, early in the fifteenth century, speaks of it as "a very noble city," and Nikitin calls it "a port of the whole India sea."

of manufactures, as well in gold, silver, iron, steel, copper, and other metals, as in precious stones, choice woods, and other valued and rare materials. For they are all cunning folk, and owe nothing to the people of the West, themselves endued with a keener intelligence than is usual with us, and hands as subtle as ours; to see or hear a thing but once, is with them to know it. A cunning and crafty race not, however, fraudulent, nor easy to defraud. And what is to be observed of all their manufactures is this, that they are both of good workmanship and cheap. I have never seen men of wit so fine and polished as are these Indians; they have nothing barbarous or savage about them, as we are apt to suppose. They are unwilling, indeed, to adopt the manner and customs of the Portuguese; yet do they readily learn their manufactures and workmanship, being all very curious and desirous of learning. In fact, the Portuguese take and learn more from them than they from the Portuguese; and they that come fresh to Goa are very simpletons till they have acquired the airs and graces of the Indians. It must then be understood that all these countries of Cambaye, Surat, and others (in the region) of the river Indus and of the Grand Mogor, are the best and most fertile of all the Indies, and are, as it were, a nursing-mother, providing traffic and commerce for all the rest; so, too, is the kingdom of Bengal, where their manners and customs are the same. The people, both men and women, are there more cultivated than elsewhere; those countries are the mart of all the ships of India, and there living is better than anywhere else.

No people in the world know so much about pearls and precious stones; and even at Goa the goldsmiths, lapidaries, and other workmen occupied with the finer crafts are all Banians and Bramenis of Cambaye, and have their own streets and shops.[1]

Cambay was encompassed with a strong brick wall, and had high and fair houses. This mart of Gujerat was "so haunted by the Portugals that you shall often find two hundred frigates at once riding there."[2]

[1] Pyrard, II, p. 230; cf. Monfart, p. 16.

[2] "Cambaya was a very fair city and had a very good and busy harbour. *Innumerable small barks went in and out of the port.* Spices, China silks, sandals, ivory, velvets of Vercini (?), great quantity of Pannina which came from Mecca, gold coins called Chickinos (=7s.) were brought in. The boats which left the harbour were *usually laden with an infinite quantity of cloth* made of bumbast (cotton) of all sortes, as white, stamped and painted with great quantity of Indigo, and conserved dried ginger, Myrabolans,

There was such a large amount of traffic with Goa that two or three times a year "*there went together from three hundred to four hundred vessels,*[1] called Cafilas, of Cambaya, like the caravans of Aleppo." At Goa the whole city looked for these fleets, as in Spain they awaited those from the Indies. At the arrival of a Cambay Fleet, we are told the joy of the merchants and the whole people was marvellous. C. Frederick says that *innumerable vessels came in and out of the harbour, and adds,* "*If I had not seen it, I could not have believed that there should be such a trade as there is.*" The outgoing ships were laden with the produce and the manifold manufactures of Gujerat. Yet the principal exports can be pointed out as indigo; great stores of precious stones, not of the fine sorts, such as diamonds and rubies, but of other kinds, which they knew how to cut skilfully and to work into a thousand pretty things; rock-crystal, iron, copper, rock-alum, wheat, rice, vegetables of various varieties, medicinal drugs, butter, oils of divers sorts, perfumes, white and black soap, sugar, conserves, paper, wax, opium, calicoes of all sorts, cloths painted with various figures, woollen carpets for rough use, cotton carpets with stripes of many colours; cabinets made in the German style and inlaid with mother-of-pearl, ivory, gold, silver, and precious stones; small cabinets, coffers, and boxes of tortoise-shell, "which were polished so clearly

dried and candied, Boraso in paste, great store of sugar, great quantity of Cotton, abundance of Opium, Assafetida, Puchio, with many other sortes of druggs, Turbants made in Diu, great stones like to Corneolaes, Granats, Agats, Diaspry, Calcidoni, hemitists, and some kinds of natural Diamonds.

During the time I dwelt in Cambaitta, I saw very marvellous things; there were an infinite number of Artificers that made Bracelets called Mannii, or bracelets of Elephants teeth, of divers colours, for the women of the Gentiles, which have their armes full decked with them."

Polo's contemporary, Marino Sanudo, called it one of the two chief ocean-ports of India, and in the fifteenth century *Conti described it as* 14 *miles in circuit.*

[1] Cf. Varthema's remark that forty or fifty vessels laden with cotton and silk stuffs sailed from Cambay every year. Again, 300 ships of different countries come and go here (p. 111). Portugal frigates came in fleets two or three times from September to December, guarded by the Portugal "Armatho (Armada) of friggatts; such that you shall see 200 friggatts in a fleete goinge or comeinge from Cambaia to helpe lade the carricks at Goa" (Jourdain).

that nothing could have a prettier effect," tents, bands, called "Parcuites," of fine white cotton, couches and bedsteads that were painted and lacquered with all manner of colours and designs ; silk-stuffs of all kinds, pillows, counterpanes, coverlets of silk, "painted with much neatness and cleverly worked."

Pyrard remarks that *cloths had the whiteness of snow and were very delicate and fine.* Gujerat was the home of textile manufacture. Its silk- and cotton-stuffs were the principal source of riches in India. Pyrard has understated the truth when he remarks that everyone from the Cape of Good Hope to China, man and woman, is clothed from head to foot with stuffs made in Gujerat. We know that all the countries of Asia, Eastern Africa, and of Europe, too, depended upon India for their cotton clothing. In fact, almost the whole planet got its supplies of fine fabrics from Gujerat, "the Lancashire of India," Bengal, the "Paradise of Nations," and the numerous cities of the Coromandel coast.

The considerable traffic of this premier port of India could not amount to less than 100,000 tons per annum. Taking the tonnage of barques plying between Goa and Cambay to be 50 tons each, we find the outward total tonnage from Cambay to Goa comes to more than 43,000 tons.[1] Assuming half of the Diu traffic with Cambay, we have 48,000 tons for the two ports alone. When we think of the Cambay trade with Mocha, Ormus, Maldives, and the numerous ports of India, we are sure that the most modest estimate could not be less than 100,000 tons per annum.

Surat, the "gate of Mecca," or the "city of the sun," was another celebrated port of Gujerat. It could not rival the traffic, wealth, prosperity, and culture of the now-forgotten port of Randir in the beginning of the sixteenth century. Both the cities suffered terribly from the destruction wrought by the Portuguese in 1512 and 1530. Randir could not recover from that mortal blow, so that much of the traffic was transferred to Surat. The Rev. Patrick Copland (1611–14)

[1] 350 barques $\times \frac{5}{2}$ times $\times$ 50 tons each barque=43,750 tons.

found in it many stone and brick houses which were fair, square, and flat-roofed. The city was adorned with goodly gardens full of various fruits continuing all the year round. The people were " grave, judicious, neat, tall, goodly cloathed in long white Callico or Silk robes."[1] It could use everything from whatever quarter in India it might come. As at Cambay and Goa, commerce was very extensive here, both in exports and imports, because the Mogul Empire and the Moslem Deccan States swallowed a great deal of goods, to which might still be added the great demand of the decaying Vijyanagar chiefs. All this meant a considerable vent of every kind of merchandise. It was also a very convenient place for the exchange of Malabar, the Deccan, and up-country goods. Hence, it was " one of the most eminent cities for trade in all India."

Surat annually exported[2] all sorts of piece-goods, white, coloured, and striped, for which Gujerat was so famous, and all the other goods provided by Cambay, besides Chinese, European, Malabar, Southern and Eastern commodities of all kinds. It was also an entrepôt for the up-country produce as far as Cashmir, Lahore, and Agra. Taking into consideration the very considerable activity of Surat, we shall find that, for reasons stated elsewhere, the aggregate gross tonnage of the ships entering or leaving Surat probably approached the amount of 20,000 tons per year. (App.)

The Decay of Malabar Ports

Next to Surat, *Daman* was a place of moderate trade under Portuguese control. It had lost its ancient importance, as had other ports on the same coast.

Bassein[3] was, however, the great shipbuilding harbour of those days. It has also rich quarries of very fine and hard

[1] Cf. Valle, I, pp. 10–16, 296; Copland in Purchas, E. S., IV, p. 140; Payton (1613), Purchas, E. S., IV.

[2] Finch in Letters Received, I, p. 30; Terry in Purchas, E. S., IX, p. 24; Samuel Bradshaw's report on Surat exports and imports; Letters, I, p. 76; Bombay Gazetteer, Vol. II.

[3] Valle, I, pp. 140–3.

freestone resembling granite, and was the favourite resort of the wealthier Portuguese, as well as the seat of the governor, who was styled the General of the North. Next to Ormus, it brought the greatest revenue into the Portuguese treasury.

Dabul,[1] a port of very great antiquity, was a place of much traffic in all sorts of merchandise in the days of Barbosa and Varthema. Although it had sadly suffered under the adverse influence of the Portuguese, yet it was not a mean place at the end of the sixteenth century. According to Green, the town had "nine ships of great burthen and draughts, the least of them drawing 18 or 20 feet, being laden." These ships yearly sallied out with very rich commodities. Jourdain informs us that two or three ships of great burden and far richer than those that went for Surat, every year sailed to the Red Sea, and two more very rich ships used to go to Ormus.

Chaul[2] had remained one of the most important seaports in Western India from long before the days of Ptolemy. It was the chief mart of Gujerat and a place of great commerce at the time of Barbosa's visit. De Barros describes it as a city which in population and size was one of the most important of that coast. It did not lose its importance during the sixteenth century on account of its excellent position as an entrepôt for the Malabar and Cambay ships. Pyrard alludes to it in these words: "The country there is vastly rich, and productive of all kinds of valuable merchandise, which the merchants from all parts of India and the East come to seek. But the chiefest are the silks, which are obtained there in such quantity that alone they almost supply Goa and all India. They are of a different quality from those of China; and at Goa no account is made of any but Chaul silk, whereof very pretty stuffs are made; it also largely supplies choice cotton fabrics."

[1] Barbosa, p. 72; Varthema, p. 114; Pyrard, II, p. 259.

[2] Barbosa, p. 69; Linschoten, I, pp. 63–4; Frederick in Purchas, E. S., X, pp. 91–2; D'Cunhe's History of Chaul and Bassein; cf. Varthema, pp. 113–14.

"Golden Goa"

Before we pass on to Goa, it should be remembered that many ports had fallen into decay during the hundred years of Portuguese domination in the Indian waters. Barbosa names about fifty seaports from Debul Sind to Comorin on the western coast of India. The Portuguese monopoly very much curtailed the activities of small ports and concentrated commerce in a few big cities alone. The works of Linschoten, Pyrard, and other travellers take no notice of the numerous port towns so enthusiastically described by Barbosa. Goa, the metropolis of the Portuguese East, had robbed all other ports of their ancient importance and fame. "Golden Goa" stood, "like imperial Rome, on seven hills." It had become a wonder of the East for its power, opulence, trade, elegant buildings, and the luxury of its inhabitants. It was the rendezvous of the merchants of all Eastern nations. Venetians, Italians, Germans, Flemings, Castilians, and Englishmen were also settled there. It was "a marvel to see the great multitude of people that came and went every day by sea and by land, on all manner of affairs." According to Pyrard, it was the finest spectacle in the world to see the vast number of ships that lay at anchor in the harbour. The mighty traffic and commerce that was done there, was such, indeed, that every day "seemed fair-day." Its population has been estimated to be 225,000 souls, three-fourths of whom were Christians, and yet the clergy were not included in this estimate. Being the seat of the Portuguese Government in the East, it was a centre of all their commercial activities. Its immense traffic is evidenced by the arrival of about one thousand Cambay barques, by a fleet of about two hundred and fifty ships bound for the south and other fleets for Ormus, Africa, and Europe. The annual tonnage of the ships entering and leaving Goa for the various parts of the world must have been far more than that of Cambay.[1]

[1] Pyrard, II, pp. 27, 67, 178; Linschoten, I, p. 184; Purchas, E. S., X, p. 101. "Goa," by Klognen, p. 20; Varthema, pp. 119–25.

The Malabar Trade

The whole strip of the sea coast from Goa to Comorin was, and is even now, known by the name of Malabar. It has been described as wonderfully fertile, vastly rich in natural resources and productive of many kinds of valuable merchandise which merchants from all over the East and the West came to seek at its numerous ports. Onore, Barcelor, Cannanore, Calicut, and Cochin were the principal ports which, with the exception of Calicut, were held by the Portuguese. Large quantities of pepper, ginger, cinnamon, cardamoms, beetle, areca, cocoanut, copra, cocoanut oil, fine timber for the manufacture of ships and house furniture, rice, butter, sugar, and palm-sugar were exported from all these ports. Different kinds of cotton cloths were also available for export.[1]

The Portuguese, however, controlled the exclusive purchase of pepper, and none others dared buy it in those parts. As the allied princes and their subjects had liberty to trade with or without the Portuguese passports, the best pepper was exported to Mocha and other places, and the worst handed over to the Portuguese on account of their offering fixed rates which had been settled by several treaties with the Malabar princes.[2] The King of Portugal had prohibited the export of ginger on the ground that it interfered with the sale of his pepper. On account of this restriction, the West Indies ginger was largely used in Europe in those days. It is strange to say that cinnamon, the third great product of Malabar, was also forbidden to be carried into Portugal; yet

[1] Pyrard, II, pp. 355–6; Frederick in Purchas, E. S., X, p. 102; Linschoten, I, p. 70. The people of Malabar, especially the Moguls, Nairs, merchants, and bankers, lived in great luxury. They wore ear-rings of very precious jewels and pearls set in gold, on their arms from the elbows upwards gold bracelets, with similar jewels and strings of very large pearls. At their wrists they wore jewelled girdles. They always used perfumes, sat upon carpets of cloth of gold and silk, and leant upon pillows of cotton, silk, and fine cloth. But the lot of the common people was very deplorable. This account of Barbosa is confirmed by Pyrard after the lapse of a century (Barbosa, pp. 40–48; Pyrard, I, pp. 377, 385–8).

[2] Portuguese Records (Doc. Remettidos, Vol. I, doc. 8).

a great quantity of it was every year shipped under the name of Ceylon cinnamon, and full customs duty was paid on it. According to Linschoten, its price was 25–30 against 100 pardaos for the Ceylon kind. The manner of Portuguese trade with the Malabar ports will be described later on. Here we will notice the great traffic of the two important ports of Calicut and Cochin.

Calicut was the greatest Malabar port before the arrival of the Portuguese. Their frequent depredations on its shipping, and continued wars both on land and sea against its King, reduced the great traffic of this famous city. The rival town of Cochin became, next to Goa, the centre of Portuguese commerce in India. The Raja of Calicut ever remained a sworn enemy of the Portuguese, and continually harassed them by an organised system of piracy conducted under his patronage by the Malabars.[1] With the decay of the Portuguese power in India, he began to regain his former supremacy. Pyrard found his country thickly populated and adorned with great and beautiful cities, of which the chief was Calicut. No country in all the Indies was, in his opinion, better furnished with all commodities. It was famous for a marvellous abundance of pepper, ginger, cinnamon, cardamoms, tamarind, cocoanuts, rice, and different kinds of wood which were the principal source of the country's wealth. A great store of precious stones of all sorts, except diamonds, very fine cotton fabrics which bear the name of "calico," and "divers sorts of painted and patterned tapestry," were exported from it.[2] It has been described as a very fair and great city, "the busiest and most full of all traffic and commerce in the whole of India." It had merchants from all parts of the world, and of all nations and religions by reason of the liberty and security accorded to them there. The circuit of the city proper was more than five leagues. It was really a large district covered with handsome, large, and magnificent buildings and spacious enclosures in such wise that a single house required a very

[1] Linschoten, I, pp. 68–73 ; Pyrard, I, p. 375, for the sound policy of the Raja.

[2] Pyrard, I, pp. 371, 398–400.

large space for all its gardens, orchards, fish-ponds, and plantations. Their markets were so full of people of all races, from the Cape of Good Hope to Japan, all the day long, that it was difficult to pass through them.

Such is the glowing description of Calicut at the beginning of the seventeenth century from the pen of Pyrard, whom eight months' residence in this famous city gave exceptional opportunities to observe the grandeur and prosperity of a great commercial town under Indian rule. Calicut was then outrivalled by **Cochin** in traffic, opulence, and elegance of buildings. The latter had become the greatest centre for the export of Malabar produce to all parts of the world. Next to Goa it was the important emporium of Portuguese trade. There were really two towns known by the name of Cochin, the one under the Moslem king of its own and the other under the Portuguese. Both were connected with each other by beautiful suburbs, and were practically one so far as trade was concerned. Their traffic must have been very considerable, because ships to and from Portugal, Malacca, and China touched here, and the whole Southern Armada made Cochin its resting-place for a few days. There was also a great direct traffic with Bengal. Many ships laden with Malabar produce and cowries brought from the Maldives left Cochin every year for Bengal, the Coromandel coast, and the Eastern countries. We learn from Bacarro (Manuscript, folio 315) that thirty ships or more used to come to Cochin every year from Bengal, and that every ship brought a capital of more than 20,000 xeraphins. In other words, the value of Bengal exports to Cochin alone was 600,000 xeraphins, or £130,000 per annum.[1]

"The Pearl Island." The fertile island of Ceylon,[2] where the Portuguese held the port of Colombo with a few other minor ports at a great expense on account of continual wars with its inhabitants, has been the seat of great traffic from the remotest antiquity. There was constant intercourse between India and Ceylon from prehistoric times. It has been

[1] Pyrard, I, pp. 433–8; Hobson-Jobson, p. 423.
[2] Barbosa, pp. 145–54; Pyrard, I, p. 404.

famous for its cinnamon, areca, cardamoms, elephants, ivory, ebony, snake-wood, precious stones, such as topaz, emeralds, garnets, water sapphire, chrysoliths, spinels, star stones, firmament stones, rubies, hyacinths, cat's eyes, ape stones and serpentine stones, and small quantities of gold, silver and iron, but above all, pearls, which have given the country the romantic name of the "Pearl Island." Coffee and tea were not among the produce in those days. There must have been a great traffic for all these valuable articles. No definite idea of the volume of its trade can be had. *Ribeiro observed that no less than a thousand small boats were loaded every year with areca alone.* According to Pyrard, areca grew in such abundance that all India was supplied with it from Ceylon, so that "a great traffic was carried on to all parts, for whole ships are laden with it for conveyance elsewhere." Then trade in cinnamon and elephants was no less considerable. These animals, being obtainable there at a small price, were carried to India and sold at from 1000 to 1500, and some even so cheap as from 400 to 600 ducats in the Malabar and Coromandel countries. We have also to take into consideration the number of ships that arrived there from Bengal and the Coromandel coast laden with cloths, rice, butter, and other provisions. At least one Portuguese galleon used to go to Ceylon every year for the lading of cinnamon, and then Indian junks from the whole western coast of India went there for exchanging Indian products with the valuable commodities to be obtained in the island. Under these circumstances 15,000 tons of shipping will be a fair estimate of the Indo-Ceylonese trade.[1]

The Coast of Coromandel was said to extend from *Negapatam*[2] to the celebrated port of Masulipatam. The former was a very great city, and "very populous of Portugals and

[1] Linschoten, I, p. 80; Pyrard, II, pp. 140–50, 358; Barbosa, p. 170. The wonderful and delicate workmanship of the Ceylonese in gold, silver, ivory, iron, steel, and other materials has been eulogised by both Linschoten (I, p. 81) and Pyrard (II, p. 142).

Some stones were half ruby and half sapphire, others were half topaz and half sapphires, and also cat's eyes (Barbosa, p. 169).

[2] Dutch Records, Vol. XXIII, 639, doc. C. Frederick, pp. 108–9. Correa (1540) saw 700 sail loading rice at Negapatam (Hobson-Jobson, p. 974).

Christians of the country and part Gentiles," though it was a place of small trade. Next came the famous port of *St. Thomé* or Mailapur, the chief city of Narsingha or the Vijyanagar state, and a town of great traffic. Though not very extensive it was, in the judgment of Frederick, the fairest in all that part of the Indies.[1] The sea was very dangerous, and yet the people could dexterously lade and unlade ships by means of their barques, called "catameroni" by Balbi, and catamarans in later times.[2] It seems to have regained its former greatness under the Portuguese, for Barbosa speaks of it as almost uninhabited. Then ten or twelve miles south of Masulipatam was *Narspur Petta*, situated on the banks of a river. It was the greatest centre of the shipbuilding industry on that coast. Moslems, Portuguese, and Hindus built their vessels in that place, since all materials, wood, iron, and other things, were found there in abundance, and also the wages of workmen were very low.

Masulipatam, immortalised by Ptolemy in his Tables and the Periplus[3] as Masalia, has been since the dawn of authentic history famous for the export of cotton piece-goods. Kalinga was already well known for its diaphanous muslins in the time of Sakya Muni Gotam (600 B.C.), as may be seen in a story related in the Buddhist annals.[4] It was a very busy seaport. Every year ships were sailing to the coasts of Bengal, Arracan, Pegu, Tenasserim, laden with all sorts of cotton cloths, glass, iron, cotton yarn, both red and white; tobacco and certain sea-shells called cowries, which were used as money in Bengal and Arracan; also some spices and sandal-wood. In return they brought rice, cotton, silk, seed of gingili, sugar, all sorts of woven fabrics, some fine quilts, rubies, sapphires, gum-lac, benzoin, gold, tin, dyeing wood, glazed and porcelain ware, and a certain beverage called "Nijpa."

Ships also sailed to Malacca, Achin, Priaman, Queda, and Perak, laden with all sorts of painted cloths and rice, bringing

[1] Barbosa, p. 174; Linschoten, I, p. 82.
[2] Balbi, Viaggio, f. 82; Fryer, p. 24.
[3] Periplus, p. 47. [4] Marco Polo, p. 349.

in return sulphur, camphor, silk, tin, and some Gujerat cloths, also pepper from Priaman, and some chinaware which they bought there from the Chinese for selling on the coast.

Other ships sailed to Ceylon and the Maldives, laden with rough cotton cloths, bringing in return "kayro"[1] for making ropes, and "cocoa-nuts which were antidotes against poison." From Ceylon they brought cinnamon, fine mats, cocoa-nuts, and some precious stones, to be sold on the coast, especially at Masulipatam.[2] *Sometimes one hundred ships were seen sailing from the Southern Islands,*[3] *"laden with spicerie, linen-cloth, and china commodities; besides stones and other wealth."*

On account of this immense traffic the whole country along the coast, except the kingdom of the Carnatic or Carnata of old, was in a most flourishing condition. A great number of magnificent temples, extensive pagodas, elegant public buildings, fortified towns and maritime cities were incontestable monuments of its vast riches, arts, and industries. The towns of Pulicat, Sadras, Conjivaram, Cuddalore, and St. Thomé were centres of maritime commerce. The manufacture of cotton fabrics of exceeding fineness and of various kinds, coloured, painted, white, was a speciality from most ancient days. *Marco Polo found the most delicate buckrams of the highest price which "in sooth looked like tissues of spiders' web" being exported to all the quarters of the planet. "There is no King or Queen in the world but might be glad to wear them,"*[4] was the concluding remark of that keen observer on the excellence of those cloths. Then at the close of the sixteenth century, Linschoten observes that "there is excellent faire linnen of cotton made in Negapatan, Saint Thomas, and Musulepatan, of all colours, and woven with divers sorts of loome workes (flowers) and figures, verie fine and cunningly wrought, which is much worne in India, and

[1] See Hobson-Jobson.
[2] Dutch Records, I, 27, doc. 16, 7–8; John Davis (1599); Purchas, II, p. 325.
[3] R. Fitch (1583–91) in Purchas, E. S., X, p. 172.
[4] Polo, p. 349.

better esteemed than silke, *for that it is higher prised then silke*, because of the fineness and cunning workmanship."[1]

Besides these piece-goods and chintz, diamonds, rubies, pearls, agate, indigo, rice, etc., used to be exported in return for spices of all sorts, sulphur, spelter, tin, lead, musk, Pegu rubies and spinels, Malabar pepper, vermilion, quicksilver, coral, alum, gum-lac, benzoin, gold, all sorts of China silk-stuffs, porcelain, sandal, copper, camphor, velvets, rose-water, opium, many Cambay and Europe goods.

From the Coromandel we pass on to **Orissa and Bengal.** The produce and manufactures of the former as described by Frederick and Fitch,[2] were in general similar to the two countries between which it lies. Bengal was rightly called the "Paradise of Nations" on account of its extraordinary fertility and the incredible abundance and cheapness of its manifold produce. Barbosa names Bengala[3] as the principal

[1] Linschoten, I, p. 91.

Barbosa describes the Hindu merchants of this coast as "very sharp, great accountants, and dexterous merchants" (p. 174).

[2] Frederick, p. 112; Fitch, p. 182. In the port of Orissa, every year were laden twenty-five or thirty ships, large and small, with rice, various sorts of fine white calicoes, oil, great store of butter, lac, long pepper, ginger, mirobolans, great store of cloth of "herbes," which was a kind of silk that "groweth amongst the woods without any labour of man" (Frederick, p. 113).

[3] *The situation of Bengala*, according to the ancient maps, is a little further east of Chatigam or Chitagong, the Porto Grande of the Portuguese. For instance, the positions of the principal ports on the Bay of Bengal, going from west to east, are given as follows:—

Map of Linschoten—Satigam, Chatigam, Bengala.
" Sir T. Roe—Angeli, Satagam, Bicanapor, Charegam, Bengala.
" N. Sanson—Ongely, Satigam, Chatigam, Bengala (A.D. 1652).
" D. Johanni—Satigam, Chatigam, Bengala.

But the position is reversed in the map of Di Giacope di Gastatchi piemontese Cosmographe (K. 115, 21): Satigam, Bengala, Chatigam.

Then we read these words in the Map of Commerce (A.D. 1638): "In Bengala are found the cities of Cattigam and Satigan, and principally for trade that of Bengala, on the banks of a Gulph known by that name."

It is very strange that Abul Fazl, Frederick, and Ralph Fitch should make no mention of the port of Bengala. If it was a very great centre of trade, it could not be left by the three keen observers who had personal knowledge of Bengal and its neighbouring kingdoms.

Mr. Mansel L. Dames has examined the whole controversy on the situation of this port in his edition of the Book of Duarte Barbosa, and arrived at the conclusion that, "Gaur taken together with its subordinate ports was the place known as Bengala in the early part of the sixteenth century" (Vol. II, p. 145, Hakl. Soc.).

mart of the province. It was a very great city with a very good harbour. Many foreigners, as the Arabs, Persians, Abyssinians, Portuguese, and Gujerats lived there. They were all great merchants and owned large ships of the same build as those of Mecca, and others of the Chinese build which they called "Jungos." These were "very large and carried a very considerable cargo." With these vessels they navigated to the numerous ports of the Coromandel, Malabar, Cambay, Pegu, Tenasserim, Sumatra, Ceylon, and Malacca, and traded in all kinds of goods. They lived in great luxury, and even the common people were well off. The latter wore white shirts half-way down the thigh and drawers, and very small head-wraps of three or four turns; all of them were "shod with leather, some with shoes, others with sandals, very well worked, sewn with silk and gold thread."[1]

One century after, both Linschoten and Pyrard[2] fully bear out this account in all its details, only the ancient port had lost its importance. Satgaon, commonly called by the Portuguese Porto Pequeno, was the traditional mercantile capital from the Pauranic age to the time of the foundation of the town of Hugly by the Portuguese. Frederick and Fitch both describe it as "a reasonable faire citie for a citie of the Moores" and one which abounded in all things.[3] Every year thirty or thirty-five ships were laden with Bengal merchandise, and the former traveller saw eighteen ships of the Portuguese at the port. Its decay commenced in the latter part of the sixteenth century, owing to the silting up of the channel of the Saraswati. Abul Fazl clearly mentions that out of the two towns of Satgaon and Hugly, situated at a distance of a mile from each other, the latter was the more important, and that both of them were in the possession of the Europeans.[4]

These were no other than the Portuguese outlaws who had

[1] Barbosa, p. 181; Varthema, p. 210: "One of the best that I had hitherto seen."

[2] Linschoten, pp. 92–7; Pyrard, I, pp. 333–4.

[3] Frederick, pp. 114–15; Fitch simply borrows his account from Frederick, p. 182.

[4] Ain-i-Akbari, II, p. 125.

no forts, nor any government, nor policy as at Goa, but "lived in a manner like wild men, and untamed horses."[1] They did much mischief by their piracies, "living in no forme of subjection to God or man."[2]

The principal exports of Bengal were its piece-goods of various sorts, named "Sarapuras, Cassas, Comsas, Beatillias, Satopassas, and *a thousand such-like names.*" *These were very fine and much esteemed in India.* They were not only carried all over India and the East, but also into Portugal and other countries of Europe. Fine and flowered tussar[3] stuffs were another speciality of Bengal. Butter, rice,[4] wheat, opium, saltpetre, raw silk, ginger, lac, cotton, long pepper, borax, musk, agate, civet,[5] elephants, furniture, and large quantities of black and red pottery, like the finest and most delicate *terre sigillee*, fruits and scented oils, sugar[6] and rattan—these might be named as the chief commodities which were imported from the province. The leather[7] industry was no less remarkable. The last, but by no means the least, articles of export were the slaves and eunuchs of Bengal. According to the testimony of Barbosa, eunuchs were sold as merchandise for 20 or 30 ducats each to the Persians, who valued them

[1] Linschoten, I, p. 95.

[2] Wm. Finch, p. 71; confirmed by many other travellers, as Pyrard, I, p. 334; Bernier, I, p. 94.

[3] *Herba cloths* were so decorated with "flowers, branches, and personages that it was wonderful to see, and they were so finely done with cunning workmanship, that they could not be mended throughout Europe" (Linschoten, I, p. 96).

[4] *Rice* was more abundant than in all the rest of the Eastern countries. Every year divers ships came there from all places, and yet there was "never any want thereof, and all other things in like sort, and so good cheap that it were incredible to declare."

[5] *Civet* was bad in Bengal on account of adulteration and was much brought into India from Portugal, where it was obtained from Guinea (Linschoten, II, pp. 95–6; Pyrard, I, pp. 327–34).

[6] *Sugar.*—Barbosa states that they did not know how to make loaves of sugar, yet many ships were laden with powdered sugar for sale to all parts (p. 179).

[7] *Leather.*—The harness of Goa horses, as, in fact, in other parts of India, was supplied from Bengal, China, and Persia; it was all of silk embroidery, and enriched with gold and silver and fine pearls. The stirrups were of silver gilt, the bridle was adorned with precious stones, silver, and with silver bells (Pyrard, II, p. 75. See the description of the Vijyanagar army by Nuniz and Paes, Sewell's Forgotten Empire).

much as guards to their wives and houses. Both Linschoten and Pyrard have given detailed accounts of the existence of slavery in Bengal.[1]

Gold and diamonds,[2] though probably not exported, were found in small quantities in the country.

In exchange for its cheap and abundant exports, Bengal received all sorts of spices, ivory, ebony, and many other sorts of fine wood for the making of house furniture ; cowries, tin, copper, spelter, salt, sandal, radix china, rhubarb, porcelain, but above all, every sort of coined money. Need we say that Bengal was annually enriched with a large influx of gold and silver, brought for the purchase of its much-needed produce and manufactures ? It yielded the palm to none in the excellence of its extremely fine and delicate fabrics, coloured as well as white. From the days of Chandergupta Mauriya[3] (fourth century B.C.) to the end of the eighteenth century, the textile industry was the mainstay of Bengal as of all India. Pyrard outdoes Linschoten in his praise of Bengal piece-goods. "*Some of these cottons and silks are so fine that it is difficult to say whether a person so attired be clothed or nude.*"[4]

The finest muslins of Bengal were known to the ancient Greeks, from whom they received the name of Gangitiki, indicating that they were made on the borders of the Ganges. They were known to the world by many picturesque names, as "flowing water," "morning dew," "woven air," and the like. This wonderful superiority continued for more than two millenniums, and made Bengal a sink of silver and gold.

The Near East. Passing from Bengal along the coast, we see many small kingdoms, like those of Arracan, Martaban,

[1] Barbosa, p. 180; Varthema, p. 258; Linschoten, p. 94; Pyrard, I, p. 332.

[2] The manner of finding out *diamonds* from river beds has been described by the native historian whose work was translated by Gladwin (p. 24).

[3] Cf. Kautilya. Of cotton fabrics, those of Madhura (southern coast of Coromandel), of Aparanta (Concan), western parts of Kalinga (Orissa and Northern Coromandel), of Kashi (Benares), of Vanga (Bengal), of Vatsa (Kausambi, near Calicut), and of Mahisha (Mahashmati), are the best (p. 94).

[4] Pyrard, I, p. 329 ; cf. Barbosa, p. 95.

Tenasserim, Pegu, Siam, Camboja, and Cochin China.[1] With all of them India had direct commercial relations. All these territories can be treated in one group. They yielded, as they do even now, large quantities of fragrant wood, as aloes wood, benzoin,[2] and the "costly sweet wood called calamba (Lignum aloes), which being good was weighed against silver and gold." Sapan wood, rhubarb, radix china, musk, camphor, lac, ivory, tin, spelter, long pepper, elephants, and glazed earthenware were the chief articles of export. The most valuable contribution to the markets of India was in gold, silver, rubies,[3] sapphires, spinels, some diamonds and emeralds, and bezoar stones which were very costly, being antidotes to poison. Cochin China was, moreover, noted for its great quantities of raw silk, silk-stuffs, marble, fine skins, and many other commodities that China proper produced.

These countries took in payment of their valuable goods a few Europe-manufactured articles through the Portuguese, but mainly white and coloured piece-goods from Bengal, Coromandel, and Gujerat; various silk-stuffs made in India, Cambay drugs, pearls, Malabar pepper, rose-water, lead, iron, steel, copper, vermilion, and quicksilver. Spices and chinaware were brought from the port of Malacca. Frederick says that one ship sailed in September from St. Thomé with white and painted cottons and a great store of red yarn, while another ship from Bengal laden with fine cotton cloth of all sorts arrived at the departure of the St. Thomé ship. A small bale of cloth cost a thousand or two thousand ducats. Many small vessels from Malacca and ships from Mecca laden with woollens used to visit these kingdoms every year.

The Spice Islands, lying to the south-east of India, next claim our attention. The Moluccas, Java, Sumatra, and Borneo have been famous for their spices, gold, and other

[1] For general description of the products of these countries, see Linschoten, I, pp. 97–104; C. Frederick, p. 125; Balbi, p. 157; Barbosa, p. 184.

[2] *Benzoin.*—"It is much trafficqued withal throughout India, for it is one of the costliest drugges in all the Orient, because it excelleth all others in sweetness" (Linschoten, pp. 96–8; Pyrard, p. 360; Monfart, p. 34).

[3] *Rubies.*—"They have such quantities that they know not what to do with them, but sell them at most vile and base prices" (Frederick, p. 13).

valuable products since the days of Rama, and later on of Ptolemy. All of them were extended limbs of India, on account of the settlements of the Indians and the great traffic carried on between them and the mainland. The wave of Moslem dominance swept away the ancient Indian civilisation, yet the economic connection was not severed. The Portuguese controlled the major part of the traffic by holding the fortified city of Malacca, the great centre of Indo-Chinese trade. Varthema asserts that more ships arrived here than in any other city in the world.[1] It continued in its prosperity all through the sixteenth century under Portuguese rule, so that Camoens has rightly styled it the Home of Opulence.[2] In the beginning of the seventeenth century Pyrard attests to its greatness by remarking that it was the richest and busiest in all the Indies, after Goa and Ormus, owing to the great cargoes from Japan, China, India, the Moluccas, and other adjacent islands.[3] All ships between Goa and Japan had to pay their dues there. It was a great market for cotton-stuffs, Cambay drugs, Malabar pepper, Bengal sailcloth, sugar, salt, opium, beads, and leather articles from various parts of India. China porcelain, Japan curiosities, Persian tapestries, European woollens and metals were in great demand.

The Clove Islands of the Moluccas consisted of a group of well-known islands, Ternate, Tidore, Mortir, Bachian, and Makian. They had such a marvellous quantity of cloves that the whole world was supplied therewith by them. They also exported camphor, gold, tin, ivory, rattan, rosin, amber, benzoin, and paradise-birds.[4]

The independent kingdom of **Banda** yielded no other

[1] Varthema, p. 224; Barbosa, p. 191.

[2] Camoens, X, p. 44.

[3] Pyrard, II, p. 150; Linschoten, I, pp. 104–6.

[4] Varthema, p. 246; Barbosa, p. 202; Linschoten, pp. 116–18; Pyrard, II, pp. 166–7; English Report for goods obtainable in these islands, Letters, I, p. 74; Roe's Embassy, p. 488; Buleau's Expedition in Harris's Voyages; Voyages under the D.E.I. Co., pp. 278–91; see observations of Saris touching the marts and merchandise of the Near and Far East in Purchas, I, pp. 386–95; description of Banda and Moluccas, by H. FitzHerbert, Purchas, I, pp. 697–9.

products but nutmegs, mace, and paradise-birds. The first two grew so luxuriantly that all the countries were supplied by them. They grew nowhere else.

The island of **Java** has been traditionally famous for its gold and silver mines. It has been called the island of gold and silver since the days of the Rámáyana, although it has no such mines in it; only the adjacent island of Sumatra deserves this name. It has a great wealth of cereals, for which it was called the "Island of Barley" by the Hindus. It yielded all sorts of spices, as nutmegs, cloves, mace, pepper, better than that of Malabar, but in small quantity; ginger, bamboos, frankincense, though not so good as that of Siam and Malacca, black benzoin, camphor, and precious stones like diamonds, emeralds, jasper, sapphire, agate, carbuncle, and bezoar. The Portuguese had not much traffic here because the people themselves carried their commodities to the various contiguous ports. The goods desired by the Javanese were all sorts of white and coloured linen from Coromandel, Bengal, and Cambay, rials, Spanish dollars, porcelain, woollen and silk stuffs, China and Japan curiosities, opium, amber, coral, and European commodities like broadcloth, iron, lead, vermilion, etc. According to the testimony of Pyrard, many Chinese were settled in the town of *Bantam*[1] carrying on an extensive trade. Every year in the month of January came nine or ten great ships from China laden with all kinds of merchandise from that country.[2] The town was also thronged with Indians, Arabs, and Christians. Evidently a great trade existed between Bantam and many of the Indian ports.

Sumatra, the "Golden Chersonese," was the nearest place for the supply of gold in India. It was probably known as the Land of Ophir in ancient days. There was a direct trade with it from India for gold, silver, brass, copper, iron, precious stones, pepper, camphor, camphor oil, benzoin, sulphur, sapan wood, tortoise-shell, brimstone, naphtha, amber of various

[1] Voyages, pp. 182–202.

[2] Linschoten, I, p. 114; Pyrard, II, p. 163; Saris, Hakl., p. 216; Barbosa, p. 198; Voyages under the D.E.I. Co., pp. 145–80.

colours, wax, dragon's blood, rattan, eagle wood, divers drugs, a great store of silk, though not so good as that of China, and paradise-birds. Pepper, however, was the principal product in Sumatra, whence the Arabs and Indians and latterly the Dutch supplied themselves with it. It was bigger and heavier than that of Malabar and hence more prized by Indians. Pyrard says that thirty ships could be laden in one year with it.[1]

The great island of **Borneo** had abundance of gold dust and bars, and the best of diamonds. The realm of Succadana yielded pepper in great quantity, as also cloves and nutmegs. It likewise produced very fine white and round pearls; abundant camphor, better than that of China; dragon's blood, bamboos, calamba, and angelica; iron, copper, and tin; bezoar, ape-stone, and goat's stone; wax, honey, and rice.[2]

From Borneo we pass on to the **Philippine Islands** or the Manillas, which were the important centre of Asiatic and American trade of those days. The Spaniards of Mexico, New Spain, and Peru came there by way of the South Seas to supply themselves with Chinese and Indian commodities. As this direct relation had seriously reduced the Spanish-American trade, bullion imports into Spain and the royal customs, the King of Spain made several restrictions to discourage the direct Manilla-American commerce.[3] For instance, trade with New Spain was prohibited to soldiers resident in the Philippines, and a law was made limiting the bullion export from Mexico to Manilla to only 500,000 dollars per annum. Yet more money found its way to the Manillas by clandestine means. The greater part of this trade was with China whence

[1] Camoens, p. 124; cf. John Davis on the produce of Sumatra, 1599, in Purchas, II, pp. 317–18; also Sir Francis Drake, *ibid.*, p. 145; Linschoten, p. 108; Pyrard, II, p. 157; Dutch Voyages, pp. 136–43.

[2] Barbosa, p. 203; Saris, Hakl., p. 222; Correa, II, p. 631; Barret in Hak., II, p. 412; Letters, I, p. 79.

"*Camphor* is one of the principallest wares in India" (Lin., II, p. 118). It was worth its weight in silver and some of it even more. It was much in demand all over India (Barbosa, p. 203; Dutch Voyages, p. 218).

[3] Cf. great stores of E.I. merchandise, calicoes, and spices in the town of Pernambuco, captured by Lancaster in 1595 (Voyages, p. 45).

from thirty to forty large ships laden with Chinese merchandise usually came to Manilla every year. A few ships full of Japanese and Portuguese merchandise also came from Japan. Then some Portuguese ships went from Malacca laden with spices, Indian and Persian goods, more particularly Indian cloths, and returned laden with civet, tortoise-shell, gold and Spanish money. The value of Manilla trade, based on the returns of customs as given in the memorable work of De Morga (1609), is as below :—

	Value of Trade.
Duties collected on Chinese goods at 3 per cent amounted to 40,000 dollars	1,333,333 dollars.
Duties collected on goods to New Spain at 2 per cent amounted to 20,000 dollars	1,000,000 ,,
Duties collected on money and goods from New Spain amounted to 28,000 dollars	1,400,000 ,,

From the foregoing figures it will be clear that the value of Indian exports to New Spain through the Manillas was not appreciable ; it was very likely below 100,000 dollars.

The Celestial Empire was culturally and commercially connected with India from the remotest antiquity. Chinese diaphanous silks were appreciated in India even as early as 1000 B.C.[1] There was also a great demand for Chinese porcelain, at least after the advent of Moslems in India, if not earlier. The great port of Randir, near Surat, was the most important centre of trade with China and Malacca in the beginning of the sixteenth century. The Chinese commodities " were concentrated there in greater perfection than in any other place soever." Every merchant had many glass shelves " filled with fair and rich porcelain of new styles " in his house for decorative purposes.[2] Akbar alone at his death left more than two million and a half rupees' worth of most elegant vessels of every kind in porcelain and coloured

[1] Mahabharata ; Sabha Parva, LI, 25–6 ; Arthashastra (about 310 B.C.), p. 94.

[2] Barbosa, Hak., II, p. 146 ; cf. Pyrard—" They import also from thence much porcelain ware, which is used *throughout India*, as well by the Portuguese as by the Indians " (Part II, p. 176 ; Part I, pp. 170, 224 ; Linschoten, pp. 129–30.) Jourdain speaks of China dishes worth Rs.50,000 each, and Hawkins, Rs.5,000 each.

glass in his treasury.[1] Much of the Randir trade was transferred to Goa and Surat during the Portuguese domination. The great realm of China annually sent its junks to Malacca and India laden with good stores of raw silk, various sorts of stuffs, damasks of all colours, satins of several kinds, and all sorts of embroidery work; rhubarb, sugar, ginger, china root, civet, musk, amber, and wax; porcelain, gold, gold-leaf and wire; steel, copper, quicksilver, tin, lead, and iron pans; flax, cotton, saltpetre, calin or spelter which was much esteemed all over Asia; likewise all sorts of varnished work, mother-of-pearl and tortoise-shell; china-beer, and a great quantity of confectionery. Rubies, sapphires, and some other precious stones, too, were carried out. There were also exported many pretty gilded things, such as very rich chests and trays of gilt wood ornamented with a thousand pretty designs, cabinets made in the German fashion, salt dishes, fans, and delicate works of ingenious men.[2]

China commonly received through the Portuguese, Japan silver, Spanish dollars, silver bullion; Portuguese and Indian wines; woollens and velvets; Malabar pepper and Sumatra spices; all kinds of crystal and glasswares; drugs from Cambay, sandal, ambergris, olive oil, benzoin, frankincense, rattan, opium, wormwood, saffron, vermilion, coral (wrought and unwrought); fine stuffs from Cambay, Calicut and Bengal; pearls, rubies, diamonds, and all other sorts of precious gems; "precious stones cut and set in rings, chains, carkanets, tokens, ear-pendants, and bracelets"; and in general, all sorts of luxurious articles, which found a very good market there.

The Chinese trade, like that of Malacca, Mozambique and Ormus, was reserved for the ships of the King of Spain. No Portuguese could trade thither, except some grandee on whom was conferred the privilege of making one trading

[1] Valentyn (Java and Surat, p. 217); Vincent's Akbar, p. 412.

[2] Pyrard, II, p. 175; Linschoten, I, pp. 128–31; Sousa, II, p. 452; Barbosa, p. 200; Pyrard, I, p. 176; Valentyn (China), p. 4.

voyage with one, two, or more vessels. In these ships there always went many private merchants for trade by paying freight to the owner of the ships and the royal dues at different ports. The whole voyage between Goa and Japan took full three years in those days, and yet it was most profitable. We are informed by Sir Thomas Roe (A.D. 1616) and others that China commodities were as dear in India as they were in England.[1] The port of Macao alone was then open to the Portuguese on the extensive coast of China, and hence there must have been an extraordinary concourse of people in that town at the arrival of the Portuguese ships. Besides this restricted trade, numerous Chinese junks plied between China, Malacca, and other parts. China was then, as it is to-day, the greatest sink of silver. Pyrard estimated that silver worth more than seven million pounds was imported into China every year from Europe, Japan, the West Indies, Peru, Mexico, and Chili. This amount, together with the merchandise carried thither, implies a considerable amount of exports from that territory. The ships returning from China were laden with valuable cargoes, being sometimes worth more than £2,000,000.[2]

Japan. Lastly, we go to the extreme Orient, or the "Land of the Rising Sun." It had not yet awakened from its slumber of ages, had then very few arts and depended upon China and India for the satisfaction of its wants. It consumed almost the same imports as China, with the exception of the great stores of Chinese silk-stuffs which were carried thither by the Portuguese. The returning ships were laden with great stores of silver and gold, some curiosities, hemp, some kind of blue dye as good as indigo, gold, rice, and some sort of varnish. Nagasaki and a few other ports were open to the Portuguese. The Japanese trade formed part of the Chinese adventure,

[1] Monsieur de Monfart says that "They will exchange or barter gold for twice as much weight in silver; for they have no coyned money" (p. 31). Rials were worth six testones or 600 rees in China, though they were worth 436 rees at Goa (Linschoten, I, p. 243). Hence the extraordinary profits in the China trade are apparent; cf. Embassy, II, p. 346 n.

[2] Pyrard, II, p. 201; cf. Fitch in Purchas, E. S., X, p. 198.

but immense profits were made on account of the monopoly and the returns in silver.[1]

This completes our survey of the whole Oriental trade and of the exact part which India played in the beginning of the seventeenth century in the commercial life of the East and the West. It will be hardly an exaggeration to say that India was the respiratory organ for the circulation and distribution of the moneys and commodities of the commercial system of the world; it was the sea wherein all the rivers of trade and industry flowed, and thus profusely enriched its inhabitants.

Liberty of Conscience

Now there are a few general features which deserve our attention. At the threshold of our period we find peoples of various nations and religions from Africa to China living in the greatest freedom in the busy seaports and inland towns of India. Liberty of conscience, supreme tolerance, free exercise of divers religions, amicable and peaceful relations among this heterogeneous population, scrupulous protection of property and person, little state interference in commercial concerns, much delegation of powers in adjusting mutual differences, and, above all, light customs duties have been enthusiastically described by our great travellers.

All these admirable features stand in astounding contrast to the disgraceful restriction of religious freedom at Goa and Cochin, and the abominable system of inquisition and high duties prevalent in Portuguese towns.[2]

[1] Linschoten, I, pp. 150–64; Pyrard, II, pp. 170–9; Saris, p. 229; Letters, VI, p. 9; Letters of William Adams in The Memorials of Japan, p. 42.

[2] For Calicut, see Barbosa, p. 146; Pyrard, I, pp. 366, 404. For Cochin, Pyrard, I, pp. 435–6; Linschoten, I, pp. 70–1. For Surat and the whole Mogul Empire, Valle, I, pp. 30, 127. For Vijyanagar, Paes in Sewell's Forgotten Empire, p. 256.

The King of Calicut gave to each one of these merchants a Nair to guard and serve him, a *chety* (scribe) for his accounts, and to take care of his property, and a broker for his trade (Barbosa, p. 146). They had among them a Moorish governor who ruled over and chastised them, without the King meddling with them.

India—the Sink of Precious Metals

India stands out prominently as the cradle of numerous arts and handicrafts at that time as it had been from the remotest antiquity. Even before the days of Solomon and Hiram, merchants of other nations came to her busy ports to supply themselves with her products and manufactures. Strabo, Niarchus, Ptolemy, Megasthenes, Polo, Conti, Nikitin, and a host of other travellers have borne testimony to her commercial greatness. In spinning, weaving, and dyeing, India excelled all other nations of the world, and this industrial supremacy continued wellnigh up to the end of the eighteenth century. No less was she supreme in many fine arts. It was in her marts that the produce of Africa, Western Asia, the Southern Islands, and countries of the Far East was collected for further distribution to the East or the West. In ancient times Pliny complained of the luxury of his countrymen and the continual drain of gold into India. But Rome does not present a solitary instance. Almost every nation on earth obtained to a very large extent its supplies of fine cotton and silk fabrics, Malabar spices, indigo, sugar, drugs, precious stones, and many curious works of art, spices of the South, and silks as well as porcelain of China from India in exchange for gold and silver. There was always a favourable balance of trade for India. This immense traffic from all parts of the world must have brought in a great amount of the precious metals. It is hazardous to estimate the quantity of gold and silver annually imported into the country, but there is no doubt that India and China were like two pits, in which the Europeans, as well as the other Asiatic peoples, stood with both feet and still sank deeper and deeper. The truth has been felicitously expressed by Terry in these words: "This I am sure, *that many silver streames runne thither as all rivers to the sea,* and there stay, it being lawful for any nation to bring in silver and fetch commodities but a crime not lesse than capitall to carry any great summe thence. The Coyen or Bullion brought thither is presently melted, and refined and then the Moguls stampe (which is his name and title in Persian letters) put upon it. This coyen is more pure than any I know made of perfect silver without any allay, so that in the Spanish Riall (the purest money of Europe) there is some losse."[1]

High Standard of Living. Living was then very cheap throughout India. All sorts of foodstuffs, clothing, and other articles were so extremely cheap throughout the Oriental world, but especially in India, in spite of its exceptional opulence and great manufacturing and commercial activities, that the people could comfortably live on a small income. Thomas Coryat spent only fifty shillings during his journey of ten months from Aleppo to Candahar, so that he spent only twopence a day! Terry remarks that all provisions were so plentiful throughout India that everyone there "may eat bread without scarceness." In Vijyanagar,[2] the biggest and richest city of the world, all things were incredibly cheap. So were they in Tatta, Diu, Cambay, Surat, Ahmadabad, and throughout Bengal. The upper classes, consisting of the military, nobility, landlords, merchants, bankers, jewellers, etc., lived in great luxury; others had varying fortunes in different parts of the vast continent of India. The people of Bengal, Vijyanagar, Golcondah, Bijapur, Gujerat, and the Punjab were very well off. The descriptions of the dress and ornaments and perfumes used by the people of Gujerat, Vijyanagar, and Malabar as given by Barbosa, Nikitin, Nuniz, Linschoten, Pyrard, Terry, and Valle are monumental evidence of the great plenty, prosperity, comfort, and culture of the Indians of those days. "This race is a people of great culture, accustomed to good clothing, leading a luxurious life, given to pleasure and vice. They feed well, and their custom is always to wash and anoint themselves with sweet-smelling unguents. They always, men and women alike, wear in their hair jasmine flowers, or others which grow there." This description of Barbosa is fully

[1] Purchas, E. S., IX; see the similar statement of Hawkins (Voyages, Hakl., p. 433).

[2] Paes, in Sewell's Forgotten Empire, pp. 257–9.

confirmed in the writings of Pyrard, Linschoten, and others. With all this opulence and luxury, there was undoubtedly a great deal of poverty. There is incontestable evidence that the lower strata of society consisting of the tillers of the soil, labourers, and mechanics lived very miserably. In many parts of Sind, Malabar, and even Gujerat, both men and women wore scanty clothing and lived in straw huts. That they were treated like helots is the observance of many reliable travellers. It was these people who used to sell themselves and their children as slaves in times of scarcity in Gujerat, Bengal, and throughout the Deccan.[1]

Slavery. Another prominent feature of the economic life of the people is a great amount of slave trade being carried on between the various parts of India and between India and other Asiatic countries. That large numbers of slaves and eunuchs were annually exported from Bengal to the various parts of India and the Moslem world has already been referred to.[2]

For the Coromandel coast, the evidence of Barbosa will suffice, and this is amply confirmed by later writers. "Although this country is very abundantly provided," writes he, "yet if it should happen any year not to rain, it falls into such a state of famine that many die of it, and some sell their own children for a few provisions, or for two or three fanoes, each of which will be worth thirty-six maravedis. *And in these times, the Malabars return with their ships laden with slaves.*" As for the slaves of Goa, we are informed by Pyrard[3] that their number was infinite; that they came from the Indian nations, and that a very great traffic was done in them. They were also exported to Portugal, and to all places under the Portuguese dominion. In Surat,[4] too, they were numerous, and so all over the Malabar coast.

Pyrard and Linschoten have fully described the slave

[1] Frederick in Purchas, X, p. 137; Purchas, X, p. 103; Bartholomeo, p. 154; Linschoten, I, p. 77; Pyrard, II, p. 142; Sonnert's Voyages, II, p. 25.

[2] Pyrard, I, p. 332; Linschoten, I, p. 94. In fact, nowhere in India were slaves of so little value as in Bengal (Pyrard, *ibid.*).

[3] Pyrard, II, p. 39.

[4] Valle, I, pp. 41, 157, calls them a black and lewd generation, going naked for the most part, or else very ill-clad.

auctions at Goa in their works. The former writes that "they drive the slaves as we do horses here, and you see the sellers come with great troops following." Linschoten[1] says that "they were sold daily as beasts are sold with us." Among the slaves were pretty and elegant girls and women from all parts of India, most of whom, it is strange to say, were very cultured ladies. All slaves were very cheap, the dearest not being worth more than 20 or 30 pardaos at Goa, or taking the pardao at 4s. 2d. to 4s. 6d., £4 10s. or £6 15s. only.[2] Some Portuguese, by keeping 12, 20, or 30 male and female slaves, made a living by their labour and nefarious doings.[3] Many of these unhappy beings had been kidnapped as children, while others were prisoners of war taken by the Portuguese and not allowed to be ransomed in any case.[4] Many of them were, however, captured and sold by the Indians themselves. Linschoten has a strongly condemnatory verdict on the Indian polity of his day as being responsible for the existence and continuance of slavery. In his opinion, the cause of bringing so many slaves and captives of all nations to sell in Goa was that at every ten or twenty miles, or rather in every village or town, there was a separate king and ruler of the people, "one of them not like another, neither in law, speech, nor manners, whereby most part of them are in wars, one against the other, and those that on both sides are taken prisoners, they keep for slaves, *and so sell each other like beasts*."[5] Moreover, in times of famine parents sold their children of eight or ten years for five or six measures of rice, and some for three or four ducats each. Even whole families came to offer themselves as slaves. The Portuguese made a living by buying and selling them, as they did with other wares.

Besides Pyrard and Linschoten, other travellers, too, noticed this awful practice of the Indians of selling themselves and their children in times of scarcity. Cæsar Frederick saw the sale of children for eight or ten larins

[1] I, p. 185. [2] Pyrard, II, pp. 65-6. [3] Linschoten, I, p. 186.
[4] Pyrard, II, pp. 39, 46. [5] Linschoten, I, p. 276.

each, which meant ten to thirteen shillings only.[1] Lastly, it has been seen in a previous section that there was a very large amount of trade in the slaves of Mozambique, Ethiopia, Abyssinia, Arabia, etc., in Goa and other places.[2] Need we remark that slavery was not a newly introduced or an exotic institution, but had been in existence in India from time immemorial ![3]

Customs and Transit Dues

According to Abul Fazl, the port duties throughout the extensive empire of Akbar did not exceed 2½ per cent. It is confirmed by Mr. Finch in 1609, who states that the duties at Surat were 2 per cent on coinage, 2½ on goods, and 3 per cent on provisions.[4] Although there are some complaints of perquisites, yet on the whole the administration of customs was very lenient and encouraging for the merchants. The case of transit dues was quite different. They were at least twice remitted by Akbar, and yet they seem to have been levied by the petty chiefs on the way. For the encouragement of internal commerce Jahangir issued proclamations in the very first year of his reign, abolishing the collection of duties arising from Tumgha[5] and Meer Bahry, together with taxes of every description, which the landholders, throughout the empire, had been used to levy for their *private benefit*. It was also ordered that no person should open any packages of merchandise on the road without the express permission of the proprietors. It is evident that no transit duties were allowed by the Mogul, and the port duties, too, were light.[6]

The low duties (2½ per cent on sold, but no duties on unsold goods) and the excellent management of the customs

[1] C. Frederick in Purchas, E. S., X, p. 90.

[2] Linschoten, I, pp. 264–5, 275–6; Pyrard, II, p. 231.

[3] Author's Articles on Slavery in Ancient India in the Vedic Magazine of Lahore.

[4] Purchas, E. S., IV, p. 423.

[5] Cf. Ain-i-Akbari, II, p. 57. Taxes other than land revenue called *Tamagha*. Sea-customs were known as *Bahry* taxes.

[6] Gladwin's History of Hindustan, pp. 96–7; cf. Valle for the custom house at Surat, I, p. 23; 'Abder Razzak (India in the Fifteenth Century, I, p. 14); Barbosa, p. 110; and Pyrard, I, p. 362.

department at Calicut have elicited the admiration of all travellers. But the same could not be said of the premier state of Golcondah, or of other states on the Coromandel coast.[1] There were numerous charges which must have depressed industry, and then their collection very much depended upon the personalities of the revenue officers and the farmers of customs. Yet it is perfectly certain that princes showed an unusual anxiety in encouraging foreign merchants to trade in their country even at the sacrifice of state revenue for the welfare of their subjects, and took immediate steps to check abuses brought to their notice.

Exports from Portugal

The chief articles of export[2] by private merchants were silver, jewels, woollen cloths and hats, swords, all manner of

[1] An idea of the various duties collected from merchants, and from which the Dutch were exempted, can be had from the following list :—

(A) Duties on hired labourers.
Duties on boat-hire.
Road duties.
Tolls or other duties on all provisions for home consumption imported either by water or land.
Duties on exports and imports.
Charges on the sale of gold and silver.
Forced sale of grain and other goods at higher prices on behalf of the King than what they are sold for in the market.
(Mack. MS., 20, I, p. 136).

(B) An inventory of duties collected at Palicut which were farmed by the King in 1629, if taken as typical of other places, will be a very important reflex of the tax-system of the Carnatic.
Toncon on the loading and unloading of ships.
Ditto of the town.
Duty on the Fanams. Toncon on exports.
Custom on trades.
Ijap of the pagodas or cash.
Toncon on arrack.
Duty on looms, saltpans, cultivated lands, Nely (Paddy), Bazar, brokerage.
Small toncon.
Vessels and all that may be cast on shore from the sea.
Duty on the Saye. Toncon in the town.
Duty on fish and gardens. All kinds of presents.
The unsold goods forced on the inhabitants.
Catta-Meady on all cloths made (*ibid.*, p. 8).

[2] Blochman in Ain-i-Akbari, p. 195 n.; Badoani, I, pp. 290, 388; Pyrard, II, p. 211; Embassy, pp. 167, 183, 480.

arms and ammunitions of war, or the material for making the same, musical instruments as trumpets, etc., pictures,[1] curiosities, tobacco, all kinds of ironware, glass[2] and mirrors, iron, lead, vermilion, coral, all sorts of dried fruits, salt, fish, wines, cheese, oil, olives, vinegar, printed books, and a host of other articles. *All these goods were in great demand and therefore brought a " profit of four for one, the provisions bring as much as six and seven to one."* It appears that the provisions were for the use of the Portuguese settled in the East, the imported money was invested in buying Indian goods at various centres, while jewels were carried to the Court, Agra, and Brahmpur, and the proceeds were employed in indigo and cloths.

Export of Money from Portugal. We have been told by Pyrard that every vessel that went out of Portugal to the East carried out at the least 40,000 or 50,000 crowns in silver, besides moneys and goods belonging to private merchants.[3]

[1] We learn from the Ain-i-Akbari that European *painting* was far superior to the Indian and that great improvements were made in the latter on account of the encouragement given by Akbar. " The wonderfull works of the European painters who have attained world-wide fame," were enthusiastically praised in the court of Akbar. At that time the Hindus excelled in this art. " Their pictures surpass our conceptions of things. Few, indeed, in the whole world are found equal to them " (Vol. I, p. 107).

[2] Several travellers have informed us that instead of glass windows the Indians used oyster-shells for panes, and this custom seems to be universally prevalent (see Monfart, p. 39 ; Fryer, p. 251). But we read of glass for windows in the Ain., 1, pp. 224, 226, the price being 1 rupee for 1¼ seer, or 4d. per pane. The account of Terry would lead one to the conclusion that no glass was used even for mirrors.

There is no doubt that presents of glass articles and mirrors were very much admired in those days. Even as late as at the end of the eighteenth century, Bartholomeo said that the most valuable present that could be made to a Malabar judge or magistrate was a mirror, a telescope, or a magnifying glass (p. 391).

[3] Pyrard, II, p. 193. My estimates for private trade rest upon these two assertions of Pyrard : (*a*) The King reserved two decks on each vessel, the other space, which was equal to 3½ decks, was left for the goods of merchants and mariners (II, p. 195). (*b*) Poor mariners even used to carry goods and money to the East by selling their berths for 300 crusados=or 15,000 sols or £85 each (40 sols=1 pardao=4s. 6d.). Everyone who came out of Portugal must have something to take out with him. They had a proverb, " He that takes nothing to the Indies will bring nothing home." Again, they had a saying that the first voyage was only to see, the second to learn, and the third to make money ; and so if in three voyages a *man did not make* a fortune he should not return (p. 196).

If twice this sum be supposed to be exported on private account for investment in valuable commodities like precious stones, jewels, spices, cloth, indigo, drugs, silks, saltpetre, copper, etc., which will really be an underestimate, then 150,000 crowns were sent out of Portugal on each ship. We find that 103 carracks sailed out to the East from 1590 to 1610, and 186 ships went out from 1580 to 1612, giving us an average of more than 5 ships per annum.[1] Therefore, at least 750,000 crowns can be taken as the average per annum of the export of bullion to the East Indies. This export of silver was very profitable to those who carried it out to the Indies, because it realised in India one-third above its value in Portugal.

Imports into Portugal and Spain. At the end of the sixteenth century the principal articles of import were pepper, spices, indigo, and cloth. The sale of pepper in Europe was monopolised by the King of Spain, while spices had been farmed out to a company established for the purpose. Since 1588, indigo had also been farmed out, so that no Portuguese could buy it in India for export into Europe or carry it into Portugal.

Linschoten[2] informs us that five ships laden with pepper used to go to Portugal every year. Each of these ships usually carried 8,000 quintals or 1,024,000 lbs. of pepper, so that the annual importation of this article amounted to 40,000 quintals. On the other hand, Fonseca states that 20,000 quintals, costing £100,833, were yearly conveyed to Lisbon towards the close of the sixteenth century, a quintal

[1] Period.	Ships that left Portugal.	Stayed in India.	Balance to be accounted for.	Returned safely.
1497–1579	620	256	364	325
1580–1612	186	29	157	100

Whereas in the first period 90 per cent of the ships, in the second only 63 per cent returned safely to Portugal (Whiteway's "Rise of the Portuguese Power," p. 42).

[2] Pyrard, II, pp. 213, 273; I, pp. 433–8; Linschoten, II, pp. 220–2; Fonseca, J. N., "Goa," p. 24 (Ed. 1878).

Linschoten says that pepper was sold at 12 ducats per quintal to the King by the Company, and that the latter got it in India at 28 pagodas the Bhar of 3½ quintals. According to this statement the price of pepper would be about 7d., or 4 annas per pound, but the price given by Fonseca is 10s. per quintal, which means a penny per pound.

being purchased at the rate of 10s. 1d., and that 10,000 quintals of spices were annually imported, from which a profit of about £45,000 accrued to the farmers. The other goods imported into the country are said to have yielded a profit of £130,000 at the rate of at least 30 per cent of their gross cost. On this basis the average annual value of these other imports was £500,000 only. Every year ships laden with cloth, indigo, and drugs sailed from Goa in the month of November to the coast of Malabar to receive their lading of pepper and other spices. They touched at several important Portuguese ports like Onore, Barcelor, Mangalor, Cannanore, Cochin, Cranganore, Quilon, etc. Having collected spices at these places, they left for Portugal in the months of January and February. Sometimes local ships were sent from Goa to collect pepper and spices on the Malabar coast, and the lading was transferred at Goa to the carracks bound for Portugal.

We cannot exactly know the value and volume of Indo-Portuguese trade, but its vague immensity has well been summed up by Mr. Wylde. "Those rich trades of India, Persia, Arabia, China, and Japan did never appear in their true lustre and splendour, so much as in the time of the Portugals who had the sole command of those trades in their own hands, before either we or the Dutch had made any discovery thereof, when *they had every year at least two millions of pounds returned home on Register, besides pearls, diamonds and other precious stones*."

The volume of the sea-borne European trade at the close of the sixteenth century was very likely 10,500 tons for the outgoing[1] carracks and 5,600 tons for the ships that arrived safely in Portugal,[2] but 9,000 tons for those which sailed from the Indies for the West.[3] At the highest it could not be more

[1] 186 ships left Portugal from 1580 to 1612, therefore the annual tonnage $=186 \times 1800 \div 32$.

[2] 100 carracks returned, therefore the yearly average $=100 \times 1800 \div 32$.

[3] Since fifty-seven ships were sunk, captured, or lost, we should add about two ships more per year to the *fleet going out of the Indies*, so that the total tonnage amounts to 9,000 tons.

than 20,000 tons both ways. This sinks into insignificance when compared with the gigantic amounts of to-day, but for those days it represented a large traffic.

Mr. Mun in 1620 stated that before the opening up of the sea-borne trade of England with India, £600,000 per annum was sent from Europe through Mocha to India for calicoes, drugs, sugar, rice, tobacco and other things, and that £500,000 was paid for Persian raw silk through Aleppo and Constantinople. He does not give any estimate of the Aleppo-Ormus trade, which was the only means of distributing Indian and European commodities over Persia, Turkey, Turkestan, Russia and many other countries of Europe. From what has already been said of the Aleppo and Persian trades, it is clear that large amounts of precious metals must have found their way to India through Ormus. As the Indian ships carried back large cargoes of valuable commodities like pearls, Persian silks, silk, woollens, carpets, horses, etc., from Ormus, it is likely that no more than £600,000 in gold and silver, including the silver exported from Persia, was usually brought back to Indian ports. Thus, about 1,200,000 pounds' worth of gold and silver was imported from Europe into India through the two most important channels of her maritime commerce.

Having now completed our survey from the Cape of Good Hope to Japan, of the character and extent of the sea-borne trade between India and Europe, we proceed to study the part played by the Portuguese in restraining and encouraging the maritime activities of India in those days.

Portuguese Restraints on Asiatic Trade. It has been seen that the pepper, spices and indigo trades were monopolised, that the importation of Malabar ginger and cinnamon into Spain and Portugal was prohibited, and that the right to trade with Mozambique, Ormus, Philippines, China and Japan was farmed out to several captains and grandees for a period of three years at every such grant. Asiatic[1] merchants were, moreover, prohibited from carrying steel, iron, lead, tobacco, ginger, cinnamon of Ceylon and several other things

[1] I. O. Portuguese Records, Doc. Rem., doc. 8.

from port to port for sale. The subjects of the King of Portugal were at complete liberty to import into Europe any and every article, except those five above-mentioned commodities from the Indies, while private merchants were allowed to go on board the ships bound for Mozambique, etc., by paying freight and several other dues to the owners of the ships. The commerce at Goa, Malacca and Ormus was also restricted to a certain extent. The King and his licencees had the right of pre-emption in these places, so that only when all the ships belonging to the King or his nominees had laden their goods, were other merchants allowed to make their purchases.[1] In the homeward-bound ships space was reserved for the goods of merchants and mariners who paid no other freight but 30 per cent duty at Lisbon. The crews of all the Portuguese ships in India were also allowed private trade. According to Fonseca, the latter had increased to such proportions that separate fleets composed of several ships were successively sailing to various parts in search of merchandise on private account. One of these fleets is related to have consisted of 240 merchantmen. There is evidence that the monopoly enjoyed by the Portuguese captains and grandees was, at the end of the sixteenth century, working to the prejudice of trade in general. There are many such complaints in the despatches from Portugal to India.

It has also been mentioned that no Asiatics except the subjects of the allied princes could stir out of their ports without obtaining passports from the Portuguese. Those who defied these sovereigns of the seas did it at the peril of their persons, ships and goods. The Malabars, Arabs and the Gujerats did sometimes steal out without permits, but they were always liable to be captured by the Portuguese ships. Within these restrictions all encouragement was given to Indian and other Asiatic merchants to resort to various ports with their goods, and Portuguese fleets were on the sea to

[1] Doc. 58 relates in detail the various oppressions committed by the Captain of the South in the trade of Malacca, and how he caused the depopulation of that town.

defend them against the depredations of the Malabars and other pirates, and to convoy them to their destination. Large fleets for the security of the sea in India and Europe were a permanent feature of the political organisation of the Portuguese. They equipped two armadas at Goa, one of which, called Armada del Nord, went as far as Ormus; the other, Armada del Sud, sailed as far as Comorin. *Each was composed of fifty or sixty war galliots, without counting the merchantmen called Navies de Chatie, which were convoyed by Navies de Armada to the various ports.* One or two grand galleys like those of Spain were also added to the fleet. These ships departed in the month of October and remained on their cruising duty for six months. Galleys were rowed by prisoners and convicts, but galliots by the Canarins, natives of Salsette, Colombo, etc. These men were called Lascars and their captain, Moncadon (Mukaddam, headman or boatswain). The ships of war were well armed. The great galleys had from two to three hundred soldiers called *Lascarits, others had a hundred each, while smaller frigates carried forty to fifty men-at-arms. These men were permitted to trade on their own account*, while making these voyages in the King's service. Thus warships should also be counted[1] as merchantmen.

Besides these two regular armadas, others went to Malacca, Sunda, Mozambique and other places where they were required. Viceroy Meneses mentions the expenses of all these fleets in detail. There were captains of the Carvels and high board ships of the like burden, captains of the Royal Galleys of twenty or twenty-five oars on one side, captains of the Galliots of chase, which had twenty or twenty-eight oars on each side, captains of the Malabar Galliots, bearing twenty oars on each side, captains of the Foysts and Catures of His Majesty, then the Captain of the Indian Seas and the Chief Captain of the Sea of Malacca.[2] Reliable data of the tonnage of the various kinds of ships is available in Pyrard. The

[1] Pyrard, I, pp. 438–9; II, pp. 117–18, 180, 208; Purchas, E. S., IX, pp. 173–4; Linschoten, II, pp. 169–70.

[2] Portuguese Records, Doc. Rem., doc. 6–7.

carracks varied from 1500 to 2000 tons and sometimes more, the gallions ranged from 700 to 800 tons, the caravels were not more than six or seven score tons, while some light round ships were of about 200 tons burden each, *although those stationed in the East were usually heavier*. The tonnage of all the war-ships for the cruise of Indian waters could not have been less than 18,000 tons.[1]

To this has to be added the tonnage of about two hundred vessels that accompanied the Southern Armada. With an average capacity of 100 tons even, the gross tonnage of the merchant ships comes up to 20,000 tons. No mention has been made of the ships convoyed by the Northern Armada.

The tonnage of the other galleys, needed for the defence of the port-towns, varied according to circumstances ; it can be taken to range from 12,000 to 13,000 tons. This is really a most modest estimate. There must have been a large number of vessels kept for the defence of the numerous port-towns in the possession of the Portuguese themselves and also to keep watch on the sea that no Indian vessel stirred out of the Indian ports without the Portuguese permit. We learn from Captain Sharpeigh that the "Portugalls *ordinarily* in the somer lye att the Bar (of Surat) *with* 40 *or* 50 *frigatts*, that no boatte can go *in or out* without their license." The same remark applies to many other ports.

In other words, we are justified in concluding that the total tonnage of the Portuguese Armadas of the Western Waters was approximately 50,000 tons.

Vast Merchant Shipping. Another outstanding feature is the marvellous presence of a great amount of merchant

[1]

Ships.		Tons each.		Tons.
50	×	50	Frigates . .	2500
25	×	130	Caravels . .	3250
25	×	250	Vessels . .	6250
6	×	1000	Gallions . .	6000
106				18,000

There were no light vessels in these fleets and hence they often failed to chase the Malabars. In 1605, orders were sent to build a large fleet to guard the coast against the pirates (Portuguese Records, Doc. Rem., doc. 6).

shipping, all built in the various parts of the country itself. Numerous cities like Decca, Satgaon, Allahabad, Lahore, Tatta, Masulipatam, Pulicat, Calicut, Surat, Bassein,[1] Goa, etc., were centres of an extensive shipbuilding industry. We have referred to the coasting fleets of three hundred to four hundred vessels plying between Cambay and Goa alone, and fleets of more than 250 ships sailing from Goa to the south,[2] a fleet of half that strength coming to the Coromandel coast from the south, and to the numerous ships plying on the coasts of Orissa, Bengal and other kingdoms. The 40,000 boats on the Indus, the fleet of 180 boats from Agra to Satgaon,[3] the Bengal flotilla of 4000 to 5000 armed boats, a fleet of 100 galliots of the Malabars, the numerous vessels of the various ports of India—all testify to the existence of hundreds of thousands of boats and ships of all descriptions plying in the rivers and seas of India. From an account of the Cambay ships by Pyrard, we learn that they had all their own ensigns, and the livery of their several lords on their flags, and that the merchants to whom they were consigned recognised them from afar. They had also war galliots for their escort.[4] Some of the ships belonging to Arabia, Surat and other neighbouring ports approached 1000 or 1200 tons burthen, though they were not

[1] Bassein was to the Indies what Biscay in Spain was in Europe, for all the vessels built for the King of Spain in the Indies were constructed there (Pyrard, I, p. 182).

[2] A caravan or a fleet of two hundred and forty sail—all belonging to the Portuguese—was seen by Captain T. Best bound for Cambay in 1612. "Every yeare there cometh the like fleet, all Portugals from the South coast, to wit, from Goa, Chaul, etc., to goe to Cambaya: and from thence they bring the greatest part of the lading which the Caracks and Gallions carrie for Portugall. By which may appeare the great Trade that the Portugals have in these parts" (IV, pp. 128, 148). Valle accompanied one such fleet of 200 ships in 1623 (Valle, I, p. 143).

[3] R. Fitch went to Satgaon in company with one such fleet. The boats were laden with salt, opium, hinge, lead, carpets, and divers other commodities (Purchas, E. S., X, p. 175). Jourdain speaks of these boats as "great barges of *four and five hundred tonns* a-piece. The merchants have their tents sett up in the barges as in a field. These barges are very large and broad and very well made according to the manner."

[4] Gladwin's History of Hindustan, I, p. 24. Frederick describes other boats called Bazars and Potuas. "They rowe as well as a Galliot, or as well as ever, I have seen any" (Purchas, E. S., X, p. 113); cf. the "Pericose" boats of 24 or 26 oars and of great burthen, described by Fitch (*ibid.*, p. 183).

so good and strong as the Portuguese carracks whose tonnage varied ordinarily from 1500 to 2000 tons, and sometimes even more. We also learn from Terry that the ships which usually went from Surat to Mocha were of "an exceeding great burthen. Some of them at the least 1400 or 1600 tons, but they were ill-built, and though they had good ordnance could not defend themselves. One of these ships had on board *seventeen hundred passengers*."

Walter Payton (1615) observes that the Gujerats loaded their great ships of nine, twelve or fifteen hundred tons at Gogo, and stole *out unknown to the Portuguese.*[1] *When we recall to mind the fact* that the crews of all the ships, whether Portuguese or Indian, were Abyssinians, Arabians and Indians, but mostly Malabars, who were the best soldiers as well as the best sailors, we can but faintly realise the vast number of sailors, mariners and gunners employed in the merchant shipping of the country in those days.[2]

A vivid idea of the extensive traffic of the busy ports of India can be given by the fact that the total shipping entering or leaving the various ports of the country amounted to 345,000 tons, out of which 85,000 tons were usually employed in carrying goods to and from countries outside India and the rest were engaged in its coastal trade.[3]

[1] Purchas, E. S., IV, p. 296. Middleton speaks of the *Rehemi* of 1000 tons carrying 1500 persons. Cf. Purchas, E. S., IV, p. 537 (John Hatch, in 1618).

[2] Ain-i-Akbari gives the monthly pay of the gunner as Rs.12 and of the common sailor as Rs.40 with food (Vol. I, p. 281).

[3] Appendix.

CHAPTER II

INDO-BRITISH TRADE IN ITS INFANCY

HAVING studied the manifold ramifications of the maritime activity of India at the close of the Akbar-Elizabethan period, we proceed to give a summary sketch of the rise, progress, extent and character of the Indo-British trade from its very commencement. It is proposed to divide the enquiry into three separate periods of half a century each, with the exception of the first which covers fifty-seven years, from 1601 to 1657. The Company's trade for the first seven years was centred in the Malaya Archipelago. The relation with India began in 1608, when William Hawkins of the *Hector* landed at Surat to secure trading facilities in the Mogul Empire. From that year the Indian trade claimed more and more attention, so that after 1622 India, and especially Surat, formed the principal centre of the Company's exports and imports. The Persian silk trade was sporadic, though at times it constituted a large part of the cargoes of the homeward-bound ships. But the Persian silk and Arabian drugs were first brought to Surat and thence transhipped to England; hence Surat was the heart of the English activities in the East.

First Decade. The Dutch and English went first to Java to procure spices, because they were informed by Linschoten that the Portuguese had no control over that island. Thus there was the least occasion to come into conflict with the masters of the Oriental trade and sovereigns of the Eastern seas. For these ten years English commerce was limited to

Java and its neighbouring islands.[1] The total value of the exports to the Indies in the years 1601 to 1610 was in—

	£		£	
Bullion	119,202	or	11,920	per year
Goods and stores	51,673	or	5,167	,, ,,
Total	170,875	or	17,087	,, ,,

Therefore during this period *the exported bullion bore a proportion to goods of a little more than* 2 *to* 1.

The value of imports cannot be ascertained, but it has been estimated by Milburn to amount to near £1,000,000 per annum! This estimate is grossly exaggerated, for it would mean that the estimated sales realised fifty-eight times the value of the stock employed and twenty-two times that of the actual money subscribed and invested in the first eight voyages. We know that the highest profit during this decade on any one voyage was 234 per cent, and that the estimates of Mr. Mun and the Company in 1620 and 1621, as hereafter stated, showed a very moderate profit, so that the *gross income of* £100,000 *per annum will be the most reasonable estimate.*[2] The amount of duty paid during the same period was £97,950, or, on an average, £9,795 per annum. *In other words,* 82 *per cent of the money despatched to the Indies was given back to the nation in the shape of duties alone.*

The nature of the exports and imports, their quantities, prices, total values, is shown by the invoices of the cargoes of the three ships of the third voyage, which is memorable for opening trade with India in 1608 through the efforts of Captain Hawkins of the *Hector*. It appears that three vessels of 1,250 tons in all, costing £19,913 for building and equipment, were sent out laden with iron, lead, tin and woollens

[1] The chief English factory in the Indies was first at Batavia and then at Bantam. After the Dutch persecution and massacre of the English, their business was largely transferred to Surat, which was raised to the status of Presidency in 1630. Since then all factories, like those of Jambee, Macassar, Masulipatam, Armagaon, etc., were made subordinate to it. English Factories, Vol. 1630–33, p. 6; Vol. 1634–36, p. 41 n.

[2] On the basis of the duties collected, it appears that imports were valued at about £200,000 per year.

to the value of £6,000. On their return they brought back pepper, mace, cloves and nutmegs from the Moluccas, their prime cost being approximately £20,000. The profit upon this voyage amounted to 234 per cent on the original subcription of £53,500. An instance of the extraordinary gain of those days is furnished by the fact that cloves costing £2,048 in the Indies were sold in England for £36,287 in 1609.

Second Decade. The Anglo-Eastern trade developed fast during the next decade. Four separate voyages were undertaken in 1611 and 1612 with five ships with a total capital of about £83,000. Out of this sum, £18,025 was sent out to the Indies in money and £10,650 in merchandise. Thus in the first twelve years, twelve separate voyages had been undertaken with twenty-six ships. It will be seen[1] that the various sums employed from 1600 to 1612 in all the twelve voyages amounted only to £464,284, out of which £200,540, or 43 per cent, was sent out to the Indies in money and goods, while the rest was spent in the purchase of ships, their equipment, provisions and in the upkeep of the various factories. *An average profit of* 138 per *cent on the total capital employed in all the twelve voyages was realised.* In some of the adventures the gains were unexpectedly great; for instance, they amounted to 234 and 218 per cent in the third and seventh voyages.[2]

In 1613 began the system of joint-stock adventures, and the *First Joint Stock* undertook four voyages, from 1613 to 1616, with a total capital of £429,000, out of which, it is said—

£111,499 was sent in money and
£78,017 in goods, while
£272,544 was spent in ships and victuals.[3]

[1] Marine Records Misc., IV.

[2] A tabular statement is as below:—

	£		£	
Merchandise	62,411	or	5,201	per year
Bullion	138,127	or	11,510	,, ,,
Ships, Stores, Provisions, etc.	263,746	or	21,979	,, ,,
Total	464,284	or	38,690	,, ,,

Mr. Moreau's East India Company's Records, p. 1.

[3] The three items total £462,060, which sum is greater than the capital raised by the First Joint Stock. Some money must have been obtained on loans.

Twenty-nine ships were in all employed, and though the cargo of one of the ships, costing only 40,000 rials of eight, or £9,000 (a rial = $4\frac{1}{2}$ shillings), was sold in England at £80,000 sterling, yet the total profits did not amount to more than $87\frac{1}{2}$ per cent in the four adventures. Looking at the detailed statement we find that out of twenty-nine ships sent out to the Indies, only fourteen could return to England, the rest were either lost, captured, worn out or kept in the Indies to fight the Dutch and Portuguese.[1]

The advantages of the Eastern trade were at this time shown by Sir Dudley Digges in his pamphlet, entitled the "Trades Increase." He pointed out that the maximum amount of goods and money exported in any one year was valued at £36,000 only, yet the nation saved annually £70,000 in the prices of pepper, cloves, mace and nutmegs for home consumption, and also vastly gained by the re-exportation of Indian commodities. For instance, spices worth £218,000 were exported in 1614, besides a valuable stock of indigo, calicoes, China silks, benjamin, aloes, etc., which had been exported to the Continent. If to this direct gain were added the King's customs, and also the employment given to ships as well as mariners in the re-exportations, the sum total of advantage accruing to the nation was undoubtedly very considerable.

Six years later the Company presented to Parliament "the estate of their trade, from the beginning thereof in 1600, to the 29th November, 1621,"[2] wherein it was stated that they had

[1] Macpherson's Commerce, II, p. 28. Milburn's Oriental Commerce, I, xv.

[2] A true estimate of the great success of the Company's adventures can be made by the number of their factories settled within fifteen years of their first establishment. In 1616 the Company possessed the following factories:—

In Java: Bantam, Jacotra (afterwards Batavia), Japara.
In Sumatra: Jambee, Tecoa.
In the Banda Islands: Banda.
In Borneo: Benjarmassing, Socodania.
In Japan: Firando.
In the Mogul's dominions: Surat, Amadavad, Agra, Azmere, Brampore,

"laden away in all those years out of the realms, as out of the Downs, Holland and other places, but £613,681," or £29,225 per annum in the shape of foreign coin. They had also shipped out of the realm, in woollens, lead, iron, tin and other English and foreign commodities, to the value of £319,211, or £15,200 per annum.

Thus the total value of exports in bullion and merchandise during those twenty-one years was £932,892, *or* £44,423 *per annum, and the ratio of money to goods sent out was a little less than* 2 : 1.

It is interesting to know that out of the large sum of £932,892, only £375,288 could be invested in Eastern goods, yet they produced in England by their sale £2,004,600, which is more than double the value of all the moneys and goods sent out of England to the Indies, and exceeds five times the prime cost of goods. All the expenses of the Company and the hazardous voyages, as well as all the losses incurred by the

On the Malabar coast: Calicut.
On the Coromandel coast: Masulipatam, Petapoli.
In Malacca: Patani.
In the Island of Celebes: Macassar.
Siam: the capital of the Kingdom of Siam.

Walter Payton: Purchas, E. S., I., p. 305.

Compare the factories and castles which the Hollanders had in the Indies on November 12, 1613 (original spelling retained in both lists):—

In Bantam	1 Factory.	
Jaquatra	,,	
Grassee	,,	
Sucquadana	,,	
Macassar	,,	
Patonia	,,	
Syam	,,	
Acheyn	,,	
Buttoone	1 Factory,	2 Bulwarks.
Amboyna	4 Factories,	1 Castle.
the Bakean	1 Factory,	1 Castle
Molu-Machean	3 Factories,	3 Castles, the whole Island theirs.
Motir	1 Factory,	1 Castle.
Tidore	1 Factory,	1 Castle.
Ternate	3 Factories,	3 Castles.
Japan	1 Factory,	1 Castle.
Benda	4 Factories,	3 Castles, besides one small Island.
Salor	1 Factory,	1 Castle, taken this year from the Portuguese.

This list leaves out their factories on the Coromandel coast.

sinking and capture of ships, were to be covered by this gross income of £95,457 per year. With all the enormous losses the Company had been able to declare large dividends to the subscribers of the India Stock, and hence the Eastern adventures were growing very popular among the English people. It was rightly stated by the Company that the *Stock which had already returned from the East Indies had "made somewhat more than five and a half of one towards charges."*[1]

The above-mentioned sum of more than 2 million pounds was estimated to be realised up to November, 1621, by the sale of imports, yet there was a large stock remaining out of £932,892 sent to the Indies. Twenty-five ships were yet in India or on their homeward passage laden with Eastern goods, and were thus sure to swell the profits of the Company to the very large sum of 5 million pounds. This estimate had already been confirmed by Mr. Mun in his "Discourse of Trade from England unto the East Indies," who calculated the investments and profits of the Company in the first nineteen years and a half as given in the note below.[2] On a comparison of the years 1611–21 with 1600–10, the rapid development of trade becomes self-evident.[3] The bullion sent out in the

[1] "The Reasons to Prove that the E.I. trade is a means to bring Treasure into this Kingdome." Home Misc., Vol. 39, p. 55.

[2] Volume of Trade with the East Indies :—

	£
Money in foreign coin exported . . .	548,090
English and foreign goods exported . .	292,286
Total in moneys and wares . . .	840,376

Imported into England :—

	£
Cost of goods	356,288
Sale value of goods	1,914,600

Besides these, there were to be returned from the Indies, after allowing a loss of about £84,000 on the remaining investment, goods worth £400,000. This sum could be expected to bring 2150 thousand pounds more into the Company's coffers. *In other words,* £840,376 *sent to the Indies would have brought* £4,000,000, *or about five times the actual investment.* It was also stated that the value of the Company's joint property was £400,000. Mun further affirmed that their trade gave employment to 10,000 tons of shipping, 2500 seamen, 500 ship-carpenters, and 120 factories in India. Purchas, E. S., V, pp. 287–8.

[3] Calendar of State Papers, Vol. 1622–24, p. 69, represents the above account to extend to July, 1620.

second decade amounts to £494,659, against £119,202 of the first, goods to £267,538, against £51,673, and the total export to £762,197, as against £170,875. The three quantities bear, roughly speaking, a ratio of 4 : 1 ; 5 : 1 ; and 4½ : 1.

It is evident that the export trade during the second decade grew to be more than fourfold as compared to the first ten years.

The change in the volume and character of the Eastern imports into England during the second decade will be visualised by two provisional invoices of goods sent home in the years 1614 and 1621. The trade in calicoes was improving fast ; while in 1614 12,500 pieces were provided, in the latter year no less than 123,000 pieces were invoiced. Similarly, although in the former year the total value of goods to be provided was about £15,000, in 1619 it was worth 720,244 mamudies or about £36,000, taking the mamudi as equal to 1s. Thus it was more than doubled as compared with 1614, and trebled in comparison to 1610.[1]

[1] Tentative invoices of goods as were thought fit for England :—

In 1614	£
Gumlac (tons 25) . .	800
Indigo Serkhej (tons 70) .	10,000
Green ginger (tons 3) .	800
Opium (tons 2) . .	100
Carpets	500
Cotton yarn . . .	500
Calicoes of all sorts (tons 15)	2802

The details of calicoes given in another consultation are as below :—

4000	baftas of	3s. per piece
2000	,,	4s. ,,
2000	Semians	6s. ,,
2000	,,	8s. ,,
1000	col. Semians	18s. ,,
1000	chintz	2s. 6d. ,,
200	sashes	5s. ,,
100	,,	8s. ,,
75	,,	10s. ,,
50	,,	15s. ,,
25	,,	20s. ,,

12,500 pieces.

Their value = £2,802 10s.

Foster's Letters, II, pp. 135–6.

In 1621

80,000 narrow baftas 2–3s. per piece
18,000 broad ,, 3–5s. per piece
5,000 Niccanees
4,000 Semianees
16,000 Duthes
200 bales Biana Indigo 26 Rs. per maund
9,000 maunds Serkhej Indigo 10 Rs. per maund
100 maunds Bengal silk 4½ Rs. per seer

Good store of gumlac, and "hoped to furnish 2,000 maunds of pepper."

Included in the baftas are (1) calicoes of all sorts to be procured at Agra, Patna and their adjacent places, 20,000 pieces at 1½ Rs. per piece ; (2) calicoes of Lahore and adjacent places, 20,000 pieces at 1½ Rs. per piece.

Fact. Rec. Misc., I, p. 113.

To have a view of the extent of the *Company's business at Surat* we should take into consideration the goods imported and exported from Surat to their factories at Bantam and other places outside India. In the year 1619 the total value of goods shipped by the Company alone, besides a great amount carried by their servants on their own account, was about £39,923, which was made up as under :[1]—

Goods shipped to the Southward, worth . . (Consisting of various sorts of cloth, cotton wool, steel, corn, spangles, English iron, toys, knives, brass ordnance for the King, and apparel.)	120,531 mamudies.
Goods shipped to the Red Sea . . . (Consisting of calicoes, indigo, gumlac, tobacco, looking-glasses, knives, broad-cloth, fowling pieces, sword blades.)	66,163 mamudies.
Goods shipped to England . . . . (Consisting of cloths, blood-stones, indigo, indigo-dust, carpets, vellum, and parchment, quilts, gumlac, turmeric, wax, various precious stones.)	720,243 mamudies.

Thus at the close of this decade the English were not only trading between England and the Indies,[2] but had a growing share in the supply of Asiatic merchandise to the Southern and Western countries of Asia. The result of twenty years' trade with the Indies was summarised in a report[3] by the Company wherein it was pointed out that the King would lose £20,000 per annum in his customs and the kingdom £100,000 per annum through having to buy spices from the Hollanders, and above £100,000 for other commodities then brought direct from the East Indies. In the end, it was also represented that, if the trade were judiciously followed, goods to the yearly value of near £300,000 could be imported from the East Indies.

At the end of the second decade the Company's trade is

[1] Eng. Factories, Vol. 1618–21, pp. 61–64.

[2] In January, 1621–2, the value of the stock at Surat was £170,000 to date and £10,000 was to be sent. About £20,000 per annum was employed at Surat. Court Bk., 5, p. 311.

[3] Calendar, Vol. 1617–20, Sect. 1025.

mirrored in the quantities of their various imports with their average prices in India and England as stated in their document entitled, "The Reasons to Prove that the E.I. trade is a means to bring Treasure into this Kingdome."

Quantities Imported.			Prices in the Indies.	Prices in England.
2,500,000	lbs. of	Pepper	2d. (Mun=2¼d.)	20d.
150,000	,,	Cloves	9d.	6s.
150,000	,,	Nutmegs	3d. (Mun= 4d.)	6s. 6d. (Mun=2s. 6d.)
50,000	,,	Maces	8d.	6s.
200,000	,,	Indigo	13d. (Mun=14d.)	5s.
107,140	,,	China raw silk	7s.	20s.
50,000	Pieces	Calicoes	7s.	20s.

The total prime cost being about £100,000 against £494,223 estimated to be realised at the Company's sales in England, it was rightly asserted that the sum of £394,223 was annually advanced towards the general stock of the kingdom, and that England saved £70,000 or more per year in the price only of spices and indigo by buying them from the E.I. Company.[1]

Third Decade. The rapid strides made in the first four years of the third decade, in spite of the inhuman tortures of the Dutch intended to oust the English from the spice trade, will be evident from *an account*[2] *presented by the Company to Parliament in* 1624. It shows that from the 25th March, 1620, to the 25th March, 1624, the exports in bullion and goods amounted to a total of £264,516 for four years, or £66,129 per year.

The imports for the like period were sold for £1,255,444 (including the sum recovered from the Dutch for the losses sustained in India), giving an average of £313,861 per annum. In other words, the average of these four years in exports showed an advance of 50 per cent over the average of the first twenty-one years, but in imports there was the sudden increase of 329 per cent due to the return of several ships laden with valuable cargoes. Over and above these returns, it was pointed out that the Company had twenty-four ships and

[1] Home Miscellaneous, Vol. 39, p. 56; cf. Malynes' Centre of Commerce, p. 109, and "The Golden Fleece."

[2] Calendar, Vol. 1622–24, p. 302.

merchandise to the value of 8 or £900,000 at the least in the Indies. Concerning the strength and wealth which the East India trade brought to the Kingdom, it was stated[1] that it would maintain 10,000 tons of shipping, and employ 2500 mariners and as many artisans; that the Company were supplying East India commodities for a quarter of the price hereto paid in Turkey and Lisbon; that pepper alone of the value of £200,000 was imported into England last year, nine-tenths of which was already exported; and that it would in future bring £50,000 yearly into the King's customs.

Although this gives an exaggerated view of the volume and importance of the Eastern trade, yet there is no doubt that the Company was in a flourishing condition, notwithstanding the heavy losses sustained by the sinking and capture of several vessels. As to the nature of the imports, we are informed by the Company that the twelve ships which returned to England out of the twenty-six despatched during these four years, brought pepper, cloves, mace, nutmegs, indigo, calicoes, drugs, China and Persian silk. The last commodity imported in the last two years alone was valued at £190,000 in England.[2] *About one-third of these goods was then consumed in the country and the rest exported to the Continent. This trade was even now so lucrative that imported goods produced four times as much as their original price in the Indies against five times in the previous years.* From the year-to-year view of the Company's exports and shipping in the first twenty-three years, it appears that there was sent out in money £753,300 and in goods £351,200, or on the average £48,000 per annum.

Richard Wylde gives an abstract of all the disbursements of the Company in India, what they sent out every year, as also what returns they had thence, for the next six years from 1624 to 1629, during which he was himself in India. Since his account is the only one available for showing the method and relative importance of trade in the various centres of the Indies, it has been given in a convenient form in Appendix B.

[1] Calendar, Vol. 1622–24, p. 350.
[2] Calendar, Vol. 1622–24, p. 267; 16th April, 1624.

Here the main results to be deduced from his account are represented in a tabular form :—

The Company's Trade during 1624–9.

	£
Money and goods sent from England to Surat[1] . . .	375,755
,, ,, ,, Eastern factories to Surat . .	43,980
Total stock available during 1624–9 at Surat . . .	419,735

Out of this sum was sent in money and goods to

Persia . .	£59,412 or 14	per cent of the whole
Bantam .	£49,147 or 11½	,, ,,
Mocha . .	£13,495 or 4	,, ,,

And was paid in customs at Surat	. £32,823 or 7¾	per cent of the whole
Left for investment for England	. 137,991 or 32¾	,, ,,
All kinds of expenses in the East	. 126,867 or 30	,, ,,

In other words, the whole business of the Company was centred in Surat. The President of the Surat factory directed the mercantile operations of all other places where Englishmen had settled down for trade. To the Southern, Persian and Red Sea trades together was allocated 29½ per cent of the whole stock available at Surat, besides the sums directly sent to Bantam from England, and 30 per cent was spent in maintaining the various establishments in the Indies, while the customs paid at Surat amounted to about 8 per cent. Then one-third of all the moneys and goods received could be invested in Indian merchandise intended for England. Taking into consideration the Indian goods sent out to Bantam, Mocha, Persia on one side, and the moneys spent in maintaining factories in those three regions on the other, *it can be safely asserted that three-quarters of the exports of the Company were spent on Indian soil during that period.*

The extent of the English trade at Surat can be roughly estimated from the customs paid there. The rate being 2½ per cent on the average, both on exports and imports, they must have passed goods and bullion worth about £1,312,920

[1] The cargoes sent out—known values only . . . £338,640
Money and goods brought into Surat 419,735
Money and goods sent to outside factories . . . 122,054

Add the unknown cost of the cargoes of the *William* and the *Blessing*—unknown sum plus . . . . £880,429 sterling during those six years. It means that *the approximate value of the English trade at Surat in those years could be placed at £220,000 per annum at the least.*[1]

To sum up, the total exports of the third decade, both in money and merchandise, amounted to more than £1,064,000 against £760,000 in the second and £171,000 sterling in the first, thus showing an advance of 40 per cent on the second decennium.

The value of imports cannot be definitely stated, since we are given their prime cost in some years and their sale values in others. However, we know that the imported goods were expected to produce in England three to four times their original cost at the least, and that £1,197,000 exported from England had produced £3,260,000 of imports in twenty years. Calculating on this basis and adding up the available data, we find that *the Company would have realised about* 2½ *million pounds at their sales during the third decade.*

It has been seen how, at the dawn of the third decade, the affairs of the Company lay "a-bleeding." It is better to recall that series of events which made it almost impossible for the Company to maintain its existence. The thrilling tragedy of the massacre of the English at Amboyna; the capture of several ships by the Dutch; the loss of about 2 millions on various occasions through the hostility of the same; the withdrawal of the English factories from all the places, except Bantam, of the Spice Islands; the exclusion of the English from China, Japan, Siam trades; little or no support from the Government; their indebtedness to the amount of £200,000 at home, and lastly the dislocation of trade due to wars begun by the Mogul against the kings of Bijapur and Golcondah—all these adverse circumstances conspired to place the Company in a precarious position. It is amusing to read that they entertained serious thoughts of withdrawing from India and of finally closing down their

[1] The above-mentioned sum represents the value of the total business handled by the Company at Surat; that is, besides the goods provided for England, it includes investments for other factories in the southern and western parts of Asia.

affairs. The unprofitable prospect of the Company's trade is reflected by the fact that in 1628 their £100 stock had fallen 20 per cent. That is, it was worth no more than £80, "whereas they had formerly divided two and three for one."

Fourth Decade. The acute distress, instead of coming to an end, was rather aggravated by circumstances which were out of the control of the Company. Their business "grew every day less and less." The fatal competition of the Courteen Association, their plundering cruises in India and the consequent stoppage of the Company's trade at Surat; and, lastly, the forcible purchase of pepper by the King accentuated the Company's difficulties. Then in India there was a universal dearth and scarcity of all things. Indian commodities were selling at double their usual rates, while English and other European goods had a sharp fall in their prices, being "in general disesteem." The despatches of those years are full of accounts regarding the severity of famine in India. We learn that thirty thousand people had died at Surat alone. One could hardly see any living persons "where heretofore were thousands of sound people. Dead bodies were lying on the highways, there being no one to bury or burn them." Peter Mundy, who was an eye-witness of the harrowing distress of the people, has recorded a realistic account of this great and universal calamity.[1]

The evil consequences of the rise in prices and the financial distress were somewhat neutralised by several circumstances. The Company had succeeded in securing the coastal trade of India; the trade in Persian silk was greatly improved; the Gombroon customs very much relieved the tension; the opening up of commercial relations with Orissa, Bengal and Sind gave new opportunities for procuring cheaper commodities; while the war between the Dutch and Portuguese and the Goa Convention of 1634 transferred a large part of the carrying trade controlled by those nations into the hands of the English.

[1] Fact. Rec. Surat, I, p. 280; Calendar, V, pp. 228, 342; Peter Mundy —Hakl.

The volume and value of imports into England during the fourth decade cannot be exactly ascertained on account of the lack of necessary material. The character of the import trade did not differ during this period, only the supplies from Persia, Coromandel and Bengal grew more in quantity. An idea of the principal imports can be had from the three invoices of separate ships from 1630 to 1640 given in the note below.[1]

The exports by the Company alone during this decade, so far as the author has been able to trace them in the various records at the India Office, amounted to more than £717,000 sterling. There is no information regarding the value of merchandise sent out to the Indies in the year 1634, nor could the invoices of the cargoes of six ships be found. On making allowance for these two missing items and adding the moneys and goods exported by the Courteen Company in more than twelve ships, it will be evident that not more than £900,000 in all could be said to have been exported to the East in these ten years.[2] *The depression in the Company's business is mirrored in the fact that the annual average of* £100,000 *of the preceding decade fell down to* £75,000 *during this.* In their returns, too, the Company seriously suffered from the piracies, rivalry and competition of the Courteen Association.

Fifth Decade. The depression of the Company's affairs was aggravated by new causes during this period. After the termination of hostilities at the conclusion of a treaty of peace between the Dutch and Portuguese, the English lost their

[1]

	Cargo of the *Charles* April 12, 1630.	Cargoes of the *Reformation* and *Discovery*, 1631.	Cargo of the *R. Mary*, 1639.
Cloth	425 bales	579	591
Indigo	596 churles	456 fardles	1,080 bales
Saltpetre	697 ,,	597 bales	331 ,,
Sugar	400 ,,	—	56 butts
Silk, Persia	150 bales	1,400 bales	353 bales
Cotton yarn	166 ,,	250 ,,	327 ,,
Wool cotton	22 ,,	—	15 ,,
Pepper, bales	2018=515,484 lbs.	4,509 maunds	1,895 cwts.

Marine Records Misc., IV ; Eng. Factories, Vol. 1630–33, p. 127.

[2] App. C to this chapter.

control in the supply of Oriental wares to the Portuguese ports, and their share in the carrying trade from port to port was also much diminished by the renewed competition of other rivals. There was also a great paralysis of trade on the Coromandel coast, caused by the wars, first, between the Vijyanagar king and his vassals and then between him and the neighbouring states of Bijapur and Golcondah. To the ravages of war were added the unbearable misery and suffering caused by a widespread famine, due to the wars on the eastern coast and to drought and inundations at Surat and many other inland places. In short, industry and trade in India were very much crippled in those years. Then came the convulsion in England caused by the civil strife. It could not but have a prejudicial effect upon the Company's trade. A serious blow was given to the trade in Persian silk. "The rigid and austere manners of the Republicans had rendered silks less an article in demand than under the polished manners of a court." Then the "tragicall storye of the king's beheadinge" threatened the loss of the Gombroon customs. Again, the Dutch captured an English ship laden with pepper and refused to give any compensation, because "the English were traitors and had no king." The Dutch reports about the English in 1642 and 1644 show that they were not doing much in the way of business. The Portuguese at St. Thomé were described as poor as church mice.[1] In fact, the business of the English was so much depressed that it was[2] a matter of surprise to the Dutch in 1646 that the English meant to continue in the Indies. An English factor's report[3] in January, 1642, can be taken as truly reflecting the state of affairs in India. The Danes "derived poore feint trade, not worth mentioning," but the Dutch flourished abundantly and were very fortunate in their undertakings. *In short, insufficient capital, civil war, active competition of interlopers, the loss of two ships laden with* £55,000 *in money and goods, war and famine in India and the*

[1] Dutch Records, Vol. XIII, doc. 411, Feb. 17, 1643.
[2] Dutch Records, Vol. XIV, doc. 450.
[3] Eng. Factories, Vol. 1642–45, p. 22.

revived competition of other European nations in the East, can be named as the principal causes of the growing depression of the Company's business during the fifth decade.

Compare the following note of the Directors to their Surat factory in 1644.

As regards shipping to be sent home, "wee desire but one ship to be returned us yearly, for these reasons: first, because we had rather have small returnes and a stock left in the country to bee profitably employed and take off all the interest then to have large returns and remaine indebted; secondly, aboundance of E.I. commodities make them disesteemed and undervalued; thirdly, our markets here being dead and quantity of E.I. goods coming will make them be sold farre under value."[1]

Hence, the annual provision at Surat was to be limited to the following quantities:—

Lahore Indico . . .	600 fardles
Cirques ,, . . .	400 churles
Cinnamon . . .	300 bales
Calicoes, narrow . .	150 bales=30,000 pieces
,, broad . .	50 bales= 8,000 pieces
Cotton yarn . .	100 bales
Cardamoms . . .	40 bags
Tincall	50 duppers
Drugs	40 bales

Considering the general depression in the trade with the Indies, it is nothing short of a surprise to learn that the Company's exports in bullion and merchandise amounted to more than £816,000 sterling for these ten years. Making allowance for the goods sent in the years of 1646 and 1649, and adding the sums exported by the Courteen Company in their twelve ships, we can safely assert that the total amount of British exports to the Indies during the fifth decade was decidedly more than that of the previous ten years. The annual average for all exports during this decade can be put at £95,000 against £90,000 of the former.

[1] Factory Records, Misc. 12, pp. 144–5. Cf. the invoice of the *Antelope* in Marine Misc., IV, doc. 17.

During the next seven years the Company's business was practically reduced to nothing, first on account of the Anglo-Dutch War and then by the Protector's declaration of leaving the navigation and commerce to the Indies free and open to all for three years. The exports of the Company from 1651 to 1656 totalled about £129,000 in seventeen ships and vanished altogether in the next year of 1657. The deficiency was, however, more than made up by the large amount of private shipping despatched in the three years of open trade. Although the amount of tonnage and exports sent by these separate adventurers is nowhere traceable in the Records of the Company, there is little doubt as to their great volume when we remember that no less than thirty-eight ships were employed for the purpose, that the prices of Indian produce were raised from 40 to 50 per cent, and those of English produce and manufactures were lowered in an equal proportion in the Indian markets by the keen competition of the numerous adventurers.

The whole English export trade with the Indies from 1601 to 1650 can now be roughly measured by the following decennial totals :—

Decades.	Exports. *Known quantities.* Thousand pounds	*Assumed values.* Thousand pounds
1601–1610	171	None
1611–1620	760	,,
1621–1630	1,064	20 Co.'s
1631–1640	717	50 ,,
—	—	100 Courteen's
—	—	30 Co.'s
1641–1650	816	100 ,,
	3,528	300

It is obvious that *four million pounds were approximately exported from England during the first fifty years of Anglo-Indian relations.* How much of this sum was actually consumed in India and what amounts were appropriated by Persia and the Spice Islands will permanently remain shrouded in mystery. If the conclusions arrived at from the returns of the years 1624–9 were to be applied to the whole period of fifty years, then *it would appear that three-quarters of the total exports were spent in India.* The actual volume of trade must have been larger than is shown by £4,000,000. We ought to add the Company's income from the customs of Gombroon, the large sums earned by Englishmen in their Asiatic commerce, and the carrying trade from port to port in India or between India and other countries, as well as the 100 per cent profits usually made by the sale of English merchandise in the East. In such a case the average money available for investment in goods for England and for expenses of the upkeep of the factories will be about £100,000 per annum during these fifty years.

CHAPTER III

INDO-BRITISH TRADE IN ITS INFANCY

(Continued)

The Twelve Voyages. A general review of the E.I. Company's resources and profits will help to throw a sidelight on the volume and extent of their commercial operations, and reveal to us the grave difficulties and discouragements against which that corporation continuously struggled to build up a rich trade with the East. In virtue of their charter, the merchants of London subscribed a stock of £57,473 in 1600 for the first voyage, which being carried over into the second voyage by an additional subscription was made up to £128,823.[1] The two accounts were amalgamated into one, and

[1] Macpherson, Macgregor, Milburn, Wisset and others who have borrowed from these authors, state £72,000 the subscribed capital of the first voyage and £600,442 for the second. I have adopted the figures of Sambrooke who, as an accountant of the Company, surely had more reliable information than any other later writer can claim.

Capital of the Voyages in Sambrooke's Report of 1654.			Profit.	
1st voyage, 2nd ,,		128,823	95%	(Same in Mill and Bruce)
3rd	,,	53,500	234%	,, ,,
4th	,, (a)	33,000	Complete loss	(Mill gives £13,700)
5th	,,	13,700		
6th	,,	80,163	121/16/4%	(Mill calls it 5th, and states capital £82,000)
7th	,,	15,634	218%	
8th	,,	55,948	211%	
9th	,,	19,614	160%	(Mill calls them 6th and 7th voyages—capital £147,936)
10th	,,	46,092	148%	
11th	,, (b)	25% from the 3rd	220%	
12th	,,	7,142	133/18/4	(Mill calls it 8th voyage, capital £7,200)

Home Misc., Vol. 40, p. 34. Cf. Marine Misc., IV.

(a) The sum was spent as below :—

£14,600 in shipping and victuals ; £3,400 in goods and £15,000 in money. Home Misc., Vol. 39.

(The loss of both ships made the fourth voyage the most unfortunate venture in the early history of the Company. A dividend of 3s. 6d. in the pound was declared, and in Nov., 1613, the stock in the Indies was valued at 28,000 Rials. C. Minutes, 2A.)

(b) £10,669 was the capital according to Scott.

the net profit divided in the form of Eastern commodities on the first two voyages has been calculated at 95 per cent.

These were followed by ten more voyages, which were undertaken on the basis of independent stocks for almost each voyage. This system gave rise to many inconveniences and quarrels, enhanced prices and multiplied expenses. At certain places there were separate factories for several accounts, each endeavouring to prefer the interest of their distinct employers. Their differences grew to such a pitch that the factors became enemies one against the other, and thus caused a "great disturbance to the benefitt of the trade."

Joint Stocks. To prevent these in the future, the adventurers resolved themselves into a Joint Stock, raising a subscription[1] of £418,691, the employment of which ultimately produced the very fair and encouraging profit of 87½ per cent on the original stock. In the year 1617, the period of four years to which the trade of the First Joint Stock was limited having expired, the Second Joint Stock arose from a subscription of near £1,600,000. During the twelve years from 1617 to 1628 the adventurers sent fifty-seven ships of 26,690 tons *besides pinnaces*[2] with £1,145,442 in money and goods, and it raised £289,643 in the Indies. Yet this proved to be the most unfortunate adventure undertaken by the Company. From an account preserved in the Home Miscellaneous, Vol. 39, on the success of the Second Joint Stock, it appears that it suffered an inexpressible financial loss on account of its continued hostilities with the Dutch and the Portuguese in defending its spice trade and in wresting the Red Sea and Persian trades from the Portuguese. It was again and again prolonged up to 1631 without ever raising a new subscription during these years. In 1628, on the failure of the attempt to raise subscriptions for the Second or Third Joint Stock, the system of calling in special subscriptions for

[1] This amount is less than what has been given in Chapter II. This difference is to be found in the Records.

[2] See our Shipping List and Appendix B to Chapter IX.

particular voyages to Surat and Persia was begun—£130,000 and £150,000 were readily subscribed for the first and second adventures. While very large profits were distributed among the proprietors of these particular voyages, no more than 12½ per cent nominal dividends were declared for all the moneys that had been contributed by the capitalists of England for the Second Joint Stock.[1]

The Third Joint Stock, with remains brought over from the Second and an additional subscription, made up a capital of £420,700 in all. It was a little more fortunate than the preceding adventure, because in spite of the loss of the *Jonas* and the *Jewel*, and of the great charges in India and England for financing the trade with large sums borrowed at a high interest, the adventurers could obtain an advance of 35 per cent on their eleven years' investment. The affairs of the Company were in such a desperate condition that no general subscription could be raised. But realising that something ought to be "done to support and uphold the E.I. trade, as, if this year is passed over, the trade may pass off so as never to be again revived," some adventurers opened a subscription for a particular stock. This First General Voyage began in October, 1641, with a subscribed capital of £105,000.[2] It was agreed to pay the proprietors of the Third Joint Stock 1 per cent in lieu of all charges at home and 6 per cent on the invoice cost of their goods for the service of factories, warehouses and small shipping in India.[3] This voyage was crowned with great success, as the adventurers could make a profit of 121 per cent.

This particular voyage was followed by the Fourth Joint

[1] The moneys invested and the dividends earned in the Persian voyages are quoted from Scott, Vol. II, p. 126. Cf. Calendar, p. 456, for second voyage.

		Profit.
1st Persian Voyage . .	£125,000 to £140,000	60%
2nd Persian Voyage . .	£150,000	80%
3rd Persian Voyage . .	£100,000	40%

[2] Macgregor has £67,000 against the above-mentioned sum taken from the Fact. Rec., Misc. 12, p. 51. See also O.C. 1791, and C. Min. 1650–54, p. 359.

[3] Court Bk., 18, pp. 40, 83.

Stock with a nominal capital of £104,540. As the First General Voyage closed its account in 1648, the two stocks ran side by side for six years. The adventurers of the former stock were fortunate in realising a profit of 121 per cent, but the Joint Stock struggling with numerous difficulties was proving a losing concern.

To tide over the financial embarrassment, the Second General Voyage was started in 1647 for a year with a paid-up subscription of £192,800.[1] The proprietors of this stock, too, agreed to allow the 1 and 6 per cent for charges at home and in India to the Joint Stock.[2] Without being fettered to any other liabilities, they could finally get a large return of 173½ per cent, while the Fourth Joint Stock could hardly fight against the misfortunes of the civil war, depressed markets, the losses of their two ships, the high rates of interest paid on loans secured in India and England, the consumption of available money in separate voyages, the keen competition of the Courteen Company and the unpaid debt for saltpetre by the State. As all these causes had conspired to exceptionally depress the affairs of the stock, a new subscription of about £200,000[3] was raised in 1650 under the name of the United Joint Stock to continue until midsummer, 1653.[4] As the Joint Stock had no more trade in India in 1653 and was only waiting to realise its estate and transfer it to the United Stock, the duty of continuing the Eastern trade devolved upon the shareholders of the latter. No dividends could be declared on the moneys invested in the Fourth Joint Stock, though the Third had a division of 25 per cent in 1653 and an unknown sum in the same year, being subsequently followed by a further profit of 16¼ per cent in 1654. No further information on the profits of the Fourth and the United Stocks can be traced in the Records, but it is certain that their depression

[1] Court Bk., 22, pp. 4, 35, 72.

[2] Court Bk., 22, p. 36.

[3] According to the Marine Misc., I, doc. i, the subscribed sum was £112,000 out of £300,000 proposed. But Macgregor states £157,000. Com. Statistics, IV, 323.

[4] Court Bk., 20, p. 474.

must have been accentuated by the Eastern trade being thrown open on the termination of the Anglo-Dutch War. On the contrary, account ought to be taken of the large sum of £85,000 received in 1655 from the Dutch in compensation for the manifold injuries sustained from them by the English Company, as also of another moderate sum of £20,000 obtained by the owners of the two stocks from their successors as the price of their estates in the East.[1]

The Dutch and English Trades Compared

As a contrast to the preceding account, a view of the Dutch trade with the East will be very interesting for comparative purposes. That the Dutch business was very much thriving in India even in the first quarter of the seventeenth century, will be seen from the detailed[2] invoice of money and merchandise demanded for the Surat factory by its President, V. d. Broocke, in December, 1622. He required about £30,000 in silver and gold and more than 100,000 pounds weight of valuable goods, exclusive of pepper, to be sold at Surat. While the English trade with the East steadily languished, the Dutch trade grew apace in subsequent years. The ever-increasing volume of their business is clearly evident from the total invoiced prices of the goods and the number of ships sent out of the Indies to Holland.

Years.	Ships.	Total Value (in thousand florins).	Annual Average (in thousand florins).
1599–1620	112	18,477	880
1621–1630	72	15,387	1,538
1631–1640	75	21,526	2,152
1641–1650	93	25,555	2,555
1651–1660	103	26,822	2,682

In other words, *Holland received 7½ ships per annum from the East during those sixty-one years against three ships*

[1] Scott gives 80 per cent profit, though it appears that the dividend in money was 60 per cent only. His statement that 50 per cent in pepper was divided on two occasions is incorrect. Court Bk., 20, pp. 79, 271 ; 21, p. 8. 170 per cent had been dividend up to March, 1658, and it was expected that further distributions of 35 per cent would be made. Court Bk., 30, p. 316.

[2] See Appendix A to this chapter.

annually arriving in England during that period. Moreover, while the Dutch imports cost on the average less than a million florins per annum during the first fourteen years, and the average remained pretty low up to 1620 by reason of the incessant wars with the Portuguese, the English and the inhabitants of the Spice Islands, they steadily rose to more than 2½ million florins per year in the 'sixties, showing that in this decade the annual imports had trebled as compared to the annual average of the first twenty-one years. During these sixty-one years *the total invoiced value of all the goods sent to Europe was* £9,806,000—a fairly large sum for those days.[1]

It has been seen that in fifty-seven years the English exported about £3,865,000 in money and merchandise, without taking any account of the large amounts sent out to the East in the three years of open trade. This sum can be taken to represent their invoices of goods imported from the East, as the charges of factories and other establishments would have been defrayed by the earnings from their Asiatic commerce, the profits on the English merchandise sold in the East, the freights realised in the carrying trade and the customs of Gombroon. Even allowing £828,000 plus the exports of 1654–7 by numerous English adventurers more for expenses, it is unlikely that the aggregate value of merchandise imported by the English up to 1657 could fall far below three million pounds sterling. One can be positively certain on the basis of the preceding data that after fighting against odds and experiencing the worst periods of depression, Englishmen spent no more than a third part of the treasure spent by their rich and prosperous Dutch rivals in the East.

The secret of the extraordinary Dutch success and prosperity lies in their monopoly of spices and drugs produced in the Southern Islands, as well as in the purchase of Chinese goods at very cheap rates. The prime cost of their imported merchandise was incomparably small, and the selling prices were excessively high. Hence, in comparison to the English

[1] Eleven florins have been taken equal to £1.

Company, the profits of the Dutch on their Eastern adventures were nothing short of the fabulous. Except for the decade 1621–30, during which only 82 per cent profit[1] was divided, *the annual average* of their net profit for the remaining years varied from 20 to 25 per cent on their capital stock! Notwithstanding the innumerable obstacles in establishing their trade and in planting colonies, to which the English had wellnigh succumbed, *the proprietors of the Dutch stock were given* 1,106 *per cent on their capital in* 56 *years!*

Private Trade. Over and above the English Company's trade we ought to take a *summary view of the business carried on by Englishmen in their private capacity in and with the East*, as it will greatly help us to understand the real volume of the business controlled by the English nation and the later developments of their commerce with India. A long struggle broke out between the Company and their servants. The former were determined to thoroughly preserve their monopoly of trade with the East to themselves, but the latter, disregarding all orders of their masters, more and more indulged in the forbidden fruit by trading in the East itself as well as in the Eastern commodities imported into England. Thus the English factors and mariners, by curtailing the sphere of the Company's operations, worked to the prejudice of their masters in India as well as in England. Hence as early[2] as 1604 the prohibition to buy spices was extended to persons of all ranks and ratings on the ships of the Second Voyage under Sir H. Middleton. Then a royal proclamation inhibiting the importation of pepper from foreign parts by any other persons than those of the East India Company was procured[3]

[1]

Years.	Total Dividends.
1605–1620	307½
1621–1630	82½
1631–1640	258½
1641–1650	257½
1651–1660	200

Total in 56 years = 1,106 per cent on the capital.

[2] Voyage of Sir H. Middleton (Hakl.), p. 17.

[3] Calendar, I, sec. 468–70.

in 1609. Mr. Adam Denton in one of his letters (1614) objected to the starting of private trade by the factors of the *James*, "because it would spoil employments in one place and sales in the other."[1] Supreme efforts were subsequently made to thoroughly suppress it, but finally realising the futility of absolutely preventing the crews of their ships from clandestine trade, when even the commanders[2] of fleets and captains of ships *were equally guilty* of the breach of trust, the Company allowed their servants and the officers of their ships to trade on their own account in a few unimportant articles of export and import, and reserved to themselves the rights of exporting and importing principal commodities. A complete list of the goods allowed to be exported and imported by private merchants in 1631 is given in the note below,[3] yet it should be observed that the servants were not satisfied with this indulgence. The correspondence of the period is full of complaints[4] from the Company on the violation of their monopoly. In spite of royal proclamations and their repeated prohibitory orders and stringent punishments, the evil grew apace. Factors in India always pleaded the manifold difficulties of detecting and preventing it. Restricting private trade in spices was described by factors as a Herculean labour ; while some years after, in 1650, it was again admitted that like "Adam's

[1] Foster's Letters, II, p. 118.

[2] Court Bk., 5, p. 163—the old veteran Captain Martin Pring was charged with carrying on private trade in 1621.

[3] A list of *goods allowed to be exported to India* in the year 1631 was as under :—Perpetuana's and drapery, pewter, saffron, woollen stockings and garters, ribband roses edged with gold lace, beaver hats with gold and silver bands, felt hats, strong waters, knives, Spanish leather shoes, iron and looking-glasses.

The *goods allowed to be imported from India* at this time :—Long pepper, white pepper, *white powder sugar*, nutmegs and ginger preserved, mirabolans, bezoar stones, drugs of all sorts, agate beads, blood stones, musk, aloes socotrina, ambergres, carpets of Persia and of Cambaya, quilts of sattin, taffaty, printed callicoes, benjamin, damask, sattins and taffaties, quilts of China embroidered with gold, quilts of Pitama embroidered with silk, galls, worm seeds, *sugar candy*, china dishes and puslanes (i.e. porcelain) of all sorts. King's Proclamation of 1631. B. Museum ; Eng. Fact., Vol. 1630–33, p. 27.

[4] Cf. the Petition and Remonstrance of the Governor and Company of Merchants requesting the suppression of Private Trade in 1641.

children, we think few of your servants are free from tasting the forbidden fruit."[1]

To make their restraints effective, the Company again issued prohibitory orders in 1650. Broadcloth, lead, quicksilver, vermilion, coral and elephants' teeth were prohibited from being exported on private account. Among imports, the Company reserved to themselves the exclusive right of bringing in raw silk, cinnamon, benzoin, pepper, musk, mace, nutmegs, aloes, saltpetre, cotton yarn, calicoes and indigo of all sorts. All other goods were allowed[2] to be imported by privileged persons in the Company's service to the extent of 5 per cent of the tonnage licensed by the Company on their own account. The articles specified in the free list do not differ much from those given in the preceding note. Yet it should be observed that the trade in musk, aloes, calicoes and benzoin was this time taken out of private hands on account of its being more profitable than before ; while the importation of sugar, precious stones and valuable silks was left to private enterprise. It also shows that Indian sugar was not an article of much importance during the first half of the seventeenth century.

The English Share in Asiatic Trade. The English at Banda and other places in the Southern Islands soon found out that their woollens and metals did not find much sale there. Indian commodities, especially cotton fabrics, were in great demand in those parts, therefore it was thought necessary to resort to India, dispose of English goods and money first in the purchase of Indian piece-goods fit for the southern market and thence to buy spices, pepper, silk and some drugs for the Eastern and European markets. The Indian merchants immediately realised the danger of this practice. We are told that the purchases of Hawkins at Surat in 1608 aroused a

[1] Eng. Fact., Vol. 1647–50, pp. 4, 22, 181, 206, 262, 281.

[2] Court Minutes, Vol. 1650–54, pp. 9, 33, 59.

The following E.I. goods were allowed to be imported :—Olibanam, tincal, gum-lacs, seed, tamarind, myrrh, cowries, dragon's blood, cassia fistula, cubebs, agate-ware of all sorts, camphor, china dishes, civits, ambergris, bezoar, diamonds, pearls, rubies, sugar, cassia lignum, lignum aloes, china roots, myribalans, conserves.

storm of opposition—the merchants grumbling very much and complaining to the Governor and Customer of the leave granted this Englishman in buying commodities "which would cut their owne throats at Priaman and Bantam."[1]

Notwithstanding these protests, the English and Dutch, both in their corporate and private capacities, began to indulge more and more in the port-to-port trade to the great detriment of Indian merchants. The great profits earned in this commerce have been stated in the Surat report of 1612. Indian commodities carried to the south were to yield three for one, and also those like indigo, calicoes, cotton yarn, etc., carried to England "will by our computation yield three for one at home at least."[2] In other words, £100 first invested at Surat could bring in £300 in the Moluccas, which reinvested at Bantam or Surat for the home market could produce £900 in England. Thus an adventure of a year and a half in going to Surat and the Moluccas, back to Surat and thence to England, could make nine times of the original investments. It is true that this enormous gain could not be pocketed without immense expense and great losses in life and property incidental to voyages in those days. Yet looking at the question from the point of view of the Indian shipowners and merchants engaged in foreign commerce, it must be admitted that their fears and complaints were fully justifiable, since they were being fast ousted from such profitable branches of trade by their stronger rivals from Europe. *The Dutch, English, Danes, French and the long-established Portuguese, were trying to appropriate as large a part of the Asiatic commerce, individually and corporately, as they could. Each of these nations, being desirous of obviating the necessity of exporting coin and bullion from their respective countries for their purchases of merchandise in the East, reduced it to the minimum by employing themselves in the carrying and foreign trades of Asia.*

So far as the English were concerned, Aldworth, Bradshaw,

[1] Purchas, E. S., III, p. 3.

[2] In 1628, £250,000 invested in the Indies was expected to produce £700,000 or £800,000 at home. Calendar, IV, p. 509.

Sir Thomas Roe and others repeatedly pointed out the imperious necessity of taking a greater share in the exchange of Indian and Asiatic commodities. Realising the extraordinary profits obtainable in it, English factors had begun it on their private account. They were, however, repeatedly prohibited by the Company, which wanted to monopolise this trade, too, for their exclusive advantage, as they had previously done the maritime trade between England and the Indies. Despite protests and threats, the private trade grew by leaps and bounds, and "had gotten such a head" that it was difficult for Sir T. Roe to suppress it in 1618; while Mr. Jones, on being asked which of the factors were private traders, stated that there was not a man free. This forced indulgence opened out for the Company's servants unimagined sources of accumulating wealth. According to Boothby, *Englishmen by their* 5 *or* 6 *years' stay in India carried home estates of* 5, 10 *or* 30 *thousand pounds a man without having carried any stock out of England.* Moreover, during their residence in India, we find them rolling in luxury and affecting the manners and style of royalty. Pietro Della Valle gave a vivid description of the luxurious life of the English and Dutch at Surat in 1623. This was fully confirmed by Mandelslo in 1635, Boothby in 1644 and Dr. Fryer in 1673.[1] They could one and all rear immense fortunes and live in luxury in that early period only by controlling a growing share in the Asiatic commerce of all the countries extending from China to the Red Sea.

The Profits of the Carrying Trade

While the spice trade was being rapidly controlled by the Dutch, the English turned their attention to Persia in the west and Siam and its neighbouring kingdoms in the east. They freighted their ships with the wares of Indian merchants and also made great profits on the goods they carried thither

[1] On considering the abuses of the factors in the Indies, the Directors remarked that the estates of Ball and Spalding "were swelled beyond the compass of servants." Calendar, II, section 1134, 21st October, 1621.

Della Valle, p. 41; Mandelslo, Harris's Voyages, I, p. 755; Fryer, p. 180.

on their own account. It has been seen how the Surat population unsuccessfully attempted to prevent the Dutch and the English from participating in the Red Sea and Persian trades. A contemporary letter, written by J. V. Hassel from Surat to the Directors at Amsterdam, dated 25th December, 1628, sums up the sentiments of the native traders in these words :—

The Moors were also not pleased that the Dutch began the trade in tobacco, rice, etc., which they brought to Persia. The *Moors complained the Dutch were taking every trade out of their hands,* the latter should be content with their cargoes bound homewards, their rich cargoes sent to the south, their friendship of the Moors should be worth more to the Dutch than the small trade ; the Dutch should, moreover, assist and protect the Moors. Also they mixed threatenings with it, they would complain to the *King, the Dutch did not give any profit to his subjects, were only here to seek their own profit and tried to turn everyone out of trade.*[1]

What the loss of the southern trade implied has been brought home in the calculation made by Mr. Wylde on the basis of the prices at which he himself sold spices at Surat in 1627. He estimates that 300,000 pounds of mace, nutmegs and cloves, costing £8,750 in all, could be sold for £90,000 at Surat,[2] thus returning ten times[3] the original cost of the transporter. It was also pointed out that in case the Company undertook this exchange, it could invest the money realised in the sale of spices in indigo, calicoes and other Indian commodities which, carried to England, would produce at the least £270,000, thus leaving a gross profit of £261,250.

That these estimates were not wild or exaggerated is proved by the Company's letter, dated 16th March, 1631, wherein it has been stated that English goods worth £45,800 were expected to give a profit of £30,000, or 56 per cent in the Indies, and that the carrying trade in the Indies was to produce £125,000 at an expense of £20,000 in shipping, mariners, factors, etc., meaning thereby that the Company expected to make a gross profit of £155,000 per annum in the Indies alone.

[1] Dutch Records, VIII, doc. 280; Dutch Records, VI, doc. 198.
[2] Wylde, p. 33.
[3] See Boothby's figures in the Appendices.

This statement is based on the following figures:—[1]

	Money.	Goods.	
The Pearle for Masulipatam . . .	£8,900	1,500	
The Jewell for Bantam . . .	4,000	1,300	
Charles, Jonas, Dolphin, Hart and Swallow for Surat	103,000	43,000	
	115,900	45,800	= £160,700
Other Sources of Income in India.	£		
Profits on Goods sent	30,000		
Persian trade	20,000		
Goods from Surat and Masulipatam to Bantam, Jambe, Macassar, etc. . .	25,000		
Goods from Surat to Bantam . . .	10,000		
Goods from Bantam to Surat, Persia, etc.	70,000		
	155,000		= £315,700
Charges in India and Persia of shipping, mariners, factors, etc. (besides freights and customs), about . . .	20,000		
Rest in India	295,700		
Out of this one great ship from Bantam .	60,000		
Two ships from Persia and Surat . .	80,000		
Stock on hand—4 ships and a store of .	£155,700		

Thus the carrying and Asiatic trades were a very substantial source of the Company's income by 1630. They were further increased by the continuance of war between the Dutch and the Portuguese for a decade, during which period the carrying trade of the latter was transferred to English and Danish ships. The Danes, we are told, carried so many Portugals from Bengal and other places to Masulipatam that it was unsafe for the Dutch to walk through its streets. The English carried Portuguese goods not only to the Oriental ports, but even to Portugal itself. They also profited by the sale of their merchandise and had the facility to obtain the productions of China through the Portuguese.

The cessation of the war and the revolution at home gave a set-back to the Company's carrying trade. Moreover, the Governor of Surat had got twelve vessels employed in carrying goods to the Red Sea and Persia on the Government account. The Dutch represent that he even forced the

[1] Letter Bk., I, p. 78. It will be seen that an error in calculation occurs in the first section.

merchants to make use of them and prohibited the Dutch from carrying any goods on freight. Thereupon the latter attempted to secure a share in carrying the Sind cloths to Persia and Bassora like the English, because they felt sure that the new opening would prove a gold mine. The coastal trade, too, suffered on account of the general depression in the business of the Company during the 'sixties.

Early Results of the Anglo-Indian Relations

Many far-reaching consequences of the direct trade carried on by the Dutch and English with the Indies become visible at a very early period in Europe as well as in Asia. In this connection we can first note some prominent tendencies which went on gathering force with the lapse of time. The Hanseatics, who carried on a very profitable sea-borne trade as far as Venice, were so completely wormed out of it by the Dutch and English that they had to sell their large ships and return home overland.[1] Then the English Levant Company made complaints, as early as 1604, on the decay of their trade into the Levant, alleging that all spices, silks, indigo and goods of the Indies, which used to be brought through Persia into Turkey, and from thence to England, were being brought direct from the Indies. The share of the Turks, Egyptians and Venetians was, however, more considerably reduced. The wealth, revenues, prosperity and population of the old commercial cities like Cairo, Alexandria, Aleppo, Constantinople, Mocha and Ormus were given a serious blow by the diversion of Oriental trade into new routes. But most of all, the direct and enthusiastic participation of the Dutch and English in the Eastern trade spelled a great disaster to the Portuguese trade and prosperity. The sinking condition of the Portuguese and the capture of their trade and possessions by the new adventurers form the prominent features of the period. Even in 1607 the Portuguese are reported to have sustained so great a loss in the East Indies that it was "thought in those places a wound almost incurable."[2] Then the trade to Lisbon for

[1] Calendar of State Papers, I, sections 342, 380. [2] Calendar, I, section 380.

spices was overthrown through the East India trade with England and Holland, and so was also the sale of cloths and kersies, which were the chief commodities before transported by the Portuguese from Europe. Their general trade was very much curtailed by the prizes that were made of their ships as well as by the scarcity and dearness of goods, because the great number of merchant ships in the Indies naturally sent up the prices of merchandise. "What formerly cost the Portuguese one sol," remarked Pyrard in 1610, "now costs them four or five, and even what they can bring in safety to Portugal they are obliged to get rid of it at a less price than they were wont; nay, it is as much as they can do to get it sold at all, because the Hollanders sell at lower prices still, and do their business with much greater despatch."[1] In fact, the trade of the Dutch and English had so shortened their returns that half their galleons did not come, and those that came from Portugal brought new supplies for the garrisons, but returned so empty that the charge was "but defraid." "Never were such opportunities," writes Sir Thomas Roe, "to discharge the Portugall from all these coasts. He is declining on all sides, and a little weight on his head now laid would sink him."

A few years after, in 1632, the Gombroon factors wrote to the Company that "the Portugals doe dayly decline in the Indies; and noe question oportunities will be offered, either at Syndie or Seland (Ceylon), or other partes there adjacente, wherby to joyne issue with those people and settle a trade may prove very bennificiall." The long wars with the Dutch, the sieges of Malacca, Goa, Mozambique, Ormus, Colombo and the capture of many places thoroughly broke the pride, power, prestige and monopoly of the Portuguese. The accounts of Lancaster, Pyrard, Best and Della Valle, as well as the despatches of the time, make it clear that the Portuguese were the poorest folk in sea-fights. They, in fact, thought more of their lives and fought no more. At last, the naval battles from 1654 to 1658 off the coast of Malabar between the Dutch

[1] Pyrard, II, p. 204.

and Portuguese and the capture of the important stations by the former entirely destroyed the remainder of the Portuguese power in India. Their empire on the sea had completely vanished and with it had disappeared all the springs of their wealth, prosperity, pomp, pageantry and luxury. Della Valle saw at Goa how the Portuguese lived in outward appearance with splendour enough, though in secret they endured many hardships. Tavernier, too, has given a pathetic description of the abject condition to which they had been reduced by 1650. They had so fallen from their former splendour that he saw men of fortune begging alms in private.

The decay of Portuguese trade can be adequately measured by the fall in the number of ships that sailed from Lisbon from 1591 onward.

Years.[1]	Ships.	Years.	Ships.
1591–1600	54	1621–1630	50
1601–1610	59	1631–1640	29
1611–1620	49		

Many of these vessels were required to guard the Portuguese Possessions from the Dutch and English invasions. Hence very few ships returned home laden with Oriental goods.

The Portuguese had thus passed off the political and maritime stages of India, but the effect on the Asiatic and Indian merchants of the increasing power of the Dutch and English was no less tragic. Ormus was a mere heap of ruins in 1625. Malacca, Cochin, Goa and many other Portuguese ports had lost their great trade. The Red Sea, Persian and Chinese trades were first mightily dislocated and then very much curtailed on account of the continued insecurity and frequent captures on the sea. It has already been seen how the port-to-port trade in India and Asia was controlled and appropriated by the Dutch and English, and how the share of the Indians in the carrying and foreign trades was being daily curtailed. The Europeans, as kings of the seas, could blockade any port, capture any vessel, shut up Asiatic merchants within their ports, and therefore they could and did slowly force the

[1] Sousa's History of Portuguese India, III, pp. 421–432.

foreign and coasting trades out of the hands of the Indians. In short, the latter had practically lost that foreign trade which was declared by Mun in his "England's Treasure by Forraign Trade" as "the great Revenue of the King; the Honour of the Kingdom; the Noble Profession of the Merchant; the School of our Arts; the Supply of our Wants; the Employment of our Poor; the Improvement of our Lands; the Nursery of our Mariners; the Walls of the Kingdom; the Means of our Treasure; the Sinews of our War; the Terror of our Enemies."

CHAPTER IV

CHARACTER OF INDO-BRITISH TRADE

Having taken stock of India's commercial position and outlook, traced the genesis and rise of British trade in the East in its quantitative aspect and indicated the great success achieved in diverting the Oriental trade into new hands, we may now turn to consider the course of development in the principal items of export and import. This study will give us outstanding facts of importance not only as to the quantity, quality and price of each of the chief articles of Indo-British commerce, but will also bring to light some of the interesting features of the up-hill work of building up that great trade.

It has already been seen that the ordinary items of the export trade from India were calicoes, indigo, saltpetre, pepper, sugar, drugs and provisions, while woollens, metals, coral, gold and silver, besides numerous curiosities like mirrors, sword-blades, knives, pictures, satins, tapestry, damasks, etc., were imported into India by the English as by the other European nations. Over and above all these things, spices were the commodity which brought the English into the East. These, though not the product of India proper, should take precedence over all other items.[1]

Spices. When Philip II, the sovereign of Spain and Portugal, prohibited to the Dutch the importation of spices, they resolved to fetch them for themselves from the Spice Islands. So did the English set out for the Indies in search of spices whose prices had been put up by the Dutch. That their

[1] The article on "English Commerce with India" by Wm. Foster in the Journal of the R. Society of Arts, April 19, 1918, is a valuable contribution on the subject.

adventures in the supply of Java and Sumatra spices were crowned with a series of unexpected successes, will be revealed by the following table :—[1]

Year.	Ship.	Prime Cost of Cargo. £	Selling Price in England. £
1608	Consent	Cloves = 2,948/15	36,287 or 12½ times
1610	Hector	Nutmegs = 1,730/15	27,064 ,, 16 ,,
		Maces = 3,521/15	12,461 ,, 3½ ,,
1611	Expedition	Nutmegs = 1,609/10	26,868 ,, 16½ ,,

When the English had thus gained the immediate object for which they had set out for the Indies, they soon extended their operations in the various branches of the Oriental trade. By the end of the second decade the annual consumption of the various spices in England with their prices in the Indies and at Aleppo, their ancient prices in England and the new prices due to the importations of the Company are stated by Mr. Mun as below :—

Articles.	Indian prices.	Aleppo prices.	Prices in England 1600	1620
400,000 lbs. Pepper	2½d.	2/-	3/6	1/8
40,000 lbs. Cloves	9d.	4/9	8/-	6/-
20,000 lbs. Mace	8d.	4/9	9/-	6/-
160,000 lbs. Nutmegs	4d.	2/4	4/6	2/6

Sir Dudley Digges, another partisan of the Company, averred that the ancient price of pepper was 8s. against 2s. in 1615. Both the Indian and English prices seem to be understated to present the Company's case in the strongest contrast, yet the enormous profits accruing to the nation as well as the adventurers are patent to all. In the Home Miscellaneous, Vol. 39, is preserved a most important document on the quantities, prime costs and selling prices of pepper from 1616 to 1630. It appears that during the three years from 1616 to 1618, 1,432,186 lbs. of pepper bought at an average cost of 2¾d. were imported into England per annum and sold at an average price of 24½d. per pound. But during the decade after the expulsion of the English from Amboyna, i.e. from 1621 to 1630, the average importation fell down to 1,428,667 lbs. per year, the price paid in the East rose from

[1] Home Miscellaneous, Vol. 39, Sambrooke's Report.

$2\frac{3}{4}$d. of the first triennial period to $4\frac{1}{2}$d. per pound during this decade, and the selling price went down to 18d. on the average. The actual quantities imported and sold from year to year will be found in the appendix to this chapter.

Here it should be noted in passing that Mr. Mun's statement as to the total quantity of pepper annually imported into England being 2,500,000 lbs. is exaggerated by at least 1,067,000 lbs. per year! Another amusing error which has been perpetuated by such well-known authors as Macpherson, Milburn, Macgregor and others is that they all give 250,000 lbs. as the average amount of pepper imported on Mun's authority, though the total price at $2\frac{1}{2}$d. per lb. stated by them as by Mr. Mun is £26,041 13s. 4d. The quantity, as already observed, should be 2,500,000 lbs. Again, the annual consumption of pepper in England is also grossly exaggerated, because fifty-five years afterwards Sir Josiah Child stated the consumption of the article in his own time to be only 186,000 lbs.[1] *Taking* 200,000 *lbs. as the annual consumption in England about the year* 1625, *it appears that about* 1,200,000 *lbs. of surplus pepper were sent to the European markets in those days. Thus, instead of consumers of Portuguese and Dutch spices, Englishmen had become the greatest suppliers of the Continent in this important commodity.*

£218,000 worth of pepper were sent out in the year 1614 alone. The return cargoes from the East, which realised in London £876,557 from 1621 to 1623, were largely in spices. This lucrative branch was, however, almost annihilated after the Amboyna tragedy. Thereafter attention was turned to securing large quantities of Malabar pepper, which could now be obtained on account of the loosening monopoly of the Portuguese. £15,000 worth of pepper was ordered by the Company in 1625, while the total value of goods demanded for home was £78,219. 2,118 bags of pepper were carried in the ship *Charles* in 1630. The war between the Dutch and Portuguese and the Goa Convention between the English

[1] Annals, II, p. 298. Oriental Commerce, I, xix. Commercial Statistics, IV, pp. 314, 350.

and Portuguese gave golden opportunity for the development of this branch. Large quantities were imported by the Company as well as the private merchants. In 1639 the Malabar pepper was sold at 3s. 6½d. on the average at the Company's sales, while a small quantity of Jambee variety was disposed of at 19½d. per lb. in 1641. Instructions were sent to the factors that the Raybag pepper was "in England preferred before the best you receive from the South Seas." In the sales of 1640–41, cloves, nutmegs and mace also figure in small quantities. The English could not directly buy them from the Spice Islands; even at Surat and Gombroon the Hollanders refused to sell spices to the English, nay, as a further security, they usually retained them either on board their own ships or in the custom house, until the English vessels had sailed away.[1] Small quantities were, however, clandestinely secured from the Dutch mariners and factors, or from the Indian and Persian merchants. In 1650 cinnamon (125 chests) and cardamoms (16 bales) are found included in the sales of the Company. These were obtainable at Cochin, Raybag, Rajapur, Kherapatam, etc., on the Malabar coast. Thus the loss of the southern supplies was being made up by the Malabar spices. The price of pepper was at this period much reduced in England on account of the large importations by private merchants. It was 9d.–11d. per lb. in 1650 and only 7d. in 1657. We find that 39,534 lbs. of pepper bought at £439, or 2½d. per lb., were laden on the *Benjamin* alone in 1657. The annual importation at that time was stated to be 7,000

[1] The Dutch policy will be revealed by the following two extracts from the I.O. Dutch Records, Series I:—

(1) "No European nation besides ourselves, is admitted to the trade in pepper on the west coast of Sumatra, the spices are most in our hands. Whoever comes for trade to these Southern shores, will return empty handed." Vol. XI, doc. 350, 22nd Dec., 1636.

(2) "The destruction of the trees having been accomplished, we shall forbid the planting of new shrubs in the island of Timor itself or any of the adjacent dependencies and continually destroy those that may shoot up naturally or may have escaped destruction."

(3) "Europeans and Indians were excluded from the ports of Ticco, Priaman and Indrapura, so that the Dutch alone could supply spices to the Asiatic as well as the European markets." A.D. 1649, doc. 617.

bags, out of which 1,400 bags were required for the home consumption, while the rest could be re-exported to Europe where the prevailing price was 1s. 8d. per lb. Although the average cost was stated to be 10d. per lb., yet pepper evidently formed a very lucrative branch of the Company's investment, and hence all private merchants were forbidden to import it from the East.

Piece-Goods. Next to pepper, we can place piece-goods as an article of great demand in the Company's investments in this period. The calicoes reported by Wm. Finch in 1609 were the very fine ones of Broach, worth from 10 to 50 mamudies per piece; the coarse cloths of Nausari, such as Sainjanes, which were broader than the calicoes and "more fitter for England than the Buffetacs," and also Dhootie, Byramy and Sheribaff, which were worth on the average 6 mamudies. Then there were Pintadoes, quilts, Comorin cloth and all sorts of painted stuffs in abundance. The advice of Bradshaw mentions several other kinds of cloth. It appears that piece-goods began to be imported into England soon after the settlement of the English in India. It will have been seen from the invoices of 1614 and 1621, given in the second chapter, that 12,500 pieces were ordered in the former year, but in the latter the quantity went up to 123,000 pieces, and to more than 165,900 in 1625. The demand for Indian calicoes was increasing so much that Thomas Keridge had to point out in 1624 that "the quantities of calicoes ordered to be provided annually will necessitate the resettling of divers factories dissolved last year." However, the wars in the Deccan so much "disjoynted all trade out of frame" that the supplies of piece-goods from Surat failed, and the prices and qualities of the cloths clearly showed "the great decay of weavers and trade in those parts." An increased quantity was therefore sought after on the Coromandel coast. There, too, for a time the wars and the famines had so much depreciated the quality and raised the price of calicoes that their demand in England decreased, while the development of the linen industry in the latter country discouraged the importation of Indian calicoes. Small quantities were, however, carried every year for re-exportation to the Continent and for meeting the requirements of a growing dyeing industry in England itself. The Company pointed out that "callicoes in general were in tymes paste a maine support of that Indian trade, and were here in good use and well requested and bin sold to som profitt. Since they have declyned in goodness and increased so much in their prises, they are nowe become here att a stand in their use, and other countrie cloathing, being better made and cheaper, succeeds in callicoes roome. All sorts of callicoes are of late very much disesteemed here; and would be more, were they not principally used in this place for dyeing into collours."

This despatch affords the most important evidence on the early growth of the weaving and dyeing industries of England.

The trade in the coast cloth was so much developed that we read of the Persian and Bantam markets as fully stocked with that "clothing and of a quantity of the same sent to England where it yielded contentable profitt." Later on, the Company advised the Surat factors to send calicoes "well-chosen and bought, clean whited, with hansome making up. The callicoes which for the most part wee have sold are of the Coromandell makeing, whoe are nowe preferr'd before anie of the Surat cloathing, because they fitt best for French and other forren sales."

So far as the qualities of cloth were concerned, we are informed that Persian taffetas were better than those from Agra, but that their colours quickly faded away and they became spotted. The Agra fabrics were also inferior to those of Surat, the yarn and weaving of the former "being more hollow and deceitfull, especially such as is bought white; which indeed can not be well judged of, by reason of the extraordinary gumming and beating, an art or custome auncienter, we believe, then your trade in these parts." To prevent these defects the factors began the practice of buying all cloth brown and having it cured at Baroda and Broach under their own superintendence.

In short, the trade in calicoes for the supply of the European markets was developing in the hands of the English. In the general depression of their business the export of cloth showed a great fall. The sales of 1650 do not indicate any great quantities of cloth put for sale, nor do the ladings of the Company's ships arriving in 1656.

Indigo. India is the original home of this dye. All the civilised nations of the ancient world got their supplies from this country. Yule has brought together some references from the works of Hippocrates, Dioscorides and Pliny, from the Periplus and other books, for showing the use of indigo among the ancient Greeks and Romans. The very word is a sufficient testimony of the source of the article. India continued to enjoy the monopoly till the middle of the seventeenth century. The English merchants used to carry it to their country during the sixteenth century from Aleppo and also got supplies from the Portuguese. When they first opened direct relations with India, we find them very anxious to secure that article. William Finch stated that the Biana kind was worth from 40 to 60 mamudies per maund, while the Sarkhej one could be procured at half the price. There was yet another coarser variety obtainable at Jambusar and Vorodca (Baroda) for 15 to 20 mamudies. In November, 1613, Aldworth reported that indigo could be had cheaper at Ahmadabad than at Surat, though the price quoted was Rs.14 or 35 mamudies, which is more than that quoted by Finch four years before at Surat. Private trade by the Company's servants in indigo was prohibited by Sir T. Roe,[1] because it was considered an important commodity for export to Europe. It formed the chief lading of the *Hope* in 1615. As the English were also opening trade with Arabia and Persia in Indian and European goods, they were anxious to explore all the principal markets in India for indigo. By 1625 Agra, Biana, Ahmadabad, Sarkhej, Jambusar, Cambay, Dholka, Lahore and the Coromandel coast had been tried. The Biana sort was most in demand in Persia and the Armenians and the Moslem merchants used to import large quantities of it into the

[1] Embassy, p. 350.

country. In 1628, 1,500 bales were sent there on English and Dutch ships alone. The English soon succeeded in capturing a large share in that trade, as is evidenced by the Surat Letter to the Company, dated December 31st, 1630, wherein *it is stated that they had begun to supply daily great quantities of indigo and calicoes to the Arabian and Persian markets, which before used to be performed by others both by sea and land.*

A few years later this lucrative branch of the Indo-European and Asiatic trades was threatened by the grant of a monopoly by the Great Mogul. The sale of this article was farmed out to one Manohar Dass for Rs.1,100,000. Thereupon both the Dutch and English entered into an agreement to oppose it by laying down that for one year neither nation should buy at a higher price than Rs.42 per Akbari maund of 50 lbs., nor convey any indigo to Persia for private merchants. The Dutch agent had, however, already purchased 300,000 lbs. at Rs.61 per maund and also paid in advance at the rate of Rs.50 per maund. Thus the object of the agreement was frustrated, but soon another trump card was played to bring pressure on the Emperor. The English sent orders to close the factories at Broach, Ahmadabad, Cambay and Agra. This move alarmed the Government, and had its desired effect. As the indigo cultivators, too, were dead against the monopoly, the Emperor very judiciously cancelled the lease, allowed both nations liberty to purchase from whomsoever they liked, and also ordered his revenue officers not to exact any tolls other than the seaport duties.

It must have been realised by this time that indigo was the most important article next to pepper and calicoes for the home investment of the English and their Asiatic trade. Yet its market was being spoiled by the keen competition of the Courteen Company and of the English Company's servants, who, in spite of prohibition, were trading in their private capacity in this and many other articles. The correspondence of those years is full of complaints on both these heads, but nothing effective could be done to suppress these internal and external competitors.

Of late years the rich Biana kind was being preferred in England as well as in Holland. The greater demand and the keener competition naturally sent up its price. It was, therefore, hoped that the slackness in the demand for the Sarkhej variety would lower its price to Rs.14–16. At the same time both the nations combined to bring down the prices of indigo. To the difficulty of higher prices was added another of the low quality of indigo sent home. Serious complaints were repeatedly made of the mixing of dust. The factors promised to do their best to improve the quality, "being sensible how that specie is one of the chief supporters of your trade." They even induced Prince Aurangzeb, who was then Viceroy of Gujerat, to prohibit the adulteration of indigo. The price of the indigo procured at Agra, Khurja and Hindaun remained at a high level, varying between Rs.45¾ and Rs.48 per maund. Taking the rupee as equivalent to 2½ mamudies, as was done in 1639,[1] we find that the price then varied from 115 to 120 mamudies per maund. This high price naturally curtailed the profits of the Company. It is therefore reported in the Surat Letter of January 10th, 1652, that indigo had "hithertofore bin your most gainful commodity," and it was then suggested that the profits in sugar were likely to exceed in future those of indigo.

It is interesting to note that the indigo trade was at this time further threatened by the importation of the West Indian indigo into England. The competition of this cheaper plantation produce was expected to tell heavily on the Company's investment in this profitable branch of its trade. To avoid future losses, the development of the Persian silk trade was suggested. But, though the Company could safeguard its interests, the decline of such a rich trade meant a serious blow to the agriculture and foreign trade of India.

Raw Silk. The other great trade which the English attempted to develop from the very beginning was that of silk supplies for England as well as the continent of Europe. The factors at Bantam were ordered in 1606 to try a trade

[1] Invoice of the *Royal Mary* in Marine Misc., IV.

with the Chinese by changing woollen cloth for silk, etc.[1] In 1608, eight bales of Lankin and Canton silk were sent home from Bantam, and small quantities of both raw silk and silks continued to be supplied afterwards. For instance, the *Gift* carried home fifty chests of silk of all sorts in 1616. Attempts were made to open direct trade with Japan and China through Richard Cocks and John Saris[2] on the one hand, and to explore the Siamese and Persian markets for silk supply on the other. We are informed that the Persian silk was procurable at Arras in Georgia and Lahijan in Ghilan at about 65–70 abassees the Shahi maund of English 12½ lbs. A very enthusiastic report was made from Ispahan by Edward Connock, who said that the silk trade was "the only richest yet known in the world," and that the annual import of Persian silk amounted to full £1,000,000 sterling at 6s. the pound of 16 ozs.[3] He believed that this trade would yield far better satisfaction than many, if not all the Indian trades put together.[4] The silk trade was diligently taken up, particularly after the tragedy of Amboyna, so that in the years 1622 and 1623 £190,000 worth of silk was imported into England by the E.I. Company. The capture of Ormus and the share in the Gombroon customs for a time gave splendid opportunity for the development of this branch, but the competition of the Dutch soon spoiled the market. It was reported in 1641 that silk was costing them 15s. or 15½s. the great pound of 24 ozs. and the price realised was only 10½s., though formerly they paid about 12s. and sold it at 22s.–25s. per lb.[5] The monopoly in the sale of silk by the king and

[1] Addl. MS., 24,934, p. 83.

[2] Diary of R. Cocks and Voyages of J. Saris (Hakl.).

[3] Letters Recd., I, p. 21 ; III, pp. 177, 242.

[4] O.C. 464, April, 1617.

[5] The discrepancy in the quotations of prices in various authors is simply perplexing. According to Olearius (1633–38), the price of raw silk was not above 2/6 or 2/8 per pound.

He states that the annual yield of silk was 20,000 bales, each bale being 216 lbs. ; that all Persia did not spend above a thousand bales of silk, and that the rest was sold in Turkey, the Indies, Italy and to the English and Dutch. In other words, the imported silk amounted to 4 million pounds, while Cannock estimates only one million pounds.

"Voyages and Trades of the Ambassadors," by Adam Olearius. London, 1669.

the gross abuses and extortions practised by the Persian officers in its sale very much discouraged the English. Having been shut out from China and discouraged in Persia, they turned more attention to the supplies of silk in India.

There is no mention of silk in the early reports of the English factors at Surat. The Company was pressed to open trade with Bengal for raw silk as early as 1613, in imitation of the Dutch who, it was stated, had invested some 100,000 rialls in wrought and unwrought silks.[1] Sir Thomas Roe was specially commissioned to attempt the acquisition of trading rights in Bengal and Persia for opening up the silk trade, but nothing could be effected by him so far as Bengal was concerned. A few years afterwards, in conformity with the Company's order for procuring 100 maunds of Bengal silk, the Surat factors included the stated quantity in their proposed investment of the year 1621.[2] A factory was established at Patna by Hughes and Parker and silk, silk stuffs, and several other commodities were sent to Agra. *The Lion*, the *Hart*, and other ships from Surat arrived in England with a parcel of Bengal silk and a trial was made by one Mr. Millward. "Nevertheless it was conceived that though it should prove somewhat better than the other sort, the Company will find no benefitt by bringing of it hither."[3]

Hence, the first factory established at Patna had to be dissolved on account of the Company's prohibition of Bengal silk. Attempts had also been made to procure Bengala silk through the Masulipatam factory, but the agents there saw no prospects of securing it in 1621. In another letter, dated February 26, 1622, they wrote home that "their longe expectacion vanisheth like smoke."

Ten years later another attempt was made to open trade with Bengal, but this time, too, the enterprise "fayled of its expected success." However, it was discovered that there were prospects of a considerable trade. Silk could be procured

[1] Court Bk., 3, p. 69.

[2] Court Bk., 4, p. 235; Surat consultations, March, 1621; Peter Mundy (Hakluyt), ii, p. 136.

[3] Court Bk., 6, p. 70, 9th Aug., 1623.

at 4 to 5 fanams the English pound. It meant that the prime cost of this article was only $2\frac{1}{4}$s. per lb. or about a rupee in 1632. At this time two bales of Bengala silk were sent to England as a sample in the *Mary*, and they were disposed of at 20s. per lb. for trial only.

The English settled factories in Orissa and also acquired the right to trade in Bengal. In the latter they were not, however, allowed to establish factories for fear of quarrels with the Portuguese.

Through the instrumentality of Dr. Boughton and Brookehaven, they obtained in 1650 such privileges as far outstripped those enjoyed by both the Portuguese and the Dutch. It was then pointed out that 200–300 bales of silk could be procured in February or March at Rs.85–90 per maund.

The prospects of developing the Bengal trade were for a time darkened on account of the breaking up of the Anglo-Dutch War. The Company, too, was then financially in direst straits. It did not even keep any record of its business in those years, "the Court considering what prejudice it might bee unto them if this business were not carryed very secret and privately" (Court Bk. 23, p. 159).

But after the cessation of the war, we find 13 bales, or 2151 lbs. of Bengala silk worth £705, included in the goods laden on the *Benjamin* at the Swally Marine on the 20th January, 1657. On the basis of its invoice value, it cost[1] the Company in India 7s. per lb. Thus it appears that prices had

[1] The following data on silk prices and importations will prove useful and interesting :—

Year.	Price.		Remarks.
1613			Large quantities sold. Court Bk., 3, pp. 184, 226.
1614 July	25/1	per ℔. of 16 oz.	Court Bk., 3, p. 394.
1615 March	31/5	per ℔. of 16 oz.	1 cwt. 1 quarter sold.
1619 Sept.	26/10	per ℔. of 24 oz.	71 bales of Persia silk.
1621			100 maunds of Bengal silk invoiced. C. Bk., 4, China silk brought, 414, 435.
1622	27/–		£93,000 worth Persian silk brought. C. Bk., 7, p. 595.
1623			£97,000 worth Persian silk brought.
1626 May	26/8		
1628 Dec.	26/8		782 bales of Persian silk.

soared to an exceptionally high level within a short time, due probably to the large purchases made by private merchants and the Dutch Company. The latter is reported to have exported goods worth £45,000 from Bengal in 1659. These included 910 bales of silk alone. (Marine Misc., IV.) Thus at the end of our period a small beginning in silk investments had been made by the English, but it was destined to develop to great proportions in the next few years.

Saltpetre[1] may be placed next to spices, pepper, silk and cotton fabrics, and indigo in importance as an article of export from India. It did not attract the attention of the English factors up to 1620. It is not mentioned in Sir T. Roe's report on the goods available at Agra and in Bengal. The earliest reference to its supply is in the reply of Thomas Kerridge in 1621 to the Company that it was not available about Surat. At that time the Dutch used to export large quantities from Pulicat and bring it back in the shape of gunpowder, because, as reported, the Indian powder "will not keepe, for being ill-corned it grows all into clodds." In 1625 the Company were informed that saltpetre could be secured very cheap, and President Kerridge promised to have a supply ready for the next ships to be despatched to England. From his letter of January 4th, 1628, we learn that large enough quantity had

Year.	Price.	Remarks.
1629 Feb.	24/-	
1630		1400 bales, "which will nearly equal the whole estate of the 1st Persia Voyage."
1635		China silk trade tried.
1636 March	21/3	Persia silk.
1637 ,,	23/-	China silk.
1639	18/4	Persian coarse silk.
	18/0	Persian coarse silk.
1640	17/- to 17/2	356 bales sold. Prime cost 10/6, formerly sold at 22/- to 25/-.
1641	15/- to 18/6	*The Supply* brought 600 bales.
1642		The *Crispian* had 527 bales of Persian silk.
1650	20/2 per lb.	

[1] Eng. Fact., Vol. 1618–21, pp. 251, 336; Vol. 1622–23, pp. 128, 229; Vol. 1624–29, pp. 83, 209, 215, 270, 275, 335; Vol. 1637–41, pp. 72, 94, 262.

been sent to ballast the ships and that they would send a like quantity on every ship, and more, if it could be got. In the same month 2000 maunds more were bought at Rs.2¼ per maund, while two months later the price fell to Rs.1½ only. The Company were informed that this commodity could not be exported without royal permit. The English and Dutch factors were imprisoned at Agra in 1628 for exporting it clandestinely. Bribes and presents, however, secured their release and the necessary permission. One year after we hear that more saltpetre than ever before was sent, and that orders had been given to purchase the whole available quantity. Its demand continued to grow. In 1638 promise was made to procure a far larger quantity of saltpetre which had proved so good. On the other hand, the Directors complained that saltpetre was expensive to buy and troublesome to carry home, as it infected and spoiled other goods. Orders were consequently sent to give preference to sugar, ginger, cinnamon, etc. Its supplies were not stopped, rather means were suggested for preventing its bad effects. Yet the quantity was curtailed in 1639 and it was bought no more the following year. The deficiency was made up by the purchases made by the Courteen Company's ships, and the Company's factors, too, indulged in it in 1643. Next year the factors were required to provide 20 or 25 tons of it for kentledge only. The general trade was so much depressed on account of the growing competition of the Portuguese, Dutch and Courteen Company that supplies were altogether stopped in 1649, and the stock at hand was sent to Bantam for sale at Macassar. It should be observed that factors had been busy in exploring new markets for the supply of this article. It was procured from Masulipatam (1637), at Armagaon (1638), Bengal (1639), Raybag (1640), Rajpore (1645) and Tatta in 1647. Best hopes of the development of this branch of trade were cherished at the foundation of the factory at Hugly. The cost at Patna was only Rs.1 per maund, though customs and freight raised the price at Hugly to Rs.1.4as. In the same year 200 tons of well-refined saltpetre was ordered to be sent for the use of the State. The Dutch were then exporting ten times as much. In 1651 private English merchants had, however, imported such large quantities that, after satisfying the needs of their Government, they had exported much to France, Sweden, Hamburg, Holland and Italy.

Now we must take a rapid glance at the supplies of **cotton-wool**[1] and yarn. The first, though now one of the principal exports from India, occupied a very insignificant place in those days. Cotton was reported by William Finch to be worth from 40 to 60 mamudies per *candy*, while yarn of all sorts, both fine and coarse, was at about 8 or 10 mamudies per *maund* or Rs.5 per maund at the highest. It was one of the principal articles in the coastal trade of the Indies, being carried to Sumatra and other adjacent islands, Persia and Arabia. As an import into England, some of it was used in packing calicoes, and some used as ballast and stowage. Sugar and saltpetre being scarce and dear, the factors sent cotton which the Company did not much desire, but it was expected to be a profitable lading, especially when it could be pressed as they did in Turkey. Instruments were demanded for its compressing. In 1628 the price of cotton was reported as 72½ mamudies per candy of 20 maunds, which meant a rise of about 25 per cent on that of 1608–9. Two years later, order was sent to provide cotton-wool only to fill up the vacant corners of the ships. The *Charles* had 22 bales of cotton as cargo in 1630 and the *Royal Mary* 15 bales in 1639. Then followed complaints of its dearness, but the price fell abnormally from 10 and 12 to 4 and 5 mamudies per maund in 1644. Even this reduced quotation was 50 per cent higher than that of 1608–9.

1608 . .	40–60	mamudies per	candy.
1628 . .	72½	,,	,,
During famine	200–240	,,	,,
1644 . .	80–100	,,	,,

Indian yarn[2] was imported into England by the Levant

[1] Letters Recd., I, p. 28; Eng. Fact., Vol. 1624–29, p. 212.

[2] Letters Recd., III, p. 83; Eng. Fact., Vol. 1619–22, pp. 41, 44, 49, 153, 157, 185; Vol. 1624–29, p. 64; Vol. 1630–33, pp. 4, 9.

Company, so its import by the E.I. Company was not a new introduction. In October, 1614, it was decided to send £500 worth of yarn to England out of a cargo of £14,802, and 316 maunds were laden on the *Hector* bound for Priaman and Ticcoo, but she seems to have proceeded with this cargo to England. The Company forbade the sending home of yarn in 1618, while the Masulipatam factors advised to procure it in their town whence the Dutch were sending large quantities to Holland. Yarn was abundant at Broach: 10 to 12 maunds a day could be got by the English all the year round at prices varying from 7 to 20 pice the seer fit for England. Its demand grew so much that in case of failure in securing other goods, yarn, either plain-reeled, as desired, or cross-reeled, was to be sent home. In 1628 525 bales were sent to England. The factors were afraid that this quantity would cloy the market, but the Company reported it to be a profitable commodity. "There is no fear," wrote the Directors, "of glutting the market here by selling cotton yarn, for much can be sold than has ever yet come from India." Order was given to provide 600 or 700 bales annually in future. When large investments began to be made at Broach, the weavers "grew into a mutiny, and combined among themselves not to bring any baftas to our house untill wee give them a writing not to buy any more cotton yarne; nor have they to this day. You may not therefore expect such great quantities as required or heretofore sent you, for except in this place (and here alsoe by stealth doe wee in a manner gett itt into our house) it is not to bee had."

It is abundantly clear from this Surat letter that the exports of yarn very much raised the price to the prejudice of native weavers, and that scarcity of yarn was felt even in such great manufacturing centres as Surat and Broach. The prices of cotton and yarn were reported as 12 and 23 mamudies per maund at Surat, Broach and Baroda, though yarn could formerly be had at 16 mamudies per maund. This abnormal rise was undoubtedly due to famine, so that in 1636 the price went down to its normal level. The demand in England had much increased for the finer sort, as the workmen had of late found many uses for it. The price of this quality of yarn in India was given as 12–14d. per lb., while two years later, in another letter dated November 27th, 1643, the price in England of good yarn is quoted 2s. 9d. per lb., meaning thereby that the prices realised at home were 2½ times those given in India. Large investments were natural, but the factors in India could not get a sufficient quantity of the requisite quality. The Agra and Ahmadabad markets, too, fell short of the desired quantity. Moreover, owing to the large investments made by the Dutch, yarn was too dear. Thereupon samples were obtained from Baroda, and these being equal to, if not better than, what was procurable at Surat, 50 bales were purchased. It was believed that Baroda would be the best source of supply in future.

During the period of general depression the Company ordered only small quantities as, for instance, 150 bales were demanded in 1653. The demand was still further reduced on the part of the Company, though the private merchants must have imported large amounts of yarn. It is clear by this survey that the demand for this commodity had very much increased in England, and that there was often difficulty in securing the requisite supply in the principal Indian towns, due undoubtedly to the intense demand for it in the country itself for the purpose of manufacturing cloth.

Sugar. The cultivation of Indian sugar-cane was introduced into various countries at different epochs, so the foreign demand for Indian sugar must have from time to time been curtailed. Most parts of Europe were supplied by the Portuguese with Brazil sugars during the sixteenth and seventeenth centuries, yet Indian sugar was not altogether excluded from Europe. The Levant Company used to supply England with this article from Alexandria, and then the E.I. Company began its import in the second quarter of the seventeenth century. Mr. Aldworth found indigo, white powdered sugar and divers other stuffs fit for England at Ahmadabad in 1613. He intended to send some of these articles for trial at home. The price of sugar was then quoted by him as Rs.2 per maund. The Surat sugar was reported as "no commodity for England," and the Ahmadabad kind was also no good. However, sugar was sent home about the year 1628–29. The Directors complained that the consignment was damaged, coarse and dear, and prohibited the Surat factors from purchasing any more in future. The latter had already despatched a quantity of the Agra kind by their last ships, and had 178 bales containing 3028 maunds of the same at hand. As it was not a very profitable concern, the Company allowed their servants and mariners to trade in this commodity. Although Indian sugar could hardly compete with the Brazil kind in the Western world, yet small consignments continued to be included even in the Company's investments all through this period. We are told that Agra was then the chief centre of sugar manufacture, and the best and the cheapest could be had there in large quantities, although in Bengal it was reported to be still better and cheaper. At the same time, "sugar being procurable in many places" a small trial was desired to be made in each variety. Thus we find the English factors exploring the various centres of sugar manufacture in India for their requirements which, it is a pity, cannot be determined now on account of the lack of necessary data in the records.

Tea and Coffee. It is interesting to mention that neither Linschoten nor Pyrard has referred to tea as a popular drink of the Chinese. The former describes the use only in Japan, where it was drunk by every man whether it be winter or summer after meals. The Chinese are represented as drinking wine made of rice and "brewed as we brew beer." But it is reasonable to assume from the accounts of other travellers that it was not universally used even in Japan. Master Arthur Hatch, Minister, and Saris, writing about the meals and drinks of the people, do not notice the use of tea. The ordinary drink of the common people was hot water or a light wine prepared by boiling water with rice. The earliest reference is in a letter from Mr. R. Wickham, the Company's

Agent at Firando, who writing in 1615, to Mr. Eaton at Miaco, asks for a pot of the best sort of Chaw. The European residents at Surat some time after began to drink tea. It has been stated by Mandelslo in his Travels that the English and Dutch were entertained at their ordinary meetings with tea, instead of which the Persians used coffee. There must have been a growing custom of tea-drinking in India, as we find that 20 maunds of tea were included in the goods landed at Surat from Batavia in 1650, and all bought by two Surat merchants. There is, however, no reference to tea being sent to England.[1]

The case is quite different with coffee. It was much used by the Turks, Arabians, Egyptians and Persians in their own country, and they continued this habit in other lands wherever they settled. Its use was noticed by Linschoten,[2] Pyrard,[3] Roe,[4] Terry[5] and others. Monfart (1610) would have us believe that it was drunk from Turkey to China. According to Terry, many of the people at Surat, who being strict in their religion, drank no wine, used cohwa or coffee, "a drink more wholesome than pleasant." The earliest reference in the official correspondence to coffee, besides that of Sir T. Roe, is in Letters Received, Vol. I, p. 122. The English began to deal in coffee about the year 1619, when Mr. Kerridge sent for the Surat market 100 Surat maunds of the very best kind of coffee from Mocha, which was brought to India in 1621. The best report on its supply and demand is from the pen of Mr. Kerridge. "Regarding coffa, they state that only Mocha and the places adjacent doth yield that seede, which serveth all Turkey, Arabia, Persia and India." According to him, the seed and husk could be bought at 11/11 and 6/6 mamudies per maund and sold at 15 and 8/9 mamudies at Surat. Both

[1] Letters Recd., I, pp. 144, 157; Purchas, E. S., Vol. X, p. 64; Hakluyt—Saris, p. 127; Harris, I, p. 755; Eng. Fact., Vol. 1646–50, p. 330.

[2] Eng. Fact., Vol. 1619 22, pp. 89, 296, 306; Vol. 1624–29, pp. 191, 213; Macpherson, pp. 11, 447; Linschoten, A.D. 1598, Vol. I, p. 157.

[3] Pyrard, A.D. 1610, Vol. I, p. 172.

[4] Roe, A.D. 1615, Embassy, p. 32.

[5] Terry, A.D. 1616, Purchas, E. S., Vol. IX, p. 21.

were used for beverage, though the seed was better and dearer than the other.

He sent samples of each sort to England. The English used to carry coffee to Persia, Gombroon, Bassora, Surat and even to Madras, but not to England up to 1660. The Hollanders introduced its use in their own country, while in England the first coffee-house was opened by Mr. Edwards, an English Turkey merchant, in 1652.

British Exports to the East

Woollens. The manufacture of woollen cloth was the principal, if not the only, industry worth mentioning in England at that period. Every attempt was consequently made to encourage the export of woollens, as it also served to reduce the export of bullion. The expanding market in the East is evidenced by several early reports. In 1608 John Saris demanded only 20 pieces of broadcloth for Bantam, i.e. for the whole sphere of English influence at that time. Next year Finch required 200 to 300 pieces of broadcloth, besides kersies and baize, of which good quantities could be sold at Surat and Agra. Then, the invoice of Thomas Aldworth for Surat alone was 1500 pieces, and he held out the hope "to vent 4000 cloths per annum." The character of the cloths required will be evident from the following invoice of Aldworth :—[1]

500 Venice red cloths whereof 30 or 40 stammels.
100 Popinjay greens, and light grass greens.
100 Straw colours, yellows and horse flesh.
100 Light blues, commonly called Hulings.
200 Murries in grave and other pleasant colours.
500 Pieces of Devon Kersies of the colours above said of 50s.

It seems that these large orders were sent without fully realising the Indian demand. Some time after it was truly represented that "for the price of covid of our cloth a man will there (at Surat) make himself two or three suits." Cotton fabrics were then and are now best suited for the Indian

[1] Letters Recd., I, 240.

climate, therefore woollens could only be used for the coverings of elephants and the making of saddles. They were fit for the use of the nobility only. In 1617 the Surat factors complained that broadcloth had "become a very drug." This slump necessitated the curtailment of the invoice to 100 pieces alone. Then Kerridge is found complaining of "a glut of broadcloth in India, though the price is not much stood on (when wanted), being used by the King and nobility." Again, in 1631, English commodities lay dead undisposed. Although the sphere of English trade had gone on increasing in India, yet even in 1629, 300 pieces were advised by the Surat factors. No English cloth was sent to India for two years, as mentioned in the Surat Letter, dated 13th April, 1630.

In this branch, too, the Dutch competition was telling heavily upon the English. Their cloth excelled the English one in fineness, colour and dressing, and yet it was "shamefully by them undervalued in price." Hence, about 400 broadcloths and kersies were ordered that year. Ten years later the situation remained unaltered. The cheaper and superior Dutch imports were thwarting the sale of English cloth. There was, moreover, the competition of the Persians, Armenians and private English merchants who were selling the same cloths at lower prices at Agra and Delhi. Notwithstanding this competition, English cloth was introduced in Persia and in all the important centres of India, as Surat, Agra, Delhi, Tatta, Masulipatam, etc. In 1647 a growing demand was reported from Bengal, Agra and Persia. It was followed by a favourable report in 1649–50 of the vent of broadcloth in India, Johore, Perak and adjacent places. The Bengal demand of 1650 for 30 or 40 pieces per year, shows how the Company could not much succeed in finding a market for woollens. Complaints of a reduced demand continue in the following years from Persia and Agra. The Company are again urged to prevent private trade in this commodity, because only then considerable profit could be made. It should also be observed that the methods of packing, dressing and colouring were not good in those days, so that we find the factors repeatedly pointing out improvements in these items. We shall see in our next survey how these defects were removed in the following half a century and how vigorously the sale of English cloth was pushed on.

Next to woollens, metals were the only produce of England needed for the East.

Metals. Iron, copper, tin, lead, quicksilver and vermilion were always in considerable demand in India. The first three were at times sent on trial, but proved to be unprofitable. The indigenous *iron* and Japan and China *copper* brought by the Portuguese and Dutch were far cheaper than those of England. *European* tin also could not compete in India with the kinds imported from China, Tenasserim and the Malaya Peninsula. The Persian market was as well supplied by the other European rivals. The Dutch were able to hold a monopoly of the supply of tin to all the Asiatic countries. The English struggled hard to obtain concessions of buying tin in Perak, Johore, etc., but did not succeed during the period under review. The case was different with lead. It was imported from Europe direct, or through Mocha and Ormus, before the advent of the English. Finding a constant demand, they carried lead even in their first voyage to Bantam. Finch mentioned the Surat prices of lead and tin to be 8½ and 40 mamudies respectively in 1609. Six years later Elkington advised the Company to send 1000 pigs of lead, but in 1617 Kerridge observed that the whole kingdom had not "disburthened them of above 9000 maunds at most," and that 9500 maunds were left in their storehouse. This was considered a sufficient supply for the following year. They always tried to find a market for lead at all their factories. The price in 1623 and 1629 had remained at the old level of about 8½ mamudies, both at Surat and Ahamadabad. At that time the annual demand amounted to 1000 pigs. Since 1632 the market was spoiled by the Governor of Surat, who did not allow any European to sell lead to anyone but himself. This monopoly very much reduced the profits. For instance, in 1639 it was sold at 7½ mamudies per maund. Even six years later the demand was slack, yet lead was here in better request than in any of the adjacent countries. The factors did not invoice it for a year or two in the hope of raising its price to 10 mamudies. In 1649–50 small quantities of the metal were sold or bartered, but even Capt. Bridgman held out no hope of selling any quantity in Bengal. Two years later still, it was reported as the King's commodity, and the price was 8 mamudies per maund. Thus throughout this period of fifty years the price of lead remains almost constant, and the demand much restricted on account of the monopoly of its purchase. It was much used in making shot, packing cloth or manufacturing red lead. The Indian Government wanted the whole supply for its own use, and hence claimed the right of pre-emption.

Quicksilver[1] was much employed from very ancient times in making vermilion and medicines, and extracting silver from its ores. Finch and Elkington both reported it to be "always a vendible commodity." The market could not be "glutted with what quantity can be attained in England." The price was stated to vary from 240 to 350 mamudies per maund, but the reported discovery of a mercury mine lowered the price to 200 mamudies. It was then feared that "in a few years it will not countervail the charge of sending hither." The demand for foreign mercury was much reduced, so that the Company were informed that "one year or two were better forborne than sent."[2] Another mine was reported to have been discovered near Lahore; there was also the competition of the Portuguese and Dutch, who as usual imported large quantities from the old source in China, and again, it was found that the metal imported by way of Mocha was cheaper than the English could afford. Still, small quantities continued to be sent for by the sea-route. In 1621

[1] Eng. Fact., Vol. 1646–50, pp. 7, 36; Kutilaya Arthasastra, p. 98; Letters Recd., III, pp. 9, 66.

[2] Letters Recd., IV, pp. 297, 337; V, pp. 106, 135.

a consignment was sold at 150 mamudies per maund, which was equivalent to $4\frac{1}{2}$s. per lb. "Two thousand maunds will sell at pleasure," was the report. From 1622 the demand seems to be very great and the prices were very high, ranging from Rs.85–98 in 1622 to Rs.125 in 1625 per maund, and 7s. 4d. per lb. in 1629.[1] In other words, the prices varied between 205 and 300 mamudies per maund during these seven years. This period of inflation was followed by a serious depression, due to famine, wars and the competition of private English merchants, but especially to the deliberate cutting down of prices by the Dutch to beat down the English. They sold it at Rs. 62–63 in 1630, 140 mamudies or Rs.60 per maund next year, 4s. 6d. per lb. in 1632 and only 90 mamudies per maund in 1633. Supplies were stopped for two years, small quantities were ordered next, but profit was doubtful even in December, 1639. However, the market recovered in 1645–47. The Company were informed that "the quicksilver was very welcome, it being a rising commodity and not any to be sold in town but yours." There were offers of Rs.70–74 per maund and a prospect of a still further rise in 1648. Large quantities imported by the Dutch and Portuguese from China sent down the price to Rs.60 per maund.[2] The English used to buy it from Holland and even Italy, so it was difficult for them to compete with their rivals. To put an end to English competition in this branch, the Dutch prohibited its exportation from their country in 1659.

Taking the metal group as a whole, it is evident that the English could not extend their business in this line during this first period of more than half a century, the chief reasons being that there was a large supply of all metals from the Southern Islands, China and Japan, and that the English were excluded from these markets on account of the exclusive control of the commerce of those countries by other rivals.

Among articles not of the growth or manufacture of

[1] From the Dutch Records, Series I, Vol. 8, doc. 267, we learn that the English had outdone the Dutch for some years in supplying India with lead, vermilion, and quicksilver, for which a great demand existed. A.D. 1629.

[2] The Surat maund was first of 28 lbs. and later on of 33 lbs.

England but imported into India by the English, **coral**[1] and **ivory** stand out prominently. Coral was much in demand from very ancient times. Several varieties of it have been spoken of in the Arthasastra of Kautilaya, probably of the fourth century before Christ. We have already seen a brisk trade in it at various ports. Naturally the English were interested in securing a share in its supply. William Finch demanded "some small quantity of red coral, the first for a trial," in 1609. Four years later Biddulph reported that coral would prove a good commodity, and held out the hope of selling a great quantity in Deccan where it was used for burning with the dead. Thomas Aldworth confirmed all the points of his predecessor, and added that 300 chests were usually brought from the Red Sea at a time and yet the market was never glutted. Afterwards Elkington advised the Company to send coral, as it would tend to a great profit. This experimental period was soon over. In 1616–17, when the question of transferring the English headquarters from Surat to Gogo, or Gogha, on the Kathiawar side of the Gulf of Cambay arose, it was pointed out that the latter place was not "so fit for the vent of three of our main commodities, which are coral, lead and teeth." The report of Thomas Kerridge is worthy of notice: "That from Mocha is of a paler hue, yet they spare not to furnish this place (Surat) with at least 300 chests at every return. You may boldly send by every shipping adventure, far greater quantities than is now supplied, and rely on a competent gain by such employment."

The Surat merchants were naturally alarmed at the ever-growing quantities imported by the English and Dutch merchants. The Company were informed that the people of the country were "in purpose to relinquish their corall trade out of the Red Sea, seeing ours so much better than theirs." The Indian merchants petitioned the Prince to prohibit the sale of foreign coral and its further supply through the Europeans. The local Governor forbade the landing of coral

[1] Letters Recd., I, pp. 33, 307, 310; III, p. 10; IV, p. 152.

from the English fleet. The English appealed against the prohibitory order, and were given permission to sell their coral at Surat or elsewhere for one year, provided they should bring no more of it. Some time after, when they insisted on selling coral in the Deccan, the Surat merchants prohibited the provision of calicoes to them. For a time they quietly complied with the wishes of the Indian traders, but they did not intend to give up such a profitable business without a struggle. The question at issue was quite clear to the prince and the people. We are informed that Prince Shah Jahan flew into a rage at the sight of the royal order granting the provisional permission referred to above, and tore it up stating, "nothing else but the profitt and bread of his people could content us."[1] No more significant testimony is required to show the growing control by the Europeans of the carrying and external trades of the country.

The English were not willing to submit to the restrictions imposed on the importation of coral. They proceeded to seize and plunder Indian ships. Dabul, Gogha, Diu and Surat vessels easily fell a prey. These high-handed adventures were followed by an ultimatum to the Governor of Surat for paying up more than 200,000 mamudies for the various wrongs they had suffered. The English piracies created consternation among the merchants of the various ports; the Dutch, too, refused to give any assistance against the English; the Governor had therefore to succumb to their demands. The dispute was accommodated by the payment of a very large sum, the purchase of the whole stock of coral in the hands of the English, and by a compact for a complete liberty of trade in future.

This was the beginning and the end of all troubles from the Surat merchants. The days of their free and independent trade with the African and Asiatic countries had almost passed away by the presence and extensive dealings of the two European nations in the Indian waters, and they succumbed to the inevit-

[1] Eng. Fact., Vol. 1618–21, p. 325; Vol. 1622, pp 1, 31, 54, 130, 137, 151, 176, 320.

able. It was not merely the question of the provision of coral that had been settled, but the right of free trade with Persia and other countries had been secured and the privilege of importing foreign goods into India on the same basis as the nationals of Asiatic countries had been enjoying till then was obtained. The latter meant the transference of one branch after another of the Oriental trade into the hands of the Europeans on account of their superiority at sea.

The English share in this coral trade went on increasing,[1] until a brief stop was put to it by the wars in the Deccan. However, it recovered in 1633, when three kinds of coral were sold at Rs.8¾, Rs.9½ and Rs.4 per seer at Surat, their prices in England being 12s.–14s. 7d., 15s. and 7s. per lb. respectively. This dealing gave a profit of about 80 per cent. Gains were naturally variable; three years before they could make only 37 per cent on Italian coral. A growing market was also found at Masulipatam and Golcondah, where 20 or 30 chests costing in England 14½s. per lb. and selling at Masulipatam at 100 pagodas the maund of 26 lbs. were advised in 1636. In the same year great prospects of its sale in China were pointed out by Bornford, who undertook a voyage to Macao "to gain an entrance into the China trade." The growth in this branch is evident from the remark of the President of the Surat Factory in 1639 that, next to broadcloth, coral was "the most staple and vendible commodity that Europe produced." The price was reported to be Rs.10½ per seer of 18 pice, a "price not of late years heard of." During the next few years we hear of sales of coral at Raybag, Bijapore, Armagaon, Bhaktal, Cochin, Agra, in Bengal, and on all the Malabar coast from Goa to Cape Comorin. The English had the whole trade to themselves on account of the war between the Dutch and Portuguese. In 1644 the price was 115 pagodas per maund against 100 in 1636 at Masulipatam, and 4000 lbs. yearly were demanded for that market. However, the tide

[1] Eng. Fact., Vol. 1634–39, pp. 204, 208, 226, 228; Vol. 1642–45, p. 86. Cf. the Dutch testimony of the flourishing and growing trade in coral in the hands of the English. It said that they had sold 46,700 Eng. lbs. at 16/8.

began to turn at the prospect of a peace between the two nations. The Company were informed that "but now the Portingales have peace and open trade, we may not expect the like opportunity, since they will undoubtedly abundantly supply those markets in the future." After that year complaints began to pour in as to coral remaining a dead commodity, so that in 1650 the Company were advised to stop further supplies and most of the coral was got rid of at a considerable loss. Yet it appears that the English continued to hold the market on the Coromandel, while the Dutch and Portuguese recovered their lost position on the Malabar coast.

As to **ivory**[1] it has been seen that large amounts of it were annually imported into India by the Portuguese and many Asiatic merchants who traded with the various countries of Africa. When the English began to take the place of both sets of importers, they turned their attention to this article also. The first sale of ivory by an Englishman consisted of two elephants' teeth captured from an Indian junk. Two years later, in 1611, an English ship brought to Surat tusks, broadcloth, kerseys, says, tin and red lead. The tusks were sold at 62½ to 64 mamudies per maund in 1613. Next year their commodities of quicksilver, lead, vermilion and teeth gave them such "reasonable profit, beyond their computation" that greater quantities were advised from home. It is strange that the English could make large profits on ivory brought from England; the African supply must have given tremendous gains to the importers. The wars in the Indian waters dislocated the Persian and African trade, and thus reduced the necessary supplies of ivory. In 1622 the price obtained at Nawpee, near Burhanpur, was Rs.32 per maund of 43 seers, but Rs.45 per Akbari maund at Agra. Ivory ceased to be brought into India by the English from 1630 to 1648. The prices were very uncertain, because they depended upon irregular supplies from Mozambique and Malinda. A Surat letter of 1646 states that "elephants' teeth are constantly in these parts a staple

[1] Eng. Fact., Vol. 1643–45, p. 230; Vol. 1646–50, pp. 290, 291; Vol. 1651–54, p. 57.

commodity. The sorts formerly sent from England are now fetching Rs.30 per maund of 40 seers, which is about 2s. per lb.; and in England they will cost 10s. or 11s. per cwt."[1] The usual price at Ahmadabad was reported Rs.32–34 only. The above prices hardly left any profit, so the imports of ivory were always very small during this period.

[1] Eng. Fact., Vol. 1622–23, pp. 8, 108; Vol. 1646–50, p. 8.

CHAPTER V

THE ANGLO-INDIAN TRADE
(1658–1707)

Nature of the Data. The first period of infancy, dependence and disappointment is succeeded by one of unbounded energy in all directions of the Company's business. The brilliant success of that body excited the envy of the mercantile classes in England and attracted many adventurous spirits to the East as "interlopers" or "pirates." In India, too, the Company's business was much depressed by cumbersome restrictions, heavy transit duties and other undue levies. It will be seen how the Company struggled hard against both sets of difficulties and how it came out successful in both. Notwithstanding those long struggles fought out in India as well as at home, the Company did mightily succeed in firmly building up the English trade with the East.

The data for the earlier part of this second period are not available in any published record, hence the returns for the export trade have been compiled from the Manuscript Letter Books of the Court in the India Office. The Court Books and Marine Records, too, occasionally afford very valuable material. The annual values of bullion and merchandise compiled for the years 1667–73 differ from the account presented to Parliament by the Company. The discrepancy is probably due to the inclusion or exclusion of a ship or ships in a different year from the one taken by the latter. The ships mentioned in an April letter, 1660–61, might sail in May; in such a case they should actually be included in the returns for the year 1661–62, but in my account which is identical with the one preserved in the Court Book 25*a*, they have been accounted for in the year 1660–61. I have followed the Letters throughout up to 1681–82, the last year for which regular returns of the cargoes of East-bound ships are given in those Records. The Minutes of the Court also do not afford any regular material for the following years, hence separate returns for money and merchandise cannot be made out for the period[1] succeeding the year 1681–2.

Development of Export Trade

It has been remarked that when the Company resumed their trade on the confirmation of their exclusive charter, in 1657, they showed an unprecedented activity. During six and one-third years, from January, 1658, to April, 1664, they sent out eighty-four ships to the East on which were exported in

Bullion	£733,748	} = £991,770.
Produce and manufactures	£258,022	

Their business was, however, very much curtailed on account of the outbreak of war with the Dutch. In the next three years the Company's trade consequently remained in a low state. Only nine ships could be despatched with small amounts of money and merchandise. The annual average for this period of three years was £14,000 for *money* against £117,400 and £18,000 for *goods* against £41,000 of the previous six years. Taking the fat and lean years together, the average annual investment during the nine years was

£86,000 . .	in money	} = £121,000 in total exports.
£35,000 . .	in goods	

After the cessation of hostilities, great enthusiasm was shown in increasing the volume of trade. In the next seven years ninety-nine ships sailed to the East with £1,165,311 in treasure and about £600,000 in goods and merchandise of the growth and manufacture of England. It implied an average of £166,473 per annum for bullion, which sum is 193 per cent of the average of the previous nine years. The annual average of exports in merchandise was doubled as compared to the preceding period of nine years. *This annual exportation of*

[1] See Appendices A and B on pp. 296–7 *infra*.

about £253,000 *stands in marked contrast to the past career of the Company, when the sum total of the Company's exports to India rarely amounted to* £100,000 *in any one year previous to* 1657 *and in some years did not amount to even* £25,000.

Comparing the septennial returns of 1667–74 with those of 1617–24, which years were marked by a great expansion of the Company's trade, it will be observed that the amount of trade as represented by exports had developed to about 2½-fold at the end of sixty years, while the annual average for goods alone in the two septennial periods stood at £30,000 and £85,500 respectively. It meant that the Company had succeeded in creating an increasing demand in the East for British woollens and other goods. Although it had to fight against odds at home and abroad for its very existence, it not only kept open the Eastern market for England, but, with all the might, wealth and grandeur of the Dutch, was also successful in supplying greater quantities of Indian products to the countries of the Continent. Sir Josiah Child in his spirited defence of the East India Company justly maintains and demonstrates that "the East India Trade is a most (if not the most) profitable and beneficial trade to the Kingdom." "It is a trade," says he, "that takes off a considerable quantity of our Native Commodities for our consumption, at the cheapest rates.

That brings us some commodities for further Manufacture.

That furnishes us with large quantities of goods for foreign markets.

That gives employment to, and so maintains, great numbers of *English* Shipping.

That occasions the building of more ships of burden and force, fit for warlike service, and defence of the Kingdom, than any other trade.

That brings a considerable Revenue to His Majesty's Exchequer by Customs, and the greatest addition to the Kingdom's Stock."[1]

[1] The E.I. Trade, p. 6, published 1677; I.O. Tracts, 485.

Such were the undeniable advantages of the India trade, which on a moderate computation was adding directly to the stock of the Kingdom £500,000 in one year.[1] We have seen how merchants other than the shareholders of the Company were keen in securing a share in that profitable trade, how the Company, too, were bent upon preserving to themselves the exclusive right of their Charter, and what a severe struggle ensued on the pressing problem.

Notwithstanding the bitter controversy restarted in the 'eighties on the necessity or otherwise of carrying on the Oriental trade by means of an exclusive Joint-Stock Company, the hue and cry raised by the Company's opponents against the importation of calicoes, silks and even raw silk to the detriment of British manufactures, and the ever-increasing share of free merchants and factors in that trade, the last quarter of the century is marked by a distinct advance in the Eastern trade. The prosperous condition of the Company is evidenced by the very high prices of the India Stock, which were 245 in 1677, 300 in 1683 and 560 to 500 in 1685.

For the eight years from 1674–75 to 1681–82 the exports to India were valued at £3,822,000, or on the average at £477,710 per annum. This means an advance of about £226,000 per annum, or of 89 per cent compared with the seven

[1] The calculation of Sir Josiah Child can be represented in a tabular form thus:—

	£
Indian imports into England—value	860,000
Expenses on factors, forts and other items deducted . .	60,000
Net Imports by the Co.	800,000
All goods imported in private trade by officers, seamen and factors, consisting of diamonds, pearls, musk, ambergris and such-like commodities	£ 250,000
Total Imports	1,050,000
Exports to the Indies by the Company	430,000
Exports to the Indies in private trade	120,000
	550,000

Hence the conclusion that there was an addition to the national wealth of £500,000 by one year's trade to India.

The E.I. Trade, pp. 7–8.

years immediately preceding 1674–75, and amounts to nine times the average for the first quarter of the seventeenth century.

The net result of our survey for the last twenty-four years, from 1658 to 1681, is represented in a tabular form below :—

Company's Exports to the East (Thousand £).

Periods.	Goods.	Money.	Total value.
1658–66 inclusive	312	776	1089
1667–73	604	1165	1770
1674–81	728	3093	3821
Aggregate	1644	5034	6680

In other words, *the exports in money and merchandise during this period amounted on an average to* £278,000 *per annum in round numbers.* Although the treasure was proportionally as large as formerly, being in the proportion of three to one in merchandise, there is little doubt that a far greater demand had been created for English goods in the East.

So far as the course of the export trade in the following years is concerned, it is necessary to recall the fact that neither the Letter Books nor the Court Minutes afford us regular data for the cargoes of the outgoing ships as they do for the twenty-four years which have been previously dealt with. Occasional returns are available, but they are useless in constructing a consecutive history of the Company's commerce. However, we are not altogether deprived of them.

Expansion of Exports

From the year 1680 regular statistics of British exports into the Indies have been preserved from the general wreck[1] by Moreau and Macgregor. Separate particulars of the exports of bullion and merchandise are, however, not available up to 1708, nor have any particulars been preserved regarding the private trade with those parts. The defective character of these returns has been discussed at large in the Appendix,[2]

[1] See Appendix B, p. 297. [2] Register of ships in Part II, p. 333.

and yet they have to be accepted for the years 1682 to 1697 inclusive by reason of the absence of anything better. Moreau's statistics for the subsequent ten years have been corrected in the light of the figures compiled in the Appendix from records of the Old and New Companies. A third set of returns has also been compiled from the Custom House Books for these years, those for the earlier period not being available.

On the basis of the returns compiled in the shipping list from 1658 to 1681–82 and 1698 to 1707 inclusive and that of Macgregor's for the years 1682–97, the values of the export[1] trade (through the channel of the Chartered Companies) with the East are stated below in decennial periods :—

Years.	Decennial Totals (Thousand £).
1658–67	1295
1668–77	3098
1678–87	4904
1688–97	2408
1698–07[2]	5856
	17,561 Total for fifty years

These figures bear a distinct testimony to the expanding activities of the Company. While the amounts of specie and merchandise in the first decade stood at £1,295,000, they rose to $2\frac{1}{2}$-fold in the next and to 4-fold during the third decade, giving an average of little less than £500,000 per annum within a comparatively small period of twenty years. The Company had, no doubt, succeeded in building up a very extensive trade with the East. The abnormal growth of the third decade is also to be accounted for by the fact that the Company had in those years launched a bold scheme of making conquests in Banda, Bengal and Chittagong. Conse-

[1] See pp. 296–7, 344–51 for the data.

[2] This sum is made up of the following amounts :—

£	
3,959,721	Old Company's exports.
1,475,707	New Company's in 1698–99—1701–2.
176,352	Less in Macgregor's in 1702–3—1707–8.
243,945	Less in Macgregor's in 1698–99—1700–1.
5,855,725	Actual total for 1698–1707.

quently more ships, specie and warlike stores were despatched during those years. A depression was but the inevitable reflex, the inexorable result of the abortive militarist adventures of the Company, and it was accentuated by the long European War on the one side and the vigorous attacks of the public and Parliament on the exclusive privileges of the Company on the other.[1] In that period of acute distress and financial bankruptcy the exports of the Company shrank down to half of the previous decade.

On the contrary, the last decade is characterised by an extraordinary expansion of Indo-British trade. For the first years when the Old and New Companies tried to worm each other out of trade their investments were very large, but the profits were comparatively small. The exports speedily went down in 1703 after their amalgamation, yet the general average remained high in spite of the European War. Separate returns for money and goods are not available in the records of both the Companies for thirteen years, but so far as the total amount of exports is concerned it averaged at £585,500 pounds per annum. What a remarkable progress is indicated by these figures, when we remember that *the English exports to the East for fifty-seven years since the establishment of that trade to* 1657 *were approximately equal to the amounts remitted in the ten years from* 1698 *to* 1707 ! *Yet this is not the true story.*

Full details for the export trade of this last period of ten years are fortunately available in the Books of the Custom House. From the annual accounts of exported specie and

[1] Pamphlets against the E.I. Co. :—

Reflections upon the East India and Royal African Companies, by Roger Coke, London, 1696.

A treatise Concerning the Regulation, etc., by Roger Coke, London, 1696.

A discourse concerning the East India Trade, by John Cary, written in 1695.

Reasons for constituting a New East India Co. in London, anonymous and dateless, seems to be written between 1695 and 1700.

A Letter to a friend concerning the East India Trade, anonymous, London, 1696.

Proposals for Settling the East India Trade, anonymous, London, 1696.

goods compiled from these books in the note below,[1] it will be seen that *goods of the value of more than* £600,000 *per annum had been sent to the East during these years, while the exports of specie came up very nearly to* £500,000 *per annum, and the total amount of gold and silver for the nine years was* £4,475,000 *against* £5,437,000 *in goods, giving us an average of* £1,101,000 *per year.*

Thus the balance of trade was mightily upset in these years. While the amount of bullion exported in the twenty-four years from 1658 to 1681 was thrice that of goods, the same fell to 82 per cent during the last decade. Never before was so large a proportion of merchandise exported out of England to the East.

It has previously been seen that the total exports of the two Companies as given in their records amounted to 5·8 million pounds. The Custom House, however, registered about £11,000,000. It is evident that this excess of exports was handled by private merchants. *It means that private trade had assumed such large proportions as to approximately equal the trade of the Company.* It will have been perfectly clear that to arrive at the real extent of the total English export trade with the East during these fifty years we should also reckon the large but unknown quantities of gold, silver, coral, amber and other merchandise exported by the mariners and officers of each ship, the "free" merchants, the clandestine traders and the "separate" traders. According to

[1] *Official Exports from* 1698 *to* 1710.

Years.	Specie.	Goods.
1698	399,230	451,196
1699	832,795	997,116
1700	807,583	932,275
1701	725,593	847,657
1702	410,762	498,247
1703	451,277	586,254
1704	303,012	496,439
1705	Not available	
1706	231,540	258,734
1707	313,283	369,258
1708	362,459	973,375
1709	506,469	674,826
1710	228,102	354,413

Sir J. Child, the proportion of private trade to the Company's trade about the year 1675 was 2 : 7, but its amount must have gone on increasing with the extending indulgence of the Company in permissive trade and the growing number of ships sent out. It cannot really be accounted at less than one-half of the Company's trade from 1678 to 1697, while from 1658 to 1677 the average ratio between the two trades can be taken to be as 1 : 4. That during the last decade it equalled the Company's trade has already been shown. On these assumptions the aggregate value of the whole English export trade with the East can be approximately represented by the following sums :—

British Exports to the East.

Years.	Value of Exports (in Thousands). £	Remarks.
1658–1681 . .	6680	Co.'s.
	1670	Private, assumed as ¼ of the Co. s.
1682–1697 . .	5032	Co.'s.
	2516	Private, assumed as ½ of the Co 's.
1698–1707 . .	9912	Both Co.'s and Private.
Total for fifty years .	25,810	

An analysis of the foregoing figures shows that, in spite of the violent fluctuations in the exports of money and goods sent to the East, the yearly average amounts to more than £500,000 sterling for the half-century from 1658 to 1707. It stands in sharp and pleasant contrast to the preceding fifty-seven years of the infancy of the Anglo-Oriental trade when the annual average touched the maximum amount of £100,000.

During the second half of the century, too, the first decade could not claim more than £150,000 in any case per year in the exports to the East, but in the last decennium the trade attained a height that startles the most optimistic student. The exports actually increased to £1,100,000 per annum. This rapid rise in the face of the inexorable Dutch competition could not but be a matter of unalloyed satisfaction to the English nation.

That it is a modest estimate and rather tends to an undervaluation of the English trade with the East cannot be doubted. The writer of "Some Considerations" maintained, without quoting his source of information, that within forty years from 1663 to 1703 the exports of coin and bullion to the East Indies had been £24,000,000 against £2,000,000 to Denmark and Sweden and £10,000,000 to France. These figures afford an eloquent testimony of the paramount importance of the Indo-English trade even in those days.

Repeated protests were heard from numerous writers on the ceaseless inrush of Indian calicoes and silks and the consequent prevention of the consumption of English and European manufactures, the increasing unemployment and impoverishment of the people, the continual exhaustion of Europe and the generous enrichment of the people of India. Dr. D'Avenant computed the gold and silver brought into Europe during the sixteenth and seventeenth centuries to be £800,000,000, and reckoned that £150,000,000 of it had been carried away and sunk in the East. "From whence I have reason to conclude," writes he, "that the European nations had been richer by a full third than they are, if that trade had never been discovered and undertaken."

What sums out of the large amount of money and merchandise exported by the Company were directly absorbed by India, and what share was appropriated by other Asiatic countries, cannot be definitely stated. Our shipping list offers all the necessary information for the years 1658–81 and 1698–1707. No separate and consecutive returns for the intervening period are available on the volume and distribution of trade in the various centres of the Company's activities.

Distribution of Trade

From the study of the detailed annual statistics, which have been relegated to Appendix D of this chapter, it appears that the amount of shipping sent to Surat and Bantam is approximately equal, being eighty-four ships in all of 32,000 tons to each place in the twenty-four years from 1658 to 1681. This gives an average of 3½ ships of 1333 tons per annum to each of those two factories. On the other hand, the Coromandel coast and the Bay of Bengal together claimed 112 ships of the total burden of 43,000 tons, or 4⅔ ships of 1766 tons burden per year. That is, 70 *per cent of all the shipping sent out of England was in the first instance meant for India and only* 30 *per cent to all other places in Asia.* The result of these twenty-four years' shipping statistics is summarised below :—

Places.	Total tonnage.	Ships per year.	Per cent.
Bantam . .	32,000	3½	30 outside India
Surat . .	32,000	3½	70 for India
Coast and Bay	43,000	4⅔	

An altogether different story is told by the returns of exports, since *by far the largest amount was invested in India. While it received* 88 *per cent of all the exports in money and goods, other Asiatic places claimed only* 12 *per cent.* Then Surat's share was 33 per cent of the whole, and the remaining 55 per cent were despatched to the Coast and Bay. But the disparity becomes more remarkable in the relative consumption of treasure and goods in each of the three centres :—

The Percentage Proportion of the Shares of each Centre in

	Surat.	Coast and Bay.	Bantam.
Total Exports .	33	55	12%
Money . . .	24	64	12%
Goods . . .	63	25	12%

That is, 64 per cent of all the treasure sent to the Indies was spent on the Coromandel coast and in Bengal, and only one-fourth of the English merchandise could be disposed of in these two extensive portions of India. The position was almost reversed in the case of Surat. It took over 63 per cent of the goods and only 24 per cent of the specie sent out to the East. On the other hand, Bantam and all other places outside India could take no more than 12 per cent of each of the two items. (See Appendix E on p. 299.)

This unequal distribution becomes still more conspicuous if we find out the percentage proportions of the specie and goods despatched to each centre separately. It appears that the Coast and Bay received 89 per cent in money and the rest, 11 per cent, in goods; the two quantities in the case of Bantam were related to each other as 77 : 33; while in Surat, which consumed the largest proportion of goods, the ratio of treasure to merchandise was raised to 56 : 44. English woollens and metals found very little market in Bengal or on the Coromandel side, but they readily made their way into the Mogul Empire through Surat, the Gate of India. In one word, the ratio of specie to goods in each of those places was for—

Surat.	Coast and Bay.	Bantam.
56 : 44	89 : 11	77 : 33

No statistical information on the relative distribution of money and goods can be traced out for the succeeding years up to 1697. It is, however, certain that on account of the war with the Mogul and the expulsion of the English from Bantam, still greater amounts must have been spent in India up to 1690. According to our shipping list, in the nine years from 1682 to 1690, inclusive, only 18 per cent of the total tonnage despatched from England to the East was destined for places outside India, and the remaining 82 per cent was meant for India alone.

Ninety-one ships were actually sent to India with a burden of 39,870 tons in all, while some twenty-nine ships with a tonnage of about 8700 tons sailed to Priaman, Tonqueen, etc. Thus the proportions in the two periods stand as below:—

Years.	Surat.	Coast and Bay.	Bantam.	
1658–81	30	40	30	Percentage of shipping
1682–90	39	43	18	

For the next six years the details of exports to Surat show that its share in English exports—both goods and money—during this short period had risen to 38 per cent of the whole export trade, though the percentage proportion of ships and tonnage respectively had fallen down to 32 and 34½ per cent of all the shipping sent to the Indies in this period.

It will have been obvious now that in the whole period of forty years the Company's business was almost wholly centred in India. Up to the year 1681 only 12 per cent of all the English exports to the East were spent out of India, while in the succeeding sixteen years the share of other Asiatic countries, on the evidence of the shipping returns, could be assumed to have shrunk down to approximately half of the above-mentioned proportion. But a big surprise awaits us in the next decade. In the absence of definite statistics it could not be fully realised how the excessive duties imposed upon calicoes and muslins on the one hand, and the prohibition of Indian silks since 1698 on the other, enormously modified the channels of Indo-British commerce. The relative distribution of this trade suddenly changed its course. From 1698 to 1707, inclusive, 160 ships of the burden of 55,700 tons were sent out[1] to the East, but only 85 were directly destined for India, and the rest had gone to Priaman, Fort York, and China. The practice of annually sending four or five ships to China was begun in these years. When these ships returned from that country, one generally went to unload its Chinese wares in Bengal, the other to Fort St. George, the third to Surat, sometimes a fourth to Mocha, and the fifth to England. These three or four vessels afterwards sailed for England laden with Indian and Arabian commodities. *Thus it is evident that the actual proportion of tonnage for India had much more increased than has been shown above. Still, so far as the appropriation of English exports is concerned, the share of India had undoubtedly been very much reduced.*

The proportions of exports and tonnage to the East during this last decade are given side by side for comparison :—

Places.	Per cent Exports.	Per cent Tonnage.
Surat	20	24
Coast and Bay	52	36
Outside India	28	40

In other words, the share of countries other than India in

[1] See pp. 355–9 *infra*.

exports had risen from 6–12 per cent in the previous years to 28 per cent, and in tonnage from 18–30 to 40 per cent during this decade. There are, however, one or two factors to be taken into account in arriving at the actual proportions. As pointed out before, the Chinese trade had been developed to supply India as well as England with Chinese goods. Instead of sending money and English goods direct to India, three ships with money and a small quantity of merchandise were usually first sent to China to buy goods and gold for the Indian markets. After the disposal of these goods at Surat, Fort St. George, Calcutta, or Hugly, the proceeds were invested in Indian commodities fit for England. Similarly, a ship sometimes went out of England direct to Mocha, Persia, or Maldives, took a lading of the articles fit for Surat, disposed them at a profit there and carried back Indian commodities to England. Although the direct English exports to India were thus lessened, yet the moneys available for investments in India were much more than would be indicated by the annual returns of exports. For instance, we should add the money paid by the Company in England for the bills of exchange drawn upon it from the various centres in India for sums borrowed by its agents from Englishmen resident in the East. The moneys earned by employing ships on freight and for convoys of native shipping were not less considerable. Then to the profits made on exported goods and in Eastern commerce are to be added the customs of Gombroon, consulage, and other profits there. Consequently it is highly essential in presenting the true proportions and amounts of English exports appropriated by various centres that account should be taken of these hidden and indirect imports[1] and sources of the Company's income.

Character of English Exports. Having studied the course of the aggregate English exports to the East, we proceed to analyse *the character of merchandise sent out by the Company.*

[1] Letter Bk., X, p. 194. See the appendices to this chapter for the detailed returns of exports and shipping upon which the conclusions of this section are based.

The main articles of the produce and manufacture of England in this half a century, as in the previous one, were lead, iron, and woollens; while quicksilver, vermilion, coral, and elephants' teeth were first procured from Europe and Africa and then sent on to India for sale. As can be expected from the growing volume of trade, far greater quantities began to be sent out than had ever been despatched before 1657. For instance, adding up the various items of the detailed account of the cargoes of ships sent by the Company in the four years of 1653–56, we find that the total value of merchandise was only £7425, which was distributed as follows:—

Goods Exported from 1653 *to* 1656.

	£
Broadcloth	1954
Lead	1722
Vermilion . . .	593
Quicksilver . . .	2211
Miscellaneous . .	945

This was a period of unparalleled slump in the Company's business, and hence the foregoing value does not represent the normal course of trade, yet it is most interesting for showing the relative importance of the different goods.[1]

Thus the annual value of exported merchandise in the four years of an acute depression in the Company's trade was merely £1856. Out of this one-fourth was invested in cloth. Things, however, changed very rapidly after 1657. In the next five years £258,000 worth of merchandise, or 26 per cent of the total exports, was despatched to the East. Then the

[1] Letter Bk., I.

Here it is well to recall a few salient facts regarding the amount of merchandise exported in the earlier period:—

1625. Total money and goods proposed were £80,000; 25 stammelles, 100 perpetuanos, 180 tons lead were proposed to be sent. Court Bk. 7, p. 146.

1633. Total more than £80,000; woollens and cloth, £6759 out of the total goods worth £18,987. Eng. Fact., Vol. 1630–33, p. 286.

1640. 320 cloths to Surat and Bantam. Court Bk., 17, p. 134.

1648. 200 cloths, 400 pigs of lead, 7 tons of teeth and 80 chests of quicksilver sent out. Court Bk., 22, pp. 29, 59, 72.

1650. 200 cloths, 20 chests of coral, £3000 worth vermilion and teeth were sent out.

following quinquennium, though characterised by another depression on account of the Anglo-Dutch War, shows the progressive tendency visible in the preceding period. For the five years of 1664–68 full details of exported goods with the prices at which they were bought by the Company are preserved in the Home Miscellaneous, Vol. 15, of the India Office.[1] They differ here and there from the returns recorded in the Letter Books, and hence there are discrepancies in the total values of goods shown in the following table and those stated in the chart of annual exports which appears as an appendix to this chapter.[2]

Value of the Articles Exported in the Years 1664–68.

Articles.	1664–65	1665–66	1666–67	1667–68	1668–69	Total.
	£	£	£	£	£	£
Woollens	10,008	15,734	843	23,046	18,636	68,267
Lead	3,243	848	298	7,246	6,234	17,869
Tin	—	—	—	4,280	5,834	10,114
Copper	2,598	—	—	6,625	11,787	21,010
Coral	1,121	477	1,012	—	13,956	16,566
Quicksilver	5,904	2,177	731	12,478	8,237	29,527
Vermilion	3,132	367	—	2,095	1,462	7,056
Miscellaneous	1,781	1,016	280	8,353	2,553	13,983
Total	27,787	20,619	3,164	64,123	68,699	184,392

On these figures it is obvious that in these five years goods worth 184$\frac{1}{3}$ thousand pounds were exported to the Indies, out of which woollens and other cloth were worth above £68,000; metals and vermilion £85,600, coral £16,500, and the various articles like sword-blades, knives, medicines, musk, alum, brimstone, mirrors, glassware, paper, shots, provisions, etc., cost about £14,000 in all. In other words, the ratio of goods to total exports had risen from 26 per cent of the last quinquennial period to 39 per cent; while 37 per cent of the goods were in cloth, 46$\frac{1}{2}$ per cent in metals, and the rest covered all other commodities. In the succeeding years not only did the exports swell to large proportions, but relatively far greater quantities of cloth were sent to India. The

[1] Pp. 1–115.

[2] Appendix A on p. 296.

following are the details of the shipment of cloth and other goods from 1676 to 1685 :—

		£
Broadcloth and other woollens	1676	48,684
,, ,, ,,	1677	52,445
,, ,, ,,	1678	24,764
,, ,, ,,	1679	32,913
,, ,, ,,	1680	51,666
Total cloth and woollens . .	1676–80	210,472
Other goods, stores, etc. . .	1676–80	194,646
Total		405,118
Cloth and woollens . . .	1681	94,855
,, ,,	1682	42,630
,, ,,	1683	24,448
,, ,,	1684	47,827
,, ,,	1685	48,414
Total cloth and woollens . .	1681–85	258,174
Other goods, stores, etc. . .	1681–85	187,440
Total		445,614[1]

It should be remembered that various methods were adopted by the Company in this period to enlarge the export of woollens and other English goods. For instance, the factors in India were ordered to oblige the merchants connected with the Company to take these goods in payment for half the merchandise supplied by them to the Company ; serious efforts were made to procure pepper in exchange for English goods in the Malabar factories ; and orders were also sent to dispose the goods at their cost price in India and China, so that the necessity of exporting money be minimised to the lowest extent. It was by these means that the proportion of woollens to other goods had soared to 52 per cent in the quinquennium of 1676–80 and 58 per cent in the following five years against 37 per cent in the quinquennium of 1664–68.

[1] In the Journals of the House of Commons, XI, pp. 99 and 110, there is a mention of the "Account of E.I. Goods Imported between 1675 and 1685," and of another "Account of the E.I. Goods Exported to the E. Indies for ten years ending 1685." The latter has been preserved in the State Papers, Domestic, James II, v, 104, and has been here reproduced from Scott's Joint-Stock Companies, II, p. 137.

Not only did the proportion become so high, but the annual value showed a considerable increase in the following manner :—

Average Annual Value of Woollens Exported to India.

	£
1664–68 inclusive . .	13,600
1676–80 " . .	42,094
1681–85 " . .	51,635

As the succeeding years are known to have been marked by a great trade depression produced by the long European War, the quantities of exported goods could not be so large as in the ten years just reviewed. Yet to satisfy the popular demand the Company were obliged by their charter of 1693 to annually export English goods to the value of £100,000.[1] The incorporation of such a clause in the charter is in itself a strong proof of the growing volume of the English exports to the East. The House of Commons was informed by the Company that in 1691 and 1692, cloth and other goods of the value of £100,000 were sent to the East,[2] while for the following three years the value was mentioned as £306,265.[3] The export of woollens seems to have suffered a set-back. It appears from an account of woollen cloth sent to India from December, 1684, to December, 1699, that in these fifteen years cloths of the estimated value of £431,864 in all were sent by the Company as under :—

Longcloth	40,482 pieces[4]
Short cloth	385 "
Spanish cloth . . .	562 "
Cloth sashes, kersies, etc. .	2,991 "
Total . . .	44,420 pieces = 15,417 lbs. weight of the computed value of £431,864.

This account can be supplemented by the official values of the principal commodities as recorded in the Books of the

[1] Court Bk., 37, pp. 37, 42.
[2] Court Bk., 36, p. 196.
[3] Court Bk., 36, p. 196.
[4] England's Almanack, 1700. British Mus., 816, M. 11–K. Cf. Home Misc., Vol. 40, p. 122.

Custom House and compiled for the first time in the Appendix.[1] The aggregate values of various items with their percentage proportion to the sum total of all exports are given below to show the remarkable progress made in this period :—

Official Values of Exports from 1698–1710.

Articles.	Total Value.	Percentage of the whole.
Woollens	£1,077,668	$57\frac{2}{3}$
Iron, English . . .	46,293	4
Iron, Foreign . . .	27,387	
Lead	78,580	$4\frac{1}{3}$
Coral, Foreign . . .	20,706	1
Miscellaneous . . .	616,051	33
	£1,866,685	

As the official values were in almost all cases, especially during war-time, below the market prices, the preceding sums fall far short of the actual value of the goods sent to the East. Hence the real progress was still more rapid than is revealed by these figures.

It is clear that the annual average for woollens had gone up to £89,806 as compared to £46,864 in the decennium of 1676–85. A comparison of the two most brisk periods of the fifty years from 1660 to 1710 shows that a remarkable change had been wrought in the relative and positive values of woollens and other goods. The situation in the two periods will be realised at a glance from the following table :—

	1676–85.	1698–1710.	Per cent Increase of II over I.
Annual value of goods . . .	£85,073	£155,557	83
,, ,, woollens . .	£46,864	£89,806	$91\frac{1}{2}$
Ratio of woollens to goods . .	55 : 100	58 : 100	

On the evidence adduced in the previous section it is evident that about one-eighth part of these exports could be disposed of outside India, and the rest, 88 per cent, was consumed in India alone !

[1] Appendix C on p. 298.

CHAPTER VI

THE VOLUME AND CHARACTER OF IMPORTS

THE whole period of fifty years from 1658 to 1707 is more or less blank with regard to the regular returns of the values of imports. The names of the ships which arrived from the East laden with Indian and Chinese goods can be found out from the manuscript Letters and Minutes of the Court or the Home Miscellaneous Series at the India Office, but neither the cost, nor real values, nor even the estimated values of their cargoes are available except for a few years only.[1] Hence the regular course of trade cannot be presented here. There are, however, available annual sale lists of the imported goods with the prices at which they were put up for sale by the Company, and also the annual orders of the Court sent to their factors in the East for providing goods for home. These two sources have been utilised for showing the growth of the Eastern trade with England.

This half a century is characterised by rapid progress in Oriental imports. Their value[2] in 1662–63 was £384,671 and rose to £432,869 in 1668–69, but very considerable progress was made in the following years. In the Whitehall Report (A.D. 1697) upon the Foreign Trade of England we are informed that from the year 1670 to 1688 the importations amounted upon the sale in England to about *one million pounds sterling per annum, of which about one-half was usually*

[1] Ladings of the ships which arrived in London in the years 1674 and 1675 are given in the Home Miscellaneous, Vol. 15, pp. 1–40. A list of ships carrying calicoes is given on pp. 598–800 for the ten years from 1711 to 1720 in the Home Miscellaneous, Vol. 49.

[2] British Museum Manuscript, Sloane, 2,902, p. 108.

re-exported. Later figures of the Company's annual sales are not available. In fact, when the Commissioners had no statistics before them up to the year of their report (1697), it is almost impossible to restore them now. We can, however, confidently assert that an unprecedented advance was made in the import trade during the period of the co-existence of the two Companies. It must have been commensurate with the extraordinary inflation of monetary exports from England. The amount of the Old Company's business was necessarily reduced from what it was before on account of the tooth-and-claw competition and the active crusade begun by privateers and the New Company against the former, but the *aggregate* business had undoubtedly swelled to large proportions.

The official values of goods directly imported from the East into England, based on their assumed and declared prime costs in places of origin, afford an adequate idea of the special boom brought about by the financial activities of the two rival Companies.[1] These prices can be taken as roughly approximating their invoices. *The average annual value of goods* as registered in the Books of the Custom House from 1698 to 1707 amounted to £580,640, while in the three years of boom (1699–1701) the average was as high as £755,871. Assuming the sale values to be only twice the prime cost of goods, which is undoubtedly an under-estimation, we find that in this decade the old level of £1,000,000 sterling realised at the Company's sales was far outstripped. In some years the total value of sales might have risen even to about £2,000,000.

The Company's trade had enabled England to become the great entrepôt and supplier of the E.I. goods to Europe and America. From 1670 to 1688—the year of the outbreak of a

[1] *Official Value of Imports in Sterling.*

Year	Value	Year	Value
1698	.. £356,509	1703	.. £596,309
1699	.. 717,695	1704	.. 757,814
1700	.. 787,731	1705	Missing in Customs Books.
1701	.. 762,188	1706	.. 644,652
1702	.. 247,014	1707	.. 355,838
		Total	£5,225,750

European war—the re-exports of the E.I. goods amounted on the average to £500,000 per annum, the basis for this calculation being the purchase prices at the sales of the Company. Pepper, indigo, silks, calicoes, and drugs were the chief commodities in constant demand throughout the Western world. The English naturally made very considerable profits by the supply of these goods. An idea of the financial benefit accruing from this trade at the end of the seventeenth century is furnished by Sir William Petty, who stated that the exports of Indian goods were valued at £600,000 and *their returns were nearly equal to twice the prime cost of the whole year's trade.*[1] There might be a tinge of exaggeration in this statement, yet the great advantages of this trade cannot be denied. It surely more than supplied all the silver and gold exported by the Company and other traders to the East.

It is stated in "the Generall Estimate of the Trade of England in 1697" that the exports of the E.I. goods formerly amounted to about £500,000 *communibus annis*, but during the last three years not above £150,000, and that "the pepper trade is in a manner quite lost—whereof *there was usually exported againe* 1000 *tunn per annum worth about* £100,000, *tho' not costing in India one-tenth of that summe—the advance wholly gained to the Nation.*"

In the next four years of brisk trade *the value of re-exports is quadrupled, having risen from* £150,000 to £634,733 *per annum!* By an account laid before the House of Commons on 13th January, 1703, it appears that the E.I. goods of all kinds, exported for four years, ending at Christmas, 1702, *according to the value put upon them by the authorities of the Custom House*, amounted to £2,538,933. Out of this there were exported :—

Manufactures mixed with silk, cotton, and herba, to the value of	£487,896
Wrought silks to Ireland and the plantations . . .	48,314
Calicoes exported in the same time	1,053,725
Total of silks and calicoes alone[2]	£1,589,935

[1] Political Arithmetic, p. 84.

[2] Remarks on the Accounts relating to the E.I. Trade. Cf. Home Misc., Vol. 11, for sales in 1704.

Thus, during this period, 63 *per cent of the E.I. goods exported out of England consisted of the silks and calicoes of the manufacture of India and China. This large amount of exported merchandise with the profits made upon it in the foreign countries must have brought back* £1,000,000 *per annum into the country. Thus the enormous gain to the nation by the E.I. trade is self-evident.*

The Progress of the Import[1] Trade in Cotton and Silk Goods. The main part of the Company's business consisted in providing piece-goods and silk stuffs for the English and European markets. Rapid progress was made in this branch of trade, and the cloth investments were particularly increased on the Coromandel and Bay sides. The complete returns of the ordered cotton and silk goods, so far as they are available in the Letter Books for the three centres of Surat, Fort St. George, and Hugly, have been compiled in Appendix A. Nothing more is desired by presenting these figures than to materialise our vague ideas and indefinite expressions regarding the vast importations of Indian calicoes, muslins, and silks. It will serve no useful purpose to separate the returns for these three classes of goods. The orders for all kinds of cloth have been added up to give a view of the cloth trade as a whole.

It will be seen that the *annual average* number of various cloths ordered from each centre during the seven years of 1658–64 was as under :—

Surat	84½ thousand pieces.
Fort	98 ,, ,,
Hugly	15 ,, ,,

In other words, one hundred and ninety-seven thousand pieces were, on the average, ordered per year from the whole of India during this septennial period.

After a temporary decline during the Anglo-Dutch War, this cloth trade was very vigorously pursued. For instance, the annual average for Surat rose from 84,500 pieces of the seven-

1 A detailed view of trade about the year 1700 from all the centres in the East is furnished by invoices given in Appendix D, pp. 304–5.

years' period, presently reviewed, to 247,000 pieces during 1669–72. That is, the quantity of cloth to be imported from Surat was just trebled in these four years.

In 1672 several artificers such as throwsters, weavers, and dyers were sent over by the Company with great quantities of English patterns, to teach Indian weavers new methods of manufacturing goods suitable to English and European markets. This gave a great encouragement to the vending of Indian cloths. Wrought silks, Bengals, painted and dyed calicoes were used in the place of "English silks, half-silks, worsted stuffs, say's, perpetuanos, and other sorts, not only for the clothing of both sexes, but for curtains for rooms, beds, etc." They ousted from England German linens, Silesia cambrics and lawns which were before imported mainly in exchange for English woollens. They became the general wear of all classes of society.

The importations of cloth must have been beyond all previous records, because the ordered goods suddenly jumped up to such vast numbers as are shown in the following table :—

Years.	Fort.	Bay.	Surat.	Total No. of Pieces in thousands.
1673 to 1678 inclusive . .	1479	549½	1875	3903½
1680 to 1683 inclusive . .	3795	1821	2948	8564
Annual av. for the 1st period	246½	91½	312½	650½
Annual av. for the 2nd period	948¾	455¼	737	2141

Thus the total number of cloth pieces ordered in the six years from 1673 to 1678 was about 3,903,000, or 650,500 pieces per year from the whole of India, but this amount immediately dwindles into insignificance before the phenomenal rise in the four years of 1680–83. *No less than 8½ million pieces were ordered from India, that is, the average had exceeded two million pieces per annum!*

While Surat[1] topped the list in providing the greatest number of pieces among the three centres of English invest-

[1] The towns which served as centres for supplying cloth to the Surat factory in this period were Surat, Nunsaree, Broach, Brodera, Nariad, Daboy, Dolka, Darboh, Dorugam, Ahmadabad, Agra, Dungarrapure, Brahmpore, Serrang, Cambaya. F. Rec., Surat, V, pp. 21–25.

ments, the continued depredations of the Mahratta armies in the city of Surat and other manufacturing districts of Gujerat, Koncan, and Malabar had their effect in transferring a large part of the European trade from Surat to Bengal and the Coromandel coast. The proportions of cloth investments in Surat as compared to the other two parts were as under :—

	Surat.	Bay and Coast.
1673–78 . . .	48 per cent	52 per cent of the total
1680–83 . . .	34 per cent	66 ,, ,,

The trade in piece-goods and other stuffs was in later years most appreciably affected by the Company's war with the Mogul; it recovered a good deal after the termination of hostilities, but again suffered a depression with the general decline in the Company's business during the European War. The total orders for the two years[1] 1696 and 1697 amounted to 2,571,000 pieces as under :—

Surat	865 thousand pieces.
Fort	844 ,, ,,
Bay	862 ,, ,,

The Extraordinary Development of the Silk Trade. The regular and certain supply of raw silk was a great necessity for the extensive silk manufacture of England. This industry had grown to be a national object of so much importance by 1655 that in the Treaty of Westminster it was specially stipulated that "the subjects of England might freely bring to France, and sell therein all sorts of silks and woollen stuffs of their own fabrication." Among the Asiatic countries Persia had hitherto been the greatest, if not the sole, source of the supplies of raw silk. The Levant Company was well known for bringing by far the largest quantities through Turkey, but the Dutch and the English Companies had succeeded in so far diverting this trade into their hands that in 1651 the Levant Company alleged "a great and almost total declination in their trade." A very heavy blow at their prosperity had thus been struck by supplanting them in the trade of Persian raw silk.

In the general stagnation of the E.I. Company's business

[1] For subsequent years see pp. 259, 264 n., 308.

this Persian trade had also been neglected. It remained at a low watermark even up to 1669, when the Dutch agent in Persia made the report that "the trade of the English need not disturb us. They are, in fact, doing nothing, but are obliged to remain there on account of the tolls of Gombroon."[1] Nor in the subsequent twenty-five years is much activity visible in the annual investments, which were on the whole limited to forty or fifty bales per year. The Persian silk was generally very poor in quality. Being a government monopoly and having been secured in taxes by the King, it could not be expected to be better.[2] It was about the year 1690 that the project of turning the course of the silk trade that used to pass through Turkey was set on foot. The Armenians were to be settled at Bombay, so that they might carry English woollens to Persia, and bring back silk for the use of the English. Thus the ancient Persia-Aleppo trade was to be changed through the help of the Armenian merchants. It was truly pointed out by the Directors that "this is no new thought or project of the present age, but was long since designed and consulted in the Reign of King James the first."[3] The Armenians were settled at Bombay, but the Persian silk trade could not be developed, because Persia was long in the grip of internal revolutions, disorders, and anarchy.

The main interest of this half a century lies in the great reduction of silk investments in Persia and the phenomenal development of the silk business of the Company in Bengal. A detailed account of the rise and extent of this investment will form a most interesting chapter in the commercial history of Bengal, but we must be very brief here.

In the first ten years the Bengal silk investment was quite insignificant. For instance, £3000 worth of silk was demanded from Hugly in 1658, and the next year a permanent order for procuring 100 bales per annum was given. It was, however, soon curtailed to only 30 or 40 bales, and these, too, were to be

[1] Dutch Records, Series I, 22, doc. 663; Vol. 29, doc. 749.
[2] Letter Bk., VIII, p. 176.
[3] Letter Bk., IX, pp. 20, 375.

provided if silk could be obtained from 6s. 7d. to 7s. 6d. per lb.[1]

From an account of Bengal written by Mr. Kenns in 1661 we learn that silk was wound into three sorts, known as the "head," "belly," and "foot." The English used to get the first two sorts, generally in the proportion of 5 : 4. This silk was called "Putta" or of short skein. The second kind of silk was known as "Puttany." It was the superfine sort of short skein and was usually priced from Rs.5¼ to Rs.6¼ per seer. There was also a third kind called "Dolleria"—a name given to the sort of silk in which "head, belly, and foot" were all mixed.[2] The exact quantities of silk ordered or imported in the 'seventies are not ascertainable. It is, however, certain that silk supplies from Bengal began to grow very fast after 1670.

The annual orders steadily rose from 580 bales in 1673 to 1200 bales[3] in 1679. The total amount of the various sorts of silk ordered in these seven years is shown in the following table :—

Head and belly . .	4200	to	4300	bales.
White silk . .	890	to	900	,,
Floretta . . .	540	to	590	,,
Total in 7 years .	5,630	to	5,790	,,

That is, the annual average approached the large figure of 800 bales during this period. Repeated orders were sent to

[1] Letter Bk., II, p. 335. The prices of the different varieties of white silk in 1678 and 1679 are given from Rs.3/8 to 4/12 per Bengal seer. Letter Bk., VI, pp. 37, 128, 132–33.

[2] British Museum, Addl. MSS., pp. 34, 123.

[3] The following returns have been compiled from the Letter Books :—

Year.	Head and Belly.	White.	Floretta.
1673 Sept. . . .	400–500 bales.	40 bales.	40 bales.
1674 Dec. . . .	500 ,,	50–60 ,,	50 ,,
1675 Dec. . . .	500 ,,	100 ,,	50–100 ,,
1677 July . . .	600 ,,	200 ,,	100 ,,
1677 Dec. . . .	600 ,,	200 ,,	100 ,,
1678–9 Jan. . . .	600 ,,	200 ,,	100 ,,
1679 Dec. . . .	1,000 ,,	100 ,,	100 ,,
1680 Sept. . .	The provision of silk of all sorts was to be increased by one-half.		

particularly *increase the investment in this article to as great an amount as could be procured.* For instance, in their Overland Letters to Fort St. George and Bengal in July, 1680, the Directors emphasised their need in these words : " You would what in you lies to promote the buying up what quantities of raw silk you can, that our shipping intended out this year may bring us large quantities thereof as can be procured.

" *Raw silk in general being a commodity that always turns us well to account, and not the worse for the largeness of the quantity how great soever it be.*"[1]

This trade was, in fact, so vigorously pushed up that during the next five years an unparalleled advance was made in the quantities to be procured in Bengal. In the earlier or subsequent history of the Company up to the battle of Plassey, such extensive amounts were never ordered. They are out of all proportion to the large quantities demanded in the preceding period.

Quantities Ordered from Bengal.

Year.	Head and Belly.	Ordinary.	White and Floretta.	
1680–81 . .	900 bales.	600 bales.	610 bales.	
1681–82 . .	900 ,,	600 ,,	710 ,,	
	And as much of yellow and white No. 1 as can be procured.		200 ,,	Tasore.
1682 . . .	10,000 bales.		1000 ,,	
			200 ,,	Thrown.
			100 ,,	Arunda.
1683 . . .	10,000 bales.[2]		1000 ,,	
	A bale=160 seers.		200 ,,	Thrown.
1684–85 . .	1,460 bales.		170 ,,	

Thus altogether 28,700 bales of 114,800 maunds of raw silk of all sorts had been adviced by the Court in these five years. *It means an average of* 22,960 maunds, or 574,000 lbs. of 24 ozs. *each* on taking the maund as equivalent to 25 lbs.

It is a pity that the actual amounts of silk exported from Bengal for the Company's account could not be ascertained, yet the considerable sums of money sent to Bengal in these

[1] Letter Bk., VI, pp. 220, 243. [2] Letter Bk., VI, p. 417.

years afford indisputable evidence of an unprecedented activity in investments at Cossimbazar, Ballasore, and Hugly. In the four years of 1678–81 a stock of £1,399,714 was despatched to the Coast and Bay against £890,182 to Surat and Bantam. In January, 1681, the Bengal factors were directed to invest £20,000 per annum in silk.[1] This sum was considered too inadequate next year. The stock for Bengal was raised to £150,000, of which £80,000 was to be sent to Cossimbazar[2] for the provision of silk. Orders for silk grow larger and more emphatic in the despatches of these years.[3]

It should also be noted that the order in the year 1681 includes 100 bales of thrown silk. It was the first time that the Company had gone out of its way to send for it. The reasons for this action are disclosed in their own words :—

> We have always declined Thrown silk, although there be no law in England against the importation of it. But now being inclined to vye with the Dutch in our owne way of trade, which we were never before put to, we would have you provide for us, and *send us home every year* as well as this, what you can procure there of (not exceeding 100 bales), so as *it lessens not our provision of raw silk, which we would have kept full to the utmost*, which, notwithstanding we do not intend to sell it in England, but after we have it here, we export it again for France or Holland.[4]

This trade was the source of so great a profit to the Company that in 1681 they prohibited all Englishmen from dealing in raw silk, because it was asserted that they of late had enhanced the prices and reduced the Company's investment in India.[5] Three years before, all the Company's servants had been prohibited from dealing in Chinese silk and wrought silks.[6] Thus the monopoly of the Company was made more extensive and severe.

The vast importations of the previous years could not be

[1] Letter Bk., VI, p. 254.
[2] Letter Bk., VI, p. 277.
[3] Letter Bk., VI, pp. 330, 360, 428.
[4] Letter Bk., VI, p. 425, 18th Nov., 1681.
[5] Letter Bk., VI, pp. 452, 471. In 1678 servants were prohibited to deal in China silk or silks. Letter Bk., VI, p. 6.
[6] Letter Bk., VI, pp. 3, 6.

long maintained. The hostilities with the Mogul Government in Bengal and elsewhere very much curtailed the investments, yet in the three years undermentioned 4850 bales of all kinds of silk were ordered, as has been shown in the note below.[1] At the outbreak of the European War the demand for Bengal silk and its supplies seems to have increased considerably. It had become an "extraordinary commodity, because the Turkey trade was so much interrupted by the French War." The orders in 1693 and 1694 require the Bengal factors to send as much silk as could be procured. Similarly, the provision of both raw silk and wrought silks was greatly increased in China. An abatement is visible at the end of the war, for altogether 195 tons and 500 bales were demanded from Bengal in the years 1697 and 1698.[2]

The prohibition of retailing and wearing E. India, Persia, and China silks, stuffs, etc., and the coming war with France and Spain which was very likely to affect the trade to Turkey and Italy, once more make the Company most eager to increase the provision of silk in Bengal as well as in Persia and China.[3] The actual quantities of raw silk imported from the East and recorded in the Custom House in the undermentioned years were :—

1698–99 . .	81,714 lbs.	40,857 lbs. per annum.
1700–1 . .	231,959 „	115,979 „ „
1702–4 . .	105,336 „	35,112 „ „
1706–10 . .	53,655 „	10,731 „ „

These figures are a sorry commentary on the havoc played by the European War and the financial difficulties of the Company. Except for the two years of 1700–1, the imports were not significant. They hover between 300 and 400 bales per year, but the last quinquennial period shows the most

[1] Year. Ordered silk.

1686–87	bales 1400	Head and Belly	130 Floretta.
1687–88	„ 1400	„ „	260 „
1688	„ 1400	„ „	260 „

[2] Letter Bk., X, pp. 36, 124.

[3] Letter Bk., X, p. 447. The quantities of raw silk ordered from China in the last three years of the seventeenth century were : 1698, none ; 1699, 30 tons ; 1700, 100,000 lbs. Letter Bk., X, pp. 126, 212, 355.

serious depression that this trade had witnessed for the last forty years or more, as the average quantities imported from Bengal, China, and possibly Persia had sunk down to a hundred bales per year!

The Preservation of the Pepper Trade. It has already been seen that the principal investment of the English at Bantam and its neighbouring islands was in pepper. The Malabar was in no way neglected by the English factors for pepper supplies, but up to the 'sixties it had not gained that importance which it obtained in the following years. The Dutch, by expelling the Portuguese from the whole Malabar coast between 1658 and 1665, tried to effectually shut out the English from a share in the pepper trade. For instance, in his despatch of 25th January, 1667, the Governor-General of Batavia pointed out that although pepper in the territory of the Samorin was 50 per cent dearer than at other places on the coast, they must retain the monopoly of export and at any cost prevent the English from getting their share. The latter could not naturally allow their enemies to control all the supplies, and consequently proceeded on the same lines as their rivals in entering into treaties[1] with those Malabar princes who were not bound down by their opponents. The Dutch with all their power and diplomacy could never succeed in dislodging the English from their factories or prevent them from securing the desired quantities of pepper. Carwar, Anjengo, Tellichery, and even Calicut were the principal places for collecting pepper on the Malabar coast; 400 to 500 tons continued to be yearly sent to England from about 1670 onwards, while in some years even as much as 1000 tons were shipped by the Company.

Feeling themselves powerless to deprive the English of the Malabar pepper, the Dutch designed to oust them from Bantam and other places and thus put an end to their flourishing trade. In their September sale of 1678 the Company sold 3350 bags at $7\frac{5}{6}$d. per lb., which produced them a net gain of

[1] Cf. the Treaty with the Queen of Attinga for delivering the whole produce of pepper to the English. Letter Bk., IX, pp. 2, 500, 516.

$2\frac{1}{8}$d. per lb., but this profit was not considered sufficient, and therefore the agent at Bantam was instructed to prevail with the Sultan to lessen the price of pepper and his customs. As they had 19,000 bags unsold with them, they resolved to send fewer ships. Furthermore, it was decided to send 1000 tons in shipping per annum[1] to Bantam.

Notwithstanding the manifold difficulties created by the Dutch in the securing of pepper, the extraordinary progress made in a few years in its trade seems incredible. From the Report touching the Pepper Warehouse, we learn that from April, 1672, to July, 1681 (including remainder), undermentioned quantities were received in England :—

Black pepper . .	35,626,373 lbs. or	115,276 bags ;
White pepper . .	553,763 lbs. or	1,914 bags ;
Falcon's pepper .	588,000 lbs. or	1,960 bags.[2]
Total in nine years .	36,768,136 lbs.	

In other words, 4,085,348 *lbs. of pepper were,* communibus annis, *imported by the Company into England during* 1672–81 ! *This stands in marked contrast with the* 2,000,000 *lbs. imported in the 'sixties and* 1,500,000 *lbs. brought into the country during the 'thirties !*

This can give us an idea what the Company and the British Isles at large must be gaining by the re-exportation of this article to the foreign countries, when it is remembered that the annual home consumption was scarcely one-tenth of the imported quantities, though according to Sir J. Child it was even less than one-twentieth part of this immense amount !

In 1682 all or a major part of this profitable trade was mightily threatened, because the Dutch expelled the English from Bantam,[3] and after allowing them to live in Batavia gave them doles of pepper at exorbitant prices. The English had anticipated the disastrous consequences. They had already sent the greatest fleet that had ever sailed to the Indies for the defence of Bantam.

[1] Letter Bk., VI, pp. 1, 5, 77. [2] Letter Bk., VIII, p. 321.

[3] Accounts of the loss of Bantam. C.O. 14—Batavia. 17th and 23rd Sept., 1682.

The feelings of the Directors on this important issue are couched in these words :—

If the present misunderstandings between the two nations should ferment to an open war, it would be thought by the vulgar, but a war for pepper which they think to be slight thing, because each family spends but a little of it. But at the Bottom it will prove a war for the Dominion of the British as well as the Indian seas, because if ever they come to be sole masters of that Commodity, as they already are of nutmegs, mace, cloves, and cinamon, the sole profitt of that one commodity pepper being of general use, will be more to them, than all the rest and in probability sufficient to defray the constant charge of a great navy in Europe.

It was to avoid these dire results that the English soon planted a new factory at Bencoolen and won over many native inhabitants to satisfy their demand for pepper. It was maintained at a cost of £200,000 in ten years to prevent the loss of the pepper trade to the nation.[1] From their first settlement here in 1685 to the 22nd July, 1702, the Company got pepper to the amount of 16,927 bahars, each bahar being 407 lbs. The total quantity of pepper was therefore 6,889,289 lbs., or 430,580 lbs. per year.[2] This is in no way a despicable amount considering the odds against the English.

The Malabar was more and more tapped as the Southern supplies became more insecure. The pepper settlements of the English on the west coast of India grew to be very important centres of trade. The quantities imported into England are available in the Customs Books from the year 1698. They include the Bencoolen supplies, yet with a previous knowledge of their annual average we can arrive at an approximate estimate of the quantities brought from India. In the five years of competitive trade, from 1698 to 1702 inclusive, 27⅓ million lbs. were brought into London. Such vast quantities stand unparalleled in the then history of English commerce, and they most impressively reveal the inexhaustible resources of the Malabar country for its supplies

[1] Letter Bk., IX, p. 463. [2] Letter Bk., XIV, p. 168.

of pepper. It should be remarked that the year 1699 alone claims 19,635,610 lbs. of pepper. If this quantity has been correctly recorded by the Custom House authorities, it appears that there was a great rush for securing this article at the establishment of the New Company.

As the imports of pepper in subsequent years up to 1710 average about $1\frac{1}{4}$ million lbs. per annum, it can be safely asserted that about two-thirds of these were on the average supplied from India and the rest from Bencoolen.

These are sufficiently large quantities, but it seems on comparing the Customs[1] returns with those of the Company from 1616 to 1630, that during the earlier period more pepper was imported into England. It would mean that even with the growing resources and greater facilities and immunities of obtaining pepper in Malabar, its trade had appreciably declined. Either this comparative decay was temporarily caused by the European War, or large quantities were clandestinely run into the country and thus could not be recorded in the Customs Books. Reduction is very likely due to both these causes, because it looks improbable that the pepper trade should have suffered a set-back with an otherwise rapidly growing commerce.[2]

The Beginnings of the Tea Trade. Tea, which was scarcely known as a commodity of Indo European traffic up to 1660, so successfully made its way into the Western world within

[1] Cf. pp. 294–5, 307.

[2] In 1703 the custom on pepper is stated to be $5\frac{1}{2}$d. per lb., and the freight $3\frac{1}{2}$d. per lb. Thus 9d. per lb. was on the average spent above the prime cost. As pepper dust could be disposed of at $2\frac{1}{2}$d. and flags and scummings at 4d. per lb., the Company was losing 6d. per lb. on these. Hence instructions were sent to provide clean and well-garbled pepper. Letter Bk., XII, pp. 134, 155.

The prices in 1684 of

Calicut pepper were $2\frac{3}{4}$d. per lb. and $\frac{1}{4}$d. charges in India
Billiapatam pepper $2\frac{1}{2}$d. ,, $\frac{1}{4}$d. ,, ,,
Carwar pepper 4d. price and charges.

(Letter Bk., VII, p. 481.)

Prices of pepper in England in March, 1683–84 :—

Billiapatam pepper $8\frac{1}{2}$d. per lb.
Malabar pepper 9d. ,,
Jambee pepper $8\frac{3}{4}$d. ,,

(Court Bk., 33, p. 228.)

fifty years that it occupied a respectable position among the Eastern imports of the Dutch and the English in the first decade of the eighteenth century. When and by whom tea was introduced into England has not been ascertained with any direct certainty, but the East India Company deserve the sole credit of developing this most lucrative branch of English trade.

In 1665 English factories were established at Tywan and Tonqueen in China, and tea began to form an article of investment there. In the season of 1667–68 the agent at Bantam was desired to send " 100 lbs. weight of the best *tey* that he could gett." The first importation made from Bantam was in 1669, when about 143 lbs. of tea were received in England. In the next three years, 346 lbs. more were imported. Then came a break for six years. In the last three years of the 'eighties the imports of tea rose to 5057 lbs. The troubles at Bantam again stopped this unimportant investment. The growing use of tea in the aristocratic circles about this period was attested by the Directors in their letter to Fort St. George in January, 1685, in these words :—

> In regard *Thea* is grown to be a commodity here and wee have occasion to make presents therein to our great friends at Court, *we would have you to send us yearly* 5 *or* 6 *canisters of the very best and freshest Thea.* That which will colour the water in which it is infused most of a greenish complexion is generally best accepted.[1]

Six years later, too, the Company were not optimistic on their tea trade. In their Bombay General, dated October, 1690, the Directors note that " *Thea* now pays the King five shillings per pound custom, so that no ordinary Thea can be bought for England for the Company's account, nor any but what is superfine will pay either freight or charges, and no thea must be loaden among pepper, nor Tutanague pots, nor in pots scented with camphor. *But we had rather have no Thea at all sent for the Company's account.*"[2] Yet increasing quantities were continued to be sent from Madras and Surat, because the

[1] Letter Bk., VII, p. 425.

[2] Letter Bk., IX, pp. 112–13.

total amount from 1685 to 1700 inclusive being 266,601 lbs., with an average of 16,662 lbs. per annum, stands in marked contrast to the preceding period. In fact, at the end of the century, the imports of tea had become fairly considerable. The orders to the China factors for the provision of tea will give an adequate idea of the importance and growth of its trade in the following years :—

Year.[1]	Ordinary Tea.	Bohea.
1698 . . .	300 tubs	2 tubs
1699 . . .	300 „	80 „
1700 . . .	100–150 „	50–60 „

These orders were from the Old Company. The investment had to be cut down on account of the severe competition from other adventurers. The actual quantity imported in the single year of 1700 far exceeds the sum total of tea brought into England in the previous nine years. The excessive importations of competing merchants had very much popularised the tea-drink. In 1704 we are informed that tea was a commodity of general use and a very considerable article in the profits and loss of the Company's investments.[2] The goods ordered for England from Canton in that year were to occupy 285 tons of shipping, but 117 tons out of these consisted of tea alone. In the next two years 200 tons were to be provided, and the quantity ordered so rapidly increased that in the years of 1710 12 no less than 150 tons were invoiced by the Company.[3]

It is clear that tea, though very dear, had established itself as an article of drink and made a somewhat startling progress in the first decade of the eighteenth century. Altogether 786,326 lbs., or on the average five times as much as in the previous sixteen years, were imported into the country in the first ten years of the eighteenth century.

The average prices of tea at the Company's sales varied from 11s. 6d. to 12s. 4d. in the years 1678–86, but in spite of far higher duties stood at 11s. 11d. per lb. in 1708–10.[4] As the

[1] Letter Bk., X, pp. 126, 212, 355. [2] Letter Bk., XII, p. 326.
[3] Letter Bk., XIV, pp. 30, 341.
[4] See Appendix on the imports of tea, p. 302.

Singlo tea was to be procured at 1s. per lb. and the Imperial as well as Bohea at 2s., the Company, after making allowance for all kinds of charges and duties, must have made enormous profits in this growing branch of their trade.

The Rise of the Coffee Trade. Although the use of coffee as a drink precedes that of tea in England, yet the former never gained that popularity which its rival was destined to attain in a short period. In fact, its progress, which was very rapid in the 'eighties, was soon retarded by the introduction of tea and the impositions of excessive duties. The quantities ordered and the prices at which coffee was sold by the Company during the first six years will adequately picture the early genesis of its trade :—

Year.	Coffee Ordered.	Coffee Sold.	Prices per cwt. £ s. d.		Reference. L. Bk., II, pp. 2, 25.
1658	30 tons	—	—		—
1660	—	48 bales	7 10 0	August	C. Bk., 24, p. 279.
			7 1 0	October	„ p. 303.
1661	—	2 bags	6 18 0		„ p. 467.
1662	20 tons	10 bales	6 1 0		„ p. 517.
1663	—	2 parc.	4 0 0	per stone	„ p. 519.
1664	5 tons	18 bales	8 10 0		„ p. 832.
1665–66	—	19 bales	5 12 0		

With the expansion of the Eastern import trade the investments of coffee grew to large proportions as under :—

Amounts of Coffee Ordered.

1669	200 bales.	
1670–71	300 „	per year.
1672–75	200 „	„
1676–77	300 „	„
1678–79	400 „	„
1680–81	600 „	„
1682	1200 „	„

The climax in the coffee investments was reached here when the quantities ordered from India had increased from 200 bales or 50 tons in 1669 to 1200 bales or 300 tons in 1682. Never after up to 1710, save in the year 1704, was so large a quantity ordered by the Company or imported into England.

The profits in this branch seem to be fairly considerable about this period. The prices of coffee as given in the Surat invoices, or the advices of the Court, usually hover between Rs.10 and Rs.11 per maund, or £4 to £5 per cwt., while in England they range between £8–9 per cwt., so that the gross profit made by the Company would amount to 80–90 per cent on this investment.[1]

The decrease in the Company's exports of bullion and goods curtailed their investments all round, so the orders for coffee, though fairly large, show no progress. The following amounts traceable in the Letter Books tell their own story :—

1683	. 800 bales.	1688	. 600 bales.
1684	. 500 ,,	1693	. 100 tons.
1687	. 500 ,,	1694	. 100 ,,

In the three years of 1698–1700 3477 cwts., and in the seven years from 1701 to 1708, there being no returns for 1705, 15,294 cwts. in all were *directly imported* into the country from India.

The whole course of trade can now be presented in total quantities and annual averages thus :—

1660–65	75	cwts. in all, or		12½	cwts.	annual	*Sale.*
1669–84	6700	bales	,,	1884	,,	,,	*Order.*
1686–88	1600	,,	,,	2400	,,	,,	,,
1693–94	200	tons	,,	1800	,,	,,	,,
1698–1700[2]	3477	cwts.	,,	1159	,,	,,	*Import.*
1701–8	15,294	,,	,,	2159	,,	,,	,,

Without taking account of the quantities imported from Turkey and Holland and fixing our attention on the direct trade between England and the Indies, we find that the coffee trade was very fitful after 1684, its course being made erratic to some extent by the imposition and withdrawal of excessive duties. Although the above orders can in no case be taken to represent the quantities actually imported into the

[1] Cf. Letter Bk., VIII, p. 554.

[2] Actual imports of coffee compiled from the books of the Custom House (see p. 307 *infra*) :—

1698	. 4½ cwts.	1703	. 1278¼ cwts.
1699	. 2181¼ ,,	1704	. 5499½ ,,
1700	. 1292 ,,	1706	. 31 ,,
1701	. 3473¼ ,,	1707	. 349¼ ,,
1702	. 2619¾ ,,	1708	. 2044 ,,

country, yet they are a sure index to the growing and large demand for coffee up to 1688 and its dull market afterwards due to the levy of an additional duty of £5 12s. per cwt. The development in the quantities imported is not at all significant when it is compared to the amazing progress made by tea during the same period in spite of discouraging impositions.[1]

The Boom and Slump in the Indigo Trade. It was pointed out in Chapter IV that the Indian indigo began to lose its ground in the English market about the year 1650. Nine years after we find that such abundant quantities had been imported from the Barbados and the West Indies that indigo was not required from India unless the Lahore variety could be bought at 18d. and the Ahmadabad one at 9d. per lb.[2] But the former was invoiced at 26d. and the latter at 12½d. per lb. at Surat in 1660. As they were expected to yield 3s. 4–6d. and 1s. 8d. per lb. respectively in England, much profit was not left after deducting the freight, insurance, custom, and other charges incurred on them.[3]

Fortunately the demand for indigo was rapidly increasing in the dyeing and manufacturing industries of England, and therefore large quantities continued to be imported from India up to the end of that century. From the inventory of the Company's annual orders for the provision of this dye given in Appendix C, it appears that from 600 to 1300 bales of the Lahore and Ahmadabad indigoes were annually required between the years 1670 and 1675, but the quantity was reduced to 500 bales in the next four years, and rose again to 940–1040 bales in the years 1680–84.

The stability of the prices of the three varieties of indigo in this whole period of a quarter of a century is simply amazing. From 1659 to 1681 the flat and round varieties of Ahmadabad are priced at 9d. to 12d. in the advices of the Court, and the Lahore or Agra kind at 18–24d. per lb. In 1675

[1] For the various duties imposed upon tea and coffee see Appendix B to Chapter X.

[2] Letter Bk., II, p. 286; Letter to Surat, 22nd Feb., 1659.

[3] Letter Bk., II, p. 338.

the total cost of importing this article into England was stated to be 1s. per lb. over and above its prime cost as under :—

Cost . . .	2s. 4d.	
Freight . . .	4d.	Total cost to the Co.=3s. 4d.
Custom . . .	4d.	per lb. of Lahore indigo.[1]
Waste and charges .	4d.	

The Ahmadabad indigo, whose prices varied from 9d. to 1s., would not have cost the Company more than 2s. at its delivery in England. This supplies us with a very good basis for calculating the profits of the Company in this branch of their trade.

The demand for the indigo dye must have much increased on account of the particular growth of the weaving industry after the migration of the French refugees in 1685. We are told by the Company that " it was a good commodity and likely to continue in great request." Yet the total order in 1687 amounted to 600 barrels of the Agra variety, and 140 barrels of both the flat and round ones. This was altogether equal to 133½ shipping tons. Next year the whole order went up to 1300 barrels, which would mean 217 shipping tons or 2604 cwts.

This year the Surat factors were informed that all the varieties of indigo had much fallen in price, " but they are always noble staple commodityes, and you need not fear over burdening us with them, if they be cheap bought and good in their kinds."[2]

Four years later, in October, 1693, order was given not to send the Coromandel indigo, as it brought in only 9d. or 10d. per lb., though it had to pay 6d. per lb. custom, while the best Agra or Lahore variety was sold for 6s. or 7s. per lb.[3]

We find the orders contracted to only 400 barrels for each of the two years of 1695 and 1696. In the past few years the Company had seriously attempted to encourage the cultivation

[1] Court Bk., 25*a*, advice for 1675.
[2] Letter Bk., IX, p. 2.
[3] Letter Bk., IX, p. 305.

of indigo, along with that of cotton, sugar, pepper, nutmegs, mace, etc., in St. Helena and Fort York.[1] Experiments had also been made in Fort St. David's, near Madras. Then small quantities were imported from China. The annual orders for goods to be provided there for England from 1698 to 1700 include 23 tons of indigo.[2] Most of all, the cheap importations from the West Indies heavily told upon this branch of Indian trade.[3]

The actual quantities imported into the country from the East, that is, both from India and China, as registered at the Custom House, show to what depths this great and profitable trade had fallen in the beginning of the eighteenth century. From 1698 to 1710, save for the year 1705 for which the returns are missing, 702,643 lbs. in all were brought into England.[4] An average of 54,000 lbs. per annum during this period stands in marked contrast to the year 1620, when the annual importation was stated to be 200,000 lbs. Thus this branch of the Indian trade had dwindled down to about one-fourth of what it used to be in the early period of the Company's commerce. As the Dutch, too, had completely succeeded in raising very large crops of indigo in Java and other islands, and in doing away with the necessity of buying it in India, *it is evident that the foreign markets for this commodity had practically been closed in the beginning of the eighteenth century.*

Cotton-wool formed a regular article of export from India, but the quantities, though wildly varying in different years, were not appreciable. The advices of the Court for the three years of 1688–90 include 600 bales of cotton per annum, while for 1695 and 1696 order was given to send as much of this article as was required for making up the tonnage of the ships consigned to Surat. But only two years

[1] Letter Bk., VI, p. 16 ; IX, p. 596.
[2] Letter Bk., X, pp. 126, 212, 355.
[3] The consignment on the *King William* cost £78 1s. 3d., but the net price obtained was £65 16s. 6d., so there was a loss of £12 4s. 9d. Letter Bk., X, p. 106, Aug., 1698.
[4] For the imports of indigo see Appendix G to Chapter VII, p. 314.

after the Surat factors were directed to send no more cotton to England as it sold at about 8d. per lb., while its cost[1] was above 11d. Subsequent years do not show any large importation of the article. For instance, in the years 1698–1700, 135,683 lbs. were brought from the East, while the total quantity for the first decade of the eighteenth century is 215,605 lbs., which means an average of only 18 shipping tons per year.

On the other hand, **cotton-yarn** was always an important article, being in great demand on account of the growing cotton manufacture in England. In 1658, 600 bales were demanded from Surat, Malabar, and Rajpore, and 20 tons from Hugly. Next year 400 bales were ordered to be provided per annum at the latter factory.[2] During 1660–63, the requirements vary from 100 to 200 bales, and the Bay supply was directed to be cut down to 200 bales per year. The quantity went up 500 bales per year in 1672–73 from Surat, but was reduced again next year to 300 and even to 200 in 1675, while Bengal factors were asked to supply only 50–60 bales in the latter year. No yarn was required in the next two years on account of its dearness. In 1679 complaints are heard from the Court to the effect that yarn had been sold at a great loss of late years and that they had 300 bales remaining on their hands. Yet 100 to 150 bales per annum were ordered from Surat to fill up the tonnage.[3] Next year this requirement was raised to 200 bales, and in the three years of 1682–84 the orders exceeded all previous records, being 2550 bales from all centres in India.[4] Since 1688 yarn of the finest sorts was much preferred, and fairly large quantities were annually required from all the centres to fill up the tonnage of ships.[5] For instance, 700 tons of yarn were to be provided at Surat and Hugly. The amount was reduced to 200 tons in 1693 and 1694, because its dearness was curtailing

[1] Prime cost=$3\frac{1}{2}$d., freight=$7\frac{2}{3}$d., and custom=$\frac{1}{2}$d. per lb.
[2] Letter Bk., II, p. 197.
[3] Letter Bk., VI, p. 48.
[4] Letter Bk., VII, pp. 20, 22, 26, 227, 358, 431.
[5] Letter Bk., VIII, p. 584; IX, p. 557.

the profit of the Company.[1] About the end of this century, it yielded only 20 to 30 per cent net profit, but the prohibition of Indian painted calicoes in 1699 made it a favourite commodity. A large quantity was demanded in 1704 with the remark that it would turn to account, because the weavers had fallen into the use of it in imitating several Indian manufactures.

The returns of the actual quantities imported into the country from India, as given in the note below, show that in the nine years for which the figures are available the average importation stood at 136,000 lbs. weight per annum. No comparison is possible by reason of the want of earlier returns, yet the importance of this trade, before the invention of spinning machines in England, cannot be denied.

Private Trade. On the resumption of their trade the Company promptly proceeded to jealously guard their exclusive right of trade to and from the Indies. They first prohibited the exportation of all kinds of ammunition, broadcloth, lead, coral, vermilion, quicksilver, amber, and elephants' teeth from England, and the importation home of calicoes, indigo, cinnamon, cloves, cardamoms, benjamin, saltpetre, pepper, white nutmegs, maces, or cotton yarn. Then a levy of very high rates of freight was ordered in 1665 to be charged on the goods carried against the Company's permission,[2] as, for instance:

£50	per ton	on	ammunition.
10s.	per lb.	,,	coral and amber.
5s.	per piece	,,	calicoes.
3s.	per lb.	,,	indigo, yarn and spices.
6d.	per lb.	,,	saltpetre and pepper.
5d.	per lb.	,,	mace.
£10	for every broadcloth.		
10s.	per cwt.	on	lead.
2s.	per lb.	,,	quicksilver, teeth and vermilion.

[1] Letter Bk., VIII, pp. 557–59, 568–70; IX, 312–14, 320–23, 506–8.

Imports of Cotton Yarn from India.

Year	Quantity	Year	Quantity
1699 .	204,378 lbs.	1704 .	166,640 lbs.
1700 .	165,453 ,,	1705 .	Missing.
1701 .	146,987 ,,	1706 .	44,725 ,,
1702 .	97,537 ,,	1707 .	299,642 ,,
1703 .	52,267 ,,	1708 .	46,846 ,,
		Total for 9 years .	1,224,475 ,,

[2] Letter Bk., II, p. 185.

In spite of all these restrictions, Eastern imports were more and more brought into the country to the prejudice of the Company. They consequently made more severe laws to suppress the growing volume of permitted and clandestine trade. It was during this period that they practised the most brutal methods to prevent privateers from sharing their immense profits in the Eastern commerce. Several Royal Proclamations were issued against interlopers, and every now and then the Court of Directors laid down restrictions on the rights of the officers and mariners to trade on their private account. For instance, in the year 1673–74 the private merchants could "not carry callicoes or pepper of any sort to Tonquene, Formosa, Japan, Cambojah, Syam, Bantam, or any other port or place in the South Seas, where the Company had or should settle a factory." They were prohibited to import sugar, tin, *tutenage*, skins, leather, hides, red earth, raw silk, sappan, or sandal-wood into, and to export copper from those countries.

The principal articles of private import from the East were pearls, diamonds, rubies, sapphires, neckcloths, bezoar stones, musk, ambergris, oil of mace and other spices, Persian carpets, damasks, gold and silver stuffs, tortoise shells, opium, cornelian rings and agates.[1]

Then the importation of tea,[2] coffee, silk,[3] etc., was withdrawn from private hands, as the demands for these articles grew more and more.

About 1680–81, the principal restrictions on the permission trade between England and the East were as follows :—

(1) No Adventurer or Freeman was permitted to send out in any one year in bullion or foreign coin for India any more or greater sum than one-fifth of his original adventure in the General Joint Stock.[4]

(2) The freight to be paid by Freemen, Adventurers, and

[1] Addl. MS., 24,934, p. 189.
[2] Court Bk., 45, p. 559.
[3] Memorial to the Commons, Court Bk., 45, p. 565.
[4] Court Minutes, 32, p. 113, 20th April, 1681.

Company's servants was £5 per ton, while all Unfree men had to pay £10 per ton.

(3) Five per cent on the outward as well as homeward tonnage was allowed to ship's officers in unprohibited goods.

(4) The diamond trade was solely appropriated by the Company "for the profit and advantage of the Kingdom in general and particularly for the interests of this Company." It was strictly prohibited to all persons whatsoever.[1]

(5) The following articles were also solely appropriated by the Company: Musk, Persia wrought silks, Ahmadabad Taffaties, silk Loongees, chercollees, and herba Taffaties. Restrictions for other articles were almost the same as in 1673.[2]

(6) The Company went so far as to send nimble vessels to look out for the India ships coming home, and prevent the goods brought by private adventurers being embezzled or smuggled in.[3]

(7) The Company's money was being continually misappropriated by its factors in the East. Hence it issued orders and rules for all persons in its service to prevent their trading with its funds.[4]

(8) The strictest measures were adopted to prevent privateers and interlopers from going to the Eastern waters. The Madagascar pirates are described by the Company as a "scandal to our Nation and Religion, being most of the English, at least four-fifths."

The clandestine trade had actually assumed large proportions, and the piracies of interlopers frequently recoiled upon the heads of the Company's servants. These in turn mercilessly persecuted those of their countrymen who dared invade their exclusive prerogatives. "Such instances of their barbarity might be produced, supported by facts, as would

[1] Court Minutes, 32, pp. 12, 13, 15, 16, 61.
[2] Court Minutes, 32, pp. 113, 114.
[3] Court Minutes, 32, pp. 121, 179. [4] Addl. MS., 31,146, p. 11.

excite horror." The condign and cruel punishments did not deter the interlopers. Phœnix-like they used to rise from their very ashes. The forbidden fruit was more vigorously sought after by them. But when once they became members of the sacred fraternity, they prevented others from tasting the forbidden fruit. Thus the struggle went on till the very dissolution of the Company.

These restrictions were, however, relaxed more and more as the agitation against them gathered strength.[1] The New Company, to attract the servants of the Old Company, practically threw all restraints to the winds, because they tolerated, or at least connived at, their officers and mariners bringing home any sorts of goods, and on easier terms than they were allowed by the Old Company.[2] After the union of the two companies comprehensive rules were made regarding the Permission Trade. The Indulgences were increased and stricter punishments for violating the rules were provided. For instance :—

(*a*) The amount of trade to be indulged by officers and men on hired ships was fixed as shown below :—[3]

For every 100 tons the ships should be let for, wherein such officers served :—

The Commander had liberty to carry out to the value of	£300
The Chief Mate	£60
The Second Mate	£40
The Third Mate and Purser	£30 each.
The Fourth Mate	£20
All other Officers, as Surgeon, Boatswain, Gunner, Carpenter, Steward, Quarter-Master	£15 each.
The Midshipmen	£10 each.

Every other seaman might carry out to the value of £10 on the whole.

(*b*) A charge of 15 per cent was to be levied on the unindulged goods, or those reserved for the Company, if these were imported by the said men. Five per cent was allowed by Act of Parliament and 2 per cent more was charged for warehouse room.

[1] General Court, Nov. 14, 1694.

[2] New Co. charged 1 per cent on money and 3 per cent on goods sent out and home, instead of 5 per cent charged by the Old Company. Letter Bk., XI, p. 74.

[3] Court Bk., 46, pp. 460–64.

(*c*) The importation of muslins was restricted, and 30 per cent was the levy on the pieces brought over and above the conceded rate.[1]

(*d*) Private imports of silk and tea often exceeded the indulged amounts, so the Company ordered these goods to be forfeited in future.[2]

(*e*) It was ordered that if coral, coral beads, amber, amber beads, pearls, emeralds, or any sort of precious stones were to be sent out to the Indies, then the produce thereof was to be returned in diamonds, diamond boart, musk, ambergris, or bezoar stones, and in no other goods whatsoever.[3]

These were the principal regulations to prevent the excess of private and clandestine trade between 1708 and 1715. The preceding summary has laid bare the rise, progress, regulation, restrictions, violations, punishments of the private trade in goods imported in the Company's ships or clandestinely by privateers from the East Indies. This history shows how supremely difficult and embarrassing it was for the Company to suppress this trade and to preserve its monopoly.

Europeans in the Asiatic Trade. It has been fully seen how the carrying and foreign trades of India were being captured more and more by the Dutch and English Companies during the first half of the seventeenth century. The constant depredations, frequent piracies, naval fights, sporadic hostilities of these Europeans amongst themselves and with the Asiatic powers intimidated Indian merchants and shippers. A positive discouragement was the result of the stringent measures which were deliberately adopted to monopolise, corner, control the purchase and sale of important merchandise, so that Indians and generally all Asiatics were excluded from every lucrative branch of the foreign trade of the country. Along with these are to be counted the great concessions of lower customs duties, freedom from transit dues, as well as from harassment and exactions on the way

[1] Court Bk., 46, pp. 380–81. [2] Letter Bk., XVI, p. 103.
[3] Letter Bk., XIV, p. 256.

at the numerous toll-houses. These three categories of causes narrowed down the activities of Indian merchants to the inland trade alone. The Indians were thus more and more cribbed, cabined and confined to their own country.

The struggle became keener as time went on. During the period under review more Western nations, like the French, Danes, Swedes, etc., came into India for trade. They, too, followed the practices of their predecessors in the field. Just as to-day there is a titanic scramble for carving out Africa and Asia amongst the Europeans, for delimiting spheres of influence in all lands inhabited by the non-European nations for the exclusive exploitation of the economic resources of the latter, so during the seventeenth century there was going on a frightful fight on the seas and continent of India for securing extensive spheres of commercial and political influence to the exclusion of all others. The Indian had literally to choose between the devil and the deep-sea. He avoided both, remained pent up in his own country, and thus handed over its commerce to the Europeans.

The English nation came out successful in North America and India during the eighteenth century. Then the same struggle for land, power, commerce, raw material, riches—which is inherently implanted in *all* animals and more in human breasts—was transferred to the new lands and fresh pastures of the continents of Africa and Asia.

The most successful nations, like the Americans, English and French, having obtained the lion's share, having no hope of getting anything more and for recouping their exhausted resources for some time to come, are most vociferous in crying halt to this grabbing spirit. They are making a virtue of the necessity and hoodwinking and gulling the general public by their profuse professions of universal peace, universal international law, League of Nations, the rights of self-determination and independence. How can the sufferers who have lost even tails in the spoil, agree in their hearts to this just or unjust exploitation? Being weak, exhausted, unarmed, disorganised, resourceless, they may succumb for a time, but they will always be on the look-out for raising their heads and winning back by the might of their arms what they have lost before on account of some weakness or another. Thus the eternal struggle for power and pelf will continue to the end of time. Only a small phase of this much-condemned but unending contest will be disclosed here in this section. It is really a sacred struggle for national or communal existence which ultimately resolves itself into a necessary strife for individual existence.

The first and third causes need not detain us long. No one can doubt that (*a*) the insecurity of the sea and in the country itself made the merchants averse to engage in extensive enterprises of trade; (*b*) the capitalists were afraid of putting out their money to interest, or of risking it in the operation of the sea-borne commerce; and that (*c*) heavy impositions, exactions, delays, harassments, discriminatory dues, heavier import duties, and many other charges on trade carried on by Indian merchants, discouraged them from engaging in it. *The European supremacy on the sea and the greater commercial privileges enjoyed by them diverted the current of trade to European hands and to cities under European control.*

The transfer of the foreign trade of India to European hands was principally due to the exacting restrictions imposed by the Dutch on Asiatic trade. In several treaties with the chiefs of the Southern Islands a clause was inserted to restrict them from navigating beyond certain limits, *under pain of being treated as pirates.* By this regulation alone the Dutch had succeeded in prohibiting all communication between the various states in the Spice Islands, and in limiting the communication of the inhabitants of the numerous islands to their own shores. Thus *the carrying trades of all these rich and commercial places was transferred into the hands of the Dutch.*

There were certain other clauses by which the inhabitants were not allowed to grant privileges to or hold any intercourse with the other Europeans.

The Dutch commercial privileges in the Spice Islands appear from the treaties *to have consisted of the following monopolies :—*

Amber. By the contract of 1646 with the chiefs of Timorlaut—a large island east of Timor—slaves, amber, tortoise-shell, seal-skins, red and yellow paint, and all other merchandise had to be sold exclusively to the Dutch.

Birds'-nests (an article of commerce between the Moluccas and China) were secured to the Dutch by treaties with the chiefs of Magonda and four other places.

Camphor and Benzoin. By several treaties with Sumatra (1668, 1672, 1684) these articles were Dutch monopolies.

Cassia-lignum or sapan-wood. By treaties with the princes of Mandar (1674), Tumbhava (1675), Timor (1616), and Sumatra (1672), it was to be sold to the Dutch alone.

Cloths. By treaty with the chiefs of Salayer (1675), Baroor (1668), Jambi (1614, 1683, 1721), Palembang (1681), cloths could be supplied to the inhabitants by the Dutch alone.

Cloves. By treaties with the Rajahs of Ternate (1607, 1621, etc.), Bachian (1609), Machian (1613), Amboyna (1605), and Banda (1616), cloves could be produced and disposed of only according to the instructions of the Dutch.

Diamonds. By treaty with Sambas (1609) they were to be exclusively sold to the Dutch.

Gold. By treaties with several chiefs on the northern part of the Island of Celebes and some of the chiefs of Sumatra and the Peninsula of Malaya, this precious metal was a Dutch monopoly.

Mace. By treaty with Damma (1646, etc.) mace could be sold to the Dutch only.

Mother-of-Pearl. By treaties with the chiefs of Tending and Sicabo (1740), and Tetoli (1676, 1683, 1736), the sole right of purchase was secured.

Nutmegs were monopolised by treaty with the chiefs of Damma (1655, etc.).

Opium. With the various chiefs of Sumatra (1670, 1683, 1721, 1758) treaties had been made for the exclusive right of selling opium.

Pepper. By treaties with the Rajahs of Cheribon and Java, of Bantam, Sumatra, Ternate, and Bootang (1607, 1649, 1661, etc.), no other nation could buy pepper from the inhabitants.

Sago was a Dutch monopoly by treaty with the chiefs of Maganito (1677).

Slaves, too, were exclusively secured by treaties with the chiefs of Solor (1646), Moa (1665), Damma (1646), and Timorlaut (1646).

Tin. By numerous contracts with the states on the Malayan Peninsula, the Islands of Sumatra, etc., this much-needed article of Indian use was monopolised by the sovereigns of the seas.

Tortoise-shell was secured by treaties too numerous to mention.

Wax. By several treaties it became a Dutch monopoly.

It is abundantly evident now that the inhabitants of those numerous islands were not free to exchange the above-mentioned articles with the products of India, China, Arabia, Persia, or Europe. *No nation or individual except the Dutch Company could have any intercourse with the inhabitants of the islands under its control.* Even the servants of the Company were prohibited from trading privately in the monopolised articles. The observations of Christopher Fryke on this point are full of significance :—

Though Pepper is as plenty in India as stones in the streets, and only serves for ballast very often, and to pack up other goods tight; and although sometimes *several whole ship loads of it be thrown into the sea, and many hundred thousand pound-weight of it burnt*, yet dares no man in the service of the Company take one single corn of it, but everyone is obliged to buy it of the Indians, who deal with the Company for it; and the same rule is observable in respect to other spices.

Further on, he says :—

None of the spices, neither the cinnamon, nor the cloves, mace, nutmegs, saffron, borrobone (used instead of saffron), etc., may be carried away by any private person upon pain of death ; *and it hath cost some men their lives for attempting to bring them over.*[1]

That spices were burnt in considerable quantities to keep up their prices and to safeguard the monopoly is borne out from another source :—[2]

In one year 70,000 trees were destroyed in one island alone, and that in all the Spice Islands about 500,000 or 600,000 trees were annually burnt down.[3]

Such were the civilised methods employed by the republican Dutch !

When the English and French were thus restricted by the Dutch, they had to follow the same means to exclude their opponents in other places. In all these rivalries and hostilities the peoples of India were the great sufferers. They were excluded by all in supplying their own marts with the products of Asia and Europe as they used to do up to the end of the sixteenth century. The English people devoted more attention to capturing the coasting trade of India, of the Near and the Far East up to China.

At first the English Company were against permitting any share to their servants in the coastal trade. After having devised every possible discouragement for private traders engaged in Indo-British trade, the Directors proceeded to make short shrift of those who, contrary to their orders, were carrying on coasting trade in the Indies. The spirit of their

[1] "A relation of two several voyages made into the East Indies by Christopher Fryke and Christopher Schewitzer." Translated from the Dutch ; London, 1700. Begun in 1680 and lasted for nine years ; pp. 113, 123.

[2] The Dutch employed persons called "Exteripators" to root up trees in the Molucca Islands, so that the cultivation of the spice trees should be restricted to Amboyna for cloves, the Banda Isles for nutmegs, and Ceylon for cinnamon. These harsh measures occasioned repeated wars with the native inhabitants, which at length terminated by the Dutch granting the chiefs annual allowances by way of compensation, and for preventing their vassals from planting trees in future. These were augmented at various periods, viz. 1652, 1662, and 1673, when they were finally settled by treaty at an annuity of 12,450 Rix Dollars per annum to the several chiefs.

[3] Factory Records, Java, IX.

policy will be disclosed by the following extract from their Surat Letter, dated April 9th, 1660 :—

Heere is a Surat report, that some of our factors (*notwithstanding our prohibition of all private trade*) have assumed that liberty to themselves, as to fraight and imploy vessels upon their owne particular accompt, from port to port, wee desire that you make a diligent enquirye who those parties bee that have or shall exercise *such unlawfull* and unwarrantable course, and give us true, and full accompt thereof. Beeing we are resolved not to permit any person whatsoever, to drive on a private trade, *which hath beene and (if not supressed) will bee, distructive, to our publique. Therefore whosoever they be that shall appeare to be guilty of this crime, shall assuredly upon notice given us, be dismissed our imployment, and returne for England, and wee shall proceed against them according to their demerritte.*[1]

The Company desired to reserve all the profits of the Indo-Asiatic and coastal trades for themselves. However, it could neither suppress the one nor the other. The exceptionally large profits tempted every servant of the Company to reap the rich harvest in as short a time as possible and return home to lead a life of comparative ease and comfort.

An idea of the profits of the carrying trade can be had by the rates of freights paid in those days :—

China Freights to Madras.

Gross goods like sugar, alum, china root, etc.	25% of the value of goods.
Tutenague and copper	20%
Fine goods, as raw and wrought silks, musk, camphor, vermilion, etc.	15%
Gold	7–8%

Thus a ship carrying goods worth Rs.100,000 will have been able to make some Rs.20,000 in one voyage alone.

Freights from Bengal to Madras.

Fine piece-goods	4–4½%
Gurrahs, sailcloth, cambays	8%

Freights from Madras to Persia.

Fine Bengal sugar	18%
China sugar	20%
Coarse Bengal sugar	23%
Fine goods, as romalls, cossaes, etc.	7–10%

[1] Surat Letter, 9th April, 1660, Letter Bk., II, p. 296.

The freights charged by the English East India Company on their ships for goods shipped by their own servants or other merchants permitted by them as fixed in 1675 and confirmed in 1680, will also serve to show the nature of trade between the various countries of the East. *Of course, far higher freights than these concession rates had to be paid by Indian merchants on the Company's ships for the same places. These concessions naturally increased the profits of the English merchants.*

The private merchants had to pay the following rates to the Company :—

From the Coast to Bantam.

Wheat, rice, and other commodities . . . . £5 per ton.

From Surat to Bantam.

Comin seed, opium, and other commodities not prohibited . . . . £6 per ton.

From Bantam to Surat.

Pepper, sugar, candy, china root, and other commodities . . . . £6 per ton.

From Bantam to Tonqueen.

Tywan and Amoy—

For coarse goods . . . . £6 per ton.
For fine goods . . . . £10 per ton.

From Tonqueen to Bantam.

All commodities not prohibited . . . . . . £10 per ton.
From Tywan and Amoy to Surat . . . . . £10 per ton.
For gold and silver from Bantam to the above three places and back 2%
For musk, ambergris, and other fine goods . . . 2%

When we think of the profits of the various articles, which often amounted to cent per cent, it is only then that the immensity of the losses incurred by Indian shipbuilders, ship-owners, shippers, and merchants can be realised. In the Java Records, Vol. IV, pp. 6–11, the profits of the Manilla and Japan trades on Indian goods are shown. *In the latter case they varied from* 420 *to* 700 *per cent in* 1667 !

Sieur Luillier has given us an idea of the *profits of various trades* at the end of the seventeenth century. They can be summarised as under :—[1]

1200%	profit on	Japan articles.
1000%	,,	China ware.
500%	,,	Chinese silks.
30–40%	,,	Bengal silks and rice to Coromandel.

We are told by the same traveller that *the Dutch had never less than forty ships, and often more, trading continually from one place to another in the East.* The English, too, drove a considerable trade, yet much inferior to the Dutch, for they received little more in return than the value of the plate they sent over from Europe; the profit of the coasting commerce went to defray the charges of their officers, forts, and factories.

Besides the Company, their servants made considerable profits in carrying the goods of Indian merchants and their own.

The English East India Company were always chary of granting a large share of coasting trade to their servants, as it was in the long run prejudicial to their own trade and interest. The way was opened by the New Company at the end of the seventeenth century. That body granted free liberty to all its merchants, factors, and writers to trade from port to port in India as they saw fit.[2]

The Old Company, too, were obliged to relax their grip, so that Englishmen freed from the restraints of their masters not only began to share but control the coasting trade and even the inland trade of India. English factors owned and hired ships and carried on a large trade. The Company then realised that these private merchant ships were a great source of strength in time of war, and that other nations were not allowed to grow in power and riches by the English monopoly of the Indo-Asiatic trade. Since then they never opposed this privilege of their servants, although frequent complaints of sacrificing their interests were made. A single instance will suffice.

Considerable Private Trade in Bengal. In their letter of 27th March, 1713–14, the Directors wrote :—

We have convincing reasons to believe that the *Private Trade investments there* (*at Patna*) *were double in value to ours,* which

[1] Voyages to the East Indies, Edition 1701, p. 332.
[2] Letter Bk., XI, p. 15.

to be sure contributed to the greatness of the general charges, and when our goods came down those came down also—this added to the charges, but we could never learn when any boats have been lost that the Private Trade suffered, all the damage was clapt to our account.[1]

There were many other abuses. No difference was made between private and official purchases and debts. Bad debts advanced in private trade, but unrealisable, were thrown upon the Company. Its servants were buyers of goods for the Company and sellers of the same to the Company at a far higher price. The worst goods were entrusted to the Company and the best goods appropriated for their own country trade.[2]

The Company was thus ill-served and defrauded by its servants and yet considerable profits were reaped by that corporation in its Eastern trade!

The Profits of Eastern Trade. The Company, reinstated in the year 1657 with a capital of £739,782 to their ancient privileges of exclusive trade, made a call of only 50 per cent upon the subscribers. Hence the original stock of the Company was £369,891 and not £786,000 as Macgregor has noted.[3] With a temporary depression during the Dutch War of 1664–67, when the value of their stock went down to 70 per cent, the Company enjoyed the longest spell of prosperity hitherto known. Up to the year 1691 an unprecedented success attended the whole affair. For instance, £390½ per cent were divided between the 1st of October, 1661, and the 1st of April, 1681. It was followed by a dividend of £150 per cent on the 18th of January, 1682,[4] out of which 100 per cent

[1] The same complaint a few years after in Letter Bk., XVIII, p. 472.

[2] Letter Bk., XVIII, p. 157.

[3] Commercial Statistics, IV, p. 325.

[4] Macpherson, Milburn, Macgregor, and Wisset are wrong in asserting that this doubling of the Company's stock took place in the year 1676. The Company's Letter of 14th January, 1681–82, expressly declares that this dividend of 150 per cent was declared in 1681:

"The Court have also resolved upon the next sale to make a dividend of 150 per cent, viz. 100 per cent of the present stock to be immediately brought to the credit of each adventurer for doubling of his adventure, and 50 per cent of the present stock to be paid in money on the 29th of September next." Letter Bk., VI, p. 438.

In the face of this evidence, it appears that all the reputed authors in blindly copying from Macpherson have committed a grave error.

Macpherson, Annals, II, p. 579; Milburn, Oriental Commerce, I, xxxiv; Macgregor, Commercial Statistics, IV, p. 330; Wisset, Compendium, I, p. 41.

was used to double their stock and 50 per cent was paid in money to the Adventurers. This climax of prosperity was reached by the arrival of six ships whose cargoes were computed at upwards of £500,000 value. The Company remained securely seated at the giddy heights of their shining fortune for another decade. After the 50 per cent dividend and the doubling of their stock in the aforesaid manner, all future dividends were made and computed upon their stock so doubled. The actual profits in the nine years from 1676 to 1685 were stated as amounting to £963,639. No dividend was, however, declared for four years since the 150 per cent division. The following entries are available for the next six years :—

A dividend of 25% on the 1st Oct., 1685.
" " 25% " 14th April, 1686.
" " 25% " 12th Oct., 1687.
" " 25% " 20th April, 1688.
" " 50% " 2nd Oct., 1689.
" " 50% " 8th April, 1691.

So that the dividends from 1658 to 1681 amounted to 440½ per cent ; and from 1681 to 1691, " doubling the same, as the stock was, according to that nominal duplication, amounted to 400 per cent." In other words, from 1658 to 1691 840½ per cent on the £369,891 original stock had been divided amongst its subscribers. Or *an unusual profit of* 21 *per cent per annum over a period of forty years had been enjoyed in the Eastern adventures.*

This tide of prosperity had, however, already begun to turn against the Company. The heavy expenses of an unsuccessful war with the Mogul, the depression of trade, and the great losses suffered at sea by the sinking and capture of twelve richly laden ships during the Anglo-French War (1689–97) developed into a disease which ended only with the dissolution of the Company.

By an order of the 3rd of May, 1693, the Court called in a new subscription of 50 per cent of the then stock from the Adventurers, so that the whole stock was increased by £325,565.[1] But this 50 per cent additional stock was after-

[1] Court Bk., 36, pp. 186, 214, 215–17, 227, 234.

wards ordered to be paid back with interest out of a new general subscription raised for the better carrying on of their trade and making it more national and extensive by allowing new Adventurers to take up the stock. As the sums proved insufficient, the Company were compelled to raise loans upon their stock; viz., of 25 per cent in October, 1695, from the Adventurers on allowing 20 per cent for prompt payment,[1] and another sum of 25 per cent in September, 1697, on their then stock from the Adventurers, too, by allowing them a bond of £120 for £100 advanced.[2] These exorbitant rates of interest on large sums of money borrowed on bonds, were sure to prove prejudicial to the existence of the Company during the period of an unusual depression. The increasing amounts of their bonded debts raised in England at exorbitant interest will show how their trade was financed by ever-recurring loans.[3]

The Adventurers, not despairing of better success for the future, had "with a Roman courage and resolution resolved to add"[4] large sums of fresh money to their stock, but the future grew darker and darker. No dividend could be declared after 1691 up to the end of the century, and the value of their stock had a sharp fall to 37 per cent. Yet in spite of depressions, disasters, and discouragements the Company had reaped very large profits and managed to outflank and outvie

[1] Court Bk., 37, pp. 34–36.

[2] Court Bk., 37, pp. 196, 198–99, 341. Court Bk., 38, pp. 99–100.

[3] Co.'s Bonded Debt at Interest :—

	Year.		Amount.			
	1662	..	137,242	0	0	Home Misc., Vol. 40, p. 50.
			120,000	0	0	Short loan.
	1664	..	165,807	0	0	
31st December,	1680	..	532,589	7	5	
	1681		613,529	7	5	
29th April,	1693	..	451,507	16	10	
18th November,	1693	..	256,359	6	11	
30th ,,	1694	..	401,813	8	5	
,, ,,	1695	..	637,296	12	0	
,, ,,	1696	..	746,808	19	6	
,, ,,	1697	..	595,896	19	9	
31st March,	1698	..	631,554	19	10	
11th March,	1695	..	1,110,981	0	0	Debt in India & England.

Journal of the House of Commons, Vol. XII, p. 313; Vol. XI, p. 507.

[4] Letter Bk., IX, pp. 444, 464.

their Dutch rivals. The course of dividends of the two Companies is presented in the following table :—

Years.		Dividend declared by	
		[1] The English Co.	The Dutch Co.
1658–81	. .	440½%	433⅓%
1681–91	. .	400%	232½%
1692–1700	. .	None.	190%
1700–10	. .	Not known.	240%

Thus the Dutch Company divided 666 *per cent in forty years against* 840 *per cent of the English Company.* Even the next decade does not place the proprietors of the Dutch stock in a much better position than their English compeers.

The next section on the aggregate values of the Dutch and English trades with the East will prove no less a disillusionment as to the proverbially gigantic volume of the Indo-Dutch commerce.

A View of the Dutch Trade

It is a recognised fact that the opulence and power of the Dutch reached their zenith during the latter half of the seventeenth century. Their political conquests and commercial monopolies in the East had made them the most dominating nation in the Indo-European trade. Goa, formerly the key of all the commerce of the Indies and the fairest city in India, had been reduced to an extreme poverty and was so shrunk that it did not contain more than 20,000 inhabitants in the 'twenties of the eighteenth century. Batavia, the Dutch metropolis, having shorn Goa of its commerce, splendour, opulence, and population, had grown to be the Queen of the East on account of the superb beauty of its buildings, its magnificent harbour, and the immense trade which it carried on throughout the East. The Dutch were known to be the wealthiest, the strongest, and the greatest dealers of all Europeans in India. They had never less than forty ships, and often more, trading from one place to another in the Indies. They annually despatched 14–15 tall ships to Europe, and as many to the East.

[1] See Appendices to this chapter.

A view of the fabulous profits earned by the Dutch is furnished by Stavorinus and Valentyne. According to the former the profits of the eleven years from 1662–63 to 1673–74 amounted upon an average annually to 520 per cent upon the finer spices, being in money £30,415 a year. They rose to 850 per cent or £46,315 a year from 1688–89 to 1697–98. During this last decade a further profit of £23,266 was made upon the other goods which amounted to $59\frac{3}{64}$ per cent upon their prime cost. But these profits gradually decreased after that period. Those upon the spices, indeed, rendered a higher proportion per cent, and in the year 1731–32 they were even 2,400 per cent upon the prime cost; but the consumption was, on the other hand, so small, that in the ten years, in which that extraordinary proportion of gain appeared, namely from 1730–31 to 1739–40, the real annual average profit in money scarcely amounted to one-fifth part of the sums before made with a lesser advance upon the prime cost. The extraordinary profits are confirmed by Valentyne, who states the Dutch gains at Surat to average :—

665%	upon	cloves	42%	upon	benzoin
1,453%	,,	nutmegs	34%	,,	gumlac
718%	,,	mace	27%	,,	quicksilver
128%	,,	copper bars	19%	,,	vermilion
31%	,,	copper plate			

Now one is apt to be deceived as to the real extent of the Dutch trade in the East and that with Europe by seeing these bloated figures of their profits. A little calculation will show that their whole import trade in the Indies on the basis of these profits amounted to :—

Years.	Prime Cost per Year.	Sale Value per Year.
1662–73	£5,842 in spices	£36,257
1688–97	£5,449 ,,	£51,764
	£39,433 in all other goods	£62,699

In other words, during the ten years of 1688–97 the annual sales of all the goods disposed of in the Indies averaged about £114,500 sterling per year. Such is the astounding insignificance of the Dutch trade at its climax during the last years of the seventeenth century when we judge it by present standards!

Their Indo-European trade, too, when expressed in cold statistics, is shorn of its greatness. *The invoiced value of all the goods sent out of the Indies falls far short of the specie and merchandise* exported out of England to finance the Indian trade. The profits made by the English Company in the port-to-port trade in Asia were sufficient to defray the charges of their officers, forts, and factories. *Hence the invoiced value of their Eastern imports can be justly taken to be equal to their exports from England.* Even deducting £2,000,000 more, or 16 per cent, for expenses and losses in the East from all the sums exported by the English into the Orient, we find that there is still a significant difference between the sums invested by the two nations in the Indies during the fifty years from 1661 to 1710 :—

The Course of Indo-Dutch Trade

Years.	Ships.	Total Invoices. (Thousand Florins.)	Increase.
1661–70	126	31,439	100
1671–80	127	33,723	107
1681–90	140	44,719	142
1691–1700	147	45,063	137
1701–10	187	54,581	173
	727	209,525 or about £19,000,000	

A sum of £19,000,000 *sterling stands against* £26,000,000 *sent out by the English in money and goods!*

During the last decade, while the Official value of Eastern imports, which was, on the whole, decidedly less[1] than the invoiced prices, was estimated by the authorities of the Custom House in England to be £5,227,000 for nine years, the Indian imports into Holland for the same nine years were invoiced at £4,962,000. *It is now evident that the business and profits of the English throughout this period of fifty years were superior to those of the Dutch, and that the former had fairly surpassed their most active, shrewd, powerful and old competitors in the Indo-European trade.*

[1] The exports amounted to 11 million pounds, the imports must have nearly equalled this sum. Surely they could not be less than half the exports.

The Company's Growing Assets

It has been shown that after 1625 the Company had to pass through many financial crises. Their commercial weakness was exhibited even by the exaggerated evaluation of their effects, which were valued at £180,511 in 1646, while their debts in England alone amounted to £122,000.[1] This languishing condition was, however, left far behind by 1664, when by a statement made on 8th December it was shown that after deducting all debts owned by the Company a balance of £495,735 was left in their favour. On the basis of this valuation the stock was worth 130 per cent.[2] The great commercial and political activities of the Company during the 'eighties and 'nineties are fully reflected in the considerable growth of their property and the number of ships owned by them. It was alleged [3] that their stock-in-trade stood at £1,700,000 in 1681, against £370,000 in 1657. This account is much exaggerated, for two years later [4] it was estimated at only £1,116,000, including even all the disparate stock. There was a rapid inflation in the Company's stock in the

[1]

Quick stock at Surat .	£83,600	£180,511
,, ,, Bantam .	60,731	
Shipping and stores .	31,180	
Gombroon Customs .	5,000	

Milburn's Oriental Commerce, Vol. 1, p. 27.

[2]

Quick and Dead Stock in India .	£435,713	
,, ,, ,, England .	76,577	
Debts for goods undelivered . .	127,935	
,, ,, delivered . .	21,316	661,542
,, owned by the Company		165,807
Balance . .		£495,735

Court Bk., 24, pp. 908–9. Cf. also Home Misc., 40, p. 47.

[3] E.I. Co.'s Answer to the Turkey Co., 1681.

[4] An account taken out of Ye Company's Bookes in January, 1682–83 :—

	Disparate.	Dead Stock.	Quick Stock.
Bantam . .	£26,399 10 0	£24,339 5 0	£112,006 19 6
Surat . .	18,784 5 9	139,373 11 0	199,299 13 4
Coast and Bay .	24,753 7 0	18,336 15 0	541,296 1 2
St. Helena . .		10,000 0 0	
	£69,937 2 9	£192,049 11 0	£852,602 14 0

succeeding three years, for in the year 1685 it was stated that their dead and quick stocks were valued at £719,464 and £2,487,312, both in India and England.

This did not include bad and disparate debts amounting to £11,413, nor were the very considerable debts of the kings of Persia and Siam owing to the Company accounted for, by reason of the uncertainty of their recovery. Thus it was proved that every hundred pounds adventure in the E.I. Stock was worth £327 10s. 3d.[1] per cent in dead and quick stock—the total of all the Adventurers' stock amounting to £739,782. The growth of their total property in the years of prosperity can now be summed up in the following table :—

Year.	Total Stock.	
1646	£180,511	
1664	£512,290	
1681	£1,700,000	
1683	£1,116,000	
1685	£3,318,189	disparate stocks excluded.

This sudden and abnormal inflation was given a sharp set-back by the war with the Mogul Emperor. The succeeding years reveal a lamentable shrinkage in the Company's prosperity. For instance, the General Account of November, 1689, shows that the Company were creditor to the amount of £1,468,233, and after deducting the debts owned by them the balance amounted to £907,595,[2] which was a little less than twofold, as compared to that of 1664. The succeeding statement of their stock is no less reflective of the rapid reduction of their commercial operations. The dead stock [3] was stated to be £498,608, and the quick stock [4] £367,761 in 1691.

Besides this, the Company had rents, revenues, duties, customs, etc., valuable and improving, though not brought in credit of the said account, amounting to £27,303. In other words, their stocks and revenues were worth more than

[1] Jure Impt., 22,185, p. 7.
[2] Jure Impt., 22,185, p. 18.
[3] Quick stock means ships and merchandise, and the other implies forts, factories, houses, etc.
[4] Journals of the House of Commons, X, p. 560.

£1,500,000. Still, they shrank from £3⅓ million in 1685 to £1½ million in the six years when the Company were passing through the wave of depression after the disastrous war with the Mogul.

The price of their capital stock had consequently fallen to 150 per cent. As the enemies of the Company, taking advantage of its decadent condition, set up a great agitation for dissolving that body, it was pointed out by the latter that the various forts, towns, and territories in India had cost them, from first to last, above £1,000,000 sterling, that these were theirs for ever by their Charters, and they "knew no law nor reason for being thus dispossessed of their Estates at an under value." The troubles at home and the continental war during the last decade of the seventeenth century very much depressed the business of the Company, which would have recovered and prospered after the Peace of Ryswick had the corporation not been thrown into convulsion by the erection of a new company. The Old Company was, to some extent, enabled to tide over the depression by the revenues of their territories in India, which were stated to be upwards of £44,000 a year in 1697,[1] and were soon after enhanced by the acquisition of Calcutta and other villages in Bengal. There is, however, no doubt that the two Companies, in spite

[1] The revenues of Fort St. George and Fort St. David's amount to, by the balance of the Books ending in April, 1697, as by Advices read from thence, viz. :—

Fort St. George 36,101 pagodas, each 9s. .	£16,285	19	0	
Fort St. David's 26,658 ,, ,, .	11,996	2	0	
Bombay by their last books ending the 31st July, 1686 (1696 ?), 113,048 rupees at 2s. 3d. .	12,717	15	0	damaged.
Customs of Persia are per annum . . .	3,333	9	8	
	£44,333	5	8	

This revenue is over and above the charges of collection and does not arise by any Customs or other duties on the Company's own goods, but by the inhabitants and particular merchants and is, too, far from being oppressive. In all probability this Revenue will in a few years increase to double what it is now, and ought not to be valued at fewer years' purchase than a plantation in America, viz. 10 years. The Company pay only 3,000 pagodas or £375 per annum in lieu of Customs and all other charges for their trade in Bengal, whereas the interlopers have been forced to pay from 3½ to 5 per cent Customs (besides considerable presents) whenever they have procured goods there.

Jure Impt., 22,185, p. 58.

of the great boom in business which followed the Peace of Ryswick, had involved themselves in excessive debts by their ruinous rivalry.

Although the English Companies trading to the East Indies gained a new strength by their amalgamation, it is true, however paradoxical it may appear, that we have now to describe the history of the commercial dealings of a bankrupt company. In the year 1709 the real state of the Company's affairs was disclosed by Lord Godolphin, who had been empowered to examine and ascertain the reciprocal credits and debts of the two Companies. By an account appended to his famous award, it appears that the debts of the London Company amounted to £1,249,807, and their assets to only £850,911, thus showing a deficiency of £398,896. A deficit of about £400,000, according to their own exaggerated valuation, does not augur a prosperous career. With the state of their finances so seriously rotten, the Company had been compelled to purchase the prolongation of their privileges with a new loan of £1,200,000 to the Government for the public use without any additional interest on so large a contribution. The absurdity of this transaction has been strongly commented on by Mill :—

> But the chief mark of the ignorance at that time of parliament in the art and science of Government, was *their abstracting from a trading body, under the name of loan to Government, the whole of their trading capital,* and expecting them to traffic largely and profitably when destitute of funds. The vast advance to Government, the *place of which they feebly supplied by credit, beggared the English Company and ensured their ruin from the first.*

CHAPTER VII

FIFTY YEARS BEFORE PLASSEY
(1708–1757)

In the preceding chapters we have sketched the rise and progress of the Indo-British trade to the year 1707. The next year marks the complete coalition of the two Companies under the name of The United Company of Merchants of England Trading to the East Indies.

From this year we have a regular account of the total amount and value of the Oriental trade, probably because it was strictly provided in the Company's Charter of that year that "an account of Several Goods of the Kingdom of Great Britain as also of other Goods and Merchandise exported from the Port of London for Account of the United Trade of the English Company Trading into the East Indies be presented to Parliament every year."[1] Moreover, the establishment of the United Company precedes, though it is a pure coincidence, by just fifty years the acquisition of political sovereignty in Bengal. Hence the two important events, like the union of the two companies in 1708 and the successful revolution in Bengal in 1757, constitute a distinct period in the history of the East India Company.

Official Statistics

A brief note on the nature of the available statistical data is pre-eminently necessary. The various sources afford two fundamentally different sets of statistics. The one set is distinguished by the name of Official Statistics, and the other is known as the Company's Returns. The former have been

[1] Cf. the Company's Charter of 1693.

regularly compiled by the authorities of the Custom House of London since 1697. They are now available in the Board of Customs Library and the Public Record Office. The volumes for the years 1697 to 1716, as well as for 1718, 1728, 1750, 1753, 1755, and 1766 are missing in the Books of the Custom House Library; however, the gap is fortunately all filled up but for the three years of 1705, 1712 and 1728 by the volumes available in the Record Office.

A general survey of the returns relating to the East India goods imported into England shows that :—

1. The values of some commodities, as chinaware, were the prices realised at the sales of the Company.

2. The prices of the articles known as "unrated goods" were, on the other hand, actual costs in the country of purchase as declared on oath by the importer.

3. The values assigned to the "rated goods" were arbitrary, and had no relation to the actual prices prevailing either in the country of origin or in England, or to their sale prices in England; and that

4. The rated values arbitrarily fixed by the Customs authorities, though constant in the majority of cases, did vary in the case of a few articles.

The variable and invariable characters of the rated values of the Oriental goods from 1590 to 1757 have been fully shown in a table given in Appendix A to this chapter. A cursory glance at these values will make it patent to all that the values which remained unalterable for more than 160 years[1] could have no relation to actual market prices. The wide divergence between the two values can be visualised in the following typical cases :—[2]

Articles.	Prices for the purpose of Customs.	Sale Prices available for 1707–13.
Tea . . .	1s. to 2s. per lb.	18s. 6d. per lb.
Coffee . . .	£2 to £3 per cwt.	£28 per cwt.
Calicoes, Quilted .	10s. per piece.	£2 1s. 8d. per piece.
,, Stitched .	10s. ,,	£3 13s. 0d. ,,

[1] Harleian MSS. 7013, pp. 36, 37, 40, 47, detail the discussion on the alteration in the rated values proposed by the Patent Officers and the Custom House authorities in 1714.

[2] Harleian MSS. 7013, pp. 36, 37, should be compared.

It is evident now that since the year 1697, whence the Official Returns become available, there is no one factor of quantity or value which can be responsible for bringing about fluctuations in the annual aggregates, as is the case in the returns based on actual prices where there are always present these two variable factors of quantity and price, the second requiring to be eliminated before we can show quantitative changes in those returns. The Official Returns, being a hotch-potch of opposite elements, are valuable neither as indicative of the quantities of goods imported, nor as indices of the variation of their values. The total money values of the goods are vitiated, even for comparative purposes, on account of their being composed of variable and heterogeneous items. Had they been collected on a basis of invariable values of *all* goods imported into and exported from England since 1660, the year of the revised rates, they would have been as useful as, if not superior to, the returns based on actual prices for showing the relative importance of the various branches of England's import trade.

The value of the Official import and export statistics has been thus commented upon by the Inspector-General of Customs in his report attached to the "Imports and Exports" of the year 1790—the first report of its kind available on the merits of these returns (Customs 17, Vol. 12).

From the very loose manner in which the Entries of Free Goods outwards are made as to Species, quantity and quality, and also from the Estimates in this office, having been formed near a century ago, when the Prices differed materially from the present times, very little reliance as to the value is to be put upon the Accounts of British Manufactures Exported, in any other respect than in a comparative view between one period and another.

The Accounts of the Foreign Merchandize exported are as accurate as can reasonably be expected, in accounts of so extensive a nature, but the same objection applies to the Rate of Value in these Accounts as in the case of British Manufactures. The Account of the Species and Quantity of Foreign Merchandize Imported is fully as accurate as the Accounts of Foreign Merchandize Exported, but this Account is likewise liable to the same objections as the two preceding with respect to the Rate of value.

The Estimates in this office by which the Goods Imported and Exported are valued, were made about the year 1697, probably by the first Appointed Officer, for the Office was instituted in that year, upon what principle he formed his Estimates it is difficult to ascertain this day, but *it is evident from various Records in the Office that the value adopted as to the Imports was the prices which the Articles were supposed to bear in the Countries from whence they came,* and that the value of Goods Exported did not include the Freight Outwards, for the Goods Imported or Exported in a British or a Foreign Bottom still continue to be valued at the same Rate. This plan appears to me to be erroneous in principle. In Estimating the Value of Exports in British Bottoms the freight ought to have been included, for the Freight I conceive is to be considered as so much additional value or labour attached to the commodity. If two Cargoes of Goods Value £1000 each were exported to Spain or any other Country, the one in a British, the other in a Foreign Bottom, that which was Exported in the British Bottom would enable the Exporter to purchase Goods in Spain to the Amount of the Additional Value which they would acquire by the Freight and if the Returns were made also in a British Bottom, the Value of the Freight is to be *excluded* in order to show the *true balance.* On the other hand, in Estimating the Value of Goods Imported and Exported in Foreign Bottoms, the Freight ought to be included in the former and excluded in the latter.

I have taken the liberty, Sir, of troubling you with these remarks upon the Rate or Estimates in this Office, in order to show *that the difference between the value of Imports and Exports is very little to be depended upon in striking the Balance of Trade, and consequently that the Arguments held both in and out of Parliament, and the voluminous writings of various Authors upon the subject of Commercial Balances, chiefly founded upon the Accounts of the Inspector-General's Office, are made upon false Data.*

As a contrast to the foregoing remarks, the opinion of a learned and laborious author like Moreau affords a great surprise. He takes for his "starting-point the year 1696, at which period a great and advantageous change took place in the books of the English Customs, by fixed rates of official value being invariably assigned to each article of importation and exportation, in lieu of the variable quotation of the prices current, which until then had served as a basis for general evaluation; the perpetual fluctuation of which occasioned much obscurity and disorder in the estimations."

Moreau is evidently unaware of the fixed and invariable rates established in 1590 and 1660, and therefore takes 1696 as a year marked by a great change. It has been previously seen that no such alteration was inaugurated in the method of levying Customs duties in 1696, nor was the system of rated and unrated goods advantageous in any respect. However, as the imports and exports have been collected on a uniform, though a defective basis, they afford useful data for tracing variations in their different items, so far as their interrelation to each other or their proportion to the total trade of England is concerned.

In passing, a note of warning must be struck on the fallacious method of finding out the balance of trade adopted by the authorities of the Custom House. Since the year 1707, the aggregate values of goods imported and exported from and to the East Indies are given at the end of each year's report. They have been reproduced by Moreau and Macgregor. The total value of exported *goods* has been subtracted from that of the imported *goods*, and the *import* excess has been taken as a measure of the *unfavourable* balance of English trade with the East. No account has been taken of the immense fortunes reared by Englishmen in the East and remitted home in the shape of goods, nor of the commercial and territorial revenues left over after defraying all charges, and sent to England in merchandise. The Import and Export Report of the year 1790 has some pregnant remarks on the subject :—

The great Excess of the Imports over the Exports in the E.I. Trade, appears as a Balance against us in the Inspector-General's Books, but this Excess consisting of the produce of the Company's Territorial Revenues, and of remittances of the Fortunes acquired by Individuals, instead of being unfavourable is an acquisition of so much additional Wealth to the Public Stock.[1]

[1] Public Rec. Office, Customs 17, Vols. 12 and 13.

In this note another extreme has been touched. The important item of exported gold and silver has been completely ignored, and the excess, which is the difference between imported and exported goods alone, has been represented as a net gain to the nation. The real favourable balance can only be found out by subtracting the exports of specie from this excess. In other words, the sum total of exported merchandise, as well as all gold and silver sent out of the country to feed the Eastern trade, ought to be deducted from the imports to arrive at the favourable or unfavourable balance of trade, and the large sums earned and remitted by Englishmen in their corporate or individual capacity should not be left out of account.

The Company's Returns of Exports to the East

So far as the Company's returns are concerned, mention should be made of two volumes in the India Office Record Department in the Home Miscellaneous Series, Nos. 72 and 449, the first of which gives on its first page figures for goods, stores, and bullion sent from England to India and China in each year from 1st March, 1732, to 1st March, 1772, and the second supplies sundry statistics from 1747 to 1795, on pages 2–9 and 12. The first set was reproduced in the Third Report of the Committee of Secrecy, 1773, p. 75, and then by Milburn in his "Oriental Commerce" (1813). I have not been able to trace the export returns for the years 1708 to 1731, collected on the same basis in the India Office Records, although they have been given by Milburn. The annual values of exported merchandise differ from those given in the Parliamentary Paper,[1] No. 152 of 1812–13. The latter were reproduced, without any reference to the document abovementioned, in Sir Charles Whitworth's "State of the Trade

[1] The title of this Parliamentary document is "An Account of Bullion and Merchandise Exported by the East India Company to India and China respectively, from 1708 to the latest period; distinguishing each year, and the Several Presidencies; with a Statement of the Mode in which the value of the Merchandise is calculated—25th March, 1813."—India Office Parliamentary Papers, Vol. 8.

of Great Britain" (1776), Abbé Raynal's[1] Atlas, Moreau[2] Cesar's "State of the Trade of Great Britain" (1822) and "East India Company's Records" (1825), and in Macgregor's "Commercial Statistics" (1848).

All these statisticians had direct access to original matter, yet it appears that Macgregor reproduces the data regarding Anglo-Asiatic trade from the earlier works of Whitworth and Moreau only in a defective manner. Corrected in the light of the Parliamentary Paper mentioned above, Macgregor's "Commercial Statistics" can be utilised with advantage. Moreau has taken care to state that all his data were taken from authentic sources, while in the introduction to his "State of the Trade of Great Britain" he writes: "Our Chart is merely a laborious compilation, the slow production of eight years' labour and uninterrupted inquiry."

As shown above, there is perfect similarity in the data of the Parliamentary Paper and of the works of Moreau and Macgregor, but their statistics on exports of merchandise differ in many items from those of Milburn. It is a pity that Moreau has not referred to the work of his predecessor, nor tried to explain the discrepancies between the two sets of figures. As no memoranda on the nature of those statistics are attached to either of these works, one could throw little light on the grave differences existing in their data.

The mystery is, however, solved by referring to the returns

[1] This useful and rare book is the last volume of Raynal's "East and West Indies." As he relies upon Whitworth for his figures of the total trade of Great Britain and for those of the Oriental trade (Livre III, Vol. II) there is nothing new for our purpose.

[2] There is an incontestable evidence of Mr. Moreau's use of the Parliamentary Paper, No. 152, because he has copied out the last table on the decennial returns of the different articles of export *en bloc.* The other statistics he has presented in a slightly different form. For instance, he has left out separate returns for Madeira, St. Helena, Madagascar, the Cape of Good Hope, Mocha, Gombroon, Borneo, Batavia, Bencoolen, and Prince of Wales's Island, probably because of their inclusion in the totals for India in the Parliamentary document. Secondly, the form of presenting these returns has also been changed by Moreau. As this new form is to be had in Macgregor's "Commercial Statistics," it appears that he must have used Moreau and not the Parliamentary Paper.

given in the India Office Records, Home Miscellaneous, Vol. 72, where it is stated that those export statistics are for goods and stores *paid for by the Company*, probably up to the end of the financial year. Now the actual exports sent out could not necessarily be equal in value to the goods for which the Company could make payments up to the end of their financial year. Variation in individual years is but natural. What we are concerned with is that the total values of both sets of figures should approximately coincide with each other when compared for a number of years, and this is exactly the case with regard to these otherwise divergent returns.

So much for the differences existing in the export figures of the Company's returns. As regards imports, no statistics of the prime costs of goods brought into the country are available in any published work. The Company's records, such as Minutes and Letters of the Court of Directors, as well as the Factory Records of Surat, Fort St. George, etc., do not afford any consecutive material worth the name. The sale values of imported E.I. goods are given since 1708 onward in the works of Moreau, Milburn, and Macgregor, while the official values of imports exist since 1698. These alone can form the basis of our conclusions regarding the progress of the Oriental trade.

Eastern Imports

Taking first the *sale statistics* of the goods imported by the Company in each year from 1708 to 1757 for our study, we find an *almost* unbroken rise in the total values realised in the sales of goods put up by the Company. Take, for instance, the last year of each decade from 1708 to 1757, and it will be seen that the sale proceeds in these years invariably show a progressive rise :—

1708	£986,516
1717–18	989,722
1727–28	1,688,752
1737–38	1,724,013
1747–48	1,739,159
1757–58	1,770,919

Looking next at the following table, it will be seen that the quinquennial totals, with the exception of the two five-years periods of 1728–32 and 1753–57, also manifest a progressive tendency, so far so that the goods sold by the Company in the last quinquennium realised two and a half times the total sale values of the five years from 1708 to 1712. Again, the decennial totals are no less indicative of the great and invariably progressive character of Eastern imports into England. While the total money value of those imports in the first decade of 1708–17 was £9,785,911, it rose in the next decade to £14,669,093, showing an increase of 50 per cent in ten years.

The next decade of 1728–37 is also of steady progress, the growth as compared to the first decade of 1708–17 being 63 per cent. The climax was achieved in the year 1735–36 when the imports were sold for £1,997,452 in that year alone. Despite the war with Spain and the general European war from 1739 to 1743 on one side, and the Carnatic War with the French in India from 1744 to 1748 on the other, the values realised for Oriental imports show no tendency to shrink, only the rate of growth is slackened, so that during the fourth decade, ending in the year of the Peace of Aix-la-Chapelle, the import trade manifests an increase of 85 per cent over the first decade against 63 per cent of the third. The years of peace following that memorable treaty are particularly marked by a great expansion of the import trade, so that the quinquennial period of 1748–52 shows 178 per cent increase over the first quinquennium of 1708–12. However, this spell of prosperity was soon broken by the Seven Years' War with the French in 1756 and the commencement of hostilities against the Nabob of Bengal in 1757. The import trade naturally suffered a shock, but it seems to have more than recovered soon after the brilliant victory at Plassey. Despite these adverse circumstances, the last ten years show greater progress than was achieved during the two decades immediately preceding them. In fact, *the total decennial value of imports during* 1748–57 *was* 219 *per cent as compared to the years* 1708–17.

The foregoing data afford eloquent testimony to the fact that a steady and growing supply of Indian and Eastern goods had been pouring into England. The demand both for home consumption and re-exportation to the Continent or the Colonies had increased to more than twofold in the fifth decade as compared to the first, or to 2½-fold when the first and the last *quinquennial periods* are taken into consideration.

A Progressive Statement of the Sale Amount of Imports.[1]

Periods.	Quinquennial Values.	Decennial Totals.	Percentage Progress.
1708–12	£4,007,052		
1713 17	5,778,859	£9,785,911	100
1718–22	6,883,939		
1723–27	7,785,154	14,669,093	150
1728–32	7,580,958		
1733–37	8,445,425	16,026,383	163
1738–42	8,463,812		
1743–47	9,599,158	18,062,970	185
1748–52	11,141,990		
1753–57	10,310,605	21,452,595	219
		£79,996,952	

Turning now to the Official Returns, which roughly indicate the quantitative character of the total Eastern imports brought by the Company and private merchants into Great Britain, we find a steady and rapid progress during the first three decades, but the advance is more than arrested during the fourth by reason of the Spanish and Carnatic Wars, as well as the oft-recurring depredations of the Marathas in Bengal, when imports fall from £9,724,548 in the third decade to £9,328,136 in the fourth. In other words, on account of the less money available for home investments due to the exorbitant expenses incurred in the war with the French, the scarcity of merchant vessels, the increased charges of freight and insurance in shipping goods from India, and many other impediments, less goods could be imported into England. However, as the sales, instead of showing a fall during this fourth decade, rather indicate a great increase, it is evident that there must have been an abnormal rise in the prices of Eastern goods. This inference is fully supported by the

[1] Based on Macgregor's figures.

prices realised at the Company's sales in England and those obtained by the French Company in France during these years.

Going to the next decade, we find that with the return of peace in Europe the import trade, so far as quantities are concerned, is soon revived, so that its value amounts to £10,841,200 during the fifth decade. On the basis of these figures, which we have taken as roughly indicative of the amounts of imports, the decennial values are serially related to each other as

100 : 170 : 173 : 165 : 193.

In other words, the import trade in its quantitative aspect expressed in decennial averages developed by 93 per cent during the fifty years under review. But expressed in quinquennial averages, which are more reliable indices of the relative growth of commerce, the quantities imported in the last five years' period are two and a half times those of the first quinquennium of 1708–12. Hence, the net rise in Eastern imports, whether measured by the quantities brought into the country or the money-values realised at the sales of the Company, was 250 per cent in terms of quinquennial progress within the fifty years under review.

Eastern Imports into Great Britain (Based on Official Returns).

Periods.	Quinquennial Totals.	Decennial Values.	Percentage Progress.
1708–12	£2,158,153		
1713–17	3,478,335	£5,636,488	100
1718–22	4,696,474		
1723–27	4,933,502	9,629,976	170
1728–32	4,707,971		
1733–37	5,016,577	9,724,548	173
1738–42	5,236,071		
1743–47	4,092,065	9,328,136	165
1748–52	5,492,223		
1753–57	5,348,977	10,841,200	193
		£45,160,348	

The preceding figures, as observed before, represent the whole import trade handled by the English nation. The Company's business is included in these aggregates and is not identical with them all. How much of it was in any one year appropriated by that body can by no means be estimated. It was seen that during 1698–1707, the private exports equalled those of the Company. The same proportion can be assumed in the import trade also.

But we experience another difficulty. The above figures are purely hypothetical, because these values are based upon fixed rates which remained almost unaltered since 1660. They are only useful for showing the relative growth of the import trade, but offer no indication to the absolute or real market prices of imported articles either in the East or in England.

It should therefore be borne in mind that neither the sale figures nor the Custom House returns reveal the true extent of the import trade with the East. The first fail to do so for the reason that the Company's sales do not include all the goods of the private merchants, while the second returns afford us no idea of the prices actually realised in England. In the years of peace the prices of Oriental goods were low, while after 1735 these were generally very high. Consequently no ratio between the prices fixed for the purposes of Customs and those actually obtained at the sales in England can be determined and agreed upon. The average sale prices for all imports may be surmised to range between two to three times the Customs rates. In any case, our conclusions are sure to be vitiated by these vague surmises, and no accurate indication of the growth and volume of the *aggregate* import trade with the East will be obtainable and admissible.

Trade in Piece-Goods

As to the nature and volume[1] of the different items of imports, it will suffice to say that although there was no difference in their character as compared to the preceding half a century, the relative importance of the several commodities had undergone revolutionary changes. Calicoes

[1] The figures of this section, having been collected by the Custom House authorities, represent all imports, both private and the Co.'s. The two cannot be separated. Hence, comparisons cannot be instituted in these items to show their growth, relative to the preceding century or half a century.

had, no doubt, during this period as in the preceding, formed the most important investments of the Company, and occupied the foremost place among the Eastern imports all through these fifty years. *The imports of calicoes were more than quintupled in* 1720 *as compared to* 1698, *maintained that position up to* 1750, *but exhibited a most serious fall from* 1,193,093 *pieces in the last-mentioned year to only* 224,983 *pieces in* 1757 *on account of the wars in India.* However, they began to recover, though slowly, after the victory of Plassey. The chintzes were subject to great fluctuations. For instance, 139,000 pieces of the year 1698 rose to about 377,000 pieces in 1740, but shrank down to 11⅓ thousands only in 1757; while after three years they recovered to 145,000 pieces, that is, to a little above their strength in 1698. The most serious blow was, however, dealt to the painted and coloured fabrics. A glance at the table in the Appendix will show the violent fluctuations and great depressions to which some of these goods were subjected since 1720. This was mostly due to the imposition of new and heavy duties on them in England for home consumption and their excessive importation by the French Company for the continental markets.

Stained calicoes, Sooseys, Shalbaftas, Taffaties, Nillas, Ginghams, Pallampores, etc., were included in the list of **prohibited goods.**[1] They could not be used in England and were therefore meant for the supply of foreign markets. White calicoes, on the other hand, were in great demand both in the British Isles and other European countries. The quantities imported from India remain fairly constant for forty years from 1711 to 1750 and are temporarily reduced in the last decade due to wars in India, Europe, and America. The following table will furnish a summary view of the whole trade in calicoes and sooseys:—[2]

Years.	Calicoes.	Stained Calicoes.	Sooseys.
1711–20	9,656,943	415,280	68,804
1721–30	9,266,980	1,272,598	93,212
1731–40	9,802,254	2,011,876	165,777
1741–50	9,334,272	2,817,996	330,107
1751–60	7,722,536	1,681,942	37,083

[1] Appendix A to Chapter X, p. 326. [2] Appendices C, F, G, to Chapter VII.

The Romance of Tea. Next to calicoes, tea and coffee demand our foremost attention, as the history of their rapid development is full of the most surprising romance of this period. They had come to occupy the topmost places, the one having risen from 22,290 lbs. in 1698 to 2,911,231 lbs. in 1760, and the other from 170 cwts. to 10,416 cwts. in those two years. There was no other item, not even calicoes, which could equal tea in Official value as an article of Eastern import into England. This Official value of white calicoes being £184,257 against £291,123 for tea in the year 1760, the latter was therefore enthroned at the top of all imports in the Books of the Custom House.

The imports of tea, though characterised by wild fluctuations in individual years, show a marked tendency to rapid growth throughout this period. The annual average for the seven years from 1711 to 1717 was 196,596 lbs.; it rose to 595,356 lbs. in the next decade, thus showing a net increase of 354 per cent over the preceding seven years. Again, it was more than doubled in the third and stood at 2,924,158 lbs. in the last decade from 1748 to 1757, indicating the wonderful increase of 1,727,562 lbs. in annual imports as compared to the first period of seven years.

Tea Imported into England and Sold by the E.I. Company.

Years.	lbs.	% Increase over the preceding.
1711–17	1,376,171	—
1718–27	5,953,566	354%
1728–37	11,687,217	196%
1738–47	14,915,549	127·5%
1748–57	29,241,585	196·9%

It means that in the forty-seven years under review the total amount of imported tea which was actually sold in England either for home consumption or re-exportation abroad was about 63,000,000 lbs., or roughly speaking, 1,344,000 lbs. per annum. *Out of this quantity* 55,500,000 *lbs. of tea was consumed at home in fifty years and the rest,* 7,500,000 *lbs. or* 12 *per cent of the total quantity imported, was re-exported either to the colonies or other European and American countries.*

The rapid growth in the consumption of tea in England during the first half of the eighteenth century presents perhaps the most interesting romance of modern times in the history of the world's commerce. Although the quantities shown in the succeeding table are much below the actual on account of the prevalence of a great illicit trade up to 1745, yet the annual consumption of tea to be 12½-fold in the 'sixties as compared to the 'twenties signifies a remarkable development in this branch of the Oriental trade and a revolutionary change in the habits of the English people.

Quantities of Tea Consumed in England.

Years.	Annual Av. in thousand lbs.	Variation in Terms of 1711–20.
1711–20	182	100
1721–30	506½	223
1731–40	1047½	575
1741–50	1460⅓	801
1751–60	2285⅔	1255

This rapid increase in the consumption of tea was attended with an almost progressive fall in the prices of all kinds of tea. *It appears from the succeeding table that the average price of tea at the sales of the Company came down from* 16*s.* 2*d. per lb. during* 1708–12 *to* 4*s.* 10*d. in* 1745–47, *and in the war-years rose to only* 5*s.* 5*d., in spite of the new duty of* 5 *per cent imposed to defray the charges of the war.*[1]

Years.	Price at the Candle.	Price for Home Consumption.	Proportion of Duties to Net Cost.
	s. d.	*s. d.*	
1708–12	16 2	16 2	36%
1713–21	12 11	12 11	82%
1722–23	7 6	7 6	200%
1724–33	6 9	10 9	64%
1734–44	4 2	8 2	128%
1745–47	4 10	7 0½	69%
1748–59	5 5	7 9	75%

The **coffee**[2] **trade** was very much linked with that of tea. The quantities of coffee imported during 1711–20 were considerably higher than those of the preceding decade, but its

[1] Milburn, II, 534–38 ; Wisset, II.

[2] Appendix B, p. 307.

imports showed a record increase in the next decade when the annual average reached 11,507 cwts. It appears that after 1730 the use of coffee went on decreasing with the growing use of tea as a drink, and when the imports of the latter declined on account of war, coffee took its place to some extent. The actual quantities and their decennial variations in terms of the first decade are as under :—

Years.	Total Quantity in cwts.		Variation.
1711–20[1]	55,251	(Nine years)	100
1721–30	103,570	,,	187
1731–40	96,398	,,	158
1741–50	52,560	,,	85
1751–60	68,724	,,	112

The sudden increase in the imports after 1720 is probably due to obtaining a Phirmaund from the Prince of Mocha for exporting 600 bales of coffee free from Customs from that port in 1719. The English, like all other Europeans, had to pay 3 per cent duty against 9 per cent charged from the Suratters, but even this was remitted in the case of coffee. We are also told that the goods of the Surat merchants were "often so overvalued as to amount to double. The difference in so short a voyage is sufficient to divert a great part of the Suratters' trade into the English Channels."[2]

The **silk industry** of Bengal was very considerably improved during this period. There was keen competition among all the European Companies for securing raw silk and the silk fabrics of Bengal. The supplies of raw silk from China were neither so good nor so excessive as those from this part of India.[3] The exports from the latter were usually far more than those from China, and were sold at a higher price. The

[1] The prices of coffee during these years are given in the Letter Book, XVII, p. 53, in the Gen. Letter from Mocha :—

1711.	55–67	Spanish dollars the	Mocha Bahar.	
1712.	68–70	,,	,,	,, ,,
1716.	110–120	,,	,,	Beettle Tuckee Bahar.
1717.	83–98	,,	,,	Mocha Bahar.
,,	156–168	,,	,,	Beettle Tuckee Bahar.
1718.	101	,,	,,	Mocha Bahar.
,,	163	,,	,,	Tuckee Bahar.

[2] Letter Bk., XVII, pp. 22, 54.

[3] Appendix D, p. 310.

quantities imported from the two countries are given side by side for decennial periods :—

Years.	Bengal Raw Silk.	China Raw Silk.	Bengal Wt. Silks.
1711–20	553,467 lbs.	59,321 lbs.	249,375 Pieces.
1721–30	806,030	58,406	519,936
1731–40	1,395,117	73,763	698,010
1741–50	841,834	75,301	372,617
1751–60	437,727	902,855	391,105

While there were practically no or little imports of raw silk from China up to 1710, the decennial amounts of silk brought from Bengal for the next forty years were $9\frac{1}{3}$, $13\frac{4}{5}$, $18\frac{9}{10}$, and $11\frac{1}{5}$ times those from China. In other words, *from nine to nineteen times as much silk was imported from Bengal into England as from China up to* 1750. But the Anglo-French wars and the wars with the Nabobs of Bengal altogether upset this splendid trade. Imports from China rose from 75,000 to 903,000 lbs., but those from Bengal dwindled from 842,000 to 438,000 lbs. during the 'sixties. Thus Bengal witnessed a very serious depression in this profitable trade during the period of its struggles against foreign conquest.

An idea of the ordinary investments of the three principal European nations has been given in the Mémoire[1] of Jean Law de Lauriston, where it is said that in 1752 the English bought about 4000 to 5000 maunds, the Dutch 2000 to 3000, and the French 6000 to 7000 maunds of silk per year. Supplies of Persian silk were very intermittent. Since the commencement of war with Spain, silk was very considerably advanced in price ; it was therefore pointed out that the overland route through Russia should be utilised for the supplies of this raw material from Persia. As the English silk industry had made great strides during the first half of the eighteenth century, the E.I. Company gave special attention to the extensive and improved culture of silk in Bengal to feed the home manufactures, and it succeeded in making sericulture the foremost industry of the province.

So far as **wrought silks** are concerned,[2] fairly large amounts were imported both from Bengal and China. The quantities

[1] Mémoire, p. xlvii, Société de L'Histoire des Colonies Françaises.
[2] Appendix C, p. 309.

of China silks cannot be made out from the volumes of Imports and Exports in the Board of Customs Library, but those from Bengal have been compiled in the Appendix. Their decennial totals in the preceding table show great variations; but even with the depression resulting from the constant depredations of the Mahrattas since 1740 and the wars of the English with the Nabobs, the imported quantities which had risen from 249,375 pieces in 1711–20 to 698,010 during 1731–40 stood at 372,617 and 391,105 pieces respectively in the next two decades, thus showing an increase of 57 per cent in comparison with the first decade.

Growth in Saltpetre Trade. The other important branch of the European trade in Bengal was the supply of saltpetre. The English Company had been obliged by clauses inserted in their charter of 1693 and the following ones to furnish the British Ordnance yearly with 500 tons of good saltpetre at £45 and £53 a ton in times of peace and war respectively. Besides this quantity large amounts were required by the Company for the provision of their ships and factories. There was also a constant demand for petre in England for dyeing, manufacturing powder and glassware. Hence the Company, by reason of their monopoly, reaped large profits in this branch of their trade. In 1717 this monopoly was threatened by a Dublin merchant, who attempted to get permission from the Irish House of Commons to import saltpetre into Ireland. The Company promptly represented against the Irish Assembly to His Britannic Majesty and pleaded not to grant its petition, because all British subjects, except those belonging to the Company, were prohibited and excluded from the E.I. trade by the Company's charters.[1]

Three years later complaints were made against the officers of His Majesty's Ordnance for having sold saltpetre to private persons, to the considerable prejudice of the Company, and it was pleaded that none of the petre supplied to the Crown for military purposes should in future be disposed of for any other use than the real service of His Majesty.[2]

[1] I.O., Miscellaneous, 4, pp. 332–33.
[2] I.O., Miscellaneous, 5, p. 326, 17th March, 1720.

Secure in their monopoly of sale in the British Isles, the Company attempted to monopolise the supply of this important article in Bengal. The Dutch and the English had both established their factories near Patna[1] for the purchase, collection, and refinement of this article. The annual despatch of saltpetre fleets down the Ganges to Calcutta and Chinsura had become a permanent feature of the commercial life of Bengal. Both the nations had from time to time tried to obtain the farm of saltpetre from the Nabob, but the political triumph of the English at Plassey made them strong enough to demand and secure it immediately after that victory. When the English reconciled Ramnarain, the Governor of Patna, to the Nabob of Bengal, quelled the disturbances in Purneah and deterred the Nabob of Oudh from attempting anything against the peace and tranquillity of Bengal, Col. Clive applied to the Nabob Mir Jaffir to grant the Company an exclusive patent for the purchase of petre on the same terms as Coja Wazeed, the prime minister of Bengal, had enjoyed for some years past. The Nabob was highly reluctant to grant such a patent, as he rightly imagined that if given in the Company's name it would become perpetual. The Calcutta Government "had reason to believe that nothing but his fear of the English and the assistance he might have occasion to demand of us (in case of any exigency) induced him to comply with our petition for that grant."[2] The Nabob being really impotent to refuse such a demand, granted to the English the exclusive privilege of the sole purchase of all petre produced in the provinces of Bengal and Bahar in return for an annual payment of Rs.40,000, and a stipulation to supply this Government with 20,000 maunds of petre per annum at the purchase price.

This important privilege was secured to (1) provide petre to the Company in India and England at very low prices; (2) to prevent the French and Dutch from being supplied

[1] The English settlements were at Fattua, Chuprey, Singia, and Chowndey (Letter Bk., XVIII, p. 472).

[2] Bengal Gen. Letters, IV, pp. 17, 63.

with that article; (3) to make immense profits from the sale of the surplus in India; and lastly (4) to undermine the power of the Nabob, who from that time became solely dependent on the English for the supply of that most essential war material.[1]

The monopoly of the sale of saltpetre was not a new thing. It had only changed hands. Coja Wazeed had held it on the same terms for many years past, the Dutch had also endeavoured to obtain grants for the sole purchase of petre and opium, hence there was made no departure by the English in securing the sole right of disposing of the whole supply of petre. The only objectionable part of the affair was the transfer of the source of an immense income and power from the natives of the country to the foreigners.[2]

The imported quantities of saltpetre must naturally vary during the years of war and peace. In the ten years of 1741–50 the annual imports amounted to 25,117 cwts. against 11,946 cwts. in the first and 19,844 cwts. in the last decade.

A View of the Saltpetre Trade.[3]

Years.	Total Quantities.	Annual Average.
1711–20	107,517 cwts.	11,946 cwts.
1721–30	87,826	9,758
1731–40	152,909	15,291
1741–50	251,169	25,117
1751–60	198,438	19,844

The Growth of the Pepper Trade. In the western parts of India the Company's trade mainly consisted in procuring large quantities of pepper and drugs and small amounts of precious stones, calicoes, cotton-yarn, and spices. The Official values and quantities of the numerous drugs imported into England from 1697 are detailed in the manuscript volumes of Imports and Exports. From a survey of those returns it appears that drugs formed a very appreciable part of the Company's investments. Diamonds,[4] bezoar stones,

[1] Bengal Gen. Letters, IV, pp. 17, 63.

[2] Bengal Gen. Letters, IV, pp. 65–67.

In 1747, Aug., 50,000 maunds of petre were bought from Omichand Deepchand at Rs.3/8 per maund (Fac. Rec., Patna, II).

[3] Appendix B, p. 307. [4] Appendix E, p. 312.

and garnets also claim considerable amounts of money. For instance, £564,904 worth of diamonds alone were registered from 1711 to 1732 in the Books of Customs. After this year there are no returns for diamonds, but the import of garnet stones becomes prominent instead. Either there was a great amount of illicit trade in diamonds, or they used to be brought into England through the Dutch and the French.[1] Spices, being monopolised by the Dutch, were brought in negligible quantities through the direct channel, but pepper was the most important item of the Anglo-Indian trade.

Notwithstanding all the efforts of the Dutch to monopolise the supplies of pepper, the English had succeeded in securing the desired quantities from their Malabar and Fort Marlborough factories.[2] From 982,860 lbs. in 1708 the imported

[1] Speaking of Pondichery, the French capital in India, M. Postlethwayt says that "the staple trade of this place is piece-goods, of which the finest are in Golconda, and the best painted here; they have likewise great quantities of silk, raw and manufactured, gold and silver brocades, perfumes, spices, and *diamonds; in which last branch of trade they have made a great progress of late.* And certain it is, that India trade of France has laid an extraordinary foundation for the increase of their European trade in general" (Great Britain's Com. Interest, p. 199).

[2] Some light will be thrown upon the question by the representations of the Company in the years 1710 and 1711.

"The Dutch in order to monopolize the pepper Trade of the Malabar Coast, have joined with the King of Cochin to make war with the Samorine, who has been obliged to deliver up to them Chittoor and Parmany clear of all customs with the sole trade (exclusive of any other European nation) of those places which are the two best on all the Malabar Coast for Pepper, the particulars whereof are as follows:

The Company does observe that the Samorine King, the most powerful of all the princes who inhabit the Pepper Countrys, being thus reduced, it may be easy for the Dutch to seize on, and secure all the other Pepper that is produced in those parts, and in that case, may sell what price they place upon it in Europe, as they do on the other four sorts of spices, whose prime cost in the Indies is less than that of pepper, and not equally necessary. This will be a means greatly to encrease their Navigation to *several parts of Europe, particularly to the Mediterranean and Turkey, where pepper is always demanded to make up the Cargoes for those places.*

Besides this, should the pepper trade be wholly engrossed by the Dutch, it would very much enhance the Freight paid by the English E.I. Co., by reason that the pepper filling up the spaces between the bales, chests, or other parcels, is a consideration for which the owners of shipping doe take a less freight by at least £10 per Tonn than otherwise they could afford the same. Whitehall, April the 26th, 1711. Representation to Her Majesty."

(Company's Representation, 16th Feb., 1710, pp. 322–32, 316–20 of B. Mus. Addl. MSS., 37,146.)

amount went up to 4,563,295 lbs. in 1720, and stood at even 3,133,884 lbs. in 1760, the year of great depression for all imports. Thus the imports in individual years show extraordinary fluctuations, and even long periods in no way eliminate these extremes. The decennial totals faithfully reflect those ups and downs as under :—

Years.	Aggregate Quantity (in thousand lbs.)
1711–20	16,197
1721–30	10,460
1731–40	22,943
1741–50	29,644
1751–60	24,664
	Total 103,908

It gives us an average of more than 2,000,000 lbs.[1] *per annum for these fifty years!* While in the second decade the imports totalled 1,000,000 lbs. per annum, they rose to a little less than 3,000,000 lbs. in the fourth decade, and stood at about 2,500,000 lbs. even in the worst years of war and universal depression. There are no means to separate the returns for the quantities imported from Fort Marlborough and the Malabar coast, but from an account of sales it appears that the quantities were related to each other as 100 : 136 from the year 1736 to 1750. If the same ratio were applied to the whole period, it would be seen that about 60,000,000 lbs. of pepper were imported from the Malabar factories during this half a century.

The following reliable figures will reveal at a glance the course of the Pepper Trade during the century and a half of British relations with the Indies :—

Years.	Thousand lbs. Imported into England.
1621–30	14,286
1672–81	36,768
1698–1707	32,614
1721–30	10,460
1741–50	29,644

[1] The Dutch imports of pepper in 1732 were 1,419,427 lbs. against 1,304,488 lbs. by the English in that year. The French imported 595,377 lbs. against 1,599,001 lbs. by the English in 1742.

The enormous extent of the depression in pepper imports during 1721–30, due to the keen competition of the Ostenders, had carried this trade to its lowest watermark, and hence the Company were justified in taking steps against these interlopers.

The prices of black pepper in India and England at different periods, as presented below, will prove of great interest :—

Years.	Prices in England.	Prices in India.
1722–32	7½d. Jambee variety.	Rs.58 per candy of 520 lbs.
	Malabar variety.	Rs.77½ ,,
1742–50	13d. av. for both.	
1751–60	12¼d. ,,	Rs.80 ,,

Thus it appears that the prices of pepper were higher by 67–73 per cent in England and by 33–37 per cent in India during the years 1742–60, as compared to the decadal period of 1722–32 ; still, this article, along with other spices, had considerably come down during the course of a century.

The average prime cost of pepper produced in the Spice Islands was 2¾d. during 1616–18 and had risen to 4½d. during 1620–30, but the same stood at only 1⅓d. about a century later, in 1720. The selling prices for the three periods were, respectively, 24½d., 18d., and 7½d. per lb. In spite of heavier duties in the third period, pepper could be sold at less than 41 per cent of the price realised a century earlier ! The net profit after deducting all kinds of charge was, according to the Company's own showing, 20 per cent[1] on the cost.

[1] The following account is interesting in presenting the various charges, the purchase and sale prices and the net profit of the Company in the Jambee pepper :—

" Prime cost of pepper on the West Coast (of Sumatra) at Eleven Bahar of 500 wt. is 11s. 8d. the wt. or per ton of 1600 wts. is £8 16s.

100 tons of pepper at said price costs . .	£880	Pepper, 100 tons or 179,200 lbs., sells at 7½d., discount deducted, £5600."
Freight at £22 a ton	£2200	
12½% for Custom, loss in breakage of pepper, warehouse, etc., charges on £5600 in contra	£700	
Demorage of ships at 6d. per ton *per diem* .	£305	
Interest on the cargo sent	£560	
Total charge	£4645	
Gained	£955	

(Letter Bk., XVIII, p. 586, 1722, March.)

As to the *other Indian imports*, sugar and rice were almost insignificant; indigo was no longer able to hold its own against the Plantation produce; cotton-yarn and carmania wool were, indeed, often imported in appreciable quantities, but during the war they suffered more heavily than all the rest. Indian sugar had altogether been beaten out of the English market by the West India product. The Dutch, Portuguese, French, and English had all made rapid strides in raising very large quantities of sugar in their colonies, and hence there was practically no demand for the Indian variety in any part of Europe. The quantity imported from 1715 to 1740 only once went up to 22 cwts., though usually it hovered about less than half of this amount. In the next twenty years, the annual average rose to about 27 cwts. out of more than 1,000,000 cwts. which were annually imported into England from 1750 to 1759.

Nearly the same remarks apply to the imports of indigo. The Dutch colonies and the West Indies supplied this important article cheaper to the European markets, and hence India had almost lost this staple trade of great antiquity. The wild fluctuations in the imported quantities pass belief. While none at all was brought in several years, in others as much as 255,000 lbs. were imported into England from India. The complete set back in this trade is indicated by the fact that while 200,000 lbs. were annually imported about the year 1620, the total quantity carried into England in the twenty years from 1741 to 1760 was only 36,215 lbs.!

So far as the Company's restrictions on the importation of Eastern goods are concerned, they were made less severe. The servants of the Company and the mariners and sailors were allowed to bring in larger quantities than before. Of course, the exclusive privilege of importing and exporting certain goods was in no way relaxed.[1] Among imports

[1] From a notice issued in 1734, we can learn the nature of the goods reserved by the Company and the commodities in which others were allowed to deal:—

Goods reserved for the Company's trade:

"Muslins, calicoes, and all sorts of goods and merchandises made and

indigo and sugar deserve mention as having no place in the Company's trade; while cotton and cotton-yarn are included in the reserved list. The other restraints were either the complete prohibition of certain goods for home consumption, or the levy of very heavy import duties upon them. The laws respecting this subject and their effects upon the Oriental trade demand special attention, and consequently we will outline them in a separate chapter.

mixed with cotton, or silk, or Herba of what denomination soever, carmenia wool, coffee, cotton, cotton-yarn, cowries, pepper, raw silk, saltpetre, red-wood, tea, turmeric."

Commodities in which commanders may trade:

"Aggats, Ambergreece, Bezoar stones, Cambogium, Camphire, China Root, Cordivants of all sorts of leather, Cotch, Diamonds, Pearls and all Precious stones, Gallingal, Goa stones, Olibanum, Oppoponax, Rangoes, Roman Vitriol, Safflower, Sanguis Draconis, Scamony, Spikenard, Tutenague, Wormseeds."

These curious words have been explained in the "Vestiges of Old Madras," II, pp. 324–25.

CHAPTER VIII

BRITISH EXPORTS TO THE ORIENT

We will now proceed to examine the growth of the export trade of England with the East during the fifty years from 1708 to 1757 *on the basis of the Company's returns.* A mere glance at the succeeding table is sufficient to impress upon the mind of the reader the steady and remarkable progress made in the vent of British merchandise in India and other parts of Asia. In the fifth decade 2·62 times more goods were supplied to India and 2·80 times more to the whole of Asia as compared to the first period of ten years. Little progress was indeed made during the first two decennial periods, as an appreciable part of that trade was then appropriated by the Ostenders and other free merchants. We are aware that more and more severe laws were made against this body of clandestine traders, and that the Company[1] did eventually, in 1731, succeed in obtaining a decree from the Austrian Emperor against those smugglers. By these measures a large part of the trade which was before carried on by the Ostenders was naturally transferred to the Company. This fact is mirrored in the rapid swelling of their exports to India, from £988,500 in the second decade to £1,299,000 sterling in the third. The remarkable growth of the next decade is, to some extent, due to the Carnatic War, for which greater amounts of military stores were required; but a large measure of it is to be attributed to the growing demand created by the Company for European goods in the Indian peninsula, as well as in other parts of Asia. In spite of wars

[1] See Court Bk., 48, pp. 126–28.

with their commercial rivals of Spain and France, the Company had succeeded in doubling the export trade during the troublous years from 1736 to 1757. The succeeding table, giving the total decennial values of exports to Greater India and Asia, respectively, is remarkable in showing the almost insignificant part played by China and Japan in consuming English goods.

Merchandise Exported from England by the East India Company to India, China, St. Helena, etc. etc.

Period.	Exports to Greater India.[1]	Exports to the East Indies.
1708–17	£966,253	£1,018,538
1718–27	988,535	1,047,395
1728–37	1,299,143	1,368,325
1738–47	1,739,595	1,829,018
1748–57	2,531,245	2,858,239
	£7,524,771	£8,121,515

It will be seen that China and Japan consumed 5, 4½, 5, 5, 11½ *per cent goods, respectively, in the five decades, while the total quantity consumed by these countries within half a century did not exceed* £596,744, *giving an average of only* £11,935 *per year, or a percentage of* 7·3 *for the fifty years' period.*

Bullion Exports to the East

The exports of bullion show a similar upward tendency, the third decade alone being characterised by a small falling off in this item. It will be seen that the share of China in the E.I. Company's bullion exports is, with the exception of the last, greatest in the third decade.

Period.	Greater India.	East Indies.	Greater India.	East Indies.
	Total Quantities in £.		Percentage Growth.	
1708–17	3,360,022	3,895,054	100	100
1718–27	4,371,034	5,216,159	130	134
1728–37	3,871,291	5,015,102	115	121
1738–47	4,575,635	5,228,333	133	135
1748–57	5,644,245	7,670,578	168	197
Total	21,822,227	27,025,226		

[1] The whole East Indies except China and Japan.

A glance at the fourth and fifth columns will show a net rise of 68 per cent in the money exports to Greater India during the fifth period, as compared to the first, but the same was doubled so far as all the Asiatic factories were concerned. In short, on the basis of the preceding decennial values, it appears that from 1708 to 1757 there was exported in money

to the East . . .	27 million	£
to Greater India . .	22 ,,	£
and		
to China and Japan .	5 ,,	£

That is, $4\frac{1}{3}$ times as much silver and gold were sent to Greater India as to China–Japan during this half a century. The amount remitted to the Celestial Empire widely varied from 14 to 35 per cent during this period, the actual ratios for the five decades being respectively :—

16 : 19 : 29 : 14 : 35 per cent of the total bullion exports.

It is a most significant fact that on the whole only 19 *per cent of the money sent out of England was spent in providing home investments in China as well as Japan, and the remaining* 81 *per cent of the precious metals was absorbed by Greater India.*

The proportion of *bullion to merchandise* during this whole period of fifty years was more than 3 : 1, although the ratios show a great fluctuation in the various decades, as, for instance, the exported money was

3·5, 5, 5·7, 2·8, and 2·7

times the value of goods sent out in the corresponding five decades. The abnormal rise in the export of bullion during the second decade is due to the great falling-off in the consumption of merchandise imported into the East by the Company on account of the large and cheaper supplies by the Ostenders, as has been previously pointed out.

The main results of our review can now be summarised thus :—

Fifty Years' Increase in

	Greater India.	Asia.
Merchandise exports to . .	162%	180%
Bullion exports to . . .	68%	97%

Quantities of Goods Exported

So far we have been dealing with the Company's returns as they are given in the Parliamentary Paper, No. 152, and reproduced by Moreau and Macgregor. Almost the same conclusions are deducible from Milburn's figures[1] for exported merchandise during the whole period.

The Official Returns, however, totally upset the foregoing results. The actual values of exports in quinquennial and decadal periods expressed in pounds sterling, and the relative progress made in the different periods, are set forth in the following table :—

British Exports into Asia.

(Based on Official Returns.)

Periods.	Quinquennial Totals.	Decennial Values.	Per cent Progress.
1708–12	649,785		
1713–17	396,615	1,046,400	100
1718–22	499,084		
1723–27	482,231	981,315	94
1728–32	707,786		
1733–37	1,093,279	1,801,065	172
1738–42	1,529,009		
1743–47	2,654,000	4,183,009	399
1748–52	2,797,862		
1753–57	3,841,573	6,639,435	634
	14,651,224	14,651,224	

It will be seen that these figures, representing the aggregate export trade, though similar to the Company's two sets in showing a decline in the second decade, are vastly different in actual and relative values. *On their basis the total export trade of England with the East Indies had developed to more than sixfold in the fifth decade as compared to the first.* But the comparison becomes startling if only two years—the first and the last of the half-century—are taken into consideration. The value of exports in 1708 was only £60,915, but it rose to £845,466 in 1757, having gone up to £874,579 in 1755, and

[1] They are respectively £1,177,126, £1,119,911, £1,389,789, £1,795,659, and £2,767,309 for the five decades.

even to £893,540 in 1746. In other words, at the end of half a century from the union of the two companies, *the British exports in goods into the East had multiplied to fourteen times their level in* 1708. It is undoubtedly a splendid record of the Company's achievements and ought to have disarmed all opposition against that body, but perhaps vested interests and factions are always blind to facts.

For a clear comprehension of the export trade in merchandise sent to the East by the Company and all other exporters, we will reproduce below in tabular form the necessary data in percentages :—

Periods.	Percentage Growth of Co.'s Export Trade.	Total Export Trade.
1708–17	100	100
1718–27	103	94
1728–37	131	172
1738–47	180	399
1748–57	280	634

A comparison of the foregoing table with the one detailing the Company's exports will indicate that the returns of the Company and the Custom House were approximately similar for the first two decades. The divergence between them grow more and more marked as years passed on. The Custom House Returns during the next three decades exceeded the Company's by £6,568,000. Now these returns for the first two decades include also private exports which in the first decade of the eighteenth century appear to equal those of the Company. It will therefore mean that during 1698–1707 the market prices were double those at which the goods were rated by the Customs authorities.

Working on this assumption, we can find the approximate market prices of all exports by doubling the Customs Values. These will then amount to £29,000,000 sterling. Now deduct the Company's exports from this sum, the remainder—£21,000,000—must have been handled by private merchants. In other words, during this half a century the average annual *exports of merchandise* from the United Kingdom approximated to £580,000.[1]

The Course of the Company's Total Export Trade

Up till now we have been separately studying the progress of the export trade in bullion and merchandise, but in the succeeding table the two items have been taken together in order to give a general view of the whole export trade of England with the East through the Company alone.

Decennial Values of Exports.

Decenniums.	Parliamentary Returns.		Milburn's Figures.	
	Value in Pounds.	Percentage.	Value in Pounds.	Percentage.
1708–17	4,913,592	100	4,992,582	100
1718–27	6,263,554	127½	6,383,078	128
1728–37	6,383,427	130	6,524,986	130
1738–47	7,057,351	143	7,023,997	140
1748–57	10,528,817	214	10,437,889	209
	35,146,741		35,362,532	

The results are almost the same in the two sets of statistics given above. Rapid progress is evidenced during the second and the last decades, the other two showing very slow advances. *The main result of the fifty years' intercourse, on the basis of the* **Company's figures,** *is a little more than the doubling of the British exports into the Orient.* For instance, on the basis of Parliamentary figures it appears that the *yearly average* of £491,359 in the first decade was raised to £1,052,881 in the fifth decennium.

In the preceding sections we have dealt with the import and export trades of Great Britain in their relation to Asia in general and China in particular. The previous study must lead us to the inevitable conclusion that, despite a falling-off

[1] The exports of treasure as registered in the books of the Custom House are very valuable for showing the total depletion of money from England for the purchase of Oriental goods. By deducting the amounts exported by the Company, we could find the actual sums sent by private merchants. It should be remembered that the necessity for exporting treasure was being yearly reduced on account of the growing profits earned by the English in the Indo-Asiatic and port-to-port trade in India.

It is a pity that my papers containing the annual returns of treasure given in the Customs books have been lost, and I have no means in India to incorporate them in this edition of the book.

here and there, the upward tendency has been persistent in both branches of trade. It is now time to investigate their mutual relation and consequently the direct gain, so far as it can be measured in money, accruing to England from this Oriental trade.

The direct advantage can be calculated by the addition of two main items—the amounts of British exports of merchandise consumed in Asia, and the excess of imports over exports of both goods and money. Having studied the first, we will limit ourselves to finding out the excess in this section. The gain will naturally differ with the source of statistics. It will be preferable to calculate that excess on the basis of the Company's returns, the Official Statistics being more or less hypothetical. The gross profit, provided all the merchandise put up at sales belonged to the Company and none to private merchants, can be presented in the

Decennial Excess of Imports over Exports.

Period.	Parliamentary Returns.	Milburn's Figures.
1708–17	£4,872,319	£4,793,329
1718–27	8,405,539	8,286,015
1728–37	9,642,756	9,501,397
1738–47	11,005,619	11,038,973
1748–57	10,923,778	11,014,706
	£44,850,011	£44,634,420

These figures have been obtained by subtracting the decennial values of exported bullion and merchandise from the decennial total sums realised from the sale of imports.

A very important item ought to be deducted from this excess, before we can calculate the gross profits of the Company. Bills of exchange were every year drawn upon the Company in England by their servants and free English merchants resident in the East for the moneys that they were to remit to England. The payments for bills of exchange being an extra charge to the Company, even though the money only changed hands in England, should be added to the usual returns regarding the export of bullion and goods.

The Third Report of the Committee of Secrecy, 1773, gives figures for the bills of exchange for the years 1732 to 1771, but the earlier figures from 1708 to 1731 are not available. By interpolating an *approximate* sum for these years, we can arrive at an estimate of the amount of money paid by the Company in bills of exchange during the fifty years in question. This sum, as detailed below, amounted to £8,864,435.

Bills of Exchange.

	Total.	Average.	
1708–31	£4,160,000	£160,000	(Interpolated.)
1732–37	1,068,838	178,139	(Based on the Third Report.)
1738–47	1,990,763	199,076	,, ,, ,,
1748–57	1,644,834	164,483	,, ,, ,,
	£8,864,435		

In other words, the total money spent by the Company on the basis of Milburn's figures, which are identical with those of the Third Report, in procuring their imports was :—

Bullion and goods exported . . .	£35,362,532
Bills of exchange paid	8,864,435
Total spent by the Company . . .	£44,226,967

An investment of £44,000,000 from England, without taking into consideration the great sums earned by the Company by their carrying trade and commerce in Eastern countries, and the revenues of Calcutta, Madras and Bombay, gave a return of imports which realised £80,000,000 sterling. *Thus the gross gain accruing to the Company during the whole period of fifty years was about* £36,000,000 *sterling, or* £715,400 *per annum on the total sum of* £44,000,000 *sent out to the East in money, bills of exchange and merchandise during the same period.*

In other words, a gross profit of 82 per cent per annum was on the average earned during the whole period of fifty years. Out of this the Company had to pay customs, freight, and demurrage, charges of merchandise in India and England, loans and donations to the state, interest on the borrowed capital, dividends to the shareholders at various rates and, above all, meet the heavy expenses of a long war with its rivals. It is strange that the rate of this gross profit continued to grow on and on during the forty years from 1708 to 1747; in the last decade alone a vehement set-back is observable, due no doubt to the expenditure incurred in wars with the French.

An idea of the excessive enhancement of expenses in India can be had from the following table of the Charges Civil and Military incurred at the various settlements in the years named below:—[1]

	1729–34.	1750–55.
Fort William	£263,207	£338,409
Fort St. George	90,948	562,577
Bombay	432,421	520,579
Fort Marlborough	43,228	106,225
St. Helena	19,918	49,440
	£849,722	£1,577,230

Dividends Paid by the Company. In 1708 the proprietors of the Company were paid 5 per cent dividends, which were increased to 8 per cent the next year and 10 per cent since anno 1711. They were, however, reduced to 8 per cent in 1722, and continued at that rate for the next ten years. As the Company had then to pay £200,000 as a free gift and also gave up 1 per cent of the interest payable by the Government on their previous loans of £3,200,000 for the renewal and extension of their charter, dividends further fell to 7 per cent in 1732 and remained at that level till Midsummer, 1743, when they were increased by 1 per cent. This rate was kept up till 1755. During this period a new loan of £1,000,000 at 3 per cent interest was advanced to Government in consideration of the Company's charter being extended to 25th March, 1780, and the rate of interest was reduced to 3 per cent on the total loan of £4,200,000 since 1750. The expense of war, new loans to Government, and reduction of interest payable by the same on their previous loans—all these were bound to tell adversely upon the Company. The dividends were therefore reduced to 6 per cent in 1756. *So far as the total amount of dividends received by the proprietors during the forty-seven and a half years*

[1] Third Report of the Committee of Secrecy, 1773, pp. 80–83.

from Christmas, 1708, *to Midsummer,* 1756, *is concerned, it was* £12,457,476, *being, upon an average,* £262,262 *for each year, or about* £8·4 *per cent per annum on* £3,194,000, *being the capital upon which the Company then divided.*[1] Compared with the Dutch Company's gains this profit is insignificant, yet it is far higher than the current interest on loans which ranged between 3 and 5 per cent in those years.

The main results of the oversea trade of England with the East, so far as it was controlled by the E.I. Company, during the whole period of fifty years from 1708 to 1757 can now be summed up as below :—

	The whole Orient.	India proper.
English money into . .	27 million pounds.	20 million pounds.
English goods into . .	8 " "	6⅘ " "
Imports into England from .	80 " "	

The Relative Distribution of British Exports in India

Having seen how much money and merchandise were exported by the Company from England into India during these fifty years from 1708 to 1757, we proceed to study the relative distribution of these exports among the various parts of India. The annual returns for the whole period, as published in the Parliamentary Paper, No. 152 of 1813, have been presented in the form of decennial totals in Appendix A. At the outset it should be remarked that, as previously pointed out in the preceding part of this section, "India" really denotes "Greater India" and not India proper. As several minor factories in other parts of Asia or Africa were controlled by the Presidencies in India, their accounts were included in the totals for India in the said Parliamentary Paper. The exports to these parts should really be deducted from the previous totals, and then alone we can find the amounts of money and merchandise imported into India proper. The result of the various calculations is summarised below :—

	Greater India.	India proper.
Total Exports . .	£29,246,998	£26,687,458
Merchandise . .	7,524,771	6,818,749
Bullion . . .	21,722,227	19,868,709

[1] Third Report of the Committee of Secrecy, 1773, pp. 72–74.

The share of English factories established in Madeira, St. Helena, Madagascar, the Cape of Good Hope, Mocha, Gombroon, Borneo, Batavia, Bencoolen, and Prince of Wales's Island, as regards both bullion and goods exported to them, came up to £2,559,540 for these fifty years, which means that a little more than 7 per cent of the total exports from England were sent to those places, while India proper absorbed 76 per cent of the total.

Out of the total sum of more than £26,500,000 imported into India by the Company, the shares of the three Presidencies were very different. The centre of importance was altogether transferred from Surat and Bombay to Madras and Bengal. The first claimed 22½ per cent of the total exports against 43½ per cent in the case of Madras and 34 per cent in that of Bengal. The last-named Presidency showed a sudden increase of activity after securing the Great Charter from Furuckseer; for instance, the bullion exports to Bengal from 1708 to 1717 amounted to £772,520, they rose to £1,331,529 in the next ten years, and stood at £1,835,629 in the last decade of 1748–57.

Similar results are to be seen in the case of merchandise. The figures for Bengal rose from £159,619 in the first decade to £227,163 during 1718–27 and £826,825 in the last decade. That is, the demand for British goods in Bengal (on the basis of decennial averages) rose to more than five times during this half a century. However, on comparing the amounts of goods exported in the years 1708 and 1757, we find in the last year ten times as much merchandise was sent into Bengal as in the first. In Madras the rate of progress was not so marked, though it went on steadily growing from £1,616,614 in 1708–17 to £2,541,498 in the last ten years in the case of specie, and from £319,661 to £581,652, respectively, in merchandise. Bombay–Surat stood last of all. The bullion exports to these parts were £652,978 during the first decade and £1,075,161 during the last, but a very considerable advance is shown in the consumption of British goods. Steady progress is visible in all decades, though the last war decade tops all. The invoiced value of goods sent in 1708–17 was £336,657, but it leaps up to £900,000 during 1748–57. The shares of the three Presidencies expressed in percentages of the *total Company's imports* into India for the fifty years from 1708 to 1757 are :—

Total Exports to

India.	Bombay.	Madras.	Bengal.
100	26·6%	43·4%	34%

Bullion Exports to

India.	Bombay.	Madras.	Bengal.
100	18%	49%	33%

Merchandise Exported to

India.	Bombay.	Madras.	Bengal.
100	38%	27%	35%

The proportions of bullion to goods show great differences in the three Presidencies. Bombay with £2,594,726 in goods to its share consumed the largest amount relatively as well as absolutely. Bengal with £2,368,432 came next, while Madras showed the least demand for British goods. The bullion exports exhibit just the opposite results. The moneys invested in procuring home investments were the greatest in Madras, then followed Bengal, while the western parts of India occupied the lowest position. The percentage proportions of bullion to merchandise in the three Presidencies, as presented in the following table, will tend to show the great differences in the commercial importance of the various ports of India.

Proportion of Bullion to Merchandise in each Presidency.

	Bombay.	Madras.	Bengal.
Bullion . .	57%	84%	74%
Merchandise .	43%	16%	26%

These figures furnish monumental evidence of the relative decay of Surat and its dependent factories, and of the great activity of the industrial towns in Madras and Bengal. The continued excursions of the Marathas, the invasions of Nadir and Abdalla, the chaos and anarchy prevailing in the central and northern parts of India, due to the decline of the Mogul Empire, naturally transferred the commercial operations of the Company from those parts to the coast of Coromandel and Bengal, which were comparatively safe from the ruinous effects of anarchy. This period of universal distraction and disturbance tended to the development of the Company's own towns of Madras and Calcutta, which rapidly grew up to be two of the greatest centres of industry, commerce and shipping.[1]

The Nature of Exports

The articles of export from Great Britain, as already stated, were practically bullion, woollens, lead, copper, iron, tin, quicksilver, hardware, stores and provisions, of which the proportions naturally varied at various times. Supreme efforts had always been made by the British nation to find new and wider markets for the woollen manufactures of the country and to protect them from foreign aggression by means of high protective tariffs.

A glance at the table in Appendix B to this chapter will show that *no other item of the exported merchandise approached in value to the* **woollens**; nay, all the other articles of export put together, leaving bullion out of account, fell far short in value of the single item of woollens. The percentage proportions

[1] During this period regular commercial intercourse was kept up with St. Helena and Bencoolen, but the trade with other Asiatic and African parts was most irregular and insignificant. For instance, commercial relations lasted from 1748 to 1765 with Madeira, where £5175 worth of goods were exported altogether. Returns from the year 1732 for Madagascar and the Cape of Good Hope continued up to 1774, giving a total of £19,035 only of exported bullion and merchandise. Borneo and Batavia show mighty fluctuations from 1712 to 1745, during which period they claimed £226,956 of British bullion and merchandise. The trade with Prince of Wales's Island began as late as 1800, so that it falls outside our period. The Persian and Red Sea trades are not very significant. The English factories at Mocha and Gombroon did but little trade with the western countries of Asia. The cheaper silk supplies from China told upon the silk trade of Persia. Though characterised by great variations during the first forty years, the trade to these parts suddenly fell down after the Peace of Aix-la-Chapelle, remained at a low level up to 1757, and lingered on up to 1772, when it ceased altogether.

of the latter to the total exported merchandise in the under-mentioned periods varied from 52½ to 71, as shown below :—

Period.	The Percentage Proportion of Woollens to Total Merchandise.
1708–20	71
1721–30	66
1731–40	52½
1741–50	59
1751–60	54

As the woollen exports by the East India Company showed a great decline in the 'twenties, the merchants raised clamours against the Company's monopoly. An enquiry was consequently made by the Lords Commissioners of Trade in 1726. The Company were asked the reasons of the diminution in the exportation of the woollen manufactures, *pari passu* with an increase in the total exports from the kingdom, in the medium of ten years from September, 1714, to 1724 as compared with the medium of the twelve years preceding (Addl. MS., 14,035, p. 34).

It was stated by the Commissioners that the total exports of manufactures, products and stores from

September, 1714, to September, 1724= £994,106
September, 1702, to September, 1714=£1,126,774

Out of this, the exports of woollen manufactures were as below :—

April, 1702, to September, 1713=	£524,400
1714=	57,000
	£581,400
April, 1714, to September, 1719=	£42,000
April, 1719, to September, 1724=	80,000
	£122,000

In other words, the percentage ratio of woollens to other goods was as high as 58 in the first period, but it fell down to only 13·5 in the second. The woollen manufacturers were naturally up against the monopoly of the Eastern trade.

The East India Company pointed out that they had tried their best to promote the vend of British manufactures, even at a considerable loss incurred by reason of the great troubles and wars in Persia and the intestine divisions in the Mogul Empire. Then the Ostenders carrying out cheaper French woollen goods could undersell the English in India. "Add to this that the Indians knowing of the entire prohibition of the use of all painted calicoes in Britain appeared more shy of dealing with the English and more inclined to the Ostenders" (I.O. Miscellaneous, 6, 279–323).

The succeeding decades do not only show a recovery, but an appreciable advance, in the vent of woollens. At the end of our period we find the Company as zealous as ever in promoting the sale of these goods. The Directors, "still desirous of promoting the national advantage," proposed to send 333 bales of woollens to Bengal Presidency although the latter had not indented for any, and sent directions that factors should exert themselves to promote the sales to the utmost of their power (27 para., 29th November, 1754).

At the same time they authorised them, in case of extreme necessity, to sell the goods at a lower rate (not under the invoice price in any case) than at an advance of 15 per cent upon the invoice price as they were used to do (paras. 24 and 28, January 31st, 1755). We find by their letter of January 31st, 1755, that they actually sent out 206 bales to Bengal and proposed 500 bales for St. George, 1130 for Bombay, and 240 for Persia. These figures show us the relative importance of the different settlements for the demand of woollen cloths. It meant that the Company had succeeded in finding a sale for about 2000 bales per annum of woollens manufactured in England.

On further examination of the table in Appendix B it will be seen that so far as absolute values are concerned, lead, iron and foreign goods show a falling off in the fifth decade, while stores manifest a distinct decrease in the fourth decennium; otherwise all along this period of fifty years there is a marked tendency towards rapid growth. *The percentage increase in several items* during each decade in comparison to the yearly average of 1708–20 has been calculated as below :—

Percentage Increase in Exports.

(The values of 1708–20 = 100.)

	Woollens.	Lead.	Copper.	Iron.	Stores.	Foreign Goods.
1708–20	100	100	—	100	100	100
1721–30	94	110	—	133	115	173
1731–40	109	193	100	159	183	356
1741–50	160	205	140	174	160	445
1751–60	239	197	432	151	343	394

It is evident that the last two decades reveal marked advances in the sale of the above-mentioned goods. Woollens, copper, and stores rose to 239, 432, and 343 per cent, respectively, in the last decade as compared with the first period of thirteen years ; while lead, iron, and foreign goods reached their highest points of 205, 174, and 445 per cent in the fourth decade as compared to the base period. These facts afford a distinct evidence to the effect that *a remarkably rapid progress had been made in all the items of the British export trade during these forty years.*

Taking the whole *metal group* as one item, we find that it was worth 12 per cent of all the exports for the first twenty-three years of this period, rose to 23 per cent during the next two decades and went up to 29 per cent in the ten years from 1751 to 1760. As a whole, it occupied 22 per cent of the total exports of the period of fifty-three years and showed a very appreciable growth in its demand. The market for tin was the weakest of them all, for only £36,402 worth of it could be exported during the fifty-three years from 1708 to 1760. Iron occupied a somewhat better position—the total amount being worth £309,052. Lead with £532,602 in value came next, and copper by reaching £1,166,781 in total worth was 32 per cent more in value as compared to the other three metals put together. The total values of all the four metals and their percentage proportions to the aggregate exports are given below :—

Metals Exported.

Periods.	Value of Metals.	% Proportions.
1708–20	£161,182	12
1721–30	129,377	12
1731–40	354,600	23
1741–50	458,066	23
1751–60	941,512	29
	£2,044,737	22

Foreign goods excelled all the other items in the rapidity and volume of their growth. They became threefold in the ten years from 1731 to 1740 and fourfold during 1741 to 1750, though in the next decade they fell down to $3\frac{1}{2}$-fold on account of the wars in India and the unsettled conditions of the continent of Europe. Their actual values and proportional strength as compared to the total merchandise were as below :—

Foreign Goods Re-exported.

Periods.	Actual Value.	Percentage of the Total Goods.
1708–20	£33,389	$2\frac{1}{2}$
1721–30	48,248	$3\frac{3}{4}$
1731–40	99,273	$6\frac{1}{2}$
1741–50	124,065	6
1751–60	109,749	3

The last item of the exports to the East is that of **stores.** Their aggregate value for the period of fifty three years being £1,162,160, they bore a ratio of $12\frac{1}{2}$ per cent to the total exports. There was an abnormal fall in the decade 1741–50, due probably to the large exportations of the previous years. The normal percentage for the whole period appears to be 13, while the extreme ranges were 9 and 15 per cent of the total exports. It must have been seen that during the fourth and fifth decades there was a considerable increase in the value of total exported goods. Mill attributes the greater part of this increase to stores and other military apparatus for the supply of forts and for maintaining the struggle against the French and the Indian princes. That his assertion is not based on facts is sufficiently clear from the percentages given above.

The preceding statements furnish remarkable evidence of

the growth of Anglo-Asiatic trade before the acquisition of political power in Bengal. The Company had marvellously succeeded in creating a permanent demand for British goods in India and elsewhere. This arduous task had been accomplished, it should not be ignored, in face of the solid opposition of equally strong competitors like the Dutch and French, and before any machinery or processes had been invented for the cheap manufacture of goods. So it is but just to conclude that the next half-century will show splendid results even without the cropping up of new causes for the favourable growth of those commercial relations.

The history of the *growth of Anglo-Asiatic trade* is profusely illustrated by presenting the same data in a different form. The following table has been prepared to give averages of the successive periods of peace and war from 1697 to 1755 inclusive. The export averages are characterised by frequent and excessive fluctuations in the periods of war and peace, but the imports, with the only exception of the third period of peace, show a wonderful tendency to advance in all periods. The following figures will, it is to be hoped, prove significant :—

Average of the Periods of War and Peace.

Periods of War ending in	Imports.	Exports.
1697	£262,837	£67,094
1712	468,941	106,908
1721	958,104	93,402
1748	968,400	432,022
Periods of Peace ending in		
1701	£656,031	£214,212
1717	695,167	79,323
1738	650,879	151,642
1755	1,119,158	714,105

In the preceding sections we have been studying the state and progress of the Anglo-Asiatic commerce by itself, without any reference to either Great Britain's trade with other parts of the world or to India's relations with other countries. The vital question whether the progress visible in the Eastern relations was a phenomenon by itself, or was due to some general causes equally operating in the extension of commercial relations throughout the world, deserves special attention. The external trade of a country is admittedly a complex phenomenon, constituting at least a binary or rather a trinal system, but it has often been treated as a unitary process. We shall always lack the exact perspective and be incapable to draw right conclusions unless we extend our researches into those binary and trinal relations. The Asiatic trade studied in its first phase of being a part of the great and growing maritime commerce of the United Kingdom, is full of strange and interesting revelations.

The annual imports and exports of the United Kingdom from 1708 to 1757 have been given by Whitworth, Moreau, and Macgregor. Their decennial totals expressed in percentages, taking the values of the first decade as base, show a steady though slow progress in both the imports and exports of the United Kingdom. But when that upward tendency is presented side by side with that part of it which was related to the East, we find that the development in the latter far outstrips that of the whole, particularly in the item of exports. The entire course of trade to and from the East as well as to and from the whole world with the United Kingdom is mirrored in the percentages given below :—

Eastern Trade versus Total Trade of the United Kingdom.

Decades.	Eastern Imp.	Total Imports.	Exports to the East.	Total Exp.
1708–17	100	100	100	100
1718–27	170	124	94	108
1728–37	173	143	172	128
1738–47	165	139	339	140
1748–57	193	162	634	176

It is therefore evident that while the *import* trade of the United Kingdom with the whole world rose by 62 per cent during the fifty years under review, the same with the East alone increased by 93 per cent. It was, however, in the manufactured and other *goods exported* from the country that extraordinary advances had been made—the two trades showing an advance of 76 and 534 per cent respectively during the same period of half a century !

Again, instead of tracing relative growth by comparing each branch of trade to its own base, we shall also measure quantitatively the part occupied by the Eastern trade in the whole commerce of the Kingdom. The following were the percentage proportions of the Eastern trade during the five decades, taking the total import and export trades of the country each equal to 100 in each decennial period :—

Oriental Trade Expressed in Percentage of the Whole British Trade.

Decades.	Eastern Imports.		Exports to the East.	
1708–17	11%	Of the total imports into the Kingdom.	1·5%	Of the total exports of the Kingdom.
1718–27	15		1·3	
1728–37	13		2·3	
1738–47	13		4·3	
1748–57	13		5·5	

Thus, while during the first decade the Oriental imports formed 11 per cent of the total imports into the Kingdom, they rose to 15 per cent during the second decennium, fell to 13 per cent in the third and maintained the same proportion for the next twenty years. Hence the net result was that at the end of half a century the proportion of the Eastern imports was enhanced by 2 per cent in the total merchandise imported into the Kingdom.

But the development of British export trade to the East was marvellous, because during the first decade those exports formed only 1·5 per cent of the total exports, but at the end of fifty years they amounted to 5·5 per cent, having quadrupled in strength as compared to their former level.

Although the amount of exports to the East appears insignificant, being only 5·5 per cent of the total exports, it should not be ignored that the East was only one part of the world and that, too, a distant and new field of exploitation. Looking upon the actual values of goods exported to the various countries in the year 1757 when the Oriental trade was much depressed owing to wars with the French and the Nabob of Bengal, we find that the East ranked sixth in the world as regards the consumption of British exports and by far the first in the supply of imports to the United Kingdom.

A Comparative Chart of British Trade to Various Colonies and Countries in 1757.

	Imports.	Exports.
East India	£1,111,908	£845,466 (6)
Flanders	52,098	225,856
France	2,117	80,665
Germany . . .	809,408	915,894 (5)
Holland	421,784	1,304,021 (2)
Ireland	687,471	960,843 (4)
Italy	402,521	295,457
Portugal	281,544	1,587,989 (1)
Russia	436,533	57,206
Spain	332,520	1,164,973 (3)
Jamaica . . .	866,124	352,797
New England . . .	27,556	363,404
New York . . .	19,168	353,311
Pennsylvania . . .	14,190	268,426
Virginia and Maryland .	418,881	426,687

It will have been obvious now that the development of the Oriental trade is not solely to be attributed to the general causes which operated in the extension of British maritime trade during these fifty years, but that there were other potent causes particular to the Oriental relation which contributed to the greater growth of Anglo-Asiatic commerce. As it has already been shown that the share of China and Japan in British exports was insignificant and had risen only from 5 per cent in the first decade to $11\frac{1}{2}$ per cent in the last decade, this remarkable progress in the Eastern trade is consequently to be explained by causes inherent in the Indo-British relations. We are therefore eventually led to those exclusive privileges which the E.I. Company had from time to time obtained from Indian Emperors and Nabobs for trading and establishing factories as the most favoured nation.

So much for the first aspect of the binary system of our Oriental trade. The other phase delineating the amount and character of that trade as part of the entire external commerce of India and other Asiatic countries is inextricably complex. Statistics of the foreign trade of all Asiatic countries as conducted by the various European and Oriental nations are not available. Yet a comparison with the course of Oriental trade shared by the French and Dutch—the two principal competitors of the British in the East—cannot but throw strong light on the growth of Euro-Asiatic commerce in general and Indo-British trade in particular.

The Fortunes of the Dutch East India Company

The values of the Dutch trade with the East Indies during the fifty years from 1708 to 1757 present an interesting contrast to the English trade; 237 ships were in all sent out of the Indies laden with Eastern goods worth 64,500,000 florins from 1710 to 1719, while in the ten years of the 'sixties the invoiced cost of goods on the 233 returning ships had risen to 86,000,000 florins, showing an increase of 33 per cent on the first decade. Thus the development of the Dutch E.I. trade falls far below that of the English. From other accounts it appears that the business of the Dutch was very much stagnant, if not positively dwindling, after the 'forties. The sums realised at the sales in the two decades of 1720–29 and 1750–59 do not exhibit any increase. They remain stationary at 19,000,000 florins per annum. The following table presents a telling story of the comparative growth of the trades of the two Companies.

Decade.	Specie Exported.	Value of Imported Goods.	
1720–29	£5,963,000	17 million £	Dutch
	5,180,000	15 ,,	English.
1750–59	7,815,000 (invoices)	17 ,,	Dutch.
	6,360,000	20½ ,,	English.

Thus, while the Dutch affairs were stagnant, the English Company had realised £5,500,000 sterling more at their sales in the second decade as compared to the first. "It cannot by any means be denied," says Mr. Van Imhof in his Considerations of the year 1742, "that the present state of the E.I. Company wears a much more disadvantageous aspect, and is not, by far, in so flourishing a condition as in former times." Ten years after, Governor-General Mossel also laments the horrid decay visible to all in the affairs of his countrymen in the East.

The comparative position of the two nations is faithfully reflected in the tendencies of their stocks and the dividends earned by the Companies. The average decennial values of the stocks from 1731 to 1780 give us a conclusive proof of the progressive decline of the Dutch. In the five decades the highest prices of the English Company's stock varied as 172½, 186, 167, 207, and 174 against 638, 410, 402, 447, and 344 of the Dutch; thus the latter showed about 46 per cent fall in average stock prices during the last decennium as compared to the first.

The history of dividends tells the same story. Abbé Raynal gives in a chart in Livre II of his Atlas the "Etat des fonds faits en 1602 par la Compagnie Hollandoise des Indes Orientales." On the basis of his figures for the annual dividends of that Company from 1708 to 1777, the last year to which the returns are given in that chart, the yearly averages of the dividends in the seven decennial periods have been calculated below and put side by side with those earned by the English E.I. Company. Very high dividends had always been declared by the Dutch Company, while the profits of the English had ever remained at a low level. The following figures, by showing a continuous and sharp fall in the incomes of the Dutch, augur a continual decay of their commercial prosperity:—

Decade.	Yearly Average of the Dutch Dividends.[1]	Yearly Average of the English Dividends.
1708–17	30	9
1718–27	27½	9
1728–37	22½	7½
1738–47	15	7½
1748–57	22	8
1758–67	16	7
1768–77	14	10½

[1] The following figures relating to the Dutch Company's dividends will be of special interest:—

Periods from	
1605–48	28% annual average. ("Le Commerce de la Hollande," B. Museum, pp. 110–75.)
1649–84	$17\frac{23}{32}$% annual average.
1685–1720	$27\frac{23}{24}$ "
1721–1756	$20\frac{4}{9}$ "
1757–80	$15\frac{35}{36}$ "

("La Richesse de la Hollande," p. 185, B. Museum.)

The Poverty of the Portuguese. No notice need be taken of the Portuguese trade with India, as it had declined to the lowest possible ebb by the year 1750. Nothing can better picture their commercial depression than the words of the Portuguese Viceroy of India, who thus summarised the then state of Goa in his letter, dated 14th December, 1758 :—

" The extreme poverty of this people is such that it seems irremediable ; all, both great and small, each in their own degree, groan under the weight of misery, in such discouragement that they dare not even dream of the means of relief.

The grave situation of this state, which renders its preservation wellnigh impossible, calls for a speedy remedy, and any delay will result in its total ruin."[1]

The Fall of the French in India

Lastly, we come to see the rise and fall of the commerce of the French in India. With their extinction as a colonial power in India, their trade, too, reached the lowest ebb. Their Company was abolished in 1769, but their Eastern trade lingered on in a languishing condition. Abbé Raynal gives reliable and very comprehensive figures of the Indo-French trade in his Chart IV, No. 2, from 1725–26 to 1770–71. The same figures are to be found quoted in the " Dictionnaire du commerce de l'Encyclopédie Methodique," article 'France." On the basis of these figures we have prepared tables of the exports and imports handled by the French Company and the number of ships employed by it (Appendix C). It will be seen that in forty-six years the Company sent out 762 ships, out of which 585 returned to France, others were almost all lost or captured in the Indies. The heavy losses during the years of war from 1738 to 1767 are self-evident from the table. It will also be seen that while in several years the Company had been making a gross profit of more than 13,000,000 livres,[2]

[1] I.O. Portuguese Records, Conselho Ultramarinho, I, Part I.

[2] " And certain it is, that the India Trade of France has laid an extraordinary foundation for the encrease of their European trade in general." " Great Britain's Commercial Interest," by M. Postlethwayt, II, p. 199.

it could earn only 353,201 and 265,327 livres in 1759 and 1762. The declining state of the Franco-Oriental trade is mirrored in the following table of the returns of money invested by the Compagnie des Indes Orientales de France in India from 1725 to 1771 :—

Years.	Annual Average of Invested Moneys.
1725–36	7,189,579 livres.
1737–46	9,485,192
1747–56	8,150,518
1757–66	3,966,008
1767–71	1,043,506

In other words, the annual average of their investments fell from 7,189,500 livres during 1725–36 to only 1,043,500 livres during 1767–71 ; that is, the operations of the Company shrank to one-seventh of their former level. The French Revolution on one side and the political preponderance of the English in India on the other, must have still more jeopardised the commercial relations of India with France in the succeeding years.

By this time it must have been abundantly clear that the other European rivals of the English were practically wormed out of the Indian foreign trade only a few years after the close of our period. The English emerged triumphant not only commercially but politically in all their struggles against Europeans as well as Indians. In fact, they were left complete masters of the foreign trade of the country whose coasting trade was already, to a large extent, controlled by them, and they had also begun to extend their withering grip on the internal trade of Bengal after 1750 in particular. In the following years their preponderance in the commercial and political spheres was so much perpetuated that, within the next fifty years, India was destined to become the brightest jewel in the Crown of England.

CHAPTER IX

THE HISTORY OF THE E.I. SHIPPING

COMPARED with the vast shipping of India, the merchant and naval marines of England at the close of the sixteenth century sink into mere insignificance. It is nothing less than a revelation to learn that the total strength of all the English *ships of war* at the defeat of the formidable Spanish fleet was 11,850 tons only, and that the so-called Invincible Armada amounting to more than 100,000 tons was completely defeated by the comparatively small English fleet of 30,000 tons. Much attention was afterwards devoted to the development of the navy, so that the carrying capacity of naval ships rose to 17,110 tons at the death of Elizabeth. Since then, such great augmentation and improvement was made, that at the Restoration the aggregate tonnage went up to 57,463 tons. It was further increased to 103,558 tons at the death of Charles II. Fast developments took place in the following years. The public navy was brought to 159,017 tons by King William, 167,071 tons by Anne, and stood at 170,862 tons at the death of George I. The war with Spain and then with France necessitated vast additions, so that the royal navy amounted to 321,104 tons at the accession of King George III.[1]

The strength of the merchant marine was also very low in the time of Elizabeth, but its development was no less rapid than that of the navy in the succeeding years. *The E.I. Company took the lead in vastly improving the mercantile marine and considerably strengthening the naval forces of the realm.* The first voyage to the East under Sir James Lancaster was undertaken with five ships of 1530 tons in all, the largest

[1] Marine Records Misc., I.

ship being no more than 600 tons, though according to Sir Dudley Digges (A.D. 1615) its burthen exceeded 1000 tons. The Company, realising the necessity of constructing large ships fitted both for war and commerce, launched the *Trade's Increase* of 1100 tons in 1610. This was the largest ship up till that time constructed in England. By 1610 the Company had employed eighteen ships and three pinnaces of the burden of 7542 tons in all, of which four were ultimately lost, the *Trade's Increase* being one of them. The next decade presents a glorious record of the increase in the number and size of vessels bound for the East Indies. It was during these years that ships of a size hitherto unknown in England were built to bring home the rich cargoes from the East. The Fifth Joint Stock Voyage of the year 1616 under the chief command of Captain M. Pring was undertaken with five ships, of which the *Royal James* was 1290 tons, the *Royal Anne* 1057 tons, and the *New Year's Gift* 867 tons.

The *Charles* and the *Palsgrave* exceeded 1000 tons each, while the *Royal Exchange*, *Unicorn*, *London*, and the *Sun* varied from 800 to 700 tons each. By the end of the year 1620–21 the Company had employed seventy-five ships and pinnaces with a total net capacity of 35,000 tons, in round numbers, which shows that the average size of the vessels then belonging to the East India Company, excluding their pinnaces, was 520 tons each against 400 tons during the first decade. Never after, up to 1667, did the Company employ so numerous and such big ships in their commerce with the East!

Speaking of the past twenty years, in their account of trade presented to Parliament on 29th November, 1621, the Company pointed out that out of the eighty-six ships which they had despatched, eleven were surprised and captured by the Dutch, nine were lost, five were worn out by long service, going from port to port in the East, and only thirty-six had returned home with cargoes, the remaining twenty-five being then in India, or on their way home. The East India trade was computed to employ near 10,000 tons of shipping, 2500 mariners, and 500 ship-carpenters.

The Company still more strengthened their merchant marine by building many large and strong ships during the next decade. The *Jonas*, *Whale*, *Blessing*, *William*, *Royal Mary*, *Discovery*, and the *Reformation* varied from 800 to 500 tons each. At least one thousand persons were supported by the building and repair of their ships, the making of their artillery, naval stores, provisions, etc. Their dock at Blackwall had grown to be an extensive and important shipbuilding centre in London. During these ten years the Company employed fifty-eight ships and pinnaces with an aggregate burden of 25,600 tons, which yield an average of 510 tons each ship after excluding the pinnaces. Thus there was a slight increase in average capacity, but a considerable fall in the number of vessels despatched to the East. Out of fifty-eight vessels, forty-eight safely returned to England, and only eight were captured, lost and wrecked. The losses from the reprisals of the Dutch and Portuguese had told heavily on the Company. The Second Joint Stock was represented to have suffered a loss of £2,000,000 sterling within six years, but only one-third of this large sum could be screwed out of the Dutch as compensation for all the injuries sustained. Many of the Company's ships were employed in the carrying trade of India and other Asiatic countries. An idea of its extent is furnished by an account of June, 1629, written in defence of the continuance and prosecution of the Company's trade, wherein it is asserted that since the establishment of the Second Joint Stock concern the Company had sent out fifty-seven ships containing 26,690 tons, besides eighteen pinnaces to be worn out by trading from port to port in the Indies. The sharp decline in the Company's trade during the fourth decade is faithfully reflected in the great fall in the number and tonnage of ships. There were sent out forty-two ships and pinnaces in all of the aggregate burthen of 24,000 tons, or about 540 tons each ship. If the thirteen ships despatched by the Courteen Association which had secured a Royal Charter for an independent trade in the East, are added to the East India Company's shipping, the total tonnage will not fall much below that of the third decennium. In the face of these figures, the Company's statement that they employed 15,000 tons of shipping of the best kind, from 300 to 600 tons each ship in 1640, is a manifest exaggeration. In the subsequent years the East India shipping fell off so much, by the general discouragement in the Eastern trade and the undermining of the Dutch, that the Company had scarcely one good ship remaining in 1657. During the seventeen years from 1641 to 1657 inclusive, the Company despatched seventy-two ships of all sizes with an aggregate tonnage of about 30,000 tons, so that the net capacity of the vessels had been reduced to 410 tons each.

The net result of fifty-seven years' trade of the Company, as regards their shipping, was that 178 ships arrived home laden with Eastern cargoes, being on the average three ships per annum, and *about* 273 vessels of the Company alone sailed out to the East, thus giving an average of five ships per year. It is a pity that the Records do not afford exact and satisfactory data regarding the tonnage of each ship. We can therefore make but a rough estimate of the total tonnage. On the basis of the figures quoted below regarding the number of vessels and their tonnage, it would appear that the average capacity of an East India ship, including pinnaces, can be taken as 440 tons, but excluding pinnaces, as 475 tons each ship, and that *during the first fifty-seven years about* 122,000 *tons were employed by the Company in their Eastern trade.*

A View of Shipping Employed in Eastern Trade.

Years.	*Company's* ships.	Tonnage in round numbers.	*Private* ships which could be traced.
1601–10	21	8,000	2
1611–20	76	35,000	1
1621–30	58	25,000	1
1631–40	46	24,000	13
1641–50	55	24,000	12
1651–57	17	6,000	37
	273	122,000	66

If the average tonnage of the Company's ships be allowed to each of the private vessels, it appears that the aggregate tonnage employed during the first fifty-seven years in the Oriental trade amounts to about 151,000 tons, or only 2650 tons per annum. What a romantic contrast this insignificant beginning presents to the colossal shipping employed in the same trade to-day!

The Freighting of Ships. In 1626 the question was debated by the Directors whether it would not be better to freight than to build ships. The matter hung on for several years. It was found that no persons were willing to let ships on freight to India, although from £30 to £45 per ton had been offered. The fear of the Dutch was worn out by degrees, and the practice of freighting was originated. During the discussion on the freighting of ships it was alleged that chartering a ship would cost £25 per ton against £31 cost to the Company in their own ships.[1] In 1642 the rate of freight was £21 per ton to Bantam, and was followed by a further reduction of one pound sterling in 1645 at the conclusion of peace between the Dutch and the Portuguese. It was still more lowered to £17 for gruff,[2] and £18 for fine goods during the years 1646–53, suddenly leapt to £25 and £28, respectively, during the Anglo-Dutch War, and came down again after its termination.

The freights for Surat and the Coromandel Coast were always higher than those for Bantam, varying from £20 to £28 per ton.

How the system of freighting ships was reluctantly adopted will be evident from the following note of the Directors :—

> We see that freighted ships are neither welcome unto you nor here much acceptable unto us, but we would not well avoyd the making triall of some without aspertions which would have bin cast upon us which being now done we shall hereafter make use of our owne which are cheaper unto us than freighted ships.[3]

[1] Court Bk., 17, Aug. 16, 1639, p. 25; 18, Oct. 6, 1641, p. 33.
[2] Coarse or heavy.
[3] Fact. Rec. Misc., 12, p. 135. Letter to Surat, 29 March, 1644.

During the 'sixties, the practice of hiring ships became general, and then a momentous decision was arrived at for freighting in future only English-built vessels,[1] and shipowners were encouraged by the Company to build special ships for Indian voyages, so that the practice of chartering more and better built bottoms became general in the succeeding years.

Remarkable Progress of the Next Fifty Years

After the restoration of their rights in 1657 the Company wrote to their factors in India that their trade, which had "layne drooping for some years," would "again be revived and vigourously followed." They did show a superabundant energy. From 1658 to 1680, inclusive, they sent out 278 ships in all, that is, about 12 ships per year. During the next thirty years, from 1681 to 1710 inclusive, 408 ships were despatched by the Company alone, so that the annual average rose to nearly fourteen ships. The tonnage of each ship, from 1658 to 1707, *so far as it was chartered by the Company*, has been stated in the Appendix. The average burden of each ship, *as far as it was freighted by the Company*, remained as low as 440 tons up to 1667, was lower in the next decade, being over 400 tons per ship despatched to the ports of Surat and Madras, and 375 tons per ship bound for Bantam. The capacity of each ship was higher during 1678–87, as the average for all ships rose to 421 tons per vessel. It slightly increased to 431 tons in the fourth decade, but was considerably lowered to 344 tons in the years 1698 to 1707 on account of the decline in the Company's trade. *This chartered tonnage, being far less than the real tonnage of East India ships, does not, in fact, reflect the true tonnage of the Eastern trade.* The tonnage occupied by the permitted merchants, the

[1] This decision was due to the passing of the memorable Navigation Act of 1651. It will suffice to say that ever since the reign of Richard II, England had endeavoured by numerous acts of navigation and trade to restrict foreign trade and shipping for the encouragement of home shipping and manufacture. It is therefore strange to see that at the close of the sixteenth century much of the carrying trade of England was in the hands of the Dutch, who had then by far the strongest mercantile marine in Europe.

Company's servants and the crews of ships was sufficiently large, as is evident from the Regulations of the Permission Trade.

So far as freights were concerned, the Company hired ships at £18 per ton for coarse goods, and £22 for fine to Surat and back in the years 1658–63. The Dutch War enhanced the freight to £21 and £25 per ton in 1665. However, it went down to £19 and £22 for gruff and fine goods, respectively, in 1667, and even to its old level of £17 and £20 in 1682 for the Coast and Bay, and £10 12s. and £12 14s. for Bantam, when 12,000 tons of shipping were ordered for India. In 1676 the Company had from thirty to thirty-five sail of large ships in their service, while in 1689 there were employed in the trade to India twenty-five Company's ships and ten Permission ships.

As war with France broke out in that year the freight went up to £27 and £30 per ton, and even to £40 in 1695–96. The cessation of hostilities sent it down to £17–£20 for a time, but the renewal of war kept the freights to various ports in the East at the very high level of £34 to £37 per ton. It is on record that from 1681 to 1698 thirty ships were lost by accidents and captures.

This could not but send up freight charges and give a staggering blow to the financial position of the Company, already burdened with the heavy expenses and reparations of a war with the Mogul. *These shipping losses explain why no dividends could be paid for several years, and why the value of the stock of the old Company fell to* 37 *per cent.*

The Carrying Trade from 1708 to 1757

During the co-existence of the two East India Companies at one time we find them employing sixty ships in India and on the homeward-bound voyage. This indicates a great augmentation in the volume of trade between the two countries, but after the coalition their shipping was naturally reduced. It stood at about 3000 tons annually in 1712, and the freights at £26 and £27. In the year 1710 the freight charges for the various ports were as follows :—[1]

	Coast and Bay.	China.	Surat.	Mocha.	Pepper Voyages.
Gruff goods .	£30 10s.	£31	£34	£33	£32
Fine goods . .	£33 10s.	£34	£37	£33	£32

After the Peace of Utrecht, freight charges came down to £21 and £26 for the Coast, and £23 and £24 for Surat. By 1724 the Company was employing annually thirteen or fourteen ships carrying between 5000 and 6000 tons, and the whole number of ships in their service was probably not less than fifty. In 1754, previous to any rumour of the war which broke out two years later, the Coast and Bay freight was at £24, and the Bombay freight at £27–£30 per ton, but the war sent up the freights by £13 per ton. The decennial averages of freights to India, from 1711 to 1760, are given below :—[2]

Years.	Bombay and Surat. Gruff and Fine.		Coast and Bay. Gruff and Fine.	
1711–20	28	29	26½	32
1721–30	24	25	22	27
1731–40	24	25	22	27
1741–50	31	32½	29	34
1751–60	32	34½	29	33

Thus in the 'fifties and 'sixties of the eighteenth century the freight charges were higher in peace as well as in war than they were in the corresponding years of the seventeenth century.

The growth of Indo-British commerce in these fifty years is likewise vividly pictured in the shipping statistics. The decade 1708–17 claims no more than 106 ships sent from England to the Indies, against 172 vessels in the preceding ten years' period, but the termination of the European War, brought about by the Treaty of Utrecht, and the Grand Charter conferred by Emperor Furuckseer in 1717 gave an extraordinary impetus to the vending of European commodities in India and of Indian merchandise in Europe. The number of ships that sailed laden with British goods to the

[1] Home Miscellaneous, 44, pp. 56–57.
[2] See Appendix.

East increased suddenly from 106 to 150 in the next decade of 1718–27, and to 152 in the third decennium. The Carnatic War brought in many more ships for the safety of the Eastern possessions, so that 189 ships arrived in the Indies during the years 1738 to 1747. This year the Peace of Aix-la-Chapelle brought the war to a nominal end.

The abatement of hostilities, though temporary, must naturally have reduced the large number of ships that were before required for carrying stores, ammunition and men to the Orient. Thus we find that 180 ships sailed from England for the Indies during the decade culminating in the battle of Plassey. The same year witnessed the recrudescence of war between the French and English which lasted for seven years and ultimately ended in the triumph of the English over the French in India and elsewhere. The Seven Years' War and the new situation in Bengal necessitated the presence of many more ships for war as well as for commerce. Consequently the number rose to 222 ships during the post-Plassey decade. On a broad survey of the facts, the result of the comparison of the two periods of fifty years each from 1658 to 1707 and 1708 to 1757, though not startling, shows considerable progress. In the second half-century as compared to the first, the number of ships sent out to the Indies was 777 and 648, respectively, and the total tonnage rose from about 200,000 to 345,500 tons, so that *the increase in the numerical strength was 20 per cent against 70 per cent in the total tonnage chartered on these ships by the Company.* It was really a splendid record of the growth and strength of the Company's shipping and trade.

Ships sent from England to the East Indies from 1658 *to* 1757 *in Decennial Periods and their Chartered Tonnage.*

Years.	Ships.	Tonnage.	Years.	Ships.	Tonnage.
1658–67	99	31,140	1708–17	106	41,235
1668–77	140	55,700	1718–27	150	62,040
1678–87	164	69,403	1728–37	152	70,241
1688–97	73	31,518	1738–47	189	84,816
1698–1707	172	59,151	1748–57	180	87,200
	648	246,912		777	345,532

The Value of Tonnage Statistics. In the preceding pages the words " shipping ton " and " weight ton " have all along been so used as if they were universally known and were invariable quantities in the days that we have been speaking of. Undoubtedly there was a rough-and-ready method of calculating the capacity of each vessel, and when once the ship was launched its burden ought to have remained constant to the time of alteration made in its build. In such a case the burthen of ships constructed and employed by the Company ought not to vary as it does in the various records. An explanation or two is, however, possible. The method of admeasuring ships was only rough, as will be seen presently, and secondly, the ton space so adjudged was, and is, naturally capable of holding different quantities of light and heavy, loose and packed goods. The old shipping ton was equivalent to a ton of wine in two butts of 252 gals. which in 1626 were estimated to occupy 60 cu. ft. of space, but surely more weight of lead and far less of loose cotton-wool could be contained in that ton-space.

As three different ways of measuring ships were prevalent in 1626, *confusion in stating the burden of the same ship was consequently natural.* These were replaced next year by the royal order which laid down the mode of admeasurement as multiplying the length of keel, leaving out the false post, by the greatest breadth within the plank, then by the depth from that breadth to the upper edge of the keel, and ultimately dividing the result by one hundred. This method reduced the burden of ships of 848 and 898 tons calculated by the old rule to 793 and 810 tons computed according to the new rule.

In other words, as the tonnage of ships preceding and succeeding 1627 *is calculated on two different methods, a reduction of at least* 7 *per cent ought to be made in the tonnage of ships built before* 1627, *prior to instituting comparisons in the tonnage of two periods.*

This new method was replaced by another probably adopted in the reign of William III, so that a new difficulty crops up in bringing the tonnage of the seventeenth century to the new basis of the eighteenth. The method followed at the Port of London and recommended for adoption in the measuring of all ships and vessels in a Circular Letter issued by the Board of Customs in 1719 is reproduced below from a manuscript record in the Custom House Library :—[1]

Take the ship's length from the inside of the Mainpost to the outward post of the stern, and the breadth from outside to outside, then take off three-fifths of the breadth from the Rake before and that gives the main length of the Keele, then multiply that breadth by the length and half breadth for the depth and the product of that divide by ninety-four and that gives the tonnage, as for example :

Admit the ship to be 72 foot in length and 20 ft. in breadth, then take off three-fifths of the breadth for the Rake before— that reduces the 72 foot to 60 foot then multiply the breadth by the length and the half breadth for the depth, and divide that by 94 and that makes her to be 127 tons and 62 parts of 94.

CUSTOM HOUSE, LONDON,
Jan. 14, 1719.[2]

Even adopting this altered basis for past and future comparisons, we are in no way at the end of our difficulty. The Superintendent of Customs in his report to the Right Hon. Wm. Pitt, attached to the annual volume of Imports and Exports of the year 1790–91, makes the following important remark :—

In order to ascertain the proportion which the declared and Registered Tonnage under the Act of the 7th and 8th of William the 3rd bore to the admeasured tonnage under the late Act of the 26th of His Majesty, I have in many instances compared the

[1] Circular Letters Issued by the Board of Customs : London and Yarmouth, 1662–1722.

[2] Compare the method given by Wm. Edgar for gauging ships : "If it be a single-Decked ship measure the keel within board (so much as she treads upon the ground) likewise the breadth on the board by the midship beam, from plank to plank, and the depth of the Hold from the Plank below the Kelsey to the underpart of the Deck plank ; and for a two deck'd ship (which carries goods between Decks) take the depth of her hold from the plank below the Kelsey to the underpart of the Upper Deck Plank, then multiply the Length by the Breadth ; and the product thereof by the Depth, and divide the whole by 94 for a Mercht. ship, and 100 for a Queen's ship, the Quotient is her tonnage." "Customs Vectigalium Systema," London, 1714 ; see also Everard's "Stereometry."

one with that of the other, and generally found the average to be nearly as two is to three, that is to say, vessels which were declared by the Master or Registered under the Act of King Wm. of One hundred Tons. But they were found to measure about one hundred and fifty Tons. Adopting this proportion, and it is a proportion which has not been taken up without much enquiry and mature consideration, the Tonnage of the Merchants Shipping employed in the Foreign Trade of Great Britain,

say from 1696 to 1760, *is increased by one-half. The differences introduced at various times in the standards of measuring ships, unless duly eliminated, are sure to vitiate our results.* It ought to be definitely borne in mind that tonnage of ships should never be taken at its face value. Various allowances ought first to be made, if a true comparative view of the merchant tonnage employed at various periods in the Anglo-Indian trade is to be secured.[1] These various complications and intricacies, which are by themselves sufficient to embarrass the ordinary reader, still more multiply when other factors are taken into consideration.

The Tonnage of Ships. Even when the practice of freighting ships had not been commenced by the East India Company, the tonnage of their ships, however varying in different records and different years, was absolutely net and not gross. In other words, *a ship of 400 tons burden was capable of bringing home at least 400 space-tons of various Eastern commodities over and above the provisions, stores, etc., necessary for the ship's crew. The cubic space occupied by a ton of wine was the original standard of measuring tonnage capacity.*

The first arithmetical rule for calculating a ship's tonnage was, according to Oppenheim, devised in 1582, and that rule made the net or cask tonnage nearly the same as the average cargo. "The unit of measurement was therefore the tun of wine in two butts of 252 gallons which in 1626 were estimated to occupy 60 cubic feet of space. The ancient wine gallon occupies 231 cubic inches and a tun measures strictly there-

[1] The original returns of tonnage have been allowed to remain intact, and no alteration has been made in the comparisons instituted above in our shipping statistics.

fore only $33\frac{11}{16}$ cubic feet, but the reckoning is by butts, and much waste of space must be allowed for in view of the usual shape of a cask." It follows that more goods could be stowed in the hold than indicated by the cask capacity of a vessel, if they were carefully packed and occupied less space than a ton of wine. In the Court Minutes of 6th May, 1618, *a ship of* 300 *tons is said to be capable of stowing* 400 *tons of dry goods like calicoes, silks, or the like.*[1]

The fact should be clearly grasped that the ship's *burden* always expressed the *net* amount of merchants' goods as measured by the ton of wine, but her "*ton and tonnage*," which was always more by one-third part of her burden, indicated on the average *dead weight* of cargo.[2] To quote an instance from the Company's Records, we find that the English captured the Dutch ship *Black Lion* of 700 tons burden in 1618. She is described as laden with 600 tons of pepper and 100 tons of other goods of great value,[3] *thus clearly showing that the burden of a ship expressed her net capacity in merchandise.*

That freighted ships were chartered for a certain net tonnage cannot be doubted. Two more instances would clear the ground. In 1647 the *Advice* of 360 tons was freighted by the Company for 300 tons only.[4] It has already been pointed out that the space for provisions, stores, etc., was separate from the hold in which merchandise was stowed away. One cause of the *Lionesse* of 350 tons burden not bringing in the chartered tonnage in 1651 was that some of the 50 tons of provisions were stowed in the hold against the usual practice.[5] Instances of chartering ships at less burden than they were

[1] Court Bk., 4, p. 306.

[2] See Oppenheim's "Administration of the Royal Navy" for a full explanation of these terms. For instance, the *Ascension* was 160 tons in merchants' goods, "but to account her in *dead weight* or her *ton and tonnage* may be added $\frac{1}{3}$ part of the same burden which maketh her tonnage $213\frac{1}{3}$."

Gross tonnage was an uncertain term, there being three different ways of expressing it. For instance, the gross tonnage of the *Sovereign of the Seas* was by depth 1466 tons, by draught 1661 tons and by beam 1836 tons. Oppenheim, p. 260.

[3] Court Bk., Aug. 26, 1619. Calendar, I, p. 292.

[4] Court Bk., 22, p. 37. [5] Court Bk., 23, p. 97.

actually capable of stowing could be multiplied indefinitely in the last quarter of the seventeenth century. The following will, however, suffice :—

Ship.	Tonnage Chartered.	Tonnage to be brought home.
Nassau .	400	500 (Court Bk., 37, p. 148).
Montague .	400	440 over and above the kentledge (Court Bk., 41, p. 287).
Tavistock .	750	800 (Court Bk., 41, p. 56).
Martha .	550	600 (Court Bk., 41, p. 159).

Ever since the permission granted to the officers and mariners of ships to indulge in private trade to the extent of 5–15 per cent on the chartered tonnage of each vessel, it became the usual practice to expressly mention in the contract, or charter party as it was called, whether the indulged tonnage was included in or excluded from that chartered for the Company. While in some cases the kentledge, consisting of iron and lead on the outward voyage and of pepper, saltpetre, red earth, cowries, callitore or other heavy wood on the homeward voyage, at greatly reduced freight rates, was also excluded from the chartered tonnage, so that *the burden of a ship expressed the net quantity of merchandise to be brought for the East India Company, exclusive of kentledge and mariners' goods, etc.* In such cases, it is reasonable to conclude that the tonnage occupied by the "Free merchants" allowed to go on almost every ship from 1680 onward was also excluded from the one chartered by the Company. Take, for instance, the case of the *Massingbird.*[1] It was chartered for 450 tons, but this tonnage was to include the 5 per cent permitted trade and half the kentledge, while in the case of the *Josia*[2] and the *Scipio*, the 5 per cent permitted tonnage alone was included.[3] *That the Company's tonnage and the tonnage chartered by private traders on the same ships were two separate quantities, the latter being excluded from the tonnage chartered by the Company, is clearly stated in the Court Minutes.*[4]

It will now be evident that the returns of shipping tonnage given in the previous sections, exclusively related as they are

[1] Court Bk., 32, p. 81 ; cf. 24, p. 227. [2] Court Bk., 32, p. 82.
[3] Court Bk., 32, p. 82. [4] Court Bk., 32, p. 47.

to the Company, fall far below the actual tonnage employed in the Indo-British trade. We have no means to calculate the burden chartered by the free merchants and that allowed to and clandestinely employed by the mariners and officers of each ship. Barring this unknown quantity the figures, which have been compiled for the first time in the history of the Company, give us a very near approximation to the real net tonnage employed by that great corporation from 1601 to 1708.

The Rating of Tonnage. The earliest information on the shipping tonnage of East Indian goods *as rated for freight*[1] is embodied in the report of the auditors appointed by the Court to consider what allowance was to be made for tonnage and freight in the ships freighted by the particular adventurers for their Persian voyages. They proposed in 1634 to allow the following quantities to a shipping ton :—[2]

Silk 10 cwts. to a ton, reckoning 112 lbs. to every cwt.
Indigo 12 ,, ,, (Here 100 lbs. to a cwt. are reckoned, because the proviso is not given.)
Cotton yarn, 9 cwts. to a ton.
Cloves 1000 lbs. ,,
Malabar pepper, 1400 lbs. subtle or net.[3]
Jambee ,, 13 cwts. ,, ,,
Calicoes, 500 pieces (fine and coarse) to a ton.

---

[1] The quantities taken as equivalent to a shipping ton by the Customs authorities in 1590 are given in the "Rates of the Custom House." Ten years after, the Company rated the provisions in equipping their ships for the first voyage as follows :—

Bread 1714 cwt. 1 qr. 4 lb.	=	150 tons or	11½ cwt.	per ton.
Meale 535 cwt. 2 qr. 24 lb.	=	30 ,,	18 cwt.	,,
Beere 30,000 gallons	=	170 ,,	176 gallons	,,
Cydre 30,000 gallons	=	170 ,,	176 gallons	,,
Wine 15,000 gallons	=	80 ,,	187 gallons	,,
Beef 538 cwt. 2 qr. 14 lb.	=	30 ,,	18 cwt.	,,
Porke 669 cwt. 2 qr. 16 lb.	=	40 ,,	17 cwt.	,,
Fish 45,000 fishes	=	25 ,,		
Otemeale 351 bishelles	=	12 ,,	30 bushells	,,
Steele wheat 351 bishelles	=	9 ,,	30 bushells	,,
Butter 80 firkins	=	2 ,,	40 firkins	,,
Oyle 2000 gallons	=	10 ,,	200 gallons	,,
Vinegar	=	30 tons		
Musterd Seeds 32 bushells	=	1 ton or	33 bushells	,,
Rice 20 bushells	=	1 ton.		

"Dawn of English Trade," pp. 34–35. Cf. the tonnage of Provisions in The 5th Voyage of 1608–9 (Court Bk., 2, p. 110).

[2] Court Bk., 13, 245.

[3] 1500 lbs. to a ton were proposed, while others proposed 12 cwts. or 1200 lbs. or 10 picults ; pp. 133 and 139.

Thus the shipping ton was rated differently for different commodities shipped on the Company's vessels. The weight ton and hundredweight, too, were varying quantities in the case of different merchandise. The hundredweight was equivalent to 100 lbs. for some articles and 112 lbs. for others.[1] In the October sales of 1624 it is expressly mentioned that 100 lbs. were usually reckoned as a hundredweight, but 112 and 110 lbs. made a hundredweight in the case of pepper and aloes respectively.

Thus we ought to be extremely cautious in finding out the exact number of pounds that composed a hundredweight,[2] *a ton, and a*

[1] Sir C. M. Watson gives the following equivalent pounds to a cwt. as current in the beginning of the 17th century :—

Hops=112 lbs. Cattle and fish=120 lbs.
Hard-fish=160 lbs. Nails, pins=120 lbs.
Sugar, spices, wax and all other things=100 lbs.

"British Weights and Measures," p. 26; cf. Rastall's Abridgment, p. 18.

[2] Here a note on the early history of the use of *ton* as a measure of weight in England will be very interesting.

Beginning with the Assize of Weights and Measures issued by Edward I in the 20th year of his reign, we find that the Troy pound of 20 shillings was from that time to be employed for weighing gold, silver, spices and "apothecaries' goods," and the Avoirdupois pound of 25 *shillings* was meant for weighing all other things. Wool, iron, lead, etc. being heavy were always weighed by the avoirdupois pound of 25 shillings. A load of lead was fixed in the above assize as equivalent to 2100 lbs., each pound being equal to 25 shillings or 15 ozs. This pound ceased to be a legal weight in the reign of Queen Elizabeth, and the pound of 16 ozs. was legalised in 1587 in its place (Watson's Weights and Measures, London, 1910).

Although it is difficult to ascertain the exact year when the use of ton of 2240 lbs., each pound being 16 ozs., came into vogue, yet it is certain that it was in much use by 1590. In the Book of Rates of the Custom House of that year *iron* is rated for the purpose of Customs duties in *tons of* 20 *cwts. each. The Amens, Spanish and Spouce varieties of iron were then expressed in ton weights. Lead,* both cast and uncast, has been rated by the "foulder," variously called "fodder, fother, or load" in the literature of that period. *Tin* has been rated by cwts. and wheat by quarters (Rates of the Custom House, London, 1590, pp. 20, 39, 41).

Then six years later, the "Pathway to Knowledge" (1596), which teaches the methods of keeping business accounts, *confirms the above information* in these words :—

"Heerafter followeth the names of divers things, *which have particular termes of reckoning proper to themselves according to their* severall kinds, as some of waight only, some of measure, others of measure and number, and the rest of number by itself.

			Waight		
Iron			*Lead*		Tinne, Copper, Lattin
Pound	2240	112	2184		112
Hundreth	20	1	19½		Hund. 1"
Tunne	1		1	Fodder	

shipping ton at the various epochs of the English commercial history.

The rating of tonnage for freight purposes was altered in 1642 when the Company themselves began the practice of freighting ships by chartering the *Ulysses* for Bantam at £21 per ton. The ships were to bring

15 cwts. net of pepper to a ton
10 „ cloves „
600 calico pieces „

Thus a ton as a measure of weight for iron was equal to the present ton of 2240 lbs. It would appear that this measure was not then extended to express the weights of other things. Yet it is very strange that the author of the "Pathway" often speaks of

(a) the prices of *rye* by "tunnes," as "bought at 55/10/0 the tun and sold at 60/0/0 the tunne ready money";

(b) and of the prices of *wheat* by tuns and of charges "paid *for* 21 *tunnes* 13 *quarters*, 2 *bushels.*"

The profit and loss on these commodities is also reckoned on *tons.*

However, it is by no means certain whether the author is really speaking of the weight-ton or capacity-ton in the case of rye and wheat, although his use of the terms tons, quarters and bushels does not leave us in doubt. In the inventory of the charges of 20 tons of wheat received, he begins by mentioning £8 per "tunne" freight, and then goes on specifying the per ton charges for primage, pilotage, measuring, custom, carriage to warehouse, etc.

Here it is difficult to reconcile the two conceptions on the scanty data before us. *Yet the use of ton as a weight equivalent to 2240 lbs. in the case of iron is established beyond doubt before* 1590.

Proceeding further, we find that in the beginning of the seventeenth century the ton was not only a measure of liquids like beer, cider, wine, oil, vinegar, water, of pitch and meal, but a measure of weight, too, in the case of iron, tin and lead at least. The Court Minutes of the E.I. Company of the very first year supply us useful information on the point. An estimate of the quantity and value of the merchandise to be sent in the ships of their first voyage is given in these words :—

Yron	tons 30 at £270
Tynn wrought	„ 5 at £330
Tynn wt. in barres	„ 5 at £420
Leade	„ 100 at £1700

(B. Mus. MSS., Addl. 24,934, p. 33; "The Dawn of English Trade in the East," by Hy. Stevens, p. 36.)

But in the accounts of the Third and Fifth Voyages in 1606 and 1609, *iron is expressed in "tunns," lead in "fothers," and "tynn" in "tunns"* (Court Bk., 2, pp. 4, 7, 8, 161).

In the invoices of 1626 and 1629 the prices of tin by tons are given (Letter Bk., I, pp. 2, 37).

Thus it appears that the use of ton as a measure of weight in the case of the above three metals had become established by the first quarter of the seventeenth century.

and the rate for other goods was to be fixed according to Turkey tonnage. No private trade was allowed on these freighted ships and no primage was to be given on them.[1] *Every ship was to carry* 22 *soldiers for every* 100 *tons of shipping and a certain number of guns.*

Here the question that naturally crops up is, "What were the rates of tonnage fixed by the Levant Company for their various imports from Turkey?" Turning to the Court Minutes of the Levant Company preserved in the Archives of the Public Record Office, we find that in their minutes of 4th February, 1631–32,[2] the Directors established the following rates of tonnage for different articles :—

A Rate of Tonnage of Commodities.

Carpetts as many as 6 chests Indico
Currence . . 20 cwt. per Tonne
Callicoes, 4 balls cont. 100 broad and 150 narrow

Cloves	10 cwt.	Cotton wool	9 cwt.
Carmania wool	9 ,,	Grogrames	6 balles
Grogrames yarn	12 ,,	Goats and Camells haire	10 cwt.
Galls Loose	15 ,,	Galls in bags	13 ,,
Gallingall	12 ,,	Gum Arabick	12 ,,
Indico	12 cwt. or 6 chests	Pepper	16 ,, [3]
Pepper long	12 cwt.	Lead Red	20 ,,
Lead white	15 ,,	Nutmegs	13 ,,
Rubarbe	8 ,,	Synamon	8 ,,
Sope	20 ,,	Silk raw	10 ,,
Seana	8 ,,	Turmeric	8 ,,
Tynn	20 ,,	Worme seed	11 ,,
Opium	10 ,,	Mastick	6 chests
Anniseed	13 ,,		

There is no evidence in the subsequent Court Minutes of the Levant Company up to 1650 of an alteration in the preceding rates, hence these alone must have been adopted by the East India Company in computing the freight charges of their cargoes since 1642. These rates remained almost unaltered up to the beginning of the nineteenth century. Only in 1685, the Committee for Shipping resolved that cotton-yarn pressed be

[1] Court Bk., 18, pp. 78 and 127.

[2] State Papers, Foreign Archives, Vol. 140. Court Bk. for 1617–31, p. 255.

[3] Here a cwt. was reckoned as equal to 100 lbs. Hence 1600 lbs. made a shipping ton for pepper. (Letter Bk., X, p. 61, March, 1698).

accounted 12 cwt. 10 lb. to the ton; cotton-wool 13 cwt. to the ton, and flax as well as hemp be accounted 12 cwt. to the ton.[1] No other *important* changes seem to have taken place in the subsequent years.

So far as other rules for freighting ships are concerned, we find them recorded in the Committee Minutes of 19th June, 1667, as follows :—[2]

1. 20 men for every 100 tons of shipping chartered.
2. 16 tons for every 100 tons to be allôwed for kentledge.
3. 40 shillings per ton to be given as Impress money.
4. 6d. per ton allowed as demurrage per day.
5. 8 tons of ballast under the pallating for every 100 tons.

The ships in August, 1667, were freighted according to these rules on £19 and £22 for gruff and fine goods respectively. Before that year the Company had to fix these various items in contracting each ship on the terms that could be acceptable to both the parties. The variation in the rates for ships hired in 1658 alone is convincing proof of the necessity of having fixed terms for hiring ships for the Company's service.[3] What alterations were afterwards effected in each of these items cannot be traced in the existing records, but they afford us sufficient data for understanding the system adopted by the Company in freighting their ships.

So far as rating of goods is concerned, the information for various years is available in the invoices of goods sent from England and India. The following table conclusively establishes the almost unalterable character of the rates fixed in 1642 :—

[1] Letter Bk., XVIII, p. 586, March, 1722. Court Bk., 34, p. 163.

[2] Court Bk., 25*a*.

[3]

Ship.	Tonnage.	Imprest Money.	Demurrage per day.
Eagle . .	500	£800	
Smyrna Mercht	—	£700	
Delight . .	250	£400	£8
Gilbert . .	250	£300	7
Advice . .	370	£600	8
Love . .			12
Society . .			6/10/0

20 men per 100 tons on the ships (Court Bk., 24, pp. 37, 39, 41, 66).

Ton Equivalents at Various Periods.

Articles.	1674.	1679 and 1680.	In the beginning of the 19th century.	
Lahore Indico	12 cwts.	12 cwts.	12 cwts.	
Sarkhej Indico	12 „	12 „	12 „	
Aloes Scotrina	15 „	16 „	16 „	
Benjamin	20 „	20 „	20 „	
Cardamons	11 „	12 „	12 „	
Carmania wool		10 „	10 „	
Coho seed	18 cwts.	18 „	18 „	
Cinnamon		8 „	8 „	as in 1631
Olibanum	18 cwts.	18 „	18 „	
Lapistutia		20 „	20 „	
Red earth		20 „	20 „	
Seena		8 „		
Lacs		16–18 „	16–18 „	
Spiknard		10 „	10 „	
Poppy		16 „		
Cotton yarn		10 „	10 „	
Turmeric		16 „	16 „	
Calicoes	400–600 cwts.	400–600 „		
Cotton			13 „	as in 1685
Cloves			12 „	
Elephants' teeth			16 „	
Pepper			16 „	as in 1631
Pepper Long			12 „	as in 1631
Quicksilver			20 „	
Raw Silk			10 „	as in 1631
Rice			20 „	as in 1600
Rhubarb			8 „	as in 1631
Sago			16 „	
Saltpetre			20 „	
Soap			20 „	as in 1631
Sugar			20 „	
Tea Green			8 „	
Tea Bohea			10 „	
Worm Seeds			11 „	as in 1631

(Court Bk., 25*a*, 170, 172; Wisset's Compendium, II, for the 3rd Column.)

Excellence of the Company's Navy. Before we conclude, it is necessary to bring out an important feature of the merchant marine of the Company. The ships owned and freighted by them were not ordinary merchant-men, nor were they men-of-war, but a new type of armed vessels useful both for commerce and war had been invented and slowly perfected to meet the exigencies of the new situations. The superiority of English ships, mariners and naval officers had been proved to the hilt by the epoch-making victory over the "Invincible Armada" in 1588. The Portuguese were admittedly very poor on the sea. They used to die in scores by scurvy on the way to the East and had no mettle to fight either the Dutch or English. In those days when no international law was recognised to bind the European and Asiatic nations, when even the European peoples were free to fight amongst themselves and surprise and capture each other's ships and even dominions beyond the Hebrides, trade was nothing but an armed commerce transacted, guarded, and preserved by means of armed vessels and armed men.

Hence the English East India Company found it expedient to equip and to navigate their ships in a manner different from what was practised in any other commerce. When factories and territories (trifling indeed in their commencement) began to unite themselves with their commerce, this attention was found to be still more requisite as the ships of the Company served for defence in time of war, and for the passage of troops which then became also essential to the Company's existence.

By various progressive measures *the Company "brought them to such a state of perfection as to make them surpass the shipping employed in almost any service whatever, the Navy of Great Britain perhaps not excepted."*

Such is the boast of the writer of an article in the Manuscript Marine Miscellaneous, Vol. I.

It was this navy which in its very infancy broke the power of the Portuguese in India and Ormus, which in its adolescence annihilated the Mogul fleet under the Seedee, which destroyed the Maratha navy under the Angrias, which expelled the Dutch from India and captured the Indian possessions of the formidable French.

Every ship of the English and Dutch that appeared on the shores of India awed her merchants and civil authorities by the show of its guns, bluejackets and men-at-arms. Each vessel was armed, so to say, to the teeth with guns. Hence the English were looked upon as "sovereigns of the seas," "Lions of the Ocean," "Lords of the Waters." Even

Aurangzeb contented himself in the enjoyment of the Indian continent thinking that God had allotted the Unstable Element for Christian rule.

This unquestioned supremacy on the sea was due to the armed and swift ships of the Company. For instance, in the 'eighties, a vessel of 500–600 tons was generally equipped with 36 guns and carried about 105 to 120 soldiers, a ship of about 400–500 tons usually carried 30 guns and 90 soldiers, the one of about 400 tons capacity for holding merchandise had 24 guns and from 75 to 90 men. There was no hard-and-fast rule on this point. The strength used, in fact, to vary according to circumstances. A cursory view of the figures supplied in Appendix C to this Chapter will reveal the variable character of this equipment.

The real import of this practice will be carried home when we cast a glance at the fleets sailing for the East in any one year to prosecute and guard the Anglo-Indian commerce. In the year 1672–73 10 ships of the aggregate burden of 4130 tons chartered by the Company alone left for the East. They carried in all an army of 918 men and 318 naval guns. Five years after, in 1677–78, 13 vessels sailed for the Indian waters. Their aggregate tonnage chartered by the Company totalled 8720 tons. They, too, were equipped with 1205 soldiers and 332 naval guns. Therefore when, during the ten years of 1681–90, 143 ships were sent to war with the Dutch and the Mogul Emperor, it is easy to realise what a large force must have been hurled into the Indies. I have not been able to trace in the Records figures for the soldiers and guns on these vessels, but on the basis of the preceding data, 143 ships of an aggregate burden of 65,000 tons could have carried about 3300 guns and 13,000 soldiers. As most of them went for war and not for commerce, the number of guns and men would really be greater. The Indian merchant-ships were without docks, had very inadequate ordnance, and inefficient gunners. Then they were generally laden to the very brim. Hence they could never successfully cope with the European vessels. They rather fell an easy prey to each and every pirate ship and depended for their safe voyage upon the security bought from the Europeans. The E.I. Company can be heartily complimented for the efficient management of their navy. No better proof can be given of the excellence of the Company's naval establishment than the very trifling losses which for a long period of time attended upon it, both in merchandise and men, through the long and perilous navigation of an Indian voyage. For a great number of years the average loss of ships was 6 per cent, that of merchandise did not exceed about 4 per cent in time of war and in time of peace 2 per cent ; and the losses in the conveyance of troops to India have not upon an average exceeded 2 per cent.

The following beautiful verses of a laureate of the English nation upon the puissance of their navies and the English dominion on sea, will be an appropriate epilogue to this chapter :—

Lords of the worlds great waste, the ocean, we
Whole forrests send to reign upon the sea,
And every coast may trouble, or relieve ;
But none can visit us without our leave.

Angels and we have this prerogative,
That none can at our happy seat arrive ;
While we descend at pleasure, to invade
The bad with vengeance, or the good aid.

The taste of hot Arabia's spice we know
Free from the scorching sun that makes it grow ;
Without the morn, in Persian silks we shine,
And without planting, drink of every wine.

To dig for wealth we weary not our limbs,
Gold, though the heaviest mettall, hither swims ;
Ours is the harvest, where the Indians mow,
We plow the deep, and reap what others sow.[1]

[1] The English and the Dutch Affairs, London, 1664, pp. 47–48.

CHAPTER X

PROTECTION AGAINST INDIAN TEXTILES

At the end of Queen Elizabeth's reign the principle of discrimination against the foreigner in favour of the nationals was the recognised basis of the Customs duties levied on the imports and exports of England. There was a uniform duty of 5 per cent on all commodities, with additional imposts on foreign wines and very discouraging levies on aliens. That no important modifications were made up to 1659 in the rates and assessments will be seen by comparing together the data of the Books of Rates of the years 1590 and 1642.[1] With the Restoration, the policy of encouraging the national industries and manufactures by passing more effective Navigation Acts and levying more discriminative duties upon manufactured goods was followed with vigour.[2] In the Act of Tonnage and Poundage of Charles II, passed in 1660 (12 Car. II, c. 4), it was provided that *all linen goods which included calicoes, lawns, damask, etc., as well as all wrought silks of India and other foreign countries,* "were to pay 'ONE FULL MOYTIE' over and above what is before rated, for which additional duty the importer giving security at the Customs House shall have twelve months time for payment of the same from the time of Importation, or in case such importer shall pay ready money he shall have ten per cent off the said duty abated to him;

[1] Consult 1 Jac. I, c. 33, and 16 Car. I, c. 36.

[2] The Act prohibiting the importing of any wines, wool, or silks into the Commonwealth of England or Ireland or any other Dominions thereunto belonging from the Kingdom of France or any Dominions belonging to the same from 7 September, 1649. Book of Rates, 1642, pp. 92–94. Custom House Library.

And if any of the said Linnens for which this said duty is paid or secured by the Importer can be exported within 12 twelve months after the Importacons, than the aforesaid Duty shall be wholly repaid, or the Security vacated, as to what shall be exported" (Statutes of the Realm, VI, pp. 194, 197).

The principal Oriental commodities, rated for the Custom House purpose at the rates given in the previous chapter, were to pay 5 per cent, less 5 per cent discount for prompt payment, as the general duty, afterwards called the Old Subsidy, but the cotton and silk goods meant for home consumption were subjected to an additional duty of 6d. in the pound. Both the cotton and silk industries had been making slow progress in England, so that the additional impost was calculated to encourage their rapid growth in the realm. It will be seen that *every piece of calico had to pay from ninepence to three shillings as Customs Duty since* 1660, yet the East India Company succeeded in creating such a great demand for them in England and Europe that their vast importations of both Indian silks and cottons began to tell heavily upon the incipient silk and cotton industries of England and curtail the demand for English woollens at home as well as on the Continent. An outcry was naturally raised that the national woollen and linen trades would be ruined.

Numerous pamphlets were written against the growing importation of Indian silks from 1670 *onward.*[1] It was asserted by one of the members of the House of Commons in 1681 that £300,000 was spent yearly in England for the East India manufactured goods, including printed and painted calicoes for cloths, bed-hangings, etc. On the other hand, it was repeatedly pointed out by the partisans of the Company that the same objections applied with a greater force to the wrought silks imported into England from France, Italy, Holland, etc.; that the silks which the Company commonly brought in were mainly taffaties and other plain or striped silks, such as were not usually made in England, but imported from France and

[1] Manchester was well known for the manufacture of cottons even as early as 1640. Baines' Cotton Manufacture in England.

other countries of Europe, so that the importation of Indian silks was working to the prejudice of the silk manufactures of foreign countries alone; and that a great part of the wrought silks from the Indies was again shipped out to France, Holland, etc., to the great advantage of the King and Kingdom. The Company succeeded in their defence, because in 1681 the petition of the silk-weavers of London against the wear of East India silks, Bengals, etc., was rejected by the House.[1]

Heavier Duties Imposed

However, the feeling against calicoes, muslins, and India wrought silks went on growing and heavier duties were laid on their importation to satisfy the popular demand. In 1685 an additional duty of £10 per £100 value with 10 per cent discount for prompt payment and full drawback on re-exportation was imposed on "all calicoes and all other Indian Linnen Imported from the East Indies and on all wrought silks or manufactures of India made of or mixed with Herba or silk and thread or cotton Imported into England from the East Indies after 18th July, 1685, and before 1st July, 1690."[2]

At the end of the above-mentioned period this additional duty, instead of being abolished, was doubled and made to cover "all calicoes and all other Indian Linnen, and all wrought silks and other manufactures of India and China, except Indigo." This levy of 20 per cent, afterwards known as the Old Impost, was continued by several Acts of Parliament and ultimately made perpetual by 9 Anne, c. 21.[3] The immediate and manifest reason for doubling the duty in 1690 was to provide "means of necessary defence of the realms, the

[1] "A Treatise," by Sir J. Child, pp. 18–19.

[2] Statutes of the Realm, Vol. VI, pp. 7–9. Cf. 1 Jac. II, c. 5. Messrs. Alton and Holland have truly asserted that a general study of the records shows that at this time the duties were not levied as percentages on the gross price at the sales ("King's Customs," Vol. II, p. 156).

[3] The Old Impost (2 Wm., c. 4) was applicable from the 25th December, 1690, to 10th November, 1695; continued until 10th November, 1697, by 4 and 5 W. and M., c. 15; 29th September, 1701, 7 and 8 Wm. III, c. 10; 1st August, 1710, 1 Anne, c. 13; 1st August, 1714, 6 Anne, c. 19; 1st August, 1720, 8 Anne, c. 13; made perpetual by 9 Anne, c. 21.

perfect reducing of Ireland and effectual prosecution of war against France." But there is little doubt that the effect of the enhancement of duty was to protect national industries from foreign encroachments.

Indian Calicoes[1] and Silks Prohibited

For thoroughly grasping the present and the subsequent legislative measures which culminated in the total prohibition of Indian silks and painted calicoes, it is here necessary to remember that continued efforts had been made from the time of James I to establish the silk industry in England in order to avoid the importations of French and other foreign silks. Within fifty years England had succeeded so far that there were in 1666 no fewer than 40,000 individuals engaged in the silk manufacture. In the following years a considerable stimulus was given to this industry by the fatal revocation of the Edict of Nantes in 1685, when 50,000 refugees, mostly silk-weavers, sought an asylum in England. Then came the war with Holland, France, and Spain which offered a splendid opportunity for the rapid development of the industry by reducing the importations from France and the Indies and increasing the demand for home manufactures.

Notwithstanding all the adverse circumstances, Indian silks and calicoes were becoming "the general wear in England." The writer of the "Naked Truth" (1696) complained that "fashion is truly termed a witch; the dearer and scarcer any commodity, the more the mode; 30s. *a yard for muslins: and only the shadow of a commodity, then procured.*" The complaints of the English manufacturers and the new settlers were considered so genuine that the question was brought before the House of Commons. It peremptorily rejected the petition of several merchants trading in the goods imported from the East Indies, *against* the Bill "for restraining the wearing of all wrought silks, Bengals, and Dyed, printed, or stained Calicoes, imported into the Kingdom of England, and the Plantations belonging there unto, of the product and Manufacture of Persia and the East Indies." This Bill for restraining the

[1] Complete list of prohibited goods on page 326.

wearing of wrought silks and painted calicoes was twice thrown out by the House of Lords, because the gentry and the ladies in general showed a great aversion to the restraints proposed by the Commons.

A battle royal raged between the parties for and against protection for the next few years. At last, in 1697, the importation of all French and other European silk goods was prohibited. This Act on the eve of the termination of the war only tended to increase the imports of Indian silks and calicoes and thus proved a veritable ruin to many centres of weaving industry in England. The seriousness of the situation will be revealed by the quantities imported from 1698 onward :—

Years.	Calicoes.	Bengal Wrought Silks.
1698	247,214 pieces	57,269 pieces
1699	853,034 ,,	24,445 ,,
1700	951,109 ,,	116,455 ,,
1701	826,101 ,,	115,504 ,,

When the object of the previous prohibition was thus frustrated, the silk-weavers of London grew tumultuous and carried their violence so far as to attempt seizing the treasure at the East India House, and had almost succeeded in it, but were in the end reduced to order. Thereupon the agitation against Indian silks culminated in several legislative enactments. The much-needed statute was passed in 1700 enacting "that from Michaelmas, 1701, all wrought silks, Bengals, and stuffs mixed with silk or herba, of the manufacture of Persia, China, or the East Indies ; and also all calicoes, painted, dyed, or stained there, should be locked up in warehouses appointed by the Commissioners of the Customs, till re-exported ; so as none of the said goods should be worn or used, in either apparel or furniture, in England *on forfeiture thereof, and also of* £200 *penalty on the persons having or selling any of them.*"

New Duty on Muslins

At the same time, to prevent the excessive importations of prohibited goods during the interim, a new duty of 15 per cent was imposed by another Act (11 and 13 Wm. III, c. 3) upon the gross price realised at sale,[1] over and above all the duties then payable on all Indian wrought silks, dyed calicoes, and muslins imported between 26th March, 1700, and 30th September, 1701, when the prohibitory Act was to operate. As the prohibited goods, being forbidden for home consumption, were meant for the European and Colonial markets, they were to pay no duty other than the 2½ per cent subsidy upon re-exportation from the country. This temporary duty of 15 per cent on muslins, instead of being abolished in 1701, was first continued to 30th September, 1708, by 12 and 13 Wm. III, c. 11,[2] and then made perpetual for further discouraging the importation of Indian manufactured cloth.

Another Act imposed a similar duty of 15 per cent on all white[3] calicoes whatsoever whether muslins or thick cloth, so that the greatest and the most lucrative branch of the Company's commerce was dealt a heavy blow.

Growth of English Manufactures

The various imposts were considered so intolerable that the Company would have much curtailed their shipping if they were not bent upon making "some show and appearance in India of not quitting the trade."[4] They did for a time highly suffer from these Acts, since they could hardly bring sufficient quantities of Indian goods; their ships had either to return dead freighted or filled with China ware, and such other commodities as did not answer their charges. The balance of trade in the Indies was mightily disturbed. The Company,

[1] Bengal General, 18th January, 1705–6. Letter Bk., XII, p. 517. *ibid.*, 7th February, 1706–7. Letter Bk., XIII, p. 98. 22d. per lb. net duty on Indian wrought silks between Mich. 1699 to Mich. 1700 amounted to £9291/8/2; and the 15 per cent duty between 25th March and 28th September, 1700, was £11,793/12/4. Public Record Office, T. 30, Vol. I.

[2] 15 per cent on muslins imposed by 11 Wm. III, c. 10, up to 30th September, 1701, continued up to 30th September, 1706, by 12 and 13 Wm. III, c. 11; allowed to be drawn back on re-exportation. Continued 24th June, 1710, by 3 and 4 Anne, c. 1; 24th June, 1714, by 6 Anne, 22, 1; for ever by 7 Anne, 7, 25.

[3] Calicoes that did not pay the duties as muslins, dimities and cotton manufactures.

[4] Fort General, 12th January, 1704–5 (Letter Bk., XII, p. 371). Every piece of calico valued at 10/– in the Book of Rates paid 3/6d. as net duty and 15 per cent more on the gross value at the Candle (Letter Bk., XV, p. 66).

seeing little hope of profit in the principal branch of their Indian business, were led to develop their China trade.

On the other hand, there is no doubt that the total prohibition of silks and painted calicoes for home consumption and the excessive duties on muslins and white calicoes imparted a great impetus to the dyeing and weaving industries of England. The importation of raw silk and cotton yarn was in a few years greatly increased. The manufacturers were so successful in producing sooseys, romalls, etc., in imitation of Bengal goods, even as early as 1703,[1] that instead of stained calicoes and linens, plain stuff was imported from India and after being printed, painted, stained and dyed in England was universally used by the people. It was truly pointed out by the Company in a petition to the House of Lords that when the Indian stuffs were first prohibited, several sorts of striped and chequered and other species of goods in imitation of them were brought into and worn in England at twice and thrice the prime cost of those prohibited; that the prohibited goods were sent to the very place those species or imitations were made at; that the protective measures had not put a stop to the importation of Indian silks and chintz, which were universally popular on account of their beauty and cheapness, but had altered the channel of their supply; that the prohibition only tended to enrich the Dutch at the expense of the English, who by appropriating this trade had replaced the British woollens with cheap Indian goods; and, lastly, that as large quantities were smuggled from the continent of Europe, the state lost the duties and the people paid more for the same goods than they would have done if these were directly imported.[2] The Legislature had, no doubt, tried to put down smuggling.

Excise on Calicoes

For instance, an Act (6 Anne, c. 3) was passed in 1707 for better securing the duties upon East Indian goods, requiring the Company to give a bond of £2500 for every 100 tons

[1] Letter Bk., X, pp. 447, 538.
[2] Miscellaneous, Vol. 5, pp. 202–69.

their ships were let for, that all goods laden upon such ships should be brought and landed in England without breaking bulk on the sea.[1] It was further supplemented by an Act of 1712 for better ascertaining and securing the payments for goods and merchandise to be imported from the East Indies, and all other places within the limits of the charters granted to the East India Company.[2] In the same year another Act (12 and 13 Anne, c. 9) was passed for laying further duties on coffee, tea, drugs, etc., for thirty-two years from 16th June, 1712.[3] Coffee was charged 12d. per lb. avoirdupois, and tea 2s. when imported from the places of the Company's charter and 5s. on importation from other places. The new additional duty on all drugs except those employed for dyeing purposes in England was 20 per cent.[4] By this time the business of calico-printing and dyeing plain Indian muslins was so firmly established in England as to lead Parliament to impose an *excise duty of* 3*d. per square yard in* 1712 *and double this amount in* 1714 *on all calicoes printed, stained, painted, or dyed in the country.* The author of the "Proposals Humbly Offered to the House of Commons" (15th January, 1706–7) had a few years before pleaded for a levy on the considerable estates acquired in a short time by those engaged in calico-printing by remarking that *there were yearly printed and glazed, in England, above twelve millions of pieces of calicoes, and linen cloth, etc., each piece containing* 18 *yards in length.* This statement affords a striking proof of the remarkable progress made in these employments set up only since the prohibiting of the importation of calicoes printed and glazed in India.[5]

[1] Journal of the House of Commons, XIII, pp. 439, 451, 453, 461.

[2] Journal of the House of Commons, XVII, p. 222.

[3] Made perpetual by 3 Geo. I, c. 7. The duty on drugs made to cease by 11 Geo. I, c. 7, and the duties on coffee and tea made to cease by 10 Geo. I, c. 10.

[4] Journal of the House of Commons, XVII, p. 229.

[5] The author of "The New Dialogues (1710) upon the Present Posture of Affairs," remarks: "I must not omit that the great variety in the sorts and Fashions of these silks and stuffs (some whereof are extremely curious and taking) would create a quickness in Trade among our own Woollen Manufacturers and Silk-weavers, who are lovers of, and sometimes gainers by Imitation," p. 197.

More Severe Penalties

As the use of printed Indian calicoes, both in apparel and household furniture, was not effectively curtailed by the numerous protective measures, and worked to the great prejudice of the woollen, silk, and dyeing industries of the Kingdom, the question was once more taken up by Parliament in 1719. The Company made many representations, but none paid any heed to their cogent reasons against the coming Bill. It was pointed out that the Company "had carried on the East India trade very much to the advantage of the nation and the woollen manufacture thereof"; that the proposed Bill would cut off a large branch of their trade, would diminish their naval force, would weaken their settlements in India, would render the English contemptible in the eyes of the Indian princes, and encourage other European nations to attempt the gradual engrossing of the whole trade and power of India; that the British revenue would suffer; and lastly, that the prohibition of Indian calicoes would evoke retaliatory policy from Indian princes to prohibit English woollen manufactures from being used in their territories.

Notwithstanding such-like frequent protests, an Act was passed (7 Geo. I, c. 7) in 1720 to preserve and encourage the woollen and silk manufactures of England by making the prohibition of the East Indian silks and calicoes more effectual. *It absolutely prohibited the wear and use of Indian silks and calicoes painted, stained, or dyed in India, under the penalty of* £5 *for each offence on the wearer, and of* £20 *on the seller.* This Act had the desired effect of discouraging the importation of painted and dyed fabrics, as will be seen in the diminishing quantities of prohibited goods brought into the country (Appendix A). The complaints against their use continued for a long time after. The ingenious writer of "A Plan of the English Commerce"[1] (1726) attributed their prevalence to female perverseness, or in his own words, the ungovernable "passion for their fashion." "Should I ask the ladies whether

[1] Petitions, 18th January, 1720; 23rd February, 1720; 30th March, 1720.

they would dress by law, or clothe by Act of Parliament, they would ask me whether they were to be statute fools, and to be made pageants and pictures of: whether the sex was to be set up for our jest, and the parliament had nothing to do but make Indian queens of them ?—that they claim English liberty as well as the man, and as they expect to do what they please, and say what they please, so they will wear what they please, and dress how they please."[1]

Even in 1735 a poet gave expression to the popular feeling in these words :—[2]

The silkworms form the wardrobes gaudy pride ;
How rich the vests which Indian looms provide ;
Yet let me here the British nymphs advise
To hide these foreign spoils from native eyes ;
Lest rival artists murmuring for employ,
With savage rage the envied work destroy.

Cotton Manufactures under Protection

These warnings were also indicative of the growing cotton industry in England. In 1740 we are told that the manufacture of cotton, mixed and plain, was arrived at so great a perfection since the exclusion of Indian cotton twenty years earlier that England manufactured not only enough for her own consumption,[3] but supplied her colonies, and even many of the nations of Europe, as will be seen from the note below. Such a rapid progress, long before the era of invention and new machinery, clearly indicates the marvellous future of the English cotton industry. The heavy duties which had brought about

[1] "A Plan of the English Commerce," p. 253.

[2] A stanza from a poem which appeared in the "Gentleman's Magazine" in 1735. Taken from the "Chronologist," p. 55.

[3]

	Imports of of cotton.	Exports of cotton manufactures.
1697	1,976,359 lbs.	£5,915
1701	1,985,868 ,,	23,253
1710	715,008 ,,	5,698
1720	1,972,605 ,,	16,200
1730	1,545,472 ,,	13,524
1741	1,976,031 ,,	20,709
1751	2,976,610 ,,	45,986

Macgregor's Commercial Tariffs, IV, 480, 494–95.

this change and excluded Indian piece-goods from the English and colonial markets have been detailed in the next section. Here it is sufficient to remark that the English commercial policy of the whole period from 1660 to 1757 is characterised by protective measures against continental and Eastern goods in general, and against the silks and painted goods of India in particular. Thoroughly shielded by the outright prohibition of such goods and the heavy imposts on others, England was fairly on the way to build up her industries. The other European countries, except Holland, had also prohibited the use of some Indian fabrics,[1] so that the European and colonial markets for Indian piece-goods were being yearly narrowed down. During the next generation the Indian cotton industry was menaced by the new revolution brought about by the introduction of machinery in manufacturing cotton goods, and within a few years more India so much lost her ancient ascendancy that instead of a producer she became the consumer of cotton goods.

Before we proceed further to unravel the complicated subject of the gross and net duties levied upon the imported East India goods, it is better to recall the various imposts levied in the beginning of the eighteenth century. Six different levies, called the Old Subsidy, Additional Duty or Half Subsidy, New Subsidy, Old Impost, Additional Impost, and 15 per cent on muslins, were prevalent in 1700. These several duties were followed by other subsidies, and additional duties on coffee, tea, drugs, and white calicoes in subsequent years.

The following memorandum of the duties imposed upon the East India goods at various periods from 1660 to 1757 will present at one view the numerous Acts relating to them :—

Memorandum Concerning Duties on the East India Goods.

12 Car. II, c. 4. *Old Subsidy* of £5 per cent; less discount 5 per cent. Net £4 5s. *on all goods.*

Additional Duty on muslins and linen= ½ net subsidy; duty being £2 7s. 6d., discount 5 per cent; net £2 2s. 9d. on *linen.*

[1] Wm. Wood's "Survey of Trade" (A.D. 1722), pp. 227–28, 550.

2 W. M., c. 4. *Old Impost* in 1690 of £20 per cent; discount $6\frac{1}{4}$ per cent on the same. Net £18 15s. *on all manufactures*, except indigo, which was free.

4, 5 W. M. c. 5. *Additional Impost* of 1692–93. £5 per cent with discount of $6\frac{1}{4}$ per cent. Net £4 13s. 9d. *on all goods* that were charged with the impost of 1690.

New Impost continued by various Acts to 1st August, 1716, continued 7 Anne, c. 31, 5 1st August, 1720, continued 8 Anne, c. 14, 5 made perpetual by 9 Anne, c. 21, 1	Statutes of the Realm, IX, pp. 133, 235.

9, 10 W. M., c. 23. *New Subsidy*—£5 per cent with discount 5 per cent. Net £4 15s. in 1698 *on all goods.*

11, 12 Wm., c. 10. Silks and printed calicoes prohibited for home wear. All wrought silks imported from the East Indies or Persia after 29th September, 1698, were to pay an additional duty of 1s. 10d. per lb. at 16 oz. avoir. over and above all other duties payable for the same.

11 and 12 Wm., c. 10. 15 *per cent on muslins* with 5 per cent discount for prompt payment.

2, 3 Anne, c. 9, in 1703. $\frac{1}{3}$ *Subsidy*—£1 13s. 4d., discount 5 per cent. Net £1 11s. 8d. All goods were liable to this duty.

3, 4 Anne, c. 4, in 1703. Additional duty on drugs. No discount—net £4. Additional duty on Japan ware. No discount—net £12. 15 per cent on white calicoes.

3, 4 Anne, c. 5, in 1703. $\frac{2}{3}$ *Subsidy*—£3 6s. 9d. with discount 5 per cent—net £3 3s. 4d. All goods liable to this duty.

10 Anne, c. 19. New duty on paper, prints and chequered linen—£15 per cent. No discount—net £15.

10 Anne, c. 26. Further duty on drugs, etc., £20 per cent. Net £20.

7 Geo. I, c. 7. Prohibition reconfirmed and made more effectual in 1720.

21 Geo. II, c. 14. *Additional Subsidy* of 5 per cent on all goods imported in 1747.

Thus new imposts were from time to time piled upon the goods imported into England. The working of the various Acts was most complicated, because some of the goods were rated and had to pay fixed percentage duties on the rates agreed upon by Parliament in their Books of Rates; some were unrated, and paid the duties *ad valorem;* while others were partly rated[1] and partly unrated.[2] The *ad valorem* duties on the unrated goods (except coffee, tea, muslins, white

[1] Goods rated (i.e. whose prices were fixed for Customs) were: Calicoes (white), canes (rattan), canes (walking), dimity, drugs, ivory, pepper, rice, sugar, saltpetre, silk, cotton yarn.

[2] Imported goods unrated were: boxes, calicoes stitched with silk, chinaware, coffee, counterpanes, cowrics, diamonds, fans, paper, lacquered ware, mulmuls flowered, muslin neckcloths, quilts, rangoes, tea, etc.

calicoes,[1] dimities and other manufactures of cotton which were under special regulations), were computed according to the gross price at the Candle, after deduction of the allowances to be made according to several Acts. There were, moreover, certain regulations with regard to allowances, discounts, and drawbacks which occasioned such a dispute between the Company and the authorities of the Custom House that it lasted for more than thirty years. It was shown by the latter that on following the method advocated by the Company, the sovereign received less, though Parliament granted more.

The great difference in the amounts of duties levied upon the principal articles of import will be at once visible from the following abstract of *the total net duties* payable upon all East India unrated goods for every £100 value according to the gross price at the Candle, both by the former method of computing and the new (1714) advocated by the Custom authorities :—

Goods—£100 value.	Old Way.			New Way.		
	£	s.	d.	£	s.	d.
Arrack, 225 gallons	49	12	3	57	3	11¾
Calicoes, white, pieces	19	10	5	19	10	5
China ware or porcelain	18	8	9¾	29	19	7½
Cotton manufactures	27	10	8¼	32	8	5¾
All other manufactures not specially mentioned	17	19	8¼	21	14	2½
Dimities, 400 yards	34	1	0	34	1	0
Drugs for dyers' use	7	7	4	7	10	10¾
Drugs of all other sorts	19	2	8¾	26	5	8
{ Muslins paying subsidies as calicoes, 30 pieces	19	10	5	19	10	5
{ Ditto, and *ad valorem*	27	12	10½	33	5	11
Coffee, 100 lbs. at importation	12	7	6	2	7	6
Upon delivery for home consumption	53	4	7	53	4	7
{ Tea, 120 lbs. at importation	3	1	2	3	5	4½
{ Upon delivery for home consumption	27	7	7¼	30	16	9½
All other unrated goods not manufactured	12	19	11½	13	18	8

After a bitter controversy, protracted over several years, the case was decided against the Company, and therefore the enhanced duties recorded in the second column came into operation. Nothing else remarkable happened up to the end of our period, except the reduction of duties on tea to prevent smuggling. It was seen that the duties realised by the

[1] See Appendix for each of these articles, pp. 326–9 *infra*.

State on tea before 1745 had been decreasing, though its importation had gone on increasing year by year. The excessive levies on the commodity whose demand was growing by leaps and bounds had very much encouraged smuggling. To put an end to it, 4s. per lb. excise was reduced to 1s. and the 14 per cent customs were raised to 28 per cent.[1] The effect of the change was a rapid inflation in imported quantities and a remarkable increase in the revenue of the State. While the net amount realised from 1741 to 1745 was £678,520 from Excise and £107,592 from Customs, the two items rose to £2,200,000 and £388,000 in the eight years from 1746 to 1753, or to a little less than £400,000 per year in 1753.

In the end, it will be better to fix our attention on the net duties—deducting all discounts for prompt payment and allowances for charges, etc.—payable on the principal Eastern imports and the sums repaid out of the same for the re-exportation of the articles from England in the last year of our survey.

It is evident that the home consumer was subjected to heavy taxation for consuming Eastern commodities, but mighty encouragement was given him for finding out markets on the continent of Europe and other foreign lands for the development of English commerce and shipping.

[1] 21 Geo. II, c. 14.

Harleian MSS., 7019, p. 40. Scoro's Observations, 23rd March, 1715. Wm. Edgar's "Customs Vectagalium Systema." London, 1714, pp. 310–19.

Arrack—from and after 1st May, 1704, the same duties were payable as upon brandy and foreign spirits imported. 7 Geo. II, c. 14.

Coffee—from British plantations in America to pay 1s. 6d. per lb. inland duty instead of 2s. 21 Geo. II, c. 1.

Tea—to pay 4 per cent more for excise ; 1s. per lb. and 25 per cent on the price at the Candle, from 24th June, 1745, and no drawback allowed since that date. 18 Geo. II, c. 26.

Indigo—of the growth of the British plantations to receive 6s. per lb. premium on importation after 25th March, 1749, which to be repaid on exportation. 21 Geo. II, c. 30.

An additional duty of 1s. per lb. laid on all goods imported from and after 1st March, 1747.

5 per cent duty on all unrated goods imported by the E.I. Company on the gross price at the Candle, the said duty to be paid without any allowance for discount and prohibited goods excepted from this duty.

Net Duties Payable Per Cent in 1757.[1]

	On Importation.			Repaid on Exportation.		
	£	s.	d.	£	s.	d.
Muslins and calicoes	38	5	11	37	2	0
China ware	39	19	7	32	18	7
Diamonds, pearls and rubies	free					
Dimities	37	8	5	36	2	9
Drugs, manufactured	28	12	7	27	2	3
„ unmanufactured	21	6	6	19	12	8
Goods for dyers' use	12	10	11	10	12	11
Tea, Customs	18	18	7	—		
„ Inland Duty	25	0	0	—		
Bengal silk per lb. = 24 ozs., rate 10s.	0	2	4	0	2	1
China silk	0	1	11	0	1	8
Dutties, rate £1	0	3	10	0	3	4
Coffee nuts, rate £2 10s. per cwt.	0	11	11	0	10	9
Coffee per cwt. and	1	13	6	1	10	2
upon home consumption	8	8	0	from British plantations.		
„ „	11	4	0	from other countries.		

In the end, a word on revenue derived from customs on the E.I. goods will furnish a useful memorandum on the benefit of the Eastern trade to the State in particular.

Sufficient data are not available for presenting a regular account of the annual total sums paid by the Company and others as customs on their Eastern imports, yet an idea of their growth during the century and a half of our period can be formed from a few items scattered here and there in the Records. The cargoes brought on the twenty-five ships belonging to the twelve separate voyages undertaken by the Merchant Adventurers under the name of the E.I. Company from 1601 to 1612, paid £81,698 as subsidies to the State; while the First Joint Stock is represented to have contributed £65,000[2] on the next four years' adventures. Multiplying those sums by twenty, in imitation of the method prevalent[3] in those days, we find that the Company's imports amounted to about £3,000,000 sterling for all their adventures in which they had invested for shipping, goods, etc., near £800,000.

[1] Langham's Net Duties (1757), p. 85
[2] Home Misc., 39, p. 24.
[3] Macpherson's Commerce, II, p. 316.

The yield of customs on the Company's goods grew with the volume of trade, so that the amount was stated in 1625 to be £30,000 per annum[1] for the preceding few years. The decline of the Company's trade during the next quarter of the seventeenth century is also faithfully mirrored in the customs returns. During the twenty-five years from 1625 to 1649, £500,000 are said to have been contributed to the public revenue, which gives us an average of £20,000 per annum for the period.[2]

It has been seen that the Company's trade lay more or less in a moribund condition for the next sixteen years, hence the share of the State must have *pari passu* decreased. It is also known that the Eastern trade was revived and pursued with vigour after the termination of the Anglo-Dutch War in 1667. From that year to 1774 the average annual yield as duties on the imported goods is mentioned as £35,000;[3] while from another account preserved in the British Museum Manuscript, Jure Impt. Coll., No. 17,019, it appears that the average for eleven years, from 1672 to 1682 inclusive, stood at £35,972 per annum.[4] As new duties were from time to time imposed on the E.I. goods since 1690 onward and the volume of trade, too, showed uninterrupted progress, the amount paid by the Company in the form of customs, excise, etc., must have increased *pari passu*.

The produce from E.I. goods in 1691–92, though a lean year,

[1] Calendar, IV, p. 116; cf. Calendar, I, pp. 138, 432.

[2] About the year 1636 the duties on Indian goods, in and out, could be valued at only £10,000 yearly (Court Minutes, 1635–39, pp. 271–72).

[3] "A particular of all Bullion shipped out by the Company since the year 1667–68 to the present year 1674."

[4] Customs paid by the E.I. Company—the year ending at Michaelmas:—

(Shillings and pence left out in each item.)

1672	£32,000	1679	£52,763
1673	27,780	1680	43,837
1674	32,639	1681	27,932
1675	27,511	1682	60,390
1676	40,958		
1677	46,595		£431,662
1678	39,257		

B. Museum MSS., Jure Impt., 17,019, p. 44.

soared high to £142,717, and the estimate for the next three years on this basis was therefore thrice this sum.[1] The total yield in 1697 stood at £122,761.[2] This is not a poor income in the last year of a long and continuous war with Europe. There are no separate entries for the net or gross yield of duties paid on the Eastern imports in the Customs Books for the following years, but an idea of the large sums contributed in several items from 1696 onward can be had from a table given on p. 330 and compiled from a manuscript volume, entitled the "Net Duties on Exports and Imports," in the Custom House Library.

At the end of our period, the *moneys paid in the exchequer as duties were on the average more than the sums exported to the East in the form of gold and silver.* In fact, the gains of the State alone in revenue from the Company's commerce were 14 per cent more than the moneys exported by that body from the whole country for investment in Oriental commodities.

For the purposes of comparison the returns of customs and bullion exported are shown side by side for the years 1750–51 to 1759–60 :—

Year.	Customs and Excise paid by the Company.[3]	Bullion exported by the Company.[4]
1750	£887,860	£809,252
1751	927,215	936,185
1752	943,792	833,394
1753	868,202	944,256
1754	904,751	668,803
1755	938,543	620,378
1756	890,132	795,008
1757	950,660	456,252
1758	770,022	172,604
1759	1,028,622	142,922
	£9,109,799	£6,379,144

In other words, while England exported $6\frac{1}{3}$ million pounds sterling to the East in ten years from 1750 to 1759, it received back, in the form of import duties, excise, etc., more than £9,000,000. The extraordinary total gains to the nation from the Oriental trade are manifest from these figures.

[1] B. Museum MSS., Harleian, 7019, p. 6.

[2] Public Record Office—Customs, III, Vol. 1.

[3] Home Misc., 61, p. 109.

[4] Parliamentary Paper, 152 of 1812–13.

It will have been evident now that from the 'thirties of the eighteenth century the Eastern trade was so immensely lucrative to England as not to deplete her by a single farthing. The total exports of treasure and goods were less than the income brought into the State by duties levied upon the goods carried in and out of the country.[1]

All the Oriental goods were obtained free of charge, so to say, by England. These re-exported goods still more multiplied the stock of the country by importing hundreds of thousands of pounds from the Continent and colonies. The shipping and shipbuilding trades were also extraordinarily benefited. Then large amounts of money were brought into the kingdom from India by Englishmen in the service of the Company as well as by those who were engaged in private trade there. England had become a supplier of Europe in Oriental products and merchandise. Her shippers, bankers, merchants, moneyed classes, the Court, the aristocracy, mariners, workmen, and capitalists—one and all—were being unusually enriched by this lucrative commerce.

Yet the State deliberately discarded these advantages. For full one century a conscious effort had been made to develop English shipping and industries and to discourage Indian and French imports. The French Court was not less anxious to retaliate and impose severe restrictions on foreign imports. To prevent the access of undesirable goods it employed effective means such as prohibitions, duties on importation and consumption, transit dues, strict restraints and harassments. Then the Court set the salutary example of using home-made manufactures and boycotted foreign goods against the will of the fashionable classes.

So in England, though the wear of Indian, Persian, Chinese silks and Indian muslins and piece-goods was the fashion of the day, the Commons first put higher and higher imposts both on the French and Oriental manufactures and then totally prohibited their use. By these methods national industries were established, encouraged, and developed. We

[1] See p. 330 *infra*.

learn from William Wood that no sooner was the Act passed for prohibiting the East India and Persian silk, stuffs, etc., than the fainting spirits of English manufacturers revived and new life and vigour seemed diffused through the nation, and the influence of it was not confined to the manufacturers only, the merchants were sharers therein. It greatly encouraged English trade to the Levant, Italy, etc.

England had done away with the necessity of importing Oriental silks and cottons. By the middle of the eighteenth century, before any machinery had been invented to revolutionise the manufacture of piece-goods, not only was the home demand fully satisfied by the English manufacturers, but large quantities were being exported to the continental and American markets.

Since 1710 almost the whole Oriental trade in manufactured goods was meant for the supply of foreign markets. These were being captured by England, and thus the demand for Indian cloth had been yearly curtailed. With the invention and growth of machinery for the manufacture and transportation of cloth, and the passing off of the French and Dutch from the political and commercial stages of the Indian continent, Indian importations into Europe began to dwindle fast and they reached the vanishing-point in a short period. Then the tide turned, India, instead of an exporter of cloth, became an importer. Therefore the spinning, weaving, dyeing, as well as their subsidiary and allied industries began to shrink and fade away before the onrushing flood of cheap English manufactures. How much of this transformation, devolution, disturbance, derangement, deterioration, decay was due to political and how much to economic causes, will be studied independently in a separate volume. Here it is essential to bear in mind that the downward process had long begun and been forced by economic causes alone.

The adverse effects of the growing cotton industry in England could not be felt up to 1760 in India. This country was still the home of cloth manufacture and the greatest and almost the sole supplier of the hundred sorts of her well-known cotton goods, precious stones, drugs, and other valuable products. By reason of her vast exports to all the countries of the world, India was still in the eyes of all the greatest sink of silver and gold.

All the currents of precious metals discharged themselves on the Indian continent. M. Bernard Picart, the voluminous and reliable author of the "Ceremonies et Coutumes Religieuses des Peuples Idolatres," remarked in 1735 that:—

Je crois que l'on peut avancer, sans crainte de se tromper, que les Etats du Grand Mogol sont les plus riches qu'il y ait au Monde; car non-seulement presque toutes les Nations de l'Europe, mais encore celles de l'Asie, y vont porter de l'Or et de l'Argent; et n'en retirent que des merchandises: de sorte que cet Empire est comme une espece de goussre, dans lequel se précipitent toutes les richesses du Monde, et d'oú aucunes ne sortent.[1]

The writer of the "Histoire de Thomas Kouli Khan," which was published at Paris in 1742, surpassed Picart in his admiration of the extraordinary riches of India.

Il y a longtemps que l'on dit, que l'Indostan est l'abîme de tous les trésors de l'Univers: tout l'or et tout l'argent que fournit l'Amérique, après avoir circulé quelque temps en Europe, vient aboutir dans le Mogol pour n'en plus sortir. Les Indiens peuvent se passer aisément de toutes les productions du reste de la terre:

Autant que l'on vient aux Indes de toutes les Nations du monde pour y chercher ce qui leur manque. Il s'en suit de là que l'argent de l'Univers trouve mille voies pour entrer dans l'Indostan et n'a presque aucune issue pour en sortie; d'autant mieux que les denrées et merchandises que l'on y apporte des pays Etrangers ne se payent jamais qu'en échange de celles du pays, et celles-ci au contraire, dont il se fait infiniment plus de consommation ne s'acquierent qu'avec de l'argent.[2]

All the gold and silver of the universe found a thousand and one channels for entering into India, but there was not a single outlet for the precious metals to go out of the country. It was this immense and constant influx of silver from all the countries of our planet which made the masses live in ease and

[1] P. 12. [2] Pp. 413–15.

comfort under a most despotic government. What James Grant has remarked about the people of the Deccan is equally true of the whole country:—

> It must be acknowledged that the peasantry of the Deccan, even under despotism, enjoy a larger portion of the fruits of the earth and their own industry, than those of other countries can boast of under the freest governments.[1]

[1] Addl. MS., 29,209, p. 402.

PART II

APPENDICES

CHAPTER I

Appendix

Tonnage Employed in the Foreign and Coasting Trades of India in the beginning of the Seventeenth Century.

Here the results of our survey of the foreign and coastal trade of India are summed up in a tabular form. They are only *rough* estimates of the *approximate* tonnage of the shipping employed in the maritime trade of India. In the absence of any positive data, personal impressions play a great part; yet an impartial attempt to express in statistics the vague descriptions of the various travellers will, it is hoped, prove very useful.

Foreign Trade of India.

Countries.	Total tonnage.
With Europe,[1] from Portugal to India	10,500
,, India to Portugal	9,000
Africa,[2] either way	5,000
Red Sea[3] ,,	10,000
Ormus[4] ,,	10,000
Maldives[5] ,,	3,500
Ceylon[6] ,,	12,000
Spice Is.[7] ,,	15,000
Pegu, Siam, Cochin-China,[8] etc.	5,000
China, Japan, and Philippines[9] directed through Moluccas	5,000
	85,000

[1] See "Imports into Portugal," *infra.* We should also add 700–800 tons of the galleon which annually left Lisbon a month or two before the fleet of carracks, to go direct to Malacca. It carried despatches thither and then loaded cargoes in China and the islands of Sunda (Pyrard, II, p. 15).

[2] One Portuguese galleon and a few Indian barques and ships seen in Zanzibar and Socotra; Lancaster speaks of a 30-ton barque from Goa (p. 7); three ships, *Pangais,* laden with calicoes, were captured near the island of Pemba (p. 121); Captain Keeling (1607) saw two ships in the Bay of Socotra (p. 119), and talks of trade carried on by the Portuguese there; Downton speaks of a ship belonging to the King of Socotra and of two Indian ships wintering there (p. 185).

C.O. 77, Vol. I, pp. 29–31, embodies an important evidence: "The Portugals do yearly send 8 ships laden with all kinds of merchandise to the

Coasting Trade at the Different Ports of India.

Tatta	10,000 tons.	Malabar Ports	50,000 tons.
Diu	10,000 ,,	Coromandel	25,000 ,,
Cambay[10]	100,000 ,,	Orissa[13]	5,000 ,,
Goa[11]	100,000 ,,	Bengal[14]	20,000 ,,
Surat[12]	20,000 ,,		

empire of Prestor John." That Zaila was the place of immense traffic has been borne out by Varthema (p. 86).

[3] and [4] "Indo-Arabian trade," *infra*, and "Euro-Asiatic centres," *infra*.

[5] Thirty to forty ships laden with cowries seen by Pyrard; many ships laden with tortoise-shells to Cambay and with fish to Sumatra and India; large amounts of cocoanut, coir, mats, etc., were also exported (Pyrard, I, 227 *et seq.*, 236–42).

[6] "The Pearl Island," *infra*.

[7] The following facts should be taken into consideration—Achin, 10 to 15 ships of diverse nations from Bengal, Calicut, Pegu, etc.

The King of Achin usually placed at sea 60, 70, and 80 galleys, besides many other vessels without any difficulty. He laid siege to Malacca with 113 sail of ships, galliots, and galleys. The Queen of *Japara* besieged Malacca with 300 sails, including 70 or 80 junks (A.D. 1575) (Conselho Ultramarinho, I, Part I, pp. 25–53). The King of *Java* led an expedition against the King of Passeruan. The latter had 2700 sails, amongst which were a thousand high-built junks and all the rest were vessels with oars. The strength of the fleet of the assailants is not given, yet it must be incredibly great (Pinto, p. 258). There passes not a year wherein, from the provinces and islands of Java, Bali, Madura, Angenio, Borneo, and Solor, there sails not thereunto at the least 1000 junks, besides other smaller vessels, wherewith all the rivers and all the harbours are full (Pinto, p. 285).

Bantam—nine or ten great ships every year from China alone.

Sumatra—thirty ships according to Pyrard. Hautman saw ten ships in the harbour of an ordinary village of Sumatra.

The King of *Tarnate* came to greet the Dutch with thirty-two very neatly built, well manned and mounted ships.

We read of fifty or more ships sailing in Java waters (Dutch Rec., Series I, Vol. IX).

Goa ship of the Captain of Malacca of 700 tons laden with Indian and European goods.

[8] Three ships of 60–80 tons, elsewhere 80 tons burden, each bound for Martaban; another ship, burden not given; Bengal and St. Thomé ships to Pegu and Arabian ships with Indian and European goods to the same (see "Near East," *infra*).

Fitch testified to the commercial greatness of Sumergan (Sunargaon), Dela, Cirion, Pegu, Martavan, Tavi, Tanaseri, Junsataon, and many others.

[9] *Canton.* We read in "Des Voyages de Jean Mocquet," begun in 1601, that at the port of Canton *there were more than three or four thousand very large ships* (p. 339, Rouen Edition, 1645).

Pinto speaks of at least 2000 merchant ships coming from China to Japan, among which were twenty-six Portuguese ships. China ships in the islands of Bali, Borneo, Java, etc., were frequently seen.

[10] and [11] Downton saw a fleet of nearly 500 Portugal frigates going to Cambay in February, 1613. Taking 60 tons as the capacity of a frigate, as we have been informed elsewhere, the tonnage of this fleet was about

In other words, the total tonnage employed in the costal trade of India amounted to 340,000 at the dawn of the seventeenth century.

30,000 tons. On November 28, 1612, he saw a flotilla of 120 Portugal frigates bound for Goa (cf. Lancaster's Voyages, pp. 194, 196).

[12] The Portuguese captured, in 1612, 120 small vessels, and ten great ships, one whereof was the *Rehemi* of 1500 tons. The tonnage will therefore be $120 \times 50 = 6000$ plus *Rehemi* of 1500 tons plus $9 \times 400 = 3600$; total being 11,100. This tonnage was captured at one time; some must have remained uncaptured in the Bar and many ships must be out on the sea. Three Indian ships were also seen ready for Sumatra at the port of Surat by Downton (Lancaster's Voyages, p. 166).

Captain Sharpeigh informs us that forty to fifty Portuguese frigates ordinarily lay at the Bar of Surat in summer, so that no boats should go in and out without their license (*ibid.*, p. 113).

Now read Wheeler's opinion on the Surat shipping: "The Moghul shipping lay pretty close together in the Surat river. Some of the vessels were more than a thousand tons burden. *Altogether there were more than a hundred good ships, besides smaller vessels.*" On the basis of such-like evidences, do we not err on the side of gross underestimation in fixing the Surat trade at 20,000 tons only?

[13] Twenty to thirty ships large and small—Frederick; then Pipli, Balasore, and Hari Harpura, city of six to seven miles in compass, were busy ports, though not visited by the travellers whose accounts have been quoted.

[14] This is an understatement, because we know that the rice export alone was very considerable. Pyrard says that "One sees arrive there every day *an infinite number of vessels* from all parts of India for these provisions" (I, 327).

Thirty to forty ships went to Cochin alone.

Thirty to forty ships returned with cowries from Maldives (Pyrard I, 237–38).

Ships to and from the Southern Islands, Ceylon, Pegu, Siam, etc.

The Bengal vessels were generally of great burden, resembling the Chinese and Arabian junks. Hence their tonnage can be taken to be 500 tons per ship.

To this Haven of Angeli come every year many ships out of India, Nagapatan, Sumatra, Mulacca, and divers other places (Ralph Fitch, p. 182).

In the end, the reader should fully weigh the pregnant words of Nicolo Conti who speaks of Indian merchants as "very rich," so much so that some will carry on their business *in forty of their own ships*, each of which is valued at 15,000 *gold pieces.*"

CHAPTER II

Appendix A

Exports by the East India Company between 1601 *and* 1619 *inclusive.*

	Money.	Goods.	Ships sent out.	Re-turned.
1601	£21,742	£6,860	4	4
1603	11,160	1,142	4	3
1606	17,600	7,280	3	3
1607	15,000	3,400	2	—
1608	6,000	1,700	1	1
1609	28,500	21,300	3	1
1610	19,200	10,081	4	4
	£119,202[1]	£51,763	21	16
1611	£17,675	£10,000	4	3
1612	1,250	650	1	1
1613	18,810	12,446	5	2
1614	13,942	23,000	9	4
1615	26,660	26,065	8	6
1616	52,087	16,506	7	3
1617 }			9	1
1618 }	298,000	152,000	9	1
1619 }			8 60	0 20
Total for 19 years	£547,626	£292,430	81	36

Ships remaining 31, lost, worn, and taken by the Dutch 14.[2]

	Money.	Goods.	Ships sent out.	Re-turned.
1620–21[3]	£62,490	£28,508	10	1
1621–22	12,900	6,523	4	1
1622–23	61,600	6,430	5	5
1623–24	68,720	17,345	7	5
	£205,710	£58,806	26	12
Total for 23 years	£753,336	£351,236	107	48

[1] Milburn's figures, £119,022, are obviously a misprint.

[2] Home Misc., 39, p. 124. Printed in full by Danvers, Marine Records, introduction.

[3] Moreau's E.I. Company's Records; Macpherson's Commerce with India, p. 110.

It is not easy to reconcile the returns of ships for the years 1622 and 1623 in the preceding statement of the Company with those given by Sainsbury in his Calendar of State Papers. They are also contradictory to another account presented in October, 1623, by the Company themselves, according to which the outgoing ships and their tonnage were as under :—

Year.	No. of ships.	Tonnage in all.
1623	3	710
1624	4	1610
1625	7	3820
1626	6	2140
1627	3	1130
	23	9410

(Calendar, IV, pp. 558–59.)

Comparing this statement with the following one based on the shipping list at the end of Part II, we find that there is an ultimate correspondence in the number of ships, but a great divergence in their tonnage, although the latter is in every case based on the Company's own records. It appears that the Company's return for the year 1623–24 in their Report to Parliament in 1625, includes the ships that have been shown as sailing in the year 1624 in the two tables preceding and succeeding these lines :—

Year.	No. of ships.	Tonnage.
1623	3	950
1624	4 (excluding pinnaces)	2350
1625	6	2930
1626	7	3500
1627	3	1550
	23	12,280 tons.

The Report of 1625 is again contradictory to another statement made by the Company to Parliament in 1621, wherein it was stated that there had been sent forth 86 ships to the Indies in the term of twenty-one years. According to the former statement, the number of ships ought to have been 95 and not 86. In short, even contemporary evidence does not confirm the validity of the table under discussion.

APPENDIX B

Wylde's Statement of the Company's Trade from 1624 *to* 1629.

	1624.	1625.	1626.	1627.	1628.	1629.
The Company sent out for Surat in money and goods	£62,000	£36,000	£90,710	£64,700	£61,345	£61,000
And from Bantam was sent in goods	—	30,061	25,486	6,541	7,378	—
Received in all for this year's investment in goods for England	62,000	66,061	116,196	71,241	68,723	61,000
	—	3,445	39,265	4,077	6,400	—
Whereof was sent to Persia in goods and money .	6,225	1,792	19,413	11,889	2,800	—
And to Bantam in Goods	13,253	—	—	6,094	6,676	5,400
And to Mocha ,, ...	705	5,310	5,817	4,763	3,547	2,500
Disbursed at Surat for Customs	7,786	6,318	4,876	5,626	1,973	2,000
Ship's expenses for provisions	5,985	—	2,256	3,916	3,375	150
House expenses in all factories	2,945	401	265	360	1,225	4,500
House rent ,, ,, ...	—	7,998	4,152	10,352	165	1,250
Charge merchandise	5,097	3,832	1,350	1,350	910	900
Factors' wages on the shore	2,230	633	698	2,964	—	—
Presents in all the factories	—	—	—	—	—	—
Disbursed in all	£58,296	£29,929	£78,092	£51,391	£27,071	£16,700
There remained for Investments for the next year .	£3,703	£10,632	£38,104	£19,850	£41,652	£44,300

APPENDIX C

Exports from England from 1624 *to* 1657.

1624 £62,000 To Surat alone (Wilde's statement).

1625 80,000 Court Minutes in Calendar, IV, p. 284.

1626 90,710 To Surat alone (Wilde's statement).

1627 64,700 To Surat alone (Wilde's statement).

1628 61,000 To Surat alone (Wilde's statement).
£21,000 in goods and £40,000 in money (cf. Court Bk., 10, p. 202; Calendar, IV, p. 458).

1629 200,000 Calendar, IV, p. 652, besides provisions of which the charge was above £15,000.
£61,000 was for Surat (Wilde's statement).

1630 150,000 On the *James*, *William* and *Blessing;*
100,000 On the *Mary*, *Exchange*, *Speedwell* and *Hopewell* (Eng. Factories, Vol. 1630–33, pp. vii, xvi).
Cargoes of the *Dove* and *Star* not found (cf. Eng. Factories, Vol. 1630–33, p. 113).
84,171 Should be added to the preceding sums on the evidence of the Court Minutes, wherein it is stated that from 1617 to 1628 there had been sent £1,145,442 in money and goods. Adding up the sums shown against these years in our list, we find a deficiency of £84,171 (Calendar, IV, p. 616).

1631 160,700 Letter Bk., I, p. 78. Cargoes of the *Palsgrave* and *London* not included in this sum. Out of it, goods were worth £43,000.

1632 22,454 Letter Bk., I, 130. Cargo of the *Swan*.

1633 80,386 £61,400 in money and the rest in goods on the *Palsgrave*, *Discovery* and *Reformation* (Eng. Factories, Vol. 1630–33, p. 28).
£66,459 in money according to Calendar, V, p. 373. Resolved to send £160,000 to the Indies (Court Bk., 13, pp. 49, 110.

1634 95,000 Money only (Calendar, V, p. 554).

1635 162,780 £29,450 on the *Swan*; £11,000 on the *Coaster*; £122,330 on the *William* and the *Crispian* (Letter Bk., I, pp. 130, 135).

1636 40,342 £10,342 on the *Hart* (Letter Bk., I, p. 82).
£30,000 on the *Mary* (Court Bk., 16, p. 149).

1637 31,719 £30,719 on the *Eagle* and the *Jonas* (Letter Bk., I, p. 170). One chest of Crusadoes was ordered on the Advice (Court Bk., 16, pp. 203, 249).

1638 22,000[1] On the *Discovery*, no information for the *Jewel* which had indeed a small stock. W. Foster mentions 20,000 Ryalls on the *Discovery*, but it really carried out 80,000 Ryalls worth £20,000 (Foster's Court Minutes, Vol. 1635–39, p. xxv. See Letter Bk., I, p. 170).

1639 42,427 £28,427 on the *Reformation*, *Hopewell* and the *Advice*. £20,000 in money was allowed to be exported on the *Hopewell*, *London* and the *William*: £6,000 was on the *Hopewell* (Court Bk., 17, pp. 41, 46, 65. Foster's C. Minutes, Vol. 1635–39, p. 304).

---

[1] This is all the shipping and stocks which you may this year expect from us for some reasons best known unto ourselves (Letter Bk., I, p. 170).

1640	£50,000	On the *Jonas*, *Crispian* and the *Swan* (Court Bk., 17, pp. 127, 130). £35,000 were for Surat.
1641	95,000	£35,000 or £36,000 for Surat (Court Bk., 17, pp. 324, 331). £10,000 for the Coast (Court Bk., 17, pp. 300, 326). £50,000 for Bantam (Court Bk., 17, p. 294).
1642	82,928	£16,064 on the *Blessing* (Fac. Rec. Misc., 12, p. 62). £58,864 on the *Crispian* and *Aleppo Merchant* (Fac. Rec. Misc., 12, p. 69). £8000 on the *Ulysses* (Court Bk., 18, p. 153). For cargo on three ships of Courten (Fac. Rec. Misc., 12, p. 59).
1643	92,130	£80,000 or £100,000 to be sent (Court Bk., 18, p. 221). 80 chests of silver on five ships. £70,000 quick stock on the *Dolphin*, *Hind* and the *Seaflower* (Court Bk., 18, p. 278). £22,130 were on the *Hart* and the *Mary* (Fac. Rec. Misc., 12, p. 89).
1644	50,000	or £60,000 resolved to be sent in money (Court Bk., 19, p. 246).
1645	60,000	£40,000 for Surat and £20,000 for Bantam (Court Bk., 19, p. 146).
1646	60,000	Money only (Court Bk., 19, pp. 423, 438, 443).
1647	80,000	£52,000 for Surat (Court Bk., 20, pp. 26–27).
1648	116,000	Court Bk., 22, pp. 4, 20, 38, 43, 48. In all, £129,673 were spent for this year's investment.
1649	70,000	Money alone (Court Bk., 20, p. 302).
1650	102,000	Sent by the U. Stock alone (Court Bk., 20, pp. 501, 507).
1651	70,000	Court Bk., 23, pp. 3, 23, 27.
1652	30,000	Money to be shipped (Court Bk., 23, pp. 65, 101).
1653 [1]	481	on the *Dove*; no information regarding the *William* (Letter Bk., I, p. 208).
1654	7,372	Letter Bk., I, pp. 231, 246, 259; Court Bk., 23, pp. 320, 340.
1655	4,215	Letter Bk., I, p. 278. Cf. Court Bk., 23, pp. 386, 390.
1656	16,622	Letter Bk., I, pp. 323, 334, 339. £17,000 sent (Court Bk., 23, pp. 463–64).
1657	None	

Appendix D

Eastern Imports into England.

1601–21	£2,004,600	Company's statement.
1620–23	1,255,444	Company's statement.
1624 .	120,000	Value of the cargo on the *Dolphin* (Calendar, III, p. 373).
1625 .	103,000	Value of the cargoes of the *Star* and the *Moon* (Calendar, IV, pp. 101, 121, 199).

[1] As a contrast to these figures, compare the statements of Wisset in his Compendium, II, p. 2, that in 1652–53–54, the exports amounted only to bullion, £8441, and goods, £3278. In 1655–56, the trade being open, there were no exports by the Company. In 1657 the Company exported in bullion £74,235 and in goods £2114. This is the only information after 1619 and that, too, is utterly wrong.

Year		Value	Particulars
1626	.	£360,000	Value of this year's imports (Calendar, IV, p. 284).
1627	.	. .	No information.
1628	.	180,000	Value of the cargo of the *William.*
		280,000	Value of the cargoes of the *Palsgrave, Dolphin* and *Discovery.*
		111,600	Value of the cargoes of the *Morris, Eagle* and the *Christopher.*
	Total	£571,600	Cost of their cargoes=£153,980 (Calendar, IV, p. 588; Eng. Factories, Vol. 1624–29, XXXV).
1629	.	53,437	Prime cost of the cargoes of the *Exchange, Blessing* and the *Star* (Calendar, IV, p. 657).
		51,150	Cost of the cargoes of the *Heart, Expedition* and *Hopewell* (Calendar, IV, pp. 657–58).
1630	.	. .	No information.
1631	.	170,000	Value of the cargoes of the *Charles* and the *Jonas* (Calendar, V, p. 156).
1632	.	70,000	Value of the pepper and cloves on the *Palsgrave;* no information for the *London* (Court Bk., 13, pp. 14, 92, 94).
1633	.	303,000	Value of the cargoes of the six ships: Pepper= £150,000; Cloves=£66,000; Sugar=£87,000 (Calendar, V, p. 460).
1634	.	58,000	Value of the cargo of the *Dolphin;* no information about two ships (Court Bk., 15, pp. 32, 58, 92–94).
1635	.	. .	No information in Court Bk., 16, p. 30.
1636	.	100,000	Value of the cargo of the *Palsgrave* wrecked in Plymouth.
		100,000	Value of the cargo of the *Discovery* (Court Bk., 16, pp. 215, 246).
1637	.	49,309	Cost of the cargoes of the two ships from Bantam. O. C. 1582, 1588. No information for the *William* from Surat.
1638	.	. .	None arrived.
1639	.	68,701	Cost of the cargoes of the *Swan* and *Mary.*
		150,000	Value of the cargo of the *Mary* (Court Bk., 17, p. 127).
1640	.	40,800	Value of the cargo of the *Discovery* (Eng. Factories, Vol. 1637–41, p. 220).
1641	.	127,507	Value of the *Crispian* (Home Misc., 39, p. 162).
1642	.	. .	No information.
1643	.	139,000	Value of the *Crispian* and the *Aleppo Merchant* for £51,000 stock sent out.
		34,000	Value of the *Reformation* (Court Bk., 19, p. 8).
1644–45	.	.	No information.
1646	.	2,229	Prime cost with charges of the cargo on the *Eagle* (Court Bk., 20, p. 52).
1647	.	100,000	Insurance policy for returning ships (Court Bk., 19, p. 194).
1648	.	80,000	Insurance policy for returning ships (Court Bk., 20, p. 199).
1649	.	. .	No information.
1650	.	50,000	Prime cost of the cargoes of the *Eagle, Anne, Greyhound* and *Farewell* (Court Bk., 20, p. 535).
1651	.	90,000	Insurance policy (Court Bk., 21, p. 100).
1652	.	40,000	Insurance policy (Court Bk., 21, p. 173).
			No information for the remaining years.

CHAPTER III

Appendix A

The Dutch Trade at Surat in 1622–23.

Memorandum of the merchandise asked for and wanted yearly at Surat, Agra, Cambaia and surrounding countries and its prices :—

100,000 Rs. of 8.

100,000 florins in Moorish or Hungarian golden ducats, quantity gold in bars, for the gold soon gives a profit and can easily be transported without duty or risk.

			Mamudi.
200,000–250,000 lbs. of clove are sold	one Man/30 lbs. Holland weight at		200–210
40–50 sachel of mace	,,	,,	40–50
40–50 picul of sandal-wood	,,	,,	25–50
20,000–30,000 lbs. of ivory	,,	,,	30–60
100,000 lbs. of lead	,,	,,	½
2,000–3,000 lbs. of tortoise-shell	,,	,,	150–200
4,000–5,000 lbs. of China-root	,,	,,	10–20
1,000–2,000 lbs. of quicksilver	,,	,,	180–200
1,000–1,500 lbs. of vermilion	,,	,,	180 200
40–50 boxes of red coral, according to its quantity.			
100 bahars of sapan-wood	,,	,,	9–10
10,000–20,000 lbs. of spionter	,,	,,	18–20
3,000–4,000 lbs. of benzoin, good quality	,,	,,	50–60
Camphor	,,	,,	50–60
Tin	,,	,,	35–40
Copper	,,	,,	25–26
Pepper	,,	,,	16–17
Wax	,,	,,	30–35

Large quantity of earthen and China ware.

20–24 pieces of fine scarlet.

6–8 ,, Italian gold cloth.

10–12 ,, velvet.

10–12 ,, satin.

Gold lace.

Some pictures, nicely painted landscapes

2–3 nice clocks, antique rings for women, nice pearls, fine falchions, 2 or 3 fine and large *English* bull-dogs.

This 29 December, 1622, at Suratte.

A mamody=10 stivers (Holl.). (signed)

P. Van den Broecke.

(Dutch Records, Vol. IV, clxvii).

APPENDIX B

Progress of the Dutch Trade.

(*a*) An account of the returns made from the East Indies to Holland, from the time the Dutch traded thither, down to the year 1724, specifying the number of ships every year and the *invoice amounts of their cargoes* :—

Years.	Ships.	Value in Florins.
1599–1613	77	13,100,000
1614	2	433,526
1615	5	511,672
1616	5	566,064
1617	4	573,007
1618	8	1,305,544
1619	5	1,074,047
1620	6	913,137
1621	6	1,094,030
1622	8	1,776,792
1623	8	1,301,909
1624	6	832,836
1625	4	983,461
1626	10	1,926,019
1627	7	1,748,099
1628	7	2,050,367
1629	7	1,132,263
1630	9	2,541,215
1631	7	1,506,669
1632	7	2,099,772
1633	7	1,861,409
1634	7	1,947,270
1635	6	2,050,037
1636	8	1,895,349
1637	8	2,673,201
1638	7	1,670,071
1639	8	3,079,413
1640	10	2,842,405
1641	10	2,906,117
1642	9	3,485,192
1643	10	3,227,882
1644	7	2,070,667
1645	8	2,921,806
1646	9	2,529,611
1647	10	2,151,033
1648	12	2,073,630
1649	9	2,243,106
1650	9	1,946,417
1651	11	2,699,991
1652	11	2,813,438
1653	16	4,745,239
1654	4	379,035
1655	10	2,467,112
1656	10	2,711,914
1657	10	3,023,855
1658	10	3,005,275
1659	10	1,782,783
1660	11	3,195,319
1661	9	2,133,791
1662	9	3,354,429
1663	10	3,324,894
1664	12	2,528,825
1665	13	3,643,492
1666	7	1,124,180
1667	12	3,119,060
1668	16	3,155,683
1669	19	4,026,481
1670	19	5,024,150
1671	18	5,186,414
1672	15	4,023,998
1673	7	1,688,316
1674	9	1,836,015
1675	14	3,549,518
1676	15	4,127,657
1677	15	3,575,483
1678	11	2,459,739
1679	12	3,889,605
1680	11	3,386,577
1681	13	5,110,897
1682	8	2,987,190
1683	11	4,909,309
1684	15	5,080,391
1685	14	4,193,729
1686	16	5,568,644
1687	16	5,630,940
1688	15	4,305,812
1689	15	3,092,896
1690	17	3,839,469
1691	8	2,400,104
1692	12	4,246,879
1693	15	3,336,236
1694	12	2,988,927
1695	15	5,154,468
1696	12	3,532,244
1697	19	5,410,517
1698	19	5,373,256

Years.	Ships.	Value in Florins.	Years.	Ships.	Value in Florins.
1699	17	5,321,290	1712	21	6,111,822
1700	18	5,298,741	1713	17	4,684,643
1701	20	6,293,703	1714	21	5,260,128
1702	21	6,725,962	1715	27	7,730,000
1703	18	6,177,447	1716	28	6,825,290
1704	21	5,382,196	1717	28	7,299,512
1705	18	4,603,338	1718	24	7,175,000
1706	17	4,719,600	1719	30	8,352,000
1707	15	4,248,532	1720	26	7,600,000
1708	18	5,219,729	1721	34	10,235,000
1709	18	5,477,439	1722	26	—
1710	21	5,732,998	1723	29	8,800,000
1711	20	5,311,869	1724	31	—

(Stavorinus, III, pp. 526–31.)

(*b*) Account of the number of ships sent out by the E.I. Company of Holland, the number of men and the amount of specie they carried, the number of ships returned, and the proceeds of sales, from 1720 to 1729 :—

Years.	Ships sent out.	Crews.	Specie thous. Florins.	Ships returned.	Proceeds of Sales. Florins.
1720	36	8,205	4,125	26	19,597,875
1721	40	8,000	6,825	34	14,985,073
1722	41	7,400	7,075	26	19,494,366
1723	38	7,785	6,887	29	16,247,506
1724	38	6,425	7,419	31	20,577,447
1725	35	6,250	7,412	36	19,385,441
1726	38	6,850	7,675	32	21,312,626
1727	40	6,400	8,092	36	18,564,987
1728	34	5,800	5,558	28	20,322,402
1729	34	6,390	4,525	25	18,100,117
Total for 10 years	374	69,505	65,593	303	188,587,840
Annual average=	$37\frac{1}{2}$	6,950	6,559,300 Florins.	30	18,858,784 Florins.

Ratio, 100 : 288.

(Stavorinus, III, p. 532.)

(*c*) Account of the number of ships returned from the Indies, with the invoice-prices and net proceeds of their cargoes for the ten years from 1750 to 1759 :—

Years.	Invoices. Florins.	Sales. Florins.	Ships.
1750	7,372,177	19,024,209	22
1751	9,630,682	16,670,614	24
1752	7,883,361	23,133,580	20
1753	10,259,866	17,317,037	22
1754	8,859,297	19,840,766	22
1755	9,652,485	19,806,077	22
1756	8,421,419	19,890,066	25
1757	8,935,720	14,829,367	26
1758	6,506,717	18,934,386	22
1759	8,437,469	18,817,328	28
Total for 10 years	85,959,193	188,263,430	233
Annual average =	8,595,919	18,826,343	23

Ratio, 100 : 219.
(Stavorinus, III, pp. 419–20.)

(*d*) Prices of the Dutch E.I. Company's stock :—

Years.	Prices.	Years.	Prices.	Years.	Prices.
1723	654	1743	350	1763	407
1724	603	1744	407	1764	374
1725	614	1745	470	1765	406
1726	658	1746	368	1766	593
1727	560	1747	434	1767	580
1728	655	1748	366	1768	518
1729	628	1749	423	1769	472
1730	715	1750	489	1770	412
1731	692	1751	603	1771	314
1732	779	1752	580	1772	369
1733	644	1753	559	1773	323
1734	754	1754	555	1774	336
1735	645	1755	515	1775	340
1736	756	1756	404	1776	340
1737	532	1757	555	1777	355
1738	585	1758	458	1778	380
1739	494	1759	386	1779	357
1740	506	1760	414	1780	328
1741	391	1761	390		
1742	403	1762	323		

(Stavorinus, III, pp. 538–39.)

APPENDIX C

Profits made in the Indo-Asiatic Trade.

A valuation of certain goods bought at *Surat* in India in December, 1629, and sold at Gombroon in Persia, February, 1630, viz. :—

	Profit.		Profit.
Sugar	90%	Gunderoon	47%
Green ginger	70	Blue Chunders	40
Indigo	50	Pentadoes	35
Rice	50	Dry ginger	75
Cotton-wool	120	Narrow Baftas	40
Mirobalanes	70	Broad ,,	40
Shashes	50	Blue Baftas	40
Sarai Benjamin	100	Sugar candy	75
Cardamum	60	Salarmoniac	65
Soap	80	Pincadies	35
Blue conches	40	Red Selcis	70
Tobacco	400		

A valuation of goods bought at *Gombroon* in February, 1629, and sold at *Surat* in 1629–30 :—

	Profit.		Profit.
Runas	50%	Royals (Rials)	8
Walnuts	100	Raisins	8
Wormseed	30	Almonds, large	30
Gold Cheekens	4	Pistaches	5
Almonds	50	Rosewater	20
Galls	50	Abareez	1½
Horses	Three for one	Rhubarb	20
Pearls	20	Assafoetida	12
Silk	12	Brimstone	30
Carpets	10	Lapis lazuli	20

Boothby sold pearls in England at five for one and diamonds at six for one, that is, made a *profit of* 400 *and* 500 *per cent respectively.*

Persian commodities made four for one profit in England.

He gives the instance of one Podemsee, a Hindu merchant, who *brought pearls to the value of* 10 *millions sterling from Persia.*

"*From Surat to Goa,* trade produces 30, 40, and 50 per cent in numerable of many divers sorts of commodities, which the Portuguese bring to Surat ; and at Cambay, 100 sale of frigates laden yearly, which I have seen, and know to be true, and *from Goa to Surat,* produces 20, 25, and 30 per cent and for cinnamon and dolium-indium 50 per cent."

From Surat to Masulipatam, Persian commodities will produce 30, 40, and 50 per cent.

From Surat to Bantam even the worst commodities produce 70 or 80 per cent; cloth 100 to 110 per cent; cotton, wool, soap, cummin seed, mustard seed, and wheat produce 8, 9, *or* 10 *for one profit.*

Persia commodities there yield 1½ and 2 for one.

From Bantam, most of these commodities are transported to Achim, Tickoo, Priaman, Jambu, Japara, Macassar, and China, which produce *one, two, three, and four for one profit.*

Surat to China: English broadcloth and kersies 20–24 *for one profit*; indigo, narrow and broad baftas, blue byrams, cankeens 6, 8, 10 *for one profit;* white pepper, cloves, maces, nutmegs, and other goods 3, 4, 5, 6 *for one profit;* China gold 40–45, 50 per cent profit in India.

Surat to Mocha: Tobacco 10–12 for one; rice 6–7 for one; chinaware 4–5 for one; spices 2 for one; sugar, candy, ginger, cotton, cardamum, soap 2–3 for one; various cloths 100 per cent.

Mocha commodities at Surat yield 2 for one and upwards.

(Boothby's Brief Discovery of Madagascar, London, 1644).

These profits can fully explain the great loss suffered by the Indian merchants by the growing participation of the Europeans in the Asiatic commerce.

CHAPTER IV

Appendix

A view of the Pepper Trade and its Profits from 1616 *to* 1630.

Pepper Bought for the First Joint Stock.

Year.	Ships.	Quantity.	Total value.	Value per lb.
1615–16, Jan. 10	N. Y. Gift	783,062	Rs.23,450	5d.
1616, Oct. 15	Dragon	828,685	23,920	2½d.
,, ,, 16	Expedition	32,560	736	1½d.
,, ,, 17	Clove	501,187	19,318	2¼d.
1616–17, Feb. 23	Peppercorn	385,625	17,279	2¾d.
1617–18, Jan. 17	Charles	1,050,750	52,345	3d.
1618, May 12	L. James	281,940	18,651	4d.
,, ,,	Hope	432,750	27,174	3¾d.
		4,296,559	Rs.192,873	2¾d.

Pepper Bought for the Second Joint Stock.

Year.	Ships.	Quantity.	Total value.	Value per lb.
1620–21, Jan. 31	James R.	980,125	Rs.75,855	4¾d.
1621, Nov. 30	Charles	822,500	62,640	4½d.
,, Feb. 18	Eagle	366,250	31,336	5d.
,, ,, 28	Star	426,125	40,559	5¾d.
1622, Aug. 29	L. James	546,875	43,618	4¾d.
,, Feb. 5	Palsgrave	510,375	40,135	5d.
1623, Dec. 12	Exchange	839,674	63,308	4½d.
,, ,,	Elizabeth	818,334	69,120	5d.
1623–24, Feb. 22	Anne	898,625	68,970	4¾d.
1624–25, Jan. 26	Moone	881,379	66,600	4½d.
,, ,,	Discovery	687,915	63,991	5½d.
,, ,,	Ruby	581,625	47,317	5d.
,, ,, 31	Charles	1,029,695	63,450	3¾d.
,, ,,	Harte	652,475	48,217	4½d.
1626–27, Feb. 8	London	818,500	51,617	3¾d.
,, ,,	Reformation	419,280	33,185	4½d.
1627, July 18	Expedition	311,250	19,831	3¾d.
1627–28, Feb. 13	Morris	516,125	27,728	3¼d.
,, ,,	Eagle	324,375	17,815	3¼d.
1628–29, Feb. 5	Mary	854,470	57,045	3½d.
,, ,,	Speedwell	210,585	11,532	3½d.
1629–30, Feb.	London	790,125	52,565	4d.
		14,286,678	Rs.1,057,334	4½d.

The difference of the *advance of price* betwixt the First and Second Joint Stocks is 1¾d.

Pepper Sold for the First Joint Stock.

Quantity sold.	Price.	Total value.	Ships.
751,616	26d.	£82,168/13	N. Y. Gift
1,955,306	26d.	212,961/8	Dragon, Expedition, Clove, Peppercorn
1,312,516	22d.	119,228/10	Charles, Hope
229,562	18d.	17,072/9	L. James
4,249,000	24½d.	£431,431	

Pepper Sold for the Second Joint Stock.

Quantity sold.	Price.	Total value.	Ships.
984,395	19d.	£80,263/8	James R.
1,642,229	19½d.	134,580/18	Charles, Eagle, Star
546,875	17½d.	40,474	L. James
510,375	17½d.	37,565	Palsgrave
1,400,000	20d.	117,000	Exchange, Elizabeth
1,152,000	18d.	86,400	Discovery, Ruby
1,515,000	18d.	113,625	Charles, Harte
1,559,000	16d.	115,500	London, Reformation, Expedition
933,000	16d.	62,200	Mary, Speedwell
776,940	15d.	46,626	London
11,019,814	18d.	£830,238	

The difference of the *sale prices* between the First and Second Joint Stocks is 6¼d. per lb. (Home Miscellaneous, Vol. 39). The averages and totals seem to be incorrect, but we have preserved the figures of the original record.

CHAPTER V

Appendix A

Total Annual Values of Exports from England separately for Goods and Bullion to the East.

Year.	Money.	Total Goods and Money.
1658–59	£242,304	£305,750
1659–60[1]	22,768	63,996
1660–61	151,077	188,033
1661–62	100,940	126,148
1662–63	91,224	138,330
1663–64	125,435	169,513
1664–65	24,130	55,010
1665–66	17,007	37,607
1666–67	1,000	3,967
1667–68[2]	143,384	206,453
1668–69	132,167	202,919
1669–70	199,678	282,340
1670–71	207,648	346,309
1671–72	197,883	304,093
1672–73	not stated	182,612
1673–74[3]	177,938	238,805
1674–75[4]	325,517	440,551
1675–76	324,039	448,193
1676–77	189,290	288,249
1677–78	289,140	363,773
1678–79	340,884	387,725
1679–80	391,474	461,211
1680–81	524,197	596,657
1681–82[5]	708,909	835,313

[1] In the face of these figures, the returns given by Milburn, Macgregor and Wisset for the years 1658, 1659, and 1660 are totally incorrect. According to them, the total value of the Co.'s exports was £251,583 and consisted of bullion, £227,820, and goods, £23,763.

[2] The Co.'s account of bullion shipped to India from 1667–68 to 1673–74 differs from mine, though it is compiled from the Co.'s books. The discrepancy can only be explained by supposing that the under-mentioned statement might have been made by taking the year to begin in June and not in May as is done in my list based on the figures given in the Court Book, 25*a*. The annual returns made by the Co. were :—

1667–68 . .	£128,606	1671–72 . .	£186,420
1668–69 . .	£162,394	1672–73 . .	£131,300
1669–70 . .	£187,458	1673–74 . .	£182,983
1670–71 . .	£186,150		

(Bruce's Annals, ii, p. 353.)

APPENDIX B

Ships, Goods, and Bullion sent to India by the Company from London during the following years.

Years.	Ships sent from England to the East Indies. No.	Tons.	Goods and Bullion Exported.
1680–81	10	4,975	£346,213
1681–82	23	9,100	834,496
1682–83	21	8,625	515,216
1683–84	22	10,880	482,147
1684–85	14	5,545	520,341
1685–86	13	7,776	649,299
1686–87	6	5,320	298,958
1687–88	6	2,908	157,491
1688–89	2	875	30,239
1689–90	4	955	131,692
1690–91	6	2,589	125,101
1691–92	7	2,786	143,728
1692–93	5	2,510	171,812
1693–94	15	5,858	677,616
1694–95	9	3,855	395,391
1695–96	7	3,126	228,622
1696–97	4	1,870	115,570
1697–98	9	3,605	388,658
1698–99	14	5,550	590,914
1699–1700	12	5,086	592,753
1700–1	7	2,675	452,716
1701–2	9	2,985	317,293
1702–3	12	4,730	220,223
1703–4	13	4,195	411,745
1704–5	17	5,025	349,711
1705–6	9	2,420	198,138
1706–7	9	3,120	333,245
1707–8	15	5,130	502,983
1708–9	10	3,410	550,358
1709–10	13	4,550	513,733

(Macgregor's Commercial Statistics, Vol. IV, p. 410.)

[3] Mark the exaggeration of the author of "Discourse on Trade," London, 1680, when he asserts that from 2nd March, 1673, to 11th March, 1674, £560,000 were exported by the Company. P. 340.

[4] The same author calculates £400,000 as the exports of private traders in 1674–75 against £120,000 to £150,000 by Sir J. Child. Cf. Child's statement that the exports in this year were £320,000 in money and about £110,000 in goods.

[5] This year's returns are taken from the B. Museum MSS., Jurc Impt., 15,898, p. 134.

APPENDIX C

Money and Principal Commodities Exported from England to the East.

(Compiled from the Custom House Books.)

Year.	Money.	Iron, English.	Lead.	Woollens.	Coral.	Iron, Foreign.
1698	£399,230	£3,194	£4,838	£19,870	£3,267	£5,087
1699	832,795	10,418	10,501	91,862	6,162	1,950
1700	807,683	6,354	6,870	86,590	2,156	1,438
1701	725,592	4,819	5,687	88,055	1,397	2,106
1702	410,762	3,973	3,351	63,851	541	1,460
1703	303,012	3,443	7,899	162,734	108	—
1704	451,277	2,411	9,129	103,731	2,120	3,010
1705	Missing	—	—	—	—	—
1706	231,500	543	5,195	15,952	—	715
1707	313,283	46	8,896	38,315	—	2,035
1708	362,459	3,827	6,224	34,112	3,656	2,535
1709	506,469	1,753	4,921	146,351	52	3,275
1710	228,102	5,511	5,069	92,245	1,247	3,776
	£5,572,164	£46,292	£78,580	£943,668	£20,706	£27,387

APPENDIX D

Number of Ships that sailed to the East with their approximate available Tonnage.

Years.	SURAT. Ships. No.	SURAT. Total Tonnage.	FORT & BAY. Ships. No.	FORT & BAY. Total Tonnage.	BANTAM. Ships. No.	BANTAM. Total Tonnage.
1658–59	9	2,820	13	4,090	3	1,025
1659–60	1	240	5	1,660	1	240
1660–61	4	1,575	6	2,100	5	1,640
1661–62	4	990	4	975	2	400
1662–63	2	760	3	1,020	2	680
1663–64	3	1,175	5	1,240	2	800
1664–65	2	470	3	805	1	included in Coast.
1665–66	1	370	2	475	none	
1666–67	1	140	none	—	none	
1667–68	4	1,100	7	2,600	3	1,050
1668–69	3	960	5	1,390	2	825
1669–70	4	1,560	6	1,680	4	1,550
1670–71	5	2,010	5	1,730	10	2,945
1671–72	4	1,670	5	2,000	9	3,000
1672–73	Separate returns not available					

	SURAT.		FORT & BAY.		BANTAM.	
Years.	Ships. No.	Total Tonnage.	Ships. No.	Total Tonnage.	Ships. No.	Total Tonnage.
1673–74	4	1,550	5	1,980	4	1,730
1674–75	5	1,750	6	2,410	4	1,600
1675–76	5	2,340	5	2,140	6	2,690
1676–77	3	1,480	3	1,610	6	2,450
1677–78	3	1,460	4	2,120	6	3,140
1678–79	3	1,480	3	1,685	2	1,150
1679–80	3	1,560	4	2,280	3	1,600
1680–81	3	1,500	5	2,690	3	1,400
1681–82	8	3,405	8	4,180	7	1,720
	84	32,365	112	42,860	84	31,635

APPENDIX E

Distribution of English Exports in India and other Asiatic Countries during 1658–81.

	SURAT.		COAST & BAY.		OUTSIDE INDIA.	
Years.	Money. In £1000	Total. In £1000	Money. In £1000	Total. In £1000	Money. In £1000	Total. In £1000
1658–67	302½	498	540	660	130	143
1668–77	403	953	1228½	1402½	269½	346½
1678–81	461½	620	1322⅔	1399⅔	180	261
	1167	2071	3091	3462	579½	750½

Percentage proportion of the share of each centre in

Exported Money	24%	64%	12%
,, Goods	62½%	25½%	12%
Total Exports	33%	55%	12%

Note.—The exports of the year 1672 are altogether excluded from this total, as the sums sent to these centres in that year are not given separately. Moreover, the separate returns for Bantam in the years 1671, 1676, and 1677 are not complete, hence the aggregates of money and goods given in this section differ from those given in Appendix A of this chapter.

Appendix F

The Number of Ships and their Tonnage chartered by the Company which were annually sent to the various centres in the Indies.

Year.	SURAT. No.	SURAT. Tonnage.	BAY & COAST. No.	BAY & COAST. Tonnage.	BANTAM. No.	BANTAM. Tonnage.
1682–83	3	870	10	5,055	5	1,485
1683–84	18	8,650	8	3,480	2	540
1684–85	5	1,380	7	3,370	2	550
1685–86	5	2,383	11	3,590	8	2,230
1686–87	3	730	3	1,810	4	1,460
1687–88	4	1,850	5	2,045	5	1,300
1688–89	2	810	2	1,435	—	—
1689–90	2	1,218	—	—	—	—
1690–91	2	970	1	225	3	1,130
	44	18,861	47	21,010	29	8,695
1698	5	2,260	10	4,063	5	1,340
1699	8	3,070	12	4,590	5	1,450
1700	2	800	4	1,600	6	2,182
1701	3	750	5	2,280	15	4,053
1702	4	1,593	2	1,200	11	3,460
1703	3	1,240	3	1,175	9	2,780
1704	3	1,020	3	1,180	9	2,820
1705	2	550	2	775	3	585
1706	1	300	3	1,250	5	1,470
1707	4	1,720	6	2,110	7	2,030
	35	13,303	50	20,223	75	22,170

Appendix G

Total Stock sent to the three centres.

Year.	Surat.	Bay and Coast.	China and other places.
1698	£245,687	£515,272	£54,183
1699	275,293	467,351	100,981
1700	110,337	484,835	644,949
1701	13,947	346,711	248,406
1702	146,488	300,000	94,968
1703	126,599	182,455	177,030
1704	83,596	138,469	115,672
1705	47,364	135,840	47,373
1706	9,119	220,488	98,486
1707	115,759	306,209	105,054
	£1,174,189	£3,097,630	£1,687,102
Per cent Ratio	20 :	52 :	28

CHAPTER VI

Appendix A

Orders for the Provision of Cloth.

Year.	Fort. Thous. pieces.		Bay. Thous. pieces.	Surat. Thous. pieces.	Reference.
1658	86		8	88	L. Bk. II, pp. 2, 14, 16, 18, 24
1659–60	72		18	—	L. Bk. II, p. 197
1660 Sept.	—		17	72	L. Bk. II, pp. 335, 339–40
1661	103		15	135	L. Bk. III, pp. 57, 84
1662	—		—	96	L. Bk. III, p. 161
1663	130		17	145	L. Bk. III, pp. 293–94, 356
1664	—		—	55	L. Bk. III, p. 424
1669	—		—	298	L. Bk. IV, p. 322
1670	—		—	290	L. Bk. IV, p. 434
1671	—		—	376	L. Bk. IV, p. 532
1672		158*		148	L. Bk. V, pp. 23–24, 32, 67
1673	205		56½	294	L. Bk. V, pp. 94–95, 100–1, 104–5
1674–75	253		72½	284	L. Bk. V, pp. 148, 154, 175, 268
1675–76	306		84½	321[1]	L. Bk. V, pp. 219–21, 237–39, 269
1676–77	204		97	346	L. Bk. V, pp. 418, 445–48, 489, 493
1677–78	186		104	353	L. Bk. V, pp. 507–9, 538
1678–79	452		123½	344	L. Bk. VI, pp. 24–26, 36, 60, 100–3
1679–80	616		99	—[2]	L. Bk. VI, pp. 126–27, 244
1680–81	612		207	408[3]	L. Bk. VI, pp. 264–66, 408
1681	605		229	536	L. Bk. VI, pp. 411, 466
1682	1342		667	1436[4]	L. Bk. VII, pp. 20–21, 30–31
1683	1236		718	568	L. Bk. VII, pp. 227, 249–51, 357–58
1684–85		517*		285	L. Bk. VII, p. 474
1686–87	151		175	175	L. Bk. VIII, p. 248
1687–88	293		282	257[5]	L. Bk. VIII, pp. 400–2, 431–37
1688	655		397	619[6]	L. Bk. VIII, pp. 557–59, 568–70
1693	458		418	305	L. Bk. IX, pp. 312–14, 320–23
1694	386		454	560	L. Bk. IX, pp. 405–9, 416–18

[1] These quantities were found too great, hence they were reduced to 179, 96 and 254 respectively (Letter Bk., V, pp. 307, 310–11).

[2] 194,000 more pieces ordered both from Coast and Bay have been added to the Coast order.

[3] 20,000 yards of sail-cloth were also ordered from the Coast.

[4] 227 bales of new kinds of stuffs were also ordered from the Bay.

[5] 40,000 yards of sail-cloth more ordered from the Coast.

[6] 100,000 shifts of sail-cloth more ordered from the Coast.

* Separate orders for Bay and Coast goods are not available.

Appendix B

Imports of Tea.

Year.	Quantity	Particulars	
1664	2 lbs. 2 ozs.	Sold at £4 5s.	
1665	$22\frac{3}{4}$ lbs.	Sold at 50s. per lb.	
1669	143 lbs. 8 ozs.		
1670	79 lbs. 6 ozs.		
1671	266 lbs. 10 ozs.		
1673–74	55 lbs. 10 ozs.	Bought by the Company from some English coffee-house.	
1675–77	No imports.		
1678	4,717 lbs.		
1679	197 ,,	from Bantam.	
1680	143 ,,	,, Surat.	
1681	None.		
1682	70 lbs.	from India.	Sold from 11s. 6d. to 12s. 4d. per lb. (1678–1686)
1683–84	None.		
1685	12,070 lbs.	from Madras and Surat.	
1686	65 ,,		
1687	4,995 ,,	,, Surat.	
1688	1,666 ,,	,, ,,	
1689	25,300 ,,	,, Amoy and Madras.	
1690	41,471 ,,	,, Surat.	
1691	13,750 ,,	permission trade.	
1692	18,379 ,,	from Madras and in the permission trade.	
1693	711 ,,	,, ,, ,, ,, ,,	
1694	352 ,,	,, ,, ,, ,, ,,	
1695	132 ,,		
1696	70 ,,		
1697	22,290 ,,	from India.	
	126 ,,	,, Holland.	
1698	21,302 ,,	,, India.	
1699	13,201 ,,	,, ,,	
	20 ,,	,, Holland.	
1700	90,947 ,,	,, India.	
	236 ,,	,, Holland.	
1701	66,738 ,,	,, India.	
1702	37,052 ,,	,, ,,	
1703	77,974 ,,	,, ,,	
1704	63,141 ,,	,, ,,	
1705	6,739 ,,	,, ,, and Holland.	
1706	137,748 ,,	,, ,,	
1707	32,209 ,,	,, ,,	
1708	138,712 ,,	,, ,,	
1709	98,715 ,,	,, ,,	Sold at 11s. 11d. per lb. on the average. (1708–1710)
1710	127,298 ,,	,, ,,	

(Compiled from Milburn's Oriental Commerce, Vol. II, pp. 531–34.)

APPENDIX C

Quantities of Indigo ordered from India.

Year.	Agra Indigo.	Sarkhej Flat.	Sarkhej Round.
1657–58	600 bales.	500 bales.	100 bales.
1658–59	200 ,,		200 or 300 both.
1659–60	None if not at 18d. per lb.	None if not at 9d. per lb.	
1660–63	None.		
1664	300 bales at Re.1	100 bales at 1 mah. per lb.	
1669	400 bales at cur. price.	200 bales at 1½ mah. per lb.	
1670	600 or 800 bales at 2 mah.	300 bales at cur. price.	
1671	600 bales at cur. price.	400 bales at 1 mah.	
	1,200 bales at 2 mah.		
1672 } each year	400 bales at cur. price.	150 bales at cur. price.	
1673 } each year	800 bales at 2 mah.	200 bales at 1 mah.	
1674	600 bales at cur. price.	150 bales.	
	900 bales at 2 mah.		
1675 } each year	400 bales at cur. price.	100 bales if under 1 mah.	
1676 } each year	800 bales at 1¾ mah.		
	1,200 bales at 1½ mah.		
1677	400 ,,	100 bales.	
1678 } each year	400 bales at cur. price.	100 bales at 9d. per lb.	
1679 } each year	200 bales at 2 mah.		
	100 ,, if dearer.		
1680	400 ,, at 18–24d.	120 bales at 9d. per lb.	
	200 ,, if dearer.		
1681	800 ,, at 18–24d.	150 bales at 9d.; none if dearer.	
	600 ,, at a rup.		
	400 ,, if dearer.		
1682	800 ,, at 18d.	130 bales at 9d. or else none.	
	600 ,, at 24d.		
	400 ,, at cur. price.		
1683	16,000 lbs. at 18d.	260 bales.	
	12,000 ,, at 24d.		
1684	800 bales.	240 bales.	
1685	600 ,,	70 ,,	
1687	300 ,,	70 ,,	
1688	600 barrels.	140 barrels, the whole lot being equal to 123½ shipping tons.	
1689	1,000 ,,	300 barrels.	

(Compiled from the Letter Books.)

APPENDIX D

Cargo of the "Martha" from Fort St. George, and of the "Anna" from the Bay of Bengal, arrived the 30th of August, 1699.

	Pieces.		Pieces.
Atlasses	828	Mobut bannies	810
Adittaes	644	Mullmulls	3,630
Allibannies	50	,, flowered	181
Allajaes	200	Neckcloths	800
Bettellees	12,340	,, flowered single	2,800
,, striped	2,100	Pallampores	100
Chints	5,780	Percallaes Book	160
Cossaes	6,149	Pegue	570
Chautars	167	Photoas	205
Callowaypoose	500	Raftaes	309
Chucklaes	1,072	Romalls	1,685
Chuckreaes	1,600	Sail-cloth	1,155
Dimities	130	Sallampores	18,000
Doreas	3,763	,, blew	1,360
Elatches	276	,, brown	4,620
Ginghams	6,300	Salpecadoes	200
,, coloured	557	Saderunches	100
Gurrahs	4,977	Sacerguntes	400
Goacon Cherulaes	200	Sallbafts	1,441
Jamwars	110	Seersuckers	1,091
Jamdhunies	136	Shirts	22,320
Izzarees	120	Soofeys	3,105
Longcloth	15,840	Taffaties	5,409
,, blew	2,610	,, striped	284
,, brown	1,100	Tanjeebs	6,444
Lungees	418	,, flowered	90
Moorees	2,400	Tepoys	446
	lbs.		lbs.
Cakelack	1,500	Red wood	121,000
Cotton yarn	18,900	Raw silk	9,400
Floretta yarn	9,000	Saltpetre	500,000
Opium	2,500	Shellack	3,300
Pepper	254,000	Sticklack	8,400

(B. Museum, Sloane MS., 2902, pp. 145, 147.)

Cargo of the "Russel" Frigate, from Bombay, arrived the 15th of April, 1700.

	Pieces.		Pieces.
Atlas Culgies	192	Mamoodies	120
Bafts, broad	2,697	Niccannees	1,366
,, narrow	1,135	Pallunpores	3,740
,, broadblue	200	Quilts	3,410
Chints	13,540	Quiltings	219
Cuttanees	613	Sovaguzzees	845
Deribands, large	2,639	,, Blew	120
,, small	7,200	Tapsiels	840
Guinea stuffs	3,100	Taffaties	101

	lbs.		lbs.
Aloes Soccatrina . .	300	Pepper	191,600
Coffee	3,300	Saltpetre	1,800
Cotton yarn . . .	45,500	Seedlack	4,200
Olibanum	43,800		

(B. Museum, Sloane MS., 2,902, p. 145.)

Cargo of the Surat-Gally arrived from China the 20th of July, 1700.

	Pieces.		Pieces.
Damasks	30	Pictures on paper . .	2,413
,, with gold flowers .	10	Fans	65,980
Golongs, white and striped .	430	Fire-fans	424
Pelongs, Nankeen . .	7	Screens, pairs . . .	2
Quilts ,, with G.F. .	8	Scriptores . . .	22
Sattins ,, . .	284	Large tables . . .	81
,, with gold flowers .	53	Tea tables . . .	2,848
Velvets	118	Lacker'd chests . .	266
Paintings on pelongs . .	115	Lacker'd wares of divers	
,, gauze . .	12,200	sorts	6,517

	lbs.		lbs.
Borax	106	Quicksilver . . .	4,353
Cambogium . . .	797	Raw silk	16,005
Copper	45,798	Sango	1,322
Cloves	358	Singlo tea	30,063
Green ginger . . .	250	Bohee tea	1,163
Pepper	112,070		

China ware, pcs. . .	146,748	Gold, ounces . . .	129
Jambee canes . . .	44,394	Musk in cod, ounces . .	228

(B. Museum, Sloane MS., 2902, p. 146.)

CHAPTER VII

Appendix A

Values fixed at various periods for the purposes of Customs as given in the Books of Rates.

Articles.	1590.	1660.	1697.	1714 & 1757.
Callicoes, fine or course	15s.	10s.	10s.	10s.
,, Cambricke—				
½ peece of 6 × ½ ells	£2 10s.	£1	10s.	10s.
The peece of 13 ells	£5	£2	10s.	10s.
Dimity, per yard	2s.	3s.	3s.	3s.
Dutties, the peece	£1	£1	£1	£1
Aloes Scotrina, per lb.	5s.	Same throughout.		
Benjamin ,,	£3	,,	,,	
Bezor stone, E.I., oz. troy	£3	£3	£1 10s.	£1 10s.
Opiam, per lb.	10s.	Same throughout.		
Cloves ,,	10s.	,,	,,	
Pepper ,,	3s. 4d.	3s. 4d.	1s. 8d.	1s. 8d.
Maces ,,	£1	Same throughout.		
Nutmegs ,,	8s.	,,	,,	
Sinamon ,,	6s. 8d.	,,	,,	
Sugar, St. Thomé, cwt. of 112 lbs.	£2	,,	,,	
,, white, per cwt.	£9	£7 6s. 8d.	Same throughout	
,, ,, from Eng. plantations	—	£5	,,	,,
,, brown	—	£1 10s.	,,	,,
Indigo, Turkey, W.I., or rich	6s. 8d.	3s. 4d.	,,	,,
,, dust	3s. 4d.	1s. 8d.	,,	,,
,, English plantations	—	1s.	,,	,,
Pintadoes, the peece	6s. 8d.	Same throughout.		
Quilts of callico, the peece	£2	,,	,,	
Rice, per 112 lbs.	£1 6s. 8d.	,,	,,	
Saffron, per lb.	£1 10s.	,,	,,	
Silk ferret or floret, 16 ozs.	£1	,,	,,	
,, China raw, 24 ozs.	£1 13s. 4d.	£1	Same throughout.	
,, Morea ,,	10s.	Same throughout.		
,, Bengal ,,	—	10s.	Same throughout.	
,, wt., E.I., per lb. in Eng. bottoms	different prices.	15s.	15s.	Prohibited
,, ,, ,, For. ,,		£1	£1	,,
Wool cotton of Eng. plantations	—	Free.	Free.	Free.
,, ,, not of ,, ,,	—	4d.	Same throughout.	
Yarn cotton, per lb.	1s.	Same throughout.		

Note.—The spelling used in the Book of Rates of 1590 has been used here.

These values have been compiled from the following Books of Rates :—

Book of Rates, 1590, British Museum Lib.
,, ,, 1660, Board of Customs Lib.
,, ,, 1697 ,, ,,
,, ,, 1714 ,, ,,
,, ,, 1757 ,, ,,

APPENDIX B

Annual Returns of Imports compiled from the Manuscript Volumes of Imports and Exports in the Public Record Office, London.

Year.	Pepper. lbs.	Coffee. lbs.	Wool. lbs.	Saltpetre. cwts.
1698	988,825	499	31,414	9,571
1699	19,573,933	244,252	34,930	1,964
1700	2,689,957	144,693	69,339	15,033
1701	2,792,546	388,993	74,517	6,374
1702	1,253,599	293,391	—	4,239
1703	413,947	143,164	—	4,841
1704	2,307,296	615,938	52,248	11,887
1705	Missing.	Missing.	Missing.	Missing.
1706	1,055,526	3,451	21,256	24,033
1707	1,538,766	39,112	4,302	28,555
1708	982,860	228,914	36,652	18,598
1709	2,039,092	14	26,358	7,748
1710	377,023	80,080	272	8,535
1711	1,717,512	752,381	117,417	12,446
1712	Missing.	Missing.	Missing	Missing.
1713	901,397	822,003	—	15,828
1714	2,157,749	1,404,928	38,890	14,662
1715	1,281,942	513,760	24,696	9,177
1716	1,166,449	335,718	19,041	8,625
1717	1,362,401	317,085	62,469	8,943
1718	2,787,642	1,124,207	129,233	18,155
1719	259,416	1,017,545	—	4,663
1720	4,563,295	573,664	115,442	15,018
1721	855,404	738,235	32,806	13,426
1722	1,096,314	1,991,083	80,106	4,733
1723	917,155	1,905,007	2,224	7,491
1724	1,362,059	2,037,056	56,804	15,390
1725	884,962	1,675,616	—	6,066
1726	2,145,086	805,625	14,287	3,496
1727	1,443,280	1,361,383	36,965	20,589
1728	Missing.	Missing.	Missing.	Missing.
1729	954,895	830,248	54,433	8,113
1730	800,632	1,616,996	44,242	8,522
1731	1,759,045	74,614	41,119	7,122
1732	1,304,488	1,096,910	41,629	17,458
1733	2,528,852	822,368	100,840	20,074

Year.	Pepper. lbs.	Coffee. lbs.	Wool. lbs.	Saltpetre. cwts.
1734	1,265,808	1,017,673	17,465	8,402
1735	3,930,701	1,184,726	211,234	27,712
1736	2,175,182	1,032,440	95,894	18,129
1737	3,144,626	1,001,290	41,773	14,005
1738	1,939,439	1,003,395	—	7,338
1739	3,182,950	1,116,135	95,292	18,506
1740	1,712,396	1,103,063	—	12,963
1741	2,571,381	1,303,597	19,635	33,854
1742	4,599,061	575,370	—	49,529
1743	2,583,557	477	23,442	39,371
1744	3,181,956	26,584	—	24,393
1745	4,314,620	1,040,947	—	26,989
1746	2,770,390	49,562	26,639	17,153
1747	2,257,216	1,053,662	16,070	12,764
1748	1,976,064	841,872	16,408	19,060
1749	3,863,437	1,017,242	20,036	25,977
1750	1,526,733	1,164,628	1,425	2,079
1751	2,229,325	1,148,805	—	12,941
1752	2,843,348	9,881	—	19,689
1753	947,846	1,180,844	1,380	14,865
1754	2,622,231	1,187,380	14,807	18,821
1755	3,838,504	2,152,048	17,030	32,586
1756	334,678	14	—	14,793
1757	4,645,439	1,046,432	71,229	23,505
1758	—	—	—	942
1759	4,068,924	971,464	19,987	22,510
1760	3,133,884	186	75,543	37,786

APPENDIX C

Year.	Calicoes White.	Year.	Calicoes White.
1698	247,214	1719	2,038,451
1699	853,034	1720	1,299,685
1700	951,109	1721	1,144,466
1701	826,101	1722	718,678
1702	320,273	1723	1,115,011
1703	674,968	1724	1,291,614
1704	654,312	1725	793,704
1705	Missing.	1726	838,063
1706	841,461	1727	1,161,935
1707	521,371	1728	Missing.
1708	502,906	1729	1,077,704
1709	480,292	1730	1,125,805
1710	361,162	1731	865,422
1711	980,002	1732	709,632
1712	Missing.	1733	1,114,584
1713	892,174	1734	821,130
1714	1,049,064	1735	1,325,815
1715	880,953	1736	1,096,538
1716	620,228	1737	835,818
1717	676,062	1738	727,158
1718	1,220,324	1739	1,398,915

Year.	Calicoes White.	Year.	Calicoes White.
1740	907,233	1751	1,193,093
1741	1,188,260	1752	938,772
1742	1,372,402	1753	795,745
1743	880,007	1754	960,391
1744	688,206	1755	736,219
1745	998,926	1756	499,818
1746	967,204	1757	638,505
1747	457,010	1758	224,953
1748	892,619	1759	746,331
1749	1,071,523	1760	988,709
1750	818,115		

Year.	Wrought Silk, Bengal.	Stained Calicoes.	Sooseys.
1698	57,269	—	—
1699	24,445	—	—
1700	116,455	—	—
1701	115,504	—	—
1702	10,518	—	—
1703	21,785	—	—
1704	73,033	—	—
1705	—	—	—
1706	39,340	—	—
1707	3,220	—	—
1708	2,330	—	—
1709	56	—	—
1710	8,709	—	—
1711	3,834	—	—
1712	Not available.	—	—
1713	34,054	2,234	10,468
1714	34,487	42,220	17,439
1715	30,623	81,735	1½
1716	2,318	28,813	4,717
1717	4,804	44,945	165
1718	78,641	40,242	2,137
1719	27,470	19,792	7,970
1720	33,144	147,022	22,647
1721	55,491	139,125	19,454
1722	18,439	129,032	4,301
1723	58,729	106,754	5,099
1724	59,324	149,468	3,653
1725	54,358	116,265	1,860
1726	71,601	181,318	10,400
1727	79,602	240,510	24,317
1728	Not available.	—	—
1729	61,421	141,173	17,090
1730	61,971	68,953	7,128
1731	32,392	149,907	8,099
1732	127,073	212,035	9,652
1733	124,486	256,144	23,171
1734	68,094	136,080	13,286
1735	119,856	338,072	29,481
1736	56,180	232,021	19,749
1737	13,384	165,741	17,903

Year.	Wrought Silk, Bengal.	Stained Calicoes.	Sooseys.
1738	37,250	154,851	16,541
1739	73,858	215,360	15,299
1740	45,437	151,665	12,596
1741	51,301	376,785	12,632
1742	62,612	324,422	151,001
1743	42,867	331,465	11,772
1744	40,536	317,064	19,578
1745	58,524	313,659	19,219
1746	14,204	206,339	9,112
1747	43,233	134,151	13,451
1748	36,002	261,051	17,649
1749	5,777	349,147	56,282
1750	17,561	203,913	25,411
1751	28,029	178,594	14,310
1752	47,156	177,732	12,393
1753	47,646	175,445	949
1754	71,591	212,085	447
1755	54,374	198,608	1,338
1756	27,902	72,698	463
1757	28,382	237,471	2,186
1758	5,114	11,376	—
1759	30,403	205,023	4,332
1760	51,108	212,910	665

APPENDIX D

Year.	Raw Silk, Bengal. lbs.	China Silk. lbs.
1698	36,534	—
1699	16,931	—
1700	85,242	—
1701	40,217	—
1702	33,169	—
1703	330,755	—
1704	306,887	—
1705	Not available.	—
1706	67,567	—
1707	19,751	—
1708	84,921	849
1709	57,768	—
1710	35,332	—
1711	46,672	11
1712	—	—
1713	13,408	3,662
1714	31,238	9,494
1715	40,307	14,936
1716	56,114	7,006
1717	97,370	—
1718	159,292	23,700
1719	52,212	—
1720	56,854	512
1721	20,084	—

Year.	Raw Silk, Bengal. lbs.	China Silk. lbs.
1722	16,062	—
1723	88,134	8,964
1724	131,491	29,705
1725	114,141	13,003
1726	91,017	2,184
1727	134,919	—
1728	Not available.	—
1729	82,821	4,550
1730	127,361	—
1731	78,561	11,272
1732	108,964	47,481
1733	176,188	12,333
1734	151,626	—
1735	191,587	—
1736	112,624	—
1737	152,665	—
1738	135,548	—
1739	160,599	2,677
1740	126,755	—
1741	154,312	—
1742	103,081	2,361
1743	76,427	—
1744	118,422	3,545
1745	117,953	47,667
1746	33,112	2,116
1747	101,145	1,903
1748	70,733	12,408
1749	22,773	5,301
1750	43,876	—
1751	35,524	61,041
1752	87,379	119,555
1753	70,203	83,124
1754	29,156	124,378
1755	58,866	124,245
1756	8,312	82,291
1757	16,675	149,283
1758	—	18,103
1759	29,627	65,142
1760	101,985	75,693

APPENDIX E

Year.	Cotton Yarn. lbs.	Diamonds. £	Dimity. Yards.	Guinea Stuffs. Pieces.
1698	—	—	—	—
1699	204,378	—	—	—
1700	165,453	92,108	—	—
1701	146,987	36,456	—	—
1702	97,537	23,414	12,663	—
1703	52,267	1,989	76,129	—
1704	166,640	12,287	26,974	—
1705	Missing.	Missing.	Missing.	—
1706	44,725	3,405	4,338	—
1707	299,642	27	3,670	—
1708	46,846	6,774	54	—
1709	—	42	82	—
1710	—	—	134	—
1711	102,134	500	638	—
1712	—	—	—	—
1713	38,875	36,216	153	41,927
1714	148,051	24,419	176	6,091
1715	39	—	27	—
1716	—	46,833	108	2,880
1717	—	—	468	—
1718	8,485	81,736	782	—
1719	21,741	1,900	12	—
1720	22,047	300	480	19,803
1721	47,447	4,000	2,144	4,881
1722	11,237	3,500	1,391	39,113
1723	27,725	24,000	11,519	30,155
1724	32,455	30,000	8,817	86,792
1725	8,580	42,500	8,075	82,095
1726	46,766	51,500	9,501	104,245
1727	29,352	49,500	7,716	7,157
1728	Missing.	Missing.	Missing.	Missing.
1729	18,436	48,500	3,711	—
1730	31,614	58,500	15,596	—
1731	21,023	27,500	14,008	—
1732	45,963	3,500	34,799	—
1733	69,952	Not available.	10,947	9,750
1734	17,945	—	2,413	—
1735	115,697	—	15,079	70,688
1736	35,599	—	7,649	6,100
1737	2,047	—	13,804	10,080
1738	3,443	—	29,276	4,480
1739	8,256	—	40,880	23,770
1740	—	—	47,391	Not available.
1741	22,338	—	41,877	—
1742	19,224	—	51,165	—
1743	20,727	—	39,040	—
1744	20,242	—	38,479	—
1745	4,981	—	28,245	—
1746	1,557	—	19,115	—
1747	—	—	28,442	—
1748	360	—	23,131	—

Year.	Cotton Yarn. lbs.	Diamonds. £	Dimity. Yards.	Guinea Stuffs. Pieces.
1749	9,036	—	15,749	—
1750	5,819	—	1,907	—
1751	5,216	—	8,506	—
1752	371	—	19,038	—
1753	3,727	—	9,843	—
1754	41,210	—	21,451	—
1755	39,637	—	21,740	—
1756	6,101	—	271	—
1757	18,906	—	16,758	—
1758	1,007	—	8	—
1759	17,427	—	25,707	—
1760	6,673	—	39,360	—

Note.—Dimity, both white and painted cloths, imported into England are included in the returns under Dimity.

Diamonds.—There are no returns for diamonds after 1732. It would appear that the import was altogether stopped through the direct channel. Probably they came through the Dutch and French. The import of garnet stones becomes prominent instead. There are no returns for Guinea stuffs after 1739, showing that none were imported into the country. It appears that their place was to some extent taken by Bombay stuffs.

APPENDIX F

Year.	Ginghams.	Lungees.	Nillas.	Pallampores.
1698	2,258	7,374	18,264	848
1699	1,380	5	—	—
1700	7,616	418	10,004	11,322
1701	15,359	—	17,341	23,508
1702	647	—	681	563
1703	4,985	6,129	11,354	655
1704	1,489	2,446	3,697	498
1705	Not available.	Not available.	Not available.	Not available.
1706	483	327	1,200	10,560
1707	74	90	93	18
1708	2,502	—	4,955	—
1709	996	4,020	4,462	3
1710	—	48	—	—
1711	1,364	1,440	4,177	1,897
1712	Missing.	Missing.	Missing.	Missing.
1713	11,960	15,526	28,073	2,151
1714	2,621	2,985	7,378	244
1715	—	—	—	—
1716	6	—	316	96
1717	—	—	—	—
1718	2,964	—	2,598	34
1719	3,161	2,230	4,926	12
1720	9,433	6,554	10,824	245
1721	8,616	7,755	12,479	62

Year.	Ginghams.	Lungees.	Nillas.	Pallampores.
1722	2,012	6,545	3,937	47
1723	2,104	4	7,689	23
1724	392	—	7,726	9
1725	1,322	238	2,346	24
1726	4,356	1,726	7,311	31
1727	10,191	2,418	16,849	910
1728	Missing.	—	—	—
1729	6,649	120	10,354	252
1730	5,469	—	12,137	113
1731	4,085	—	4,403	128
1732	2,609	—	4,644	386
1733	1,956	—	13,109	167
1734	82	—	521	23
1735	7,601	1,001	7,573	153
1736	2,900	1,293	5,011	375
1737	2,551	401	7,067	62
1738	2,810	399	9,445	52
1739	2,606	1,955	11,827	38
1740	1,314	601	7,807	51
1741	2,888	—	13,679	14
1742	2,321	600	13,833	231
1743	1,704	—	11,276	111
1744	1,518	—	5,134	53
1745	1,005	—	5,708	92
1746	983	—	5,986	195
1747	236	—	2,423	6
1748	790	—	8,990	24
1749	1,833	—	14,717	129
1750	240	—	6,206	168
1751	243	3	3,148	54
1752	384	—	2,686	317
1753	86	—	2,540	72
1754	786	145	2,195	53
1755	324	585	1,784	34
1756	—	—	—	20
1757	294	427	445	13
1758	—	—	—	—
1759	376	447	833	68
1760	1,550	444	3,892	34

APPENDIX G

Year.	Penniascoes.	Shalbaftas.	Taffetas.	Indigo.
1698	8,187	1,333	3,586	1,999
1699	—	2,605	554	950
1700	1,566	7,492	8	73,240
1701	4,030	3,376	1,099	132,363
1702	—	50	1,874	227
1703	382	—	2,600	—
1704	—	—	1	75,133
1705	—	—	—	—
1706	—	—	—	29,041

Year.	Penniascoes.	Shalbaftas.	Taffetas.	Indigo.
1707	433	4	—	200,552
1708	—	—	—	145,958
1709	513	7	1,231	—
1710	—	—	—	43,180
1711	1,580	—	710	254,819
1712	Missing.	—	—	—
1713	9,094	6,752	2,614	63,837
1714	3,626	1,802	1,265	81,567
1715	—	—	—	233
1716	—	—	—	—
1717	—	—	—	—
1718	1,196	—	236	—
1719	1,125	—	1,947	—
1720	6,051	2,557	6,380	—
1721	5,865	1,919	16,975	—
1722	1,901	278	2,455	—
1723	—	—	4	33
1724	—	—	118	21,209
1725	421	154	1	2,158
1726	1,406	736	2,157	705
1727	6,155	1,704	2,602	31,415
1728	Missing.	—	—	—
1729	2,679	673	1,543	60,920
1730	6,171	345	—	—
1731	5,214	163	—	—
1732	446	—	54	—
1733	525	933	2	—
1734	—	—	1	—
1735	1,523	1,157	6	9
1736	1,175	1,432	—	—
1737	2,027	1,030	2	147
1738	2,465	964	1	—
1739	2,149	609	—	—
1740	1,004	1,001	816	4,067
1741	3,051	821	—	2,901
1742	2,997	—	171	2,941
1743	1,799	—	20	—
1744	1,131	—	3	23
1745	—	—	—	—
1746	—	—	—	—
1747	11	—	—	73
1748	1	—	24	—
1749	2	—	1	—
1750	9	—	—	—
1751	—	5	3	—
1752	—	—	1	154
1753	60	—	—	—
1754	352	—	44	6,903
1755	753	329	351	—
1756	—	—	420	—
1757	197	269	371	11,535
1758	—	—	—	—
1759	287	722	307	11,636
1760	578	220	—	47

APPENDIX H

Per cent Prices of the East India Stock.

Year.		Note	Year.	
1661	90– 94		1693	146– 90
1664	—		1694	97– 66
1665	60– 70		1695	93– 50
1668	130		1696	67– 38
1669	108–130		1697	65– 47
1670	111		1698	75– 33¼
1672	80		1699	59– 41
1677	245		1700	142– 58½
1680	300–245		1701	119– 75½
1681	365–460		1702	120– 77¾
1682	150–260	Prices of the Doubled Stock	1703	134–106¾
1683	170–122½		1704	139½–117¼
1684	210		1705	128½– 93½
1685	500–360		1706	$123\frac{3}{1}$– 87½
1690	300		1707	115¾–103¾
1691	200–158		1708	108¾– 98¼
1692	158–131		1709	105 –104½

Prices of the Stock of the New Company.

Year		Year	
1699	50¾–106½	1705	258¼–234
1700	154 –126	1706	260 –238½
1701	140½–100	1707	272 –254½
1702	161 –125¾	1708	258½–240¼
1703	219 –151¾	1709	114 –112
1704	260 –202½		

(Scott's Joint-Stock Companies, Vol. II, pp. 177, 179, 189.)
(Roger's History of Agriculture and Prices in England, Vol. VI, pp. 721–25.)

CHAPTER VIII

Appendix A

Decennial Totals of the Exports of Bullion to

Years.	Bombay.	Madras.	Bengal.
1708–17	£652,978	£1,616,614	£772,520
1718–27	797,727	1,561,238	1,331,529
1728–37	475,001	1,825,894	1,063,447
1738–47	447,499	2,169,066	1,702,908
1748–57	1,075,161	2,541,498	1,835,629
	£3,448,366	£9,714,310	£6,706,033

Decennial Totals of the Exports of Merchandise to

Years.	Bombay.	Madras.	Bengal.
1708–17	£336,657	£319,661	£159,619
1718–27	392,357	303,970	227,163
1728–37	400,052	324,125	511,347
1738–47	565,612	326,183	643,478
1748–57	900,048	581,652	826,825
	£2,594,726	£1,855,591	£2,368,432

Total Bullion and Merchandise Exported to

Years.	Bombay.	Madras.	Bengal.
1708–17	£989,635	£1,936,275	£932,139
1718–27	1,190,084	1,865,208	1,558,692
1728–37	875,053	2,150,019	1,574,794
1738–47	1,013,111	2,495,249	2,346,386
1748–57	1,975,209	3,123,150	2,662,454
	£6,043,092	£11,569,901	£9,074,465

(Based on Parliamentary Paper No. 152 of 1813.)

Appendix B

Amount of the Principal Articles of Co.'s Export in the under-mentioned periods, viz.:

Years. Periods from	Woollens.	Lead.	Copper.	Iron.	Tin.	Stores.
1708–20	£963,574	£74,399	—	£53,977	£32,806	£162,507
1721–30	699,334	71,681	—	54,100	3,596	143,341
1731–40	804,024	125,455	173,513	65,632	—	229,548
1741–50	1,190,201	133,251	242,395	72,520	—	198,287
1751–60	1,768,749	127,816	750,873	62,823	—	428,477
	£5,425,882	£532,602	£1,166,781	£309,052	£36,402	£1,162,160

Years. Periods from	Foreign Goods.	Charges.	Total Merchandise.	Bullion.	Total.
1708–20	£33,389	£38,163	£1,358,815	£5,516,907	£6,875,722
1721–30	48,248	34,922	1,055,222	5,274,742	6,329,954
1731–40	99,273	36,064	1,534,023	4,822,018	6,356,027
1741–50	121,065	49,546	2,010,265	6,257,194	8,267,459
1751–60	109,749	51,876	3,300,363	5,661,028	8,961,391
	£414,724	£210,571	£9,258,688	£27,531,889	£36,790,553

(Based on Parliamentary Paper No. 152 of 1812–13, and Macgregor's Commercial Statistics, Vol. IV, p. 410.)

Appendix C

The Returns relating to the French Company.

Years.	Vessels returned.	Prix d'achat aux Indes.	Prix de vents en France.
1725–36	221	86,274,958 livres.	162,816,767 livres.
1737–46	159	94,851,921 ,,	179,731,336 ,,
1747–56	108	81,505,103 ,,	154,656,696 ,,
1757–66	59	39,660,087 ,,	64,887,906 ,,
1767–71	38	41,740,249 ,,	73,870,825 ,,
Total	585	344,032,318	635,963,530

Years.	Vessels sent out.	Yearly av. of such vessels.	Value of merchandise sent to India.
1725–36	252	21	24,313,790 livres.
1737–46	206	20½	28,919,349 ,,
1747–56	180	18	41,891,214 ,,
1757–66	96	9½	22,807,246 ,,
1767–71	28	7	13,699,694 ,,
Total	762		131,631,293

(Based on Abbé Raynal's Chart, IV, No. 2 Atlas.)

APPENDIX D

An Annual Statement of

Year.	PRICES OF INDIA STOCK. Lowest.	Highest.	BANK STOCK. Lowest.	Highes
1731	174	198	144	148
1732	154	178	147	152
1733	136	163	145	151
1734	135	149	132	140
1735	145	169	138	146
1736	169	178	148	151
1737	174	181	142	151
1738	121	176	140	145
1739	121	169	134	144
1740	104	164	138	144
1741	155	164	135	143
1742	157	178	136	143
1743	186	195	145	148
1744	168	194	142	148
1745	163	187	127	147
1746	154	184	124	136
1747	151	177	119	128
1748	156	184	118	129
1749	174	191	127	140
1750	184	188	131	136
1751	184	195	135	143
1752	187	195	141	148
1753	191	191	135	144
1754	182	192	129	135
1755	148	180	120	131
1756	133	145	115	121
1757	133	142	113	120
1758	132	148	117	122
1759	123	141	110	117
1760	134	142	106	114

APPENDIX E

Decennial Abstract of Imports (in thousand pieces).

Years.	Calicoes.	Stained calicoes.	Sooseys.
1697–1700	2,158	—	30
1701–10	5,183	—	53
1711–20	9,657	415	69
1721–30	9,267	1,273	63
1731–40	9,802	2,012	166
1741–50	9,334	{1,033 1,785	— 330
1751–60	7,723	1,682	37

Years.	Wrought silks.	Bengal raw silk.	Chinese raw silk.
1697–1700	109	182	—
1701–10	274	976	—
1711–20	249	553	59
1721–30	520	806	58
1731–40	698	1,395	74
1741–50	373	842	75
1751–60	391	438	903

Years.	Cotton yarn.	Pepper.
1697–1700	399	23,359
1701–10	855	12,761
1711–20	341	16,197
1721–30	254	10,460
1731–40	320	22,943
1741–50	104	29,644
1751–60	141	24,664

CHAPTER IX

Appendix A

Shipping Freights from 1626 to 1760.

1626	£50 per ton for indigo. £30 per ton for pepper. } Brought on the Co.'s ships for private account. (C. Bk. 9, p. 214.)
1627	£112 per ton of 2240 lbs. for indigo. £224 ,, ,, silk. £75 ,, ,, pepper and cotton-wool. £56 ,, ,, ginger and aloes. 2s. 6d. per piece of calico. } Co.'s rates on private trade. (C. Bk. 9, p. 423.)
1629	£40 per ton offered by the Co. for freight, but no tenders. (C. Bk. 10, p. 426.) £40 charged by the Co. to the Adventurers of the Persian voyages on their ships, viz. the *Discovery* and the *Reformation*, bound to Surat and Persia. (C. Minutes, April 13, 1629.)
1630–34	£40 charged by the Co. for the Persian voyages. (C. Bk. 13, p. 245.)
1635–40	No ships were freighted.
1639	The *Ænas* offered for £25 per ton, while it cost the Co. £35 per ton on their own ships. (C. Bk. 17, p. 25.)
1641	£20 per ton of 16 cwts. for pepper. £30 for calicoes, indigo, and other goods. (C. Bk. 18, pp. 36, 87.)
1642	£21 for pepper, 15 cwts. net to a ton. £21 for cloves, 10 cwts. net to a ton. (C. Bk. 18, p. 127.)
1643–45	No ships freighted by the Co.
1646 (?)	
1647	£17–£18 for Bantam. (C. Bk. 20, p. 412.)
1648	£25 for Surat and £20 for Bantam. (C. Bk. 22, p. 43.)
1649 (?)	
1650	£17–£18 for Bantam. (C. Bk. 23, pp. 88, 113.)
1651	£17 for gruff like pepper and saltpetre, and £21 for fine goods to Surat; £19 for gruff and £23 for fine goods to the Coromandel Coast. (C. Bk. 23, p. 75.)
1652 (?)	
1653	£17 and £18 for gruff and fine goods respectively to Bantam. £23 and £25 ,, ,, ,, Surat. £25 and £28 ,, ,, ,, the Coromandel.
1654	£25 and £28 for gruff and fine goods. (C. Bk. 23, pp. 345–6.)
1655 (?)	
1656	£17 and £21 for the Coast as well as Bantam.
1657	No ships sent.
1658–63	£18 and £22 respectively for gruff and fine goods to the Coast and Jambee. (C. Bk. 24, pp. 41, 188, 223.) £18 and £22 respectively for Surat. (C. Bk. 24, pp. 37, 56, 229.) £17 and £21 respectively for Bantam. (C. Bk. 24, pp. 28, 56, etc.)

1664 £21 and £25 for Bantam.

1665 { £21 10s. and £25 10s. for Bantam. (C. Bk. 24, p. 927.)
One month's more pay to ship's company on Surat ships. (p. 928.) }

1666 (?)

1666–68 £19 and £22 respectively for gruff and fine goods to all parts of the Indies. The ships were to serve in trade and war. (C. Bk. 25*a*, p. 35.)

1669–79 Not found.

1680 £18 and £20 for Surat, Bantam, and Amoy; £17 and £20 for Bantam and Amoy. (C. Bk. 32, p. 8.)

1681 £17 for Siam. (C. Bk. 32, p. 144.)

1682 { £17 and £20 for the Coast and Bay.
£12 and £14 for Bantam on square-sterned ships, English-built.
£10 and £12 for Bantam on round-sterned ships, English-built. These rates were fixed for the future.
£18 and £21 for Bengal. (Marine Misc. I, doc. i.) }

1683 { £16 and £19 to Surat and China. (C. Bk. 33, p. 40.)
£17 and £19 to the Bay. (C. Bk. 33, p. 69.)
£17 and £20 to Surat. (C. Bk. 33, p. 88.) }

1684 £17 and £20 fixed for the future for Surat ships. (C. Bk. 33, p. 61.)

1685 £18 and £21 to Priaman. (C. Bk. 33, p. 129.)

1686–87 No information.

1688 £18 and £21 to Surat before the outbreak of the European War. (C. Bk. 35, p. 226.)

1689–90 £27 and £30 to Surat, and £30 to the pepper settlements. (C. Bk. 35, pp. 228, 244.)

1691 £28 and £30 to Surat. (C. Bk. 36, p. 69.)

1692–93 £30 for both fine and gruff goods, for all parts. (C. Bk. 36, pp. 163, 193.)

1694 £34 for both fine and gruff goods for all parts. (C. Bk. 36, pp. 211–12.)

1695–96 £40 for both fine and gruff goods. (C. Bk. 37, p. 139.)

1697, Feb. £36 for both fine and gruff goods. (C. Bk. 37, p. 148.)

" Oct. £24 and £21 for fine and gruff goods respectively. (C. Bk. 37, p. 205.)

" Dec. £20 and £18 for fine and gruff goods respectively. (C. Bk. 37, p. 215.)

1698 £17 and £20 for gruff and fine goods to all places in the East. (C. Bk. 37, p. 309.)

1699–1700 { £17 and £20 for China, Coast, and Bay. (C. Bk. 37, p. 348.)
£18 and £21 for China, Coast, and Bay. (C. Bk. 37, pp. 35, 41, 42, 99.) }

1701 £15 for Bencoolen. (C. Bk. 38, pp. 41, 42, 99.)

	BOMBAY & SURAT.		COAST & BAY.	
Year.	Gruff.	Fine.	Gruff.	Fine.
1702	£30	£30	£30	£30
1703	33	36	33	36 & 30[1]
1704	33/10	36/10	33/10	36/10
1705	32	34	31	35
1706	—	—	30	33
1707	33	34	31	36
1708–11	34	33/10	30/10	37

[1] For pepper ships. C. Bk. 41, p. 141.

Year.	BOMBAY & SURAT. Gruff.	Fine.	COAST & BAY. Gruff.	Fine.
1712	£26	£27	£24	£29/10
1713	24/5	25	22	27/5
1714–17	23	24	21	26
1718	25	26	23	28
1719–20	26	27	24	29
1721	26	25/10	22/10	29
1722–32	24	25	22	27
1733–39	23	24	21	26
1740	32–33	33–34	30–31	35–36
1741	33	34	31	36
1742	32–31	33–32	30–29	35–34
1743	31	32	29	34
1744–47	34	35	32	37
1748	28	29	26	31
1749	27	28	25	30
1750	26/10	27/10	24/10	29/10
1751–52	27	27	24	30
1753–54	27	30	24	27
1755	28	31	25	28
1756	34/10	37	31/10	34
1757	36	39	33	36
1758	37	40	34	37
1759	38	41	35	38
1760–62	40	43	37	40

(Wisset's Compendium, Vol. II.)

APPENDIX B

A view of the number and aggregate Tonnage of Ships that sailed to the East Indies from 1601 *to* 1707.

Year.	No.	Tonnage.	Year.	No.	Tonnage.
1601	5	1,530	1623	3	950
1604	6	1,740	1624	7	2,900
1606	3	1,250	1625	7	4,230
1608	2	660	1626	7	3,500
1609	1	260	1627	7	2,190
1610	6	2,542	1628	4	1,560
1611	5	2,469	1629	5	2,600
1612	4	1,633	1630	6	2,900
1613	5	2,350	1631	14	7,720
1614	13	4,063	1632	1	400
1615	9	4,363	1633	5	2,430
1616	5	2,950	1634	5	2,170
1617	10	5,096	1635	4	2,260
1618	8	2,736	1636	2	1,300
1619	12	7,644	1637	3	1,600
1620	5	1,930	1638	2	750
1621	10	4,306	1639	5	2,490
1622	3	1,600	1640	5	2,500

Year.	No.	Tonnage.	Year.	No.	Tonnage.
1641	6	3,250	1677–78	13	6,720
1642	4	1,950	1678–79	8	4,260
1643	6	2,200	1679–80[1]	10	5,420
1644	4	1,910	1680–81[1]	11	5,430
1645	4	1,920	1681–82	23	9,160
1646	6	2,380	1682–83	19	7,700
1647	4	1,700	1683–84	28	12,980
1648	8	3,350	1684–85	14	5,300
1649	3	1,100	1685–86	27	9,783
1650	10	4,180	1686–87	10	4,020
1651	4	1,400	1687–88	14	5,195
1652	4	1,450	1688–89	4	2,245
1653	2	390		2 Private	
1654	3	1,050	1689–90	2	1,218
1655	1	260		1 Private	
1656	3	1,250	1690–91	6	2,325
1657	None by the Co.			1 Private	
1635–57	60 ships other than those of the Co. have been traced as having sailed to the East.		1691–92	7	3,510
			1692–93	6	3,400
			1693–94	10	3,640
			1694–95	8	2,830
			1695–96	10	4,310
1658–59	25	7,935	1696–97	5	1,420
	4 Private		1697–98	15	6,420
1659–60	7	2,140		4 Private	
1660–61	15	5,415	1698–99	13	5,025
1661–62	10	2,365	New Co.'s	6	2,338
1662–63	7	2,460	Private	1	300
1663–64	10	3,215	1699–1700	12	4,860
1664–65	5	1,275	New Co.'s	11	3,750
1665–66	3	845	Private	2	500
1666–67	3	840	1700–1	12	4,770
1667–68	14	4,750	New Co.'s	13	4,070
1668–69	10	3,175	1701–2	8	2,570
1669–70	14	4,790	New Co.'s	15	4,463
1670–71	20	6,685	1702–3	17	6,043
1671–72	18	6,670	1703–4	15	5,195
1672–73	10	4,130	1704–5	15	4,720
1673–74	13	5,260	1705–6	9	2,660
1674–75	14	5,760	1706–7	9	3,020
1675–76	16	7,170	1707–8	17	5,860
1676–77[1]	12	5,350			

Mill's account of the Company's shipping from 1689 to 1697 is summed up below to show the scanty and inaccurate information on this important subject :—

1689–90	3 ships.	1694–95	no information.
1690–91	small shipping.	1695–96	8 ships.
1691–92	no information.	1696–97	8 ships.
1692–93	11 ships.	1697–98	4 ships.
1693–94	13 ships.		

(Mill's *History of India*, Vol. I, p. 74.)

[1] The tonnage differs in Macgregor's Com. Stat., p. 44.

APPENDIX C

Equipment of the E.I. Company's Ships.

The under-named ships carried men and guns to the numbers given against their names :—

1672–73[1]	Men.	Guns.
London	96	30
President	120	36
Sampson	91	30
Cæsar	120	36
Ann	100	34
Bombay	91	30
Massingbird	103	36
E. I. Merchant	84	30
Unity	74	26
Antelope	91	30

1677[2]	Men.	Guns.
Phœnix	90	30
Expectation	68	20
Lancaster	75	24
Berk. Castle	80	24
Eagle	90	24
Johanna	90	24
Williamson	120	36
Nathaniel	114	36
Society	114	36
Falcon	76	30
Sampson	120	36
President	104	36
Unicorne	64	26
Loy. Subject	83	24
Cæsar	90	24
Success	105	36
George	116	36
Fleece	116	36
Beng. Mert.	105	36
W. London	106	36
Ann	85	36
Falcon	64	16
Society	90	24
Nathaniel	90	24
President	110	36
Eagle	118	36
Sampson	120	36
Castle	106	36
Johanna	106	36
Williamson	110	36
Lancaster	90	36

1709–10[3]	Tons.	Men.	Guns.
Sherborne	250	50	22
Windsor	200	40	18
Hester	300	60	22
Darby	450	90	30
Dartmouth	440	88	30
Averilla	300	60	22
Thistleworth	250	50	22
London	500	100	36
Jane Frig.	180	36	16

[1] Court Bk., 25*a*, p. 113. Letter Bk., V, p. 21.
[2] Court Bk., 25*a*, pp. 157–59. [3] Rec. Office, C. O. 16.

CHAPTER X

Appendix A

The List of Prohibited Piece-goods of India taken from the MSS. volume, Customs 17, Vol. XXVII, in the Public Record Office :—

Alatches.	Dotties, blue.	Nillas.
Allejars.	Dysooksoys.	Pallampores.
Atlas gold.	Emmerties, blue.	Peniascoes.
,, silver.	Gauze.	Photaes.
Atchbannies.	Ginghams.	Romalls, cotton.
Bandannoes.	Handkerchiefs, chintz.	,, silk.
Bejutapauts.	,, cotton.	Sallampores, blue.
Brawls.	,, silk.	Sarries, silk.
Byrampauts, blue.	Habashes.	Sastracundies.
Calicoes, blue.	Herbal.	Sattins.
Callowapores.	Khallah Gilles.	Seersuckers.
Carradarries.	Kincobs.	Silks.
Chelloes.	Kissersoys.	Sooseys.
Chintz.	Lalla Gillees.	Stuffs, Guinea.
Chucklaes.	Longees Herba.	,, India.
Cloths, long, blue.	Mugga Sarries.	Succotoons, blue.
Coopees.	Moonoos.	Taffaties.
Cuttanees.	Nawanbys.	Tapseils.
Cushtaes.	Neganepauts.	Tepoys.
Damask.	Niccanees.	Other articles.

Appendix B

A sketch of the Duties imposed upon Tea and Coffee.

Years.	Tea.	Coffee.	Act.
1660–88	5 per cent.	5 per cent.	(12 Car. II, c. 4.)
1689–94	5s. per ℔. more in lieu of the excise of 2s. collected before.	£5 12s. more per 112 ℔s.	(1 W. & M, c. 6.)
1692	5 per cent additional, but the former duty of 5s. per ℔. was reduced to 1s.	5 per cent additional. But the former duty of £5 12s. was reduced to £3 6s,	(4 W. & M., c. 5.)

Years.	Tea.	Coffee.	Act.
1695	The duty of 1s. per ℔. continued on tea imported from the place of its growth; but increased to 2s. 6d. if imported from Holland.	The cwt. duty reduced to £2 16s.	(6 & 7 W. & M., c. 7.)
1699	5 per cent additional.	5 per cent additional.	New Subsidy.
1703–4	5 per cent additional.	5 per cent additional.	$\frac{1}{3}$ & $\frac{2}{3}$ subsidies.
1704	1s. per ℔. additional if imported from the place of its growth; 2s. 6d. per ℔. additional if imported from Holland.	£2 16s. per cwt. additional.	(3 & 4 Anne, c. 18; 6 Anne, c. 50.)
1707	These duties made perpetual by		(7 Anne, c. 7.)
1712	2s. per ℔. additional if imported from the place of its growth; 5s. per ℔. additional if imported from Holland. The total gross duties were 20 per cent and 4s. per ℔. if imported from the place of its growth, but 10s. per ℔. if imported from Holland.	1s. per ℔. additional. Total gross duties were 20 per cent or net £18 18s. 9d. and £10 per 100 ℔s. Therefore 400 ℔s. or £100 worth had a net duty of £58 18s. 9d. for home consumption and £5 14s. 2d. for exportation.	(10 Anne, c. 19.)
1723	4s. per ℔. additional duty converted into excise or inland duty.	2s. additional duty converted into 2s. per ℔. excise.	(10 Geo. I, c. 10.; 18 Geo. II, c. 26.)
1745	4s. excise reduced to 1s. and all duties replaced by 25 per cent on the price at the Candle.	1s. 6d. per ℔. excise on plantation coffee.	(21 Geo. II, c. 1.)
1747	5 per cent additional subsidy.	5 per cent additional.	(21 Geo. II, c. 14.)

(Statutes of the Realm, Vols. V–IX.)

APPENDIX C

A view of the Duties payable on Pepper.

1660. The Old Subsidy of 5 per cent on a valuation of 1s. 8d. per ℔.

1690. The Old Impost of 28s. per 112 ℔s. over and above what is charged in the Book of Rates. (2 Wm., c. 4.)

1692. The New Impost of 5 per cent.

1703–4. The one and two-third Subsidies—5 per cent for both.

1712. A new impost of 1s. 6d. per ℔. for home consumption, the duty to be paid by the buyers when taken out of the warehouse. (8 Anne, c. 7, and Letter Bk., XV, p. 67.)

The gross duty at this time was 2s. per ℔. on pepper imported directly from the place of its growth, but it was 2s. 3d. per ℔. on pepper brought from places other than those of its immediate growth.

1721. The duty was reduced to 4½d. per ℔. for home consumption and ½d. for exportation.

1747. A further 5 per cent duty on the valuation of 3⅓d. per ℔. (22 Geo. II, c. 2.)

APPENDIX D

Method of calculating the Duties charged on Muslins *of* £100 *value at the Candle.*

Acts.	Gross duty. £ s. d.	Allowance for prompt payment. £ s. d.	£ s. d.
Old Subsidy	5 0 0	5 0	All these duties according to the Book of Rates.
Additional Duty . .	2 10 0	7 3	
Old Impost	20%	1 5 0	
New Subsidy	5%	5 0	
⅓ Subsidy	1 13 4	1 8	
⅔ Subsidy	3 6 8	3 4	
	£37 10 0	£2 7 3	£35 2 9[1]
15 per cent on muslins .	£15 0 0	15 0	£14 5 0[2]

		£ s. d.
Gross price at the Candle . .		100 0 0
Allowance to buyers	£6 10 0	
Allowance to the Co.	6 0 0	
The net duty of 15 per cent chargeable on the gross price	14 5 0	26 15 0
		£73 5 0

[1] Net duty.

[2] The further net duty at the gross price at the Candle.

As £135 2s. 9d. : £35 2s. 9d. : : £73 5s. : £19 0s. 11d., the net duty on the reduced value.

All duties except 15 per cent are . .	£19	0	11
The 15 per cent is	14	5	0
The total duties to be paid . . .	£33	5	11

Therefore £33 5s. 11d. were the duties payable by the proposed method but by the Co.'s method only £27 12s. 10d. were to be paid as follows:—

Net duties	£35	2	9	according to the Book of Rates
Other duty and charges .	26	15	0	on the gross price.
Total duties	£61	17	9	
These to be deducted from the gross price at the Candle give the Reduced value of	38	2	3	

Therefore as 100 : £35 2s. 9d. : : £38 2s. 3d. : £13 7s. 10d.

Net duty on reduced price =	£13	7	10
Net duty on gross price =	14	5	0
Total to be paid by the Co. =	£27	12	10

APPENDIX E

A view of the Duties on China ware according to the two methods:

Duties.	Gross amount.		
Old Subsidy .	£7	10	0
Old Impost .	20	0	0
New Subsidy .	7	10	0
$\frac{1}{3}$ Subsidy .	2	10	0
12% by 3 Anne	12	0	0
$\frac{2}{3}$ Subsidy .	5	0	0
	£54	10	0

Discount for prompt payment =	£2	7	6
Net duties payable . . =	52	2	6
Discount and Charges . . =	12	10	0

As £152 2s. 6d. : £87 10s. : :
£52 2s. 6d. : 29 19 $7\frac{1}{2}$

87	10	0	
29	19	$7\frac{1}{2}$	Duties allowed.
£57	10	$4\frac{1}{2}$	Reduced value.

But according to the Co. £100 − £64 12s. 6d. = £35 7s. 6d. is the reduced value on which duties are calculated.

Duties payable . . .	£29	19	$7\frac{1}{2}$
Duties paid by the Co. . .	18	8	$9\frac{1}{2}$

Appendix F

Duties Collected on Indian Imports.

Year.	15 per cent on muslins.	Impost 1690 on silks.
1700	£88,062	£231,805
1701	19,313	203,150
1702	56,527	152,224
1703	36,695	192,891
1704	17,751	149,164
1705	11,615	136,063
1706	33,319	145,657
1707	25,755	102,399
1708	58,924	115,999
1709	5,248	120,330
1710	30,628	87,657
1711	29,835	108,191

Appendix G

50 *Years' Chart of Tea Income.*

Years.	Revenue from Tea.	Sale Amount less discount.	Duty %.
1711 and 1712	£83,523	£232,008	36
1713–21	1,391,143	1,956,576	82
1722–23	1,386,014	693,007	200
1724–33	2,052,387	2,443,318	84
1734–44	4,466,199	3,489,218	128
1745–47	874,418	1,267,273	69
1748–59	6,288,588	8,384,784	75

(Moreau's E.I. Co.'s Records, p. 8.)

Appendix H

Abstract of the yield of Revenue from Oriental Goods.

Years.	
1601–12	£6,808 per year.
1613–17	16,250 ,,
1618–25	30,000 ,,
1625–49	20,000 ,,
1667–74	35,000 ,,
1672–82	35,972 ,,
1691	142,717 ,,
1697	122,761 ,,
1750–59	900,000 ,,

REGISTER OF SHIPS

A Complete List of Ships that left England for the East Indies with their tonnage and destination from the establishment of the Indo-British Commerce to the year 1707.

Introductory Remarks.—A few preliminary observations on the value of the list of ships and their tonnage which has been *compiled for the first time in the history of the E. I. Company* are absolutely indispensable. The whole shipping list for 107 years, from 1601 to 1707 inclusive, has involved an immense amount of labour, but it is a matter of great satisfaction that the task is almost complete. The Marine Journals, Court Minutes, Letter Books, and the Home Miscellaneous Records at the India Office have been pressed into service for finding out the names and tonnage of the various ships that sailed from England to the East Indies. *Yet this stated tonnage is not absolutely exact, but a reliable approximation to the actual amount.*

A cursory glance at the tonnage of the ships of the first and third voyages of the Company will show what mighty differences exist in the figures given by Sir Dudley Digges, the Court Minutes of the Company, and the Marine Records. Similarly, the returns given by Purchas for some of the early voyages do not always tally with those contained in some of the Company's Records, as in the case of Martin Pring's fleet of 1616. *What an amount of embarrassment one has to undergo when one finds different tonnage stated for the same ship in the different or even the same records*, as in the case of the *Palsgrave* (1625), the *Royal Mary* (1630), the *Crispian* (1635), the *Advice* (1637), the *William* (1648), and others.

Such discrepancies existing in the Company's own shipping become almost confusing in the case of freighted ships.[1] The

[1] The discrepancies in the tonnage of the same ships as stated in the Court Book 25*a* can be seen at a glance in the following table :—

Ship.	P. 140	P. 157	P. 159
Lancaster . . .	470	550	450
Eagle . . .	525	600	590
Johanna . . .	515	600	530
Williamson . .	—	600	550
Nathaniel . . .	550	570	600
Society . . .	550	570	600

Thus it will be evident that discrepancies are unavoidable, but they have been reduced to a minimum by a careful scrutiny of the available data.

same ship was chartered by the Company at different tonnage in its various voyages to the East, and hence the variance in the tonnage of the same ship is but natural. Sometimes the burden of a certain ship sailing in a particular year could not be traced out; in such a case I had to adopt its tonnage as given for the previous or subsequent voyages. Moreover, the tonnage of a few ships could not be traced at all. In such cases I have assumed their tonnage on the basis of the information scattered here and there, and explicitly mentioned the fact against the names of those ships. It is perhaps needless to remind the reader that in spite of every effort to make the list of ships complete and authentic there is a likelihood of omissions and mistakes in preparing it from the unpublished records of the Company; records, too, which have neither contents nor indices. Fortunately more than one-half of the whole list could be confirmed from other important and independent sources.

A synthesis of the evidence for the first period of fifty-seven years is as below:—

1601–13. Confirmed by Sir Dudley Digges' Trades Increase, published in 1615.
1613–16. William Foster's Letters Received, Vol. VI.
1617–21. No corroboration. See references in the list.
1622–34. Sainsbury's Calendars of State Papers, E. Indies.
1635–57. Compiled from the printed volumes of the English Factories and the Court Minutes by Wm. Foster. No other corroboration See references for tonnage in the list itself.

So far as the remaining fifty years are concerned the list could not be confirmed from any independent collateral record for the years 1658–63.

Since January, 1664, to March, 1669, the register of ships with full details of their cargoes and tonnage has been preserved in the India Office as Home Miscellaneous, Vol. 15. I have invariably followed the Letter Books for the values of their cargoes and the Home Miscellaneous for the tonnage of the ships. The latter document is also important for recording the prices of the various commodities bought by the Company for sending to the East Indies.

There is yet another valuable document—Court Book 25*a*—which preserves the details of ships and exports from the year 1667 to 1679. My list has, in the first instance, been compiled from the Letter Books and afterwards confirmed and supplemented from the above-mentioned record. Thus there is a moral certainty of the absolute correctness of the number of ships and their tonnage and the cargoes sent to the Indies from the year 1664 to 1679 inclusive.

The succeeding years present great difficulty. Macgregor has given a table of the number of ships and the annual exports sent to the East by the Company since 1680 to 1709 inclusive. He does not quote his authority for these returns and hence it is impossible to go to his original source. I have invariably followed the Letter and Court Books for these years also, and am quite unable to tally my returns with those of Macgregor. I have quoted my authority for every ship, its tonnage, and the cargo on it wherever the latter was available. Hence the disparity in our returns more or less explains itself. For the six years from April, 1685, to June, 1691, there are available two "lists of ships that left England for the East with the value of their cargoes" in the Marine Records Miscellaneous, Vol. IV. One would naturally suppose them to be complete for the period, but it is not the case. Hence the Letter Books and Court Minutes had again to be relied upon for these years.

The task for the next nine years became comparatively easy by the possession of a list of ships sent to the Indies from November, 1691, to January, 1700, which was traced out by me in the "England's Almanack" of 1700. It does not, however, give the tonnage of ships, nor their destination and value of cargoes for the first six years. The usual records were again pressed into service for these purposes. Except for the four ships that have been added to the above-mentioned list, it is otherwise complete. But the returns of this period, too, do not coincide with those of Macgregor. He is also at variance with the Company's statement for the three years from 1692–93 to 1694–95 made in their petition to the House of Commons in November, 1695. It is stated that the Company sent out to the Indies in

	Ships.	Burden.
1692–93	6	3,380
1693–94	11	4,073
1694–95	8	3,390

Cargo for three years=£306,265. (Court Bk. 37, pp. 37, 42.)

Macgregor's returns have another serious defect. He does not evidently include the ships sent out by the New E.I. Company erected in 1698 by an Act of Parliament. This Company with their offshoot of the "Separate Traders" were the legal successors of the Old Company, and hence the ships and cargoes sent by them ought to have been added to those despatched by the latter. My list takes cognisance of all the ships sent to the E. Indies and thus presents the Anglo-Indian trade in its true light.

LIST OF SHIPS

Separate Voyages.

1601. 1st voyage, Capt. James Lancaster. To Bantam—Acheen.

Ship	Tons	Remarks
Dragon . .	600 tons	Danvers' Report on the Marine Records in the India Office ; 700 tons, Marine Misc., IV ; 1060 tons, Digges.
Hector . .	300 ,,	500 tons, Marine Misc., IV ; 800 tons, Digges.
Ascension . .	260 ,,	400 ,, Digges.
Susan . .	240 ,,	400 ,, Digges.
Gift . . .	130 ,,	

1604. 2nd voyage, Capt. Henry Middleton. To Bantam—Amboyna.

Ship	Tons	Remarks
Dragon . .	600 tons	
Hector . .	300 ,,	
Ascension . .	260 ,,	
Susan . .	240 ,,	Lost near the Cape of Good Hope.

Sir E. Michelbourn's ships—Captain John Davis. To Bantam.

Ship	Tons	Remarks
Tiger . . .	240 tons	Lediard's Naval History of England, p. 401.
Tiger's Whelp .	100 ,,	Assumed.

1606. 3rd voyage, Capt. Wm. Keeling. To Bantam.

Ship	Tons	Remarks
Dragon . .	600 tons	
Consent . .	150 ,,	105 tons, Marine Misc., IV; 115 tons, Purchas, I, p. 224 ; 240 tons, Digges.
Hector . .	500 ,,	with Capt. John Hawkins for Surat.

1607. 4th voyage, Capt. Alex. Sharpey.

Ship	Tons	Remarks
Union . .	400 tons	(Digges) to Priaman in Sumatra ; *sunk* on the coast of Brittany on homeward voyage in Febuary, 1611.
Ascension . .	260 ,,	To Surat ; *sunk* at Gundavi near Surat. (Marine Journals, Vol. VII.)

1608–9. 5th voyage, Capt. David Middleton. To Java and Banda.

Ship	Tons	Remarks
Expedition .	260 tons	320 tons, Digges.

1610. 6th voyage, Commander Sir Hy. Middleton. To Surat.

Ship	Tons	Remarks
Trade's Increase .	1293 tons	Digges. 1000 tons, Purchas, I, p. 247 ; 1100 tons in other books.
Peppercorn .	342 ,,	Digges. 250 tons, Purchas.
Darling[1] . .	150 ,,	,, 90 tons, Purchas.
Samuel, pinnace .	180 ,,	Lediard's Naval History, p. 426.
Relief . .	50 ,,	Assumed.

1610–11. 7th voyage, Capt. Anthony Hippon. To Coromandel Coast.

Ship	Tons	Remarks
Globe . .	527 tons	Digges.

1610–11. 8th voyage, Capt. John Saris. To Arabia, South Seas and Japan.

Ship	Tons	Remarks
Hector . .	800 tons	Digges.
Clove . .	527 ,,	,,
Thomas . .	342 ,,	,,

Interloping voyage, Capt. Samuel Castleton.

Ship	Tons	Remarks
Pearl . . .	200 tons.	

[1] 50 to 60 tons according to Coen on p. 364 of Jourdain.

1611–12. 9th voyage, Capt. E. Marlowe. To Surat.

James . .	600 tons	Digges.

1611–12. 10th voyage, Capt. Thomas Best. To Surat.

Dragon . .	700 tons	Digges.
Hosiander . .	213 ,,	,,

1611–12. 11th voyage, Capt. Ralph Wilson. To Surat.

Solomon . .	400 tons	Digges.

1612–13. 12th voyage, Capt. Christopher Newport. To Diul, Tecco and Bantam.

Expedition .	320 tons	Digges.

First Joint Stock Voyages.—1613–17.

1613–14.

Concord . .	213 tons	Digges, pp. 19–22. Capt. Hawkins. To Bantam.
Concord . .	230 ,,	Digges, p. 31.
New Year's Gift .	867 ,, [1]	Digges. 650 tons in Marine Misc., IV, p. 21.
Merchant's Hope	533 ,,	,, 400 ,, ,, ,,
	,,	,, 300 ,, in Lediard's Naval History.
Hector . .	800 ,,	,, 500 ,, in Marine Misc., IV.
Solomon . .	400 ,,	,, 300 ,, ,, ,,
		200 ,, in Court Bk. 3, p. 1.

The whole fleet was under Capt. N. Downton and was bound for Surat.

1614–15. Fleet under Capt. David Middleton. Bound for Bantam.

Samaritan . .	453 tons	Digges. Cf. Court Bk. 3, pp. 40, 45, 93.
Thomas . .	342 ,,	,,
Thomasine . .	133 ,,	,, £3,300 in all were sent on these ships.
Advice . .	160 tons	Digges. Capt. R. Youarte. Bound for Bantam.
Attendance .	100 ,,	Assumed. Taken by the Dutch.
Dragon . .	700 ,,	Digges. Capt. Wm. Keeling. Bound for Surat.
Lion . . .	386 ,,	,,
Peppercorn .	342 ,,	,,
Expedition .	320 ,,	,,
Lannerett . .	200 ,,	,, Court Bk. 3, p. 130; Court Bk. 5, p. 313.
Speedwell . .	?	
Defence . .	400 ,,	,, Capt. S. Castleton. Bound for Bantam.
Clove . .	527 ,,	,,

1615–16. Capt. Benjamin Joseph.

Charles . .	1000 tons	Court Bk. 3, pp. 480, 578. Bound for Surat.
Unicorn . .	700 ,,	,, ,, ,,
James . .	600 ,,	,, ,, ,,
Globe . .	527 ,,	,, ,, ,,
Swan* . .	400 ,,	,, ,, ,, Bantam.
Rose, pinnace .	140 ,,	,, ,, ,, ,,
Hosiander . .	213 ,,	Court Bk. 5, p. 313 ,, ,,

[1] Sir T. Roe states the tonnage to be 650, 500, 300 and 200 tons, respectively, for the four ships. (Embassy, p. 34.)

Hope . .	533 tons	Digges. Capt. Christopher Newport. Bound for Bantam.
Hound* . .	250 ,,	Assumed.

1616–17. Capt. Martin Pring. Bound for Surat and Bantam.

James Royal .	1000 tons	To Surat under Alex. Child (Purchas, I, p. 606.
Anne . .	700 ,,	Fact. Rec. Surat, I, p. 102. Digges, 900 tons; same by Macpherson and Harris.
New Year's Gift .	700 ,,	Court Bk. 4, p. 456; 800 tons by Macpherson and Harris.
Bull . . .	400 ,,	
Bee . . .	150 ,,	Purchas, I, p. 631; Foster's Letters, VI, p. xlii.

Second Joint Stock Voyages

1617–18. Commander Sir Thomas Dale. Bound for Bantam.

Globe . .	527 tons	Court Bk. 4, pp. 29–30, 126 for this fleet.
Sun . . .	700 ,,	Stated value £10,000 against £3,000 for the Lion of 386 tons. (Home Misc., 39, p. 156.) Lost.
Clove . .	527 ,,	
Peppercorn .	342 ,,	
Defence* . .	400 ,,	
Discovery . .	500 ,,	
Unicorn . .	700 ,,	
Samson* . .	600 ,,	Assumed.
Moon . .	600 ,,	Stated value £6,000. (Home Misc., 39, p. 158.) Lost.
Flour . .	200 ,,	Assumed.

Ships marked with an asterisk were taken by the Dutch.

1618–19. Capt. Rob. Bonner's Fleet to Malabar and Bantam:—

Dragon . .	600 tons	
Expedition .	280 ,,	Purchas, I, p. 488.
Lion . . .	386 ,,	
Anne Royal .	750 ,,	Calendar, III, p. 558.
Bull . . .	400 ,,	Calendar, II, p. 287.
Rose . .	140 ,,	
Dragon's Claw .	100 ,,	Assumed.
Lion's Claw .	200 ,,	Assumed.

1619–20. Capt. J. Bitkell's Fleet. See Court Bk. 4, p. 254; Calendar, II, pp. 175, 245.

Charles . .	1000 tons		To Surat.
Diamond . .	300 ,,	Court Bk. 4, p. 306.	,,
Ruby . .	700 ,,	,, ,,	,,
Supply . .	100 ,,	Assumed.	,,
Elizabeth . .	978 ,,		To Bantam.
Palsgrave . .	1083 ,,		,,
Hope . .	533 ,,		,,
Star . . .	250 ,,	Marine Misc., IV.	,,

Capt. Fitzherbert's Fleet :—

Royal Exchange .	700 tons	Calendar, II, p. 40.
	800 ,,	Fac. Rec. Surat, p. 102.
White Bear .	900 ,,	If it was the old ship bought from the navy see Lediard's Naval History, p. 394.
Unitie . .	300 ,,	Calendar, II, p. 483.
Centaur . .	100 ,,	Assumed.

1620–21. Capt. Andrew Shilling's Fleet to Surat and Persia.[1] See Marine Journal No. 30 ; Purchas, I, p. 723.

London . .	800 tons	
Hart . .	500 ,,	
Roebuck . .	300 ,,	
Eagle . .	280 ,,	
Godspeed . .	50 ,,	

1621. Capt. John Weddell's Fleet :—

Jonas . .	700 tons	
Dolphin . .	500 ,,	Court Bk. 7, p. 230.
Whale . .	700 ,,	Estimated. Lost.
Lion . . .	386 ,,	Lost.

Capt. Walter Bennet's Fleet :—

Lesser James .	500 tons	
Anne Royal .	700 ,,	Lost.
Fortune . .	200 ,,	
Trial . .	500 ,,	Court Bk. 5, pp. 25, 85. Lost.
Rose . .	100 ,,	
Richard . .	20 ,,	

1622. Capt. John Hall.

Blessing . .	700 tons	Court Bk. 5, pp. 218, 301.
Discovery . .	500 ,,	,, ,,
Reformation .	400 ,,	

1623.[2] See Court Bk. 5, pp. 398, 431 ; Eng. Factories, Vol. 1622–23, p. 260.

Hart . .	500 tons	To Surat.
Abigail . .	150 ,,	To Bantam.
Roebuck . .	300 ,,	

1624.

Royal James .	1000 tons	Court Bk. 6, p. 430.
Jonas . .	700 ,,	Boothby.
Eagle . .	400 ,,	
Star . .	250 ,,	Marine Misc., IV.
	350 ,,	Eng. Fac., Vol. 1624–29, xxxiv.
Spy . .	100 ,,	Assumed.
Scout . .	100 ,,	,,

---

[1] Macgregor says that Shilling sailed in Feb., 1619. It was Feb., 1620.

[2] Eight ships were proposed to be sent this year to Surat and Bantam (Court Bk. 4, p. 413.)

1625.

Ship.	Tonnage.	Reference.	Destination.
Palsgrave	. 1083	Court Bk. 4, p. 254.	Surat.
	800	Marine Misc., IV.	
Dolphin .	. 500		Surat.
Lion .	. 386	Burnt by the Portuguese.	
Falcon .	. 560	Calendar, IV, p. 614.	Surat & Bantam.
Swallow .	. 100	Calendar, III, LX.	Bantam.
London .	. 800		
		1626.	
Discovery	. 500	Calendar, IV, p. 643.	Surat.
William .	. 700		,,
Blessing	. 700		
Morris .	. 400	Lost. Home Misc., 39, p. 158.	,,
Christopher	. 300	Assumed.	,,
Exchange	. 700		,,
Expedition	. 200	Boothby.[1]	
		1627.	
Mary Royal	. 800	Marine Misc., IV.	Persia & Bantam.
Hart .	. 500		Surat & Bantam.
Star .	. 250		,, Persia.
Hopewell	. 240	Bruton.[2]	,, ,,
Refuge .	. 150	Assumed	,, ,,
Scout, pinnace	100	,,	,, ,,
Speedwell	. 150		
		1628.[3]	
Jonas .	. 800		
Dove .	. 300	Assumed.	
Expedition	. 200	Marine J., No. 50.	
Little James	. 260	Court Bk. 15, p. 14. It was a prize ship.	
		1629.	
Charles .	. 700	Calendar, IV, p. 643.	Surat.
Discovery	. 500	,, and Marine J., No. 52	,,
Reformation	. 500	,,	,,
Samuel .	. 300	Lediard's Naval History, p. 459.	,,
London .	. 600	Calendar, IV, p. 643.	Bantam.
		1630.	
		Ships of the 2nd and 3rd voyages to Persia :—	
James Royal	. 1000	Marine J., No. 55 ; Court Bk. 13, p. 117.	
William .	. 700		
Mary Royal	. 800	Marine Misc., IV, doc. 17 ; Court Bk. 18, p. 233.	

[1] A Brief Discovery of Madagascar, by Richard Boothby, London, 1644.

[2] News from the East Indies ; or a Voyage to Bengalla, by Wm. Bruton. London, 1632.

[3] Two ships of the Earl of Warwick have to be added. The Co.'s President and Factors at Surat were imprisoned in 1628 for robberies committed by these ships.

Ship.	Tonnage.	Reference.	Destination.
Star	250	Marine Misc., IV, doc. 17; Court Bk. 18, p. 233.	Masulipatam.
Dove	150	Joint Stock Ship.	Surat & Persia.
Seahorse	150	Pirate Quail's ship. Court Bk. 4, p. 521.	
		1631.	
Blessing	700		Surat & Persia.
Exchange	700		,, ,,
Speedwell	200		,, ,,
Hopewell	240		,, ,,
Palsgrave	1083		Surat.
London	800		Bantam.
Pearl	250	Calendar, V, p. 283.	Masulipatam.
Jewell	250		Bantam.
Charles	700		Surat.
Jonas	800		,,
Dolphin	300	Court Bk. 22, p. 26.	,,
Hart	500		,,
Swallow	100		,,
Intelligence	100		,,
		1632.	
Swan	400	Court Bk. 12, p. 104.	Masulipatam.
		1633.	
Comfort	200	Court Bk. 15, p. 142.	Surat.
Palsgrave	1083	Wrecked. Court Bk. 16, pp. 215, 246.	,,
Discovery	500		,,
Reformation	400		Bantam.
Jewell	250	Letter Bk. I, p. 130.	Coromandel Coast.
		1634.	
Expedition	260	Court Bk. 15, p. 14.	Bantam.
London	800		Surat.
Blessing	700		,,
Hopewell	240		,,
Consolation	170	Court Bk. 15, p. 142.	Jambee.
		1635.[1]	
Coaster	260	Assumed.	Bantam
William	700		Surat.
Crispian	400	Court Bk. 15, p. 109.	
	500	,, 13, p. 45.	,,
Swan	400	,, 13, p. 104.	Coromandel.
		1636.	
Mary	800	Court Bk. 16, p. 129.	Surat.
Hart	500		Bantam.

The tonnage of English ships given in Dutch Records, B. II,

[1] The Co.'s Factors were imprisoned at Surat for piracies committed by the two ships of Cobb and Ayres in 1635.

Vol. III, docs. 106 and 113, is generally half of that stated in the English Company's Records. The reader should not be misled by the Dutch figures. Some examples are given below:—

Ships.	Tonnage.	Ships.	Tonnage.
Pearl . .	175	Maria . .	400
Palsgrave .	400	Hart . .	300
Reformation .	200	Thomas . .	100
London . .	400	Eagle . .	100
Hopewell .	75	Speedwell .	80
Expedition .	125	Providence .	50
William .	350	Swan . .	150
Crispian . .	200	Discovery .	300
Great James .	450	Comfort . .	100
Exchange .	400	Blessing . .	400
Dolphin . .	250		

1637.

Ship.	Tonnage.	References.	Destination.
Advice . .	350	Court Bk. 20, p. 444.	Coromandel and Bantam.
	500	,, 22, p. 113.	,,
Eagle . .	600	,, 16, p. 226; Marine Misc., IV, doc. 23.	Surat.
Jonas . .	500	,, 19, p. 159.	,,

1638.

Ship.	Tonnage.	References.	Destination.
Discovery .	500		Surat.
Jewel . .	250	Lost on the sea.	Bantam.

1639.

Ship.	Tonnage.	References.	Destination.
London . .	800	Court Bk. 18, p. 310.	Surat.
Reformation .	400		Bantam and Masulipatam.
William . .	700		Bantam.
Hopewell .	240		Coromandel and Bantam.
Advice . .	350		Bantam.

1640.

Ship.	Tonnage.	References.	Destination.
Blessing . .	700	Court Bk. 19, p. 173.	Bantam.
Jonas . .	500	Lost on the sea.	,,
Swan . .	400		,,
Cæsar . .	400	Court Bk. 18, pp. 55, 72. Freighted ship.	,,
Crispian .	500	Court Bk. 17, pp. 130, 159.	Surat.

1641.

Ship.	Tonnage.	References.	Destination.
Mary . .	600	Fac. Rec. Misc., 12, p. 39.	Bantam.
Discovery .	500	Court Bk. 17, p. 306; Court Bk. 18, p. 233.	Surat.
London . .	800		,,
William . .	700		Bantam.
Hopewell .	250	Marine Misc., IV.	Coromandel.
Reformation .	400	Court Bk. 17, p. 300.	,,

1642.[1]

Ship.	Tonnage.	References.	Destination.
Blessing	700		Bantam.
Ulysses	350	Court Bk. 18, p. 127.	,,
Aleppo Mert.	400	,, 22, p. 113.	Surat.
Crispian	500		,,
		1643.	
Dolphin	300	Court Bk. 18, pp. 263, 266.	Surat.
Hind	300	,, 18, pp. 263, 271.	,,
Seaflower	180	,, 18, p. 234.	,,
Hart	220	,, 18, pp. 210, 214, 272, 278.	Coromandel.
Endeavour	400		,,
Mary	800		Bantam.
		1644.	
William	650	Fac. Rec. Misc., 12, p. 91. A new ship.	Bantam.
Blessing	260	Fac. Rec. Misc., 12, p. 91. A new ship.	,,
John	500	Court Bk. 19, p. 150.	Surat.
Crispian	500		,,
		1645.	
Eagle	400	Court Bk. 21, p. 58.	Surat.
Falcon	560		,,
Lanneret	160		,,
Mary	800		Bantam.
		1646.	
Antelope	350	Marine Misc., IV, doc. 21.	Surat.
Greyhound	400	Its first name was Swan.	,,
Dolphin	300		,,
William	700		Bantam.
Ulysses	330	Court Bk. 22, pp. 24, 32.	,,
Endymion	300	,, 23, p. 74.	,,
		1647.	
Mary	800		Bantam.
Eagle	400		Surat.
Blessing	260		,,
Farewell	140	Court Bk. 20, p. 27.	Coromandel.
		1648.	
Dolphin	300	Court Bk. 22, p. 26.	Coromandel.
Bonito	400	,, 18, pp. 262, 266.	,,
Advice	300	,, 22, p. 37.	Bantam.
William	700	,, 23, p. 4.	,,
Endymion	300	,, 23, p. 74.	,,
Aleppo Mert.	400	,, 22, p. 113.	Surat.
Golden Fleece	550	,, 22, p. 24, but 450 tons in Court Bk. 23, p. 74.	,,
Greyhound	400		Coromandel.
		1649.	
Ruth	400	Court Bk. 22, p. 80.	Bantam.
Anne	300	,, 21, p. 63.	,,
Eagle	400		Surat.

[1] A ship was proposed to be sent for *Bombay*. (Court Bk. 18, p. 234.)

1650.

Ship.	Tonnage.	References.	Destination.
E. I. Merchant	330	Court Bk. 23, p. 74, but 350 on p. 358.	Bantam.
Advice .	. 500	Court Bk. 22, p. 113, but 350 in Court Bk. 23, p. 74.	,,
William .	. 700		,,
G. Fleece	. 550		,,
Love .	. 450	Court Bk. 23, p. 74, but 400 in Court Bk. 20, p. 444.	Surat.
Aleppo Mert.	. 400		,,
Lioness .	. 350	Court Bk. 22, p. 113.	Coromandel.
Bonito .	. 400	,, 22, pp. 19, 32.	,,
Supply[1]	. 250	Marine Misc., IV, doc. 22.	,,
Assada Mert.	. 250	Assumed.	Madagascar.

1651.

Ship.	Tonnage.	References.	Destination.
Eagle .	. 600	Marine Misc., IV; but 500 in Court Bk. 23, p. 463.	Surat.
Blessing .	. 260		,,
Anne .	. 300	Court Bk. 21, p. 63.	Bantam.
Welcome	. 240	,, 23, p. 14.	Assada.
Recovery	.	Permission ship.	,,

1652.

Ship.	Tonnage.	References.	Destination.
Smirna Mert.	. 450	Court Bk. 23, p. 74.	Surat.
E. I. Merchant	300		Bantam.
Roebuck	. 250	,, ,, but 350 in Court Bk. 22, p. 32.	,,
Love .	. 450	Court Bk. 23, p. 74, but 400 on p. 358.	Coromandel.

1653.

Ship.	Tonnage.	References.	Destination.
Dove .	. 150		Surat.
Welcome	. 240		,,

1654.

Ship.	Tonnage.	References.	Destination.
Eagle .	. 500		Surat.
Katherine	. 200	Court Bk. 23, p. 239.	Coromandel.
E. I. Merchant	350	,, 23, p. 458.	Bantam.

1655.

Ship.	Tonnage.	References.	Destination.
Three Brothers	260	Court Bk. 24, p. 13.	Coromandel.

1656.

Ship.	Tonnage.	References.	Destination.
William .	. 450	Court Bk. 23, p. 358.	Bantam.
Endymion	. 300	,, 23, p. 74.	,,
Eagle .	. 500		Surat.

1657.

None was sent by the Company.

---

[1] Supply was the first Indian-built ship that went to England. (Court Bk. 20, p. 509.)

Ships of the Courteen Company.

1635.

Ship.	Tonnage.	References.
Dragon . .	—	Foster's Court Min., Vol. 635–39, pp. 35, 130; Court Bk. 16, pp. 228–29.
Sun . .	—	,, ,, ,, ,,
Katherine .	—	,, ,, ,, ,,
Panther . .	—	,, ,, ,, ,,
Anne . .	—	,, ,, ,, ,,
Discovery .	—	,, ,, ,, ,,
Samaritan .	250	,, ,, ,, ,,
Roebuck .	100	,, ,, ,, ,,
		1639.
William .	—	Eng. Fac., Vol. 1637–41, xxi.
Talbot . .	—	,, ,,
Thomasine .	—	,, ,,
		1640–41.
Paradox . .	—	Fac. Rec. Misc., 12, 147.
William .	—	,, ,,
Thomas & John	—	,, ,,
Sun . .	—	,, ,,
Loyalty . .	—	,, ,,
Unity . .	700	,, ,,
Hester . .	700	,, ,,
James . .	700	,, ,,
		1641–42.
Bonasperance .	700	Eng. Fac., Vol. 1642–45 pp. 26, 29.
Bonadventure .	700	,, ,, ,,
Hampton Mert.	700	,, ,, ,,
		1645.
James . .	—	Eng. Fac., Vol. 1642–45, xxii.
Lioness . .	—	,, ,,
Friendship .	—	,, Vol. 1646–50, p. 100.

Private Ships from 1654 *to* 1657.

Allum Frigate.	Persian Mert.	Expedition.	Friendship.
Jonathan.	Constantin. Mert.	Richard & Martha.	Society.
Hopeful.	William & John.	Two Sisters.	Dethic.
Benjamin.	Adventure.	Rose.	Vine.
Mayflower.	Reformation.	Aleppo Mert.	Virgin.
Constantin. Mert.	Lion.	Loyalty.	Good Hope.
Goodwill.	Peter & Jane.	E. I. Merchant.	Love.
Smyrna Mert.	African Frigate.	John & Thomas.	Olive Branch.
Greyhound.	Coast Frigate.	Little Eagle.	Marigold.

During this period of open trade there were probably sent out many more vessels of which no trace occurs in the Records. Eng. Fac., Vol. 1654–60, pp. 49, 77, 117, 131–33, 136–37; Letter Bk. I, p. 365; II, pp. 143, 154.

We learn from the Dutch Records, B. II, doc. 137, that in 1655 thirteen private vessels were to sail between Guinea and India.

January, 1658, to April, 1659.

Reference for Exports.	Ship.	Tonnage.		Destination.	Money.	Goods.
L. Bk. I, pp. 395, 400; II, pp. 50, 61	Love	400		Hoogly	£21,560	£21,940
,, I, p. 387; II, pp. 9, 30, 47	Marigold	200	C. Bk. 24, p. 7	Guinea & Coast	None	4,645
,, II, pp. 20, 47, 95 . .	Anne	230	,, 24, p. 11	Coast	9,000	12,567
,, II, pp. 20, 47, 95 . .	Blackmore	240	,, 24, p. 12	Guinea & Coast	15,522	23,945
,, I, p. 405 . . .	Mayflower	250	,, 23, p. 74			
,, II, p. 81 . . .		300	,, 24, p. 30	Coast	8,048	8,118
,, II, p. 81 . . .	Merchant's	350	,, 23, p. 74	Coast		
	Delight	250	,, 24, p. 13	Hugly	10,033	10,993
,, II, p. 47 . . .	London	380	,, 23, p. 74	Coast	21,560	21,940
,, II, p. 55 . . .	Welcome	250	,, 24, p. 13	Surat	6,000	7,222
,, II, p. 71 . . .	Persia M.	360		Coast	7,558	7,558
,, II, pp. 132–33 . .	Surat Frig.	150		Guinea & Surat		6,956
				(£4,000 or £5,000 more for Surat, pp. 146–47)		
,, II, p. 151 . . .	Samaritan[1]	250		Guinea & Coast	None	8,218
,, II, p. 168 . . .	Coast Frig.	250		Guinea & Surat	None	8,955
Eng. Fac., Vol. 1654–60, p. 77 .	Gilbert	250	C. Bk. 24, pp. 57, 61, 77	Coast & Bantam	7,500	7,500
L. Bk. II, p. 90. . . .	Eagle	500		Surat	31,290	33,299
,, ,, ...	Smirna Mer.	450		,,	23,301	24,545
,, ,, ...	Society	240		,,	12,449	13,338
,, ,, p. 175 . . .	Vine	150		,,	4,006	6,326
,, ,, p. 183 . . .	London	400		,,	5,596	5,842
,, ,, p. 217 . . .	Constant. M.	430		,,	11,216	18,766
,, ,, p. 194 . . .	Discovery	500		Coast & Jambee	4,927	7,327
,, I, pp. 410, 414–18 .	Katherine	250		Coast & Bantam	7,186	7,222
,, ,, ...	Mert. Adventure	430		Coast & Bay	8,485	9,903
,, ,, ...	Madraspatan M.	250		Coast & Bay	7,000	8,278
,, II, p. 112 . . .	Advice	375		Bantam	9,000	9,266
,, ,, ...	Dragon	400		,,	6,067	6,081
Eng. Fac., Vol. 1654–60, p. 160n.	King Fernandez			China & India	Private ship	
,, ,, pp. 114, 135n.	Amity				,,	
L. Bk. II, p. 276 . . .	Thomas & William				,,	
,, ,, ...	Virgin				,,	

[1] 400 marks or about £10,560 were to be laden on her for the Coast (L. Bk. II, p. 253).

May, 1659, to April, 1660.

Ref. for Exports.	Ship.	Tonnage.	Destination.	Money.	Goods.
L. Bk. II, p. 226	Truroe	270	Guinea & Coast	£ None	£11,501
,, 256	Barbadoes M.	240	,, ,,[1]	,,	9,091
,, 278	E. I. Merchant	400	Coast	6,000	7,010
,, 278	Concord	300	Coast & Persia	6,776	8,319
,, 278	Smirna M.	450	Coast & Bay	9,992	12,262
,, 266–67	Blackmore	240	Guinea & Surat[2]		8,423
,, 310	Castle Fr.	240	,, Bantam[3]		7,380
		1660–61.			
L. Bk. II, p. 295	Eagle	500	Surat	5,828	12,392
C. Bk. 24, p. 227	Richard & Martha	450	,,	6,372	10,713
,, ,,	American	225	,,	3,983	5,308
L. Bk. III, p. 16	Constnt. M.	400	,,	19,314	30,027
,, II, p. 325	R. James & Hy.	400	Guinea & Coast	None	10,458
,, ,, 348	Bowen Frig.	150	,, ,,	,,	1,522
,, III, p. 44	Roy. Charles	500	,, ,,	,,	15,780
,, ,, 61	Coronation	400	,, ,,	,,	16,567
,, II, p. 364	Discovery	500	Coast	21,367	23,509
,, III, p. 5	Coast Frig.	250	,,	23,885	30,290
,, II, p. 317	Restoration	400	Bantam	4,000	5,930
,, ,, 359	African	240	,,	8,000	8,130
,, III, p. 8	Loyal Mert.	450	,,	10,000	10,629
,, ,, 26	London	400	,,	4,000	6,780
	Surat Frig.	150	,,	Not traced.	
		1661–62.			
L. Bk. III, p. 85	Marigold	200	Bantam	10,000	10,431
,, ,, 137	Starling Adv.	200*	,,	8,000	8,379
,, ,, 86	Good Hope	200*	Coast	20,999	25,521
,, ,, 97	Madras Mert.	250	,,	20,416	23,009
,, ,, 152	George & Martha	300*	Guinea & Coast	None	2,756
,, ,, 171	American	225	,, ,,	,,	34
,, ,, 117	Richard & Martha	450	Surat	20,235	35,266
,, ,, 118	Convertine	240	,,	8,499	10,753
,, ,, 118	Rose	150*	,,	5,000	5,000
,, ,, 118	Dunkirk	150*	,,	5,000	5,000
		1662–63.			
L. Bk. III, p. 185	E. I. Merchant	400	Coast	23,036	28,343
,, ,, 228	Roy. Katherine	380	,,	19,804	24,654
,, ,, 199	Castle Frig.	240	Guinea & Coast	Not traced.	
,, ,, 241	Coast Frig.	250	Bantam	8,000	9,431
,, ,, 210	Constant. Mert.	430	,,	10,000	10,760
,, ,, 255	Loy. Merchant	520	Surat	25,947	41,971
,, ,, 255	African	240	,,	14,436	23,172

[1] £10,000 or £12,000 in gold to be laden on her for the Coast (L. Bk. II, p. 256).

[2] £10,000 or £12,000 in gold to be laden on her for Surat (L. Bk. II, pp. 266–67).

[3] £3,000 in gold to be laden on her for Bantam (L. Bk. II, p. 310).

* The tonnage of ships with asterisks is *assumed*.

Ref. for Exports.	Ship.	Tonnage.	Destination.	Money.	Goods.
			1663–64.		
L. Bk. III, p. 269	Royal Oak	400*	Bantam	£12,000	£12,736
,, ,, 368	Richard & M.	400	,,	12,000	12,827
,, ,, 312	American	225	Guinea & African Coast for discovery of trade		
,, ,, 329	Marigold	200	Guinea & Coast	10,514	10,514[1]
,, ,, 357	Rebecca	200	Coast	Not found	11,908
,, ,, 361	Coronation	400	Bay	,,	15,990
,, ,, 389–90	Happy Entrance	240	Coast	13,970	17,262
,, ,, ,,	Morning Star	200	,,	13,951	17,146
,, ,, ,,	Roy. Charles	550	Surat	18,209	38,381
,, ,, ,,	London	400	,, & Mocha	16,892	32,749
			1664–65.		
,, 430,515	Constan. Mert.	300	Bantam	1,000	1,495
	,, ,,		Coast	9,384	14,204
,, ,, 440–41	Greyhound	280	,,	11,001	16,249
,, ,, 457	American	225	Hugly	2,745	6,476
,, ,, 476	African	240	Surat	None	10,604
,, ,, 476	St. George	230	,,	,,	5,983
			1665–66.		
L. Bk. III, p. 515	Dorcas	75	Hugly	1,236	2,789
,, IV, p. 5	Constant. Mert.	400	Coast	9,384	14,204
,, ,,	Return	370	Surat	6,388	20,615
			1666–67.		
L. Bk. IV, p. 43	Charles	140	St. Helena & Surat	1,000	3,967
	Eagle	500	Guinea	For bringing back the Co.'s remains there	
	Barbados Mert.	240	,,		
			1667–68.		
L. Bk. IV, p. 101	Bantam Pink	120	Surat	2,425	8,181
,, ,, 147	Return	380	,,	13,074	29,102
,, ,, 147	Constant. Mert.	400	,,	12,914	28,551
,, ,, 147	Rebecca	200	,,	5,171	14,643
C. Bk. 25*a*, p. 42	Roy. Katherine	380	Coast & Bay	13,000	13,000
L. Bk. IV, p. 111	Loy. Merchant	520	,, ,,	17,783	23,850
,, ,, 112	Blackmore	240	,, ,,	8,245	11,082
,, ,,	Rainbow	380	,, ,,	12,985	17,220
,, ,,	Madras Mert.	250	,, ,,	8,644	8,788
,, ,,	Unicorne	330	,, ,,	11,360	15,258
C. Bk. 25*a*	Loy. Subject	500	,, Bantam	24,783	31,736
L. Bk. IV, pp. 130–31	Richard & M.	400	Bantam	5,000	5,457
,, ,,	Coast Frigate	250	,,	3,000	3,079
,, ,,	London	400	,,	5,000	6,506

[1] Gold to be laden on her not mentioned; here the whole cargo has been taken to be sent in money to the Coast.

1668–69.

Ref. for Exports.	Ship.	Tonnage.	Destination.	Money.	Goods.
L. Bk. IV, p. 185	Castle Frig.	240	Coast	£17,475	£19,757
,, ,,	Morning Star	200	,,	12,475	14,244
,, ,, 198	Antelope	400	,,	24,756	30,110
,, ,, 201	John & Martha	300	,,	19,140	22,507
,, ,, 201	Crowne	250	,,	14,475	16,752
,, ,, 231	Sampson	340	Surat	8,221	30,395
,, ,, 231	Bone Bay Mert.	300	,,	6,956	24,238
,, ,, 231	Humphrey & Eliz.	320	,,	6,171	21,115
,, ,, 214	John & Margaret	425	Bantam	13,000	13,198
,, ,, 259	London	400	,,	9,500	10,603

1669–70.

Ref. for Exports.	Ship.	Tonnage.	Destination.	Money.	Goods.
L. Bk. IV, p. 293	Return	340	Fort & Bay	26,926	29,224
C. Bk. 25*a*, p. 57	Rainbow	380	,, ,,	33,500	36,770
	Coast Frig.	280	,, ,,	18,391	21,975
	Zant Frig.	180	,, ,,	15,273	17,283
	Mediterranian M.	240	,, ,,	18,986	19,859
	Happy Entrance	260	,, ,,	20, 803	26,529
L. Bk. IV, pp. 320–21	Loyal Subject	450	Surat	10,922	28,896
C. Bk. 25*a*, p. 69	Hannibal	350	,,	8,383	21,092
	Berkley Cast.	500	,,	10,009	32,946
	Experiment	260	,,	6,485	15,636
L. Bk. IV, p. 343	Loy. Merchant	550	Bantam	11,000	11,587
	Anne	450	,,	8,000	9,072
	Constant. Mert	300	,,	6,000	6,471
	Rebecca	250	,,	5,000	5,000

1670–71.

Ref. for Exports.	Ship.	Tonnage.	Destination.	Money.	Goods.
L. Bk. IV, p. 359	Greyhound	270	Bantam	10,000	10,143
	Ann	300	,,	12,510	12,510
,, ,, 412	Advance	220	,,	2,000	5,343
,, ,, 416–17	Jn. & Margaret	425	,,	7,075	7,394
	Satisfaction	400	,,	6,075	6,108
	Jn. & Martha	300	,,	5,050	6,293
	Unity	300	,,	5,050	6,272
C. Bk. 25*a*	Crowne	230	,,	{ Not	5,650
	Flying Eagle	120	,,	given }	475
	Unicorne	360	,,		3,766
L. Bk. IV, pp. 389–90	Sampson	300	Coast & Bay	27,821	33,480
	E. I. Merchant	360	,, ,,	27,780	31,647
	Humphrey & Eliz.	340	,, ,,	24,176	28,381
	European Mert.	380	,, ,,	26,804	30,726
	Bombay Mert.	370	,, ,,	25,469	32,741
,, ,, 431–32	London	400	Surat	3,362	19,122
C. Bk. 25*a*, p. 78	Phœnix	380	,,	4,425	19,054
	Massingbird	470	,,	9,146	28,376
	Falcon	360	,,	5,971	18,836
	Antelope	400	,,	4,946	19,355

1671–72.

Ref. for Exports.	Ship.	Tonnage.	Destination.	Money.	Goods.
L. Bk. IV, pp. 452, 475, 515	Anne	450	Bantam	£10,000	£10,190
	Return	340	,,	—	13,928
C. Bk. 25*a*,	Experiment	260	,,	—	11,187
pp. 90–91	Zant Frig.	180	,,	—	2,017
	Mary	330	,,	5,000	5,887
	Barnardistan	340	,,	5,000	6,891
	Expectation	400	,,	5,000	5,010
	Haniball	350	,,	5,000	6,675
	Surat Mert.	350	,,	5,000	5,065
L. Bk. IV, pp. 497–98	Berkley Cast.	500	Coast & Bay	34,247	41,673
	Johanna	500	,, ,,	33,044	40,002
	Loy. Subject	450	,, ,,	31,080	36,695
	Ann	300	,, ,,	16,294	10,401
	Rebecca	250	,, ,,	19,608	23,444
L. Bk. IV, pp. 530–31	Gold. Fleece	500	Surat	8,195	26,251
	Loy. Merchant	550	,,	10,000	28,822
	Rainbow	380	,,	7,000	18,258
	Mediterran. M.	240	,,	3,414	11,695

1672–73.

Ref. for Exports.	Ship.	Tonnage.	Destination.	Money.	Goods.
L. Bk. V, 22, 30	London	400	No mention	Not	18,026
C. Bk. 25*a*, p. 113	President	500		given	23,201
	Sampson	380			16,949
	Cæsar	500			20,225
	Ann	450			19,567
	Bombay M.	370			16,342
	Massingbird	430			19,814
	E. I. Merchant	400			17,159
	Unity	320			15,127
	Antelope	380			16,202

1673–74.

Ref. for Exports.	Ship.	Tonnage.	Destination.	Money.	Goods.
L. Bk. V, pp. 93–94, 114–15, 118	Advice	100	Bay		211
	Loy. Merchant	580	Coast & Bay	27,977	31,533
	Phœnix	400	,, ,,	24,777	27,557
	Lancaster	450	,, ,,	24,764	27,978
	Falcon	370	Surat	10,662	18,228
	Gold. Fleece	500	,,	16,858	32,300
	Mary	320	,,	13,970	23,417
	Rainbow	360	,,	14,873	26,212
	Eagle	500	Bantam	10,000	10,914
	Jonah	500	,,	8,000	88,000
	Surat M.	300	,,	8,000	8,150
	Berkley Cast.	500	,,	6,000	6,000
	Expectation	380	Fort	12,038	13,239

1674–75.

Ref. for Exports.	Ship.	Tonnage.	Destination.	Money.	Goods.
L. Bk. V, pp. 140, 144–45, 162, 173–74	Barnardistan	340	Bantam	Not given	£18,460
	London	400	,,	£4,000	4,858
C. Bk. 25*a*, p. 139	Cæsar	500	,,	15,000	16,833
	Unicorn	360	,,	8,500	8,500
	Ann	440	Fort	26,173	30,199
	Success	460	,,	39,340	43,876
	Loy. Subject	470	,,	32,060	37,027
	Bombay M.	370	,,	28,974	31,871
	Unity	320	,,	29,309	32,374
	Sampson	350	,,	24,859	27,359
	Ann	360	Surat	17,299	35,642
	New London	540	,,	26,370	47,313
	Massingbird	480	,,	21,273	42,823
	E. I. Merchant	370	,,	15,471	30,352
	Unicorn	360	,,	18,889	33,061

1675–76.

Ref. for Exports.	Ship.	Tonnage.	Destination.	Money.	Goods.
L. Bk. V, pp. 218–19, 250	Eagle	525	Fort	48,506	56,453
	Johanna	515	,,	48,959	57,137
C. Bk. 25*a*, p. 140	Falcon	380	,,	34,713	41,586
	Surat Mert.	390	,,	42,733	42,733
	Mary	330	Fort & Bantam	37,454	37,454
	Lancaster	470	Bantam	10,000	11,781
	Phœnix	450	,,	9,000	9,876
	Loy. Merchant	580	,,	11,000	11,909
	Expectation	470	,,	8,993	10,084
	Formosa	200	,,	Not	8,104
	President	520	,,	given	8,141
L.Bk.V,pp.266–88	Berkley Cast.	490	Surat	12,124	37,582
	Nathaniel	550	,,	14,726	40,664
	Society	550	,,	13,508	37,644
	Persia Mert.	360	,,	7,739	17,606
	Scipio Afric.	390	,,	8,339	20,037

1676–77.

Ref. for Exports.	Ship.	Tonnage.	Destination.	Money.	Goods.
L. Bk. V, pp. 376–77, 390, 401, 413–15	Cæsar	500	Fort & Bay	48,019	58,354
	New London	540	,, ,,	48,091	57,878
	Bengala M.	500	,, ,,	51,426	60,451
	Success	460	Surat	10,084	34,655
	George	500	,,	9,881	39,750
	Ann	449	Bantam	8,000	8,381
	E. I. Merchant	370	,,	6,000	6,245
	Bombay M.	370	,,	7,790	22,536
C. Bk. 25*a*, p. 155	Loy. Subject	470	,,	Not given	
	Barnardistan	380	,,		
	Unity	320	,,		
	Gold. Fleece	500	,,		

1677–78.

Ref. for Exports.	Ship.	Tonnage.	Destination.	Money.	Goods.
L. Bk. V, pp. 509–10, 536–37, 559	Falcon	380	Fort & Bay	25,706	40,646
	Williamson	600	,, ,,	59,253	63,575
	Society	570	,, ,,	55,886	61,072

Ref. for Exports.	Ship.	Tonnage.	Destination.	Money.	Goods.
	Nathaniel	570	Fort & Bay	£57,320	£61,445
	Sampson	600	Surat	28,748	50,653
	President	560	,,	26,123	44,143
	Unicorn	320	,,	16,004	30,688
	Eagle	600	Bantam	5,000	6,241
	Johanna	600	,,	5,000	5,309
C. Bk. 25*a*	Phœnix	450	,,		
	Expectation	450	,,		
	Lancaster	500	,,	Not given	
	Berk. Castle	540	,,		
		1678–79.			
L. Bk. VI, pp. 4, 22–23, 58–59, 80	Loy. Subject	550	Bantam	25,000	33,571
	Cæsar	600	,,	12,014	14,609
	Success	525	Fort	63,237	63,611
	Gold. Fleece	580	,,	69,696	69,989
	George	520	,,	69,237	69,799
	Bengal Mert.	525	Surat	40,748	52,851
	Ann	430	,,	20,657	30,423
	New London	530	,,	40,294	52,873
		1679–80.			
L. Bk. VI, pp. 110, 125, 138–39 128, 163, 194	Sampson	600	Fort & Bay	61,960	72,622
	Berk. Castle	630	,, ,,	54,670	62,287
	President	550	,, ,,	57,818	65,257
	Eagle	500	Fort	61,395	68,602
	Williamson	590	Surat	36,530	45,940
	Johanna	500	,,	33,785	40,609
	Lancaster	470	,,	29,315	36,462
	Falcon	380	Bantam	25,000	37,689
	Nathaniel	600	,,	16,000	16,723
	Society	600	,,	15,000	15,020
		1680–81.			
L. Bk. VI, pp. 224, 261–62, 277, 305–6	Barnardistan	350	Bantam–Amoy	27,000	42,997
	New London	530	Bantam	9,000	14,225
	Persia Mert.	360	,,	6,000	10,987
C. Bk. 32, p. 82	Bengal Mert.	570	Fort	76,257	81,556
	Gold. Fleece	500	,,	73,123	75,210
	Cæsar	600	,,	70,488	72,880
	Ann	440	Bengal	61,483	63,991
	George	580	,,	76,346	79,505
	Success	500	Surat	39,811	49,862
	Josiah	570	,,	46,437	57,942
	Massingbird	430	,,	38,253	47,533
		1681–82.			
L. Bk. VI, p. 399	Scipio Afr.	430	China & Fort	12,000	15,721
,, 363–64, 372	Amoy Mert.	310	,, ,,	20,000	26,979
	China Mert.	170	Bantam	None	335
	Oaklander	150	,,	4,000	7,857
	Kent	130	,,	4,000	7,428

Ref. for Exports.	Ship.	Tonnage.	Destination.	Money.	Goods
L. Bk. VI., pp. 390, 392	Tonqueen M.	130	Bantam		
,, 485, 489, 506	E. I. Mert.	370	,,		
,, 501	Surat Mert.	390	,,		
,, 467	Sampson	600	Surat		
,, 439	Falcon	400	,,		
,, 513	Persia M.	360	,,	£17,501	£24,855
	President	560	,,	26,147	32,213
	Barnardistan	380	,,		
	Loy. Eagle	250	,,	29,251	46,117
	Berk. Castle	650	,,	10,110	12,252
,, 429–30	Defence	650	Bay	87,985	100,920
	Resolution	650	,,	109,038	118,519
,, 403	Lancaster	550	,,		
,, 408	Johanna	600	Coast		
,, 439	Welfare	250	,,		
,, 447	Nathaniel	600	,,		
,, 451, 453	Williamson	600	,,		
,, 389–90	Dragon	180	Persia		
,, 472, 476	Crown		Permission ship		
	William & Jn.		,,		

1682–83.

Reference.	Ship.	Tonnage.	Destination.
L. Bk. VI, p. 530	Charles	370	Surat
,, VII, pp. 75–81 ;	Laurell	250	Surat & Mocha
C. Bk. 33, p. 30 ;	Prudent Mary	350	Bay
Marine J., No. 78	Rainbow	250	Mocha–Surat
	Caroline	315	China
	Smyrna M.	190	,,
L. Bk. VII, pp. 7, 12	Kempthorn	640	Bantam
,, VI, p. 536	Society	600	Bay
C. Bk. 33, pp. 25, 30, 71, 88, 127; L. Bk. VII, pp. 99, 102	New London	550	Coast
	Herbert	650	Bay
L. Bk. VII, pp. 104, 126, 128	Josiah	570	Coast
	Gold. Fleece	560	Bay
	George	570	,,
C. Bk. 33, pp. 69, 74 ; L. Bk. VII, p. 124	Mexico M.	200	Siam
C. Bk. 33, p. 69 ;	Wm. & Herbert	240	China
L. Bk. VII, p. 119	Delight	100	,,
C. Bk. 33, pp. 88, 90 ; L. Bk. VII, p. 109	Hare	500	Bay
	Hy. & William	500	,,
C. Bk. 33, p. 9	Maryland	300	not confirmed by L. Bk.

1683–84.

Reference.	Ship.	Tonnage.	Destination.
C. Bk. 33, pp. 137, 154	Massingbird	450	Surat & Persia
,, ,, 137	Success	480	Surat
,, ,, 159	Anne	460	,,
,, ,, 137	Scipio Afr.	430	,,
,, ,, 149	Coast Frig.	250	,,
,, ,, 189	Bengal M.	570	,,
,, ,, 164	Cæsar	530	,,
,, ,, 164, 186, 189	Rochester	775	,,

Reference.	Ship.	Tonnage.	Destination.
	E.I. Merchant	370	Surat
C. Bk. 33, pp. 135, 164, 186	Beaufort	775	,,
,, ,, 211, 223, 233	Asia	600	(Assumed) Surat and Maldives
,, ,, p. 211	Sampson	600	Surat
L. Bk. VII, p. 287	Nathaniel	600	,,
	Falcon	370	,,
,, ,, 287	Barnardistan	350	,,
,, ,, 320	Williamson	590	,,
,, ,, pp. 142, 164, 186	Society	600	,,
,, ,, p. 294	Bengal Sloop	150[1]	Bombay
,, ,, pp. 139, 145, 178	Charles II	370	Bantam
,, ,, p. 164	China Mert.	170	,,
,, ,, 164	Roy. James	650	Coast & Bay
,, ,, pp. 155, 211	Resolution	650	,, ,,
,, ,, 211, 225, 253	Eagle	600	,, ,,
,, ,, 211, 225	Defence	650	Bay
,, ,, 164, 186	Amoy Mert.	310	Coast
,, ,, p. 273	Jn. & Mary	300[1]	Coast & Bay
C. Bk. 33, p. 223	Syam Mert.	200[1]	Bay
,, p. 211; L. Bk. VII, p. 321	Tonqueen Mert.	130	Madagascar, Bay and Persia
	1684–85.		
Marine Misc., IV	Mary	150	Fort
C. Bk. 34, p. 20	Kempthorn	640	Fort & Bay
	Chandois	660	,, ,,
	Persia Mert.	370	Bay
,, ,, pp. 20, 59	George	570	,,
,, ,, p. 83	Josiah	620	,,
,, ,, 20	Shrewsbury	360	,,
,, ,, 35	Prudent Mary	350	Surat
,, ,, pp. 59, 62	Welfare	250	,, Private ship
Marine Misc., IV	Loy. Adventure	220	,,
C. Bk. 34, p. 59	Kent	130	,,
,, ,, ,,	Scipio Afr.	430	,,
,, ,, pp. 80–81	Charles	370	Borneo
,, ,, p. 36	Dragon	180	Tonqueen
	1685–86.		
L. Bk. VIII, pp. 60–61, 98, 136	New London	510	Surat Cf. His Majesty's
	Worcester	220	,, Commission to 19
Marine Misc., IV	Modena	775	,, ships for war with
	Charles II	775	,, the Mogul
	Emerald	103	,,
,, ,, p. 71	Nathaniel	550	Coast & Bay
	Nathaniel Frig.	100	,, ,,
	Success	480	,, ,,
	Rochester	775	,, ,,
,, ,, p. 71	Rochester Frig.	100	,, ,,
	Beaufort	775	,, ,,
,, p. 71	Beaufort Frig.	100	,, ,,
,, ,, pp. 92–93	Curtana	140	,, ,,
,, ,, ,,	Rebecca	170	,, ,,
,, ,, ,,	Saphire	320	,, ,,

[1] Tonnage is assumed.

Reference.	Ship.	Tonnage.	Destination.
Marine Misc., IV, pp. 92–3	Pearl	80	Coast & Bay
	Loy. Captain	150	Priaman & Bay
	Rose	120	,, ,,
,, ,, p. 19	Roy. James	650	,, ,,
	Diamond	80	Priaman
	Ruby	80	,,
,, ,, p. 30	Pryaman	150	,,
	Herbert	750	Tonqueen
	Rainbow	250	,,
	1686–87.		
Marine Misc., IV	Bengal Mert.	570	Coast & Bay
L. Bk. VIII, p. 232	Williamson	590	,, ,,
,, ,, 238	Resolution	650	,, ,,
,, ,, 276	Bowden	150	Surat
,, ,, 232	Cæsar	500	,,
,, ,, 263	Jonas Frig.	80	,,
	Berk. Castle	650	Priaman
	Carolina	200[1]	,,
	Orange	350	,,
	Welfare	260	,,
L. Bk. VIII, p. 266	Welcome		Private ship
	Andalusia		,, ,,
,, ,, 302	Blessing		,, ,,
	Beare		,, ,,
	1687–88.		
L. Bk. VIII, p. 319	Roy. James & Mary	670	Bombay
,, ,, pp. 393, 408	John & Mary	200	Surat
,, ,, p. 522	Shrewsbury	360	Bombay
	Josia	620	,, (Josia's former name was Society)
,, ,, 448	Princess of Denmark	670	Coast & Bay
,, ,, 480	Defence	730	,,
C. Bk. 35, p. 34	James	300	,, Private.
L. Bk. VIII, p. 512	Anne	120	,, £36,000 in
Marine Misc., IV	Dorothy	225	,, money
L. Bk. VIII, p. 346	Loy. Mert.	450	Priaman
,, ,, 475	Mary	150	Bencoolen Private ship
,, ,, 516	Persia Mert.	370	,, ,, ,,
,, ,, 452	Rainbow	250	Tonqueen
,, ,, 351	Little James	80	China
	1688–89.		
L. Bk. VIII, p. 544	Diana	170	Bombay
Marine Misc., IV	Kempthorn	640	,,
	Chandois	660	Fort
C. Bk. 35, pp. 248, 296	Rochester	775	,,
,, ,, p. 140	Crown		Permission ship
,, ,, p. 140	Endeavour		,, ,,

[1] Tonnage is assumed.

1689–90.[1]

Reference.	Ship.	Tonnage.	Destination.
Marine Misc., IV	Benjamin	468	St. Helena & Bombay
,, ,,	Herbert	750	Bombay
C. Bk. 35, pp. 228, 244	Loy. Mert.	450	Permission ship

1690–91.

Reference.	Ship.	Tonnage.	Destination.
Marine Misc., IV	Wm. & Mary	170	Bombay
,, ,,	Orange Tree	350	Bencoolen
L. Bk. IX, p. 117	King William	800	Bombay
C. Bk. 36, pp. 33, 39, 225	Dorothy	225	Fort
L. Bk. IX, p. 127	Tonqueen M.	130	Bencoolen
,, ,, 142	Defence	650	China
C. Bk. 36, p. 16	James	300	Permitted ship

1691–92.

Ships mentioned below in italics were captured by the French during 1693 to 1695. Five ships more were lost up to May, 1698.

Reference.	Ship.	Tonnage.	Destination.
England's Almanack	Little Josiah	200[2]	
C. Bk. 36, p. 188	Samuel	200[2]	
,, ,, 69	Charles II	780	Bay
,, ,, 60	Samson	600	
,, ,, 69	*Berk. Castle*	650	Surat
,, ,, 69	*Modena*	800	,,
,, ,, 88	Elizabeth	280	

1692–1693.

Reference.	Ship.	Tonnage.	Destination.
C. Bk. 36, pp. 69, 178	Resolution	670	Fort
England's Almanack	America M.	240	
C. Bk. 37, p. 10	*Prince Ann*	670	
	Roy. James & M.	670	
	Hawk	400	
	Defence	750	Surat

1693–94.

Reference.	Ship.	Tonnage.	Destination.
England's Almanack	*Seymore*	200	Private ship, Co.'s share in it
	Henry	350	
C. Bk. 37, p. 10	*Success*	400	Coast & Bay
,, 36, pp. 180, 196, 211, 213, 218, 220, 228, 232	Mary	420	Persia & Bengal
	Nassau	520	Persia & Surat
	Dorothy	200	Amoy–England
L. Bk. IX, p. 342	London Frig.	350	Coast
	Thomas	400	Surat
	Amity	120	St. Helena & Bencoolen
	Martha	700	Coast & Bay

1694–95.

Reference.	Ship.	Tonnage.	Destination.
L. Bk. IX, p. 372	Mocha Frig.	150	Mocha & Surat
C. Bk. 37, pp. 108–9	*Sarah*	340	(assumed)
L. Bk. IX, p. 342	Benjamin	470	Surat
C. Bk. 36, p. 296	Tonqueen M.	280	,,
,, 37, p. 10	Fleet Frig.	280	Bengal
	America M.	240	Surat
,, 36, p. 264	King William	720	Fort
,, ,, 258	*Russel Frig.*	350	,,

[1] The returns of ships for the years 1689 to 1700 detailed here differ from those of the Rawlinson MS. A 302 of the Bodleian Lib. I have given the sources of my figures, and hence the list of that MS. must be incomplete. [2] Tonnage is assumed.

1695–96.

Reference.	Ship.	Tonnage.	Destination.
C. Bk. 37, p. 33	*Defence*	650	
,, ,, ,,	*Hawke*	400	
,, 36, p. 298	*Jn. & Express*	200[1]	
England's Almanack	Dorill	300	Surat
C. Bk. 37, p. 33	Chambers Frig.	350	Coast & Bay
	Charles II	780	Gombroon and Surat
	Sceptre	360	Surat & Bombay
	Antelope	470	
	Maynard	200[1]	
	Sampson	600	Coast & Bay

The names of ships in italics in the years 1694–5 and 1695–6 have been added by me to the list given in the England's Almanack. The *Edward* of 500 tons ought to be included, as it returned from India in June, 1695 (C. Bk. 37, p. 10.)

1696–97.

Reference.	Ship.	Tonnage.	Destination.
England's Almanack	Sedgwick	100	Fort
	E.I. Mert.	450	Surat & Bombay
	Madras	250	Bay
	Sidney	500	,,
	Amity	120	China

1697–98.

Reference.	Ship.	Tonnage.	Destination.	
England's Almanack	Tavistock	750	Fort–China	
	Dorothy	225	Surat & Bencoolen	
	Bedford	750	Surat	
	Nassau	400	China	
	Trumball	250	,,	
	Duke of Glou.	400[1]		
	London Frig.	350		
	Sarah Gal.	340		
	Martha	625	Coast & Bay	
	Anna	350	Bay	
	Fame	120	Coast & Bay	
	Eagle	240	China	Private ship
	Thorndon	500	Coast & Bay	
	Wm. & Richmond	220	Borneo	Private ship
	Thomas	380	Surat & Bay	
	Mary	400	Surat	Private ship
	Mary	350	Bombay	
	Russel Frig.	330	Bombay	
	Shrewsbury	180	Surat	Private ship

1698–99.

Ref. for Exports.	Ship.	Tons.	Destination.	Cargoes.
Aug.	Buckhurst (p)	300	Muscat	Not found
Sept., L. Bk. X, p 138	Northumberland (o)[2]	250	Bombay	£32,799 18 6
Nov. ,, ,,	Fleet Frigate (o)	280	China	37,554 3 7
,, ,,	Benjamin (o)	450	Fort	50,856 13 11
,, ,,	Josiah (o)	400	Bay	61,912 18 0
Dec. ,, ,,	Sidney (o)	500	,,	91,398 11 9

[1] Tonnage is assumed.

[2] The figures of exports are somewhat different for the Old Co.'s ships in L. Bk. X, pp. 411–12.

Ref. for Exports.	Ship.	Tons.	Destination.	Cargoes.		
Dec., L. Bk. X., p. 138	Gracedew (o)	300	Bay	£34,385	11	5
Jan. ,, ,, ,,	Neptune (o)	275	Fort	29,944	14	5
,, XI, p. 36	London (n)	400	Coast & Bay	64,691	2	9
,, X, p. 138	Armenian Mert. (o)	220	St. Helena	7,925	12	4
,, XI, p. 36	Antelope (n)	468	Bay	62,931	8	11
Feb. ,, X, p. 138	E.I. Mert. (o)	450	,,	36,299	16	5
,, ,, ,,	Sceptre (o)	300	Fort	32,869	4	0
,, XI, p. 36	Degraves (n)	520	Coast & Bay	49,981	9	8
,, ,, ,,	Macclesfield (n)	280	China	Not stated		
,, X, p. 138	Bedford (o)	750	Surat	82,764	7	8
,, ,, ,,	Hampshire (o)	400	,,	41,697	18	8
,, XI, p. 47	Montague (n)	410	,,	47,771	1	0
,, X, p. 173	Ruby (o)	450	Persia & Bombay	40,653	7	1
,, XI, p. 57	Julian (n)	260	Borneo	8,703	13	10
	1699–1700.					
L. Bk. XI, p. 61	Norris (n)	520	Surat	39,615	13	1
,, X, p. 173	Frederick (o)	350	,,	42,351	6	5
,, ,, 226	Loyal Mert. (o)	400	Bombay	40,000	0	0
,, XI, p. 76	Rook Frig. (n)	250	Surat	39,136	0	0
,, ,, 99	Trumball (n)	300	Borneo & China	13,074	0	0
	Herne (p)	200	India	—		
	Gosfright (p)	300	China	—		
Cf. L. Bk. X, p. 311	Dorrell (o)	240	Fort & China	38,126	0	0
	Wentworth (o)	350	,, ,,	38,080	0	0
	K. William (o)	600	Fort	71,350	0	0
C. Bk. 38, p. 99	Chamber Frig. (o)	350	Bay	51,655	0	0
L. Bk. X, p. 311	Madras (o)	250	Bombay	6,300	0	0
	Howland (o)	400	Fort	45,677	0	0
	Fame (o)	420	Bay	69,377	0	0
,, ,, 279	Colchester (o)	400	Fort & Bay	68,885	0	0
,, ,, 279	Anna (o)	350	Bay	32,994	0	0
,, ,, 312	Tavistock (o)	750	Surat	73,713	0	0
,, XI, p. 115	Eaton (n)	340	China	3,500	0	0
	Tuscan Gal. (n)	220	Coast & Bay	—		
,, ,, 135	Tankerville (n)	430	,, ,,	66,950	0	0
,, ,, 146	Sommers (n)	480	,, ,,	35,565	0	0
,, ,, 147	Panther (n)	350	Borneo	4,415	0	0
,, ,, 157	Liampo (n)	160	Japan	3,786	0	0
,, ,, 172	Canterbury (n)	350	Fort	24,898	0	0
,, ,, 184	Albemarle (n)	350	Surat	34,177	0	0
	1700–1701.					
	Old Company's Ships.					
L. Bk. X, p. 312	Martha	550	Surat	£61,754		
C. Bk. 38, pp. 191, 205	Nathaniel	250	,,	15,000[1]		
,, ,, 125, 135	Advice Frig.	130	Fort	10,000[1]		
,, ,, 186, 188	Phœnix	400	,,	50,000[1]		
L. Bk. X, p. 424	Dashwood	320	Coast & Bay	40,000		

"p" denotes Private ships. "o" denotes Old Co.'s ships. "n" denotes New Co.'s ships. The figures of exports are somewhat different for the Old Co.'s ships in L. Bk. X, pp. 411–12.

[1] Money.

Ref. for Exports.	Ship.	Tons.	Destination.	Cargoes.
C. Bk. 38, pp. 165, 173	Bedford	750	Bay	£100,000
,, ,, ,,	Sidney	475	China & Coast	90,000
,, ,, ,,	Northumberland	250	,, ,,	35,000
,, ,, ,,	Hampshire	375	,, ,,	60,000
,, ,, p.196	Loyal Cooke	330	,, ,,	42,313
,, ,, pp.183, 188	Dutchess	450	,, ,,	60,000
,, ,, ,,	Josiah	500	China & Bay	90,000

New Company's Ships.

Ref. for Exports.	Ship.	Tons.	Destination.	Cargoes.
L. Bk. XI, p. 202	Borneo[1] }	600	Borneo	3,374
,, ,, 211	Rising Eagle }		Bay	40,000[2]
,, ,, 233	Seaford	240	China	31,203
,, ,, 228	Discovery	500	Mocha	6,367
,, ,, 246	Sarah Gal.	275	China	50,611
,, ,, 246	China Mert.	170	,,	20,923
,, ,, 233	Rising Sun	140	,,	15,673
,, ,, 260	Streathem	350	Coast & Bay	84,161
,, ,, 253	Neptune	260	China	36,485
,, ,, 275	Bengal Mert.	390	Coast	80,965
,, ,, 278	Degrave	300	Coast & Bay	66,709
,, ,, 291	Katherine	495	Bay	12,000
,, ,, 285	Sussanna	350	Surat	33,583

1701–1702.

Old Company's Ships.

Ref. for Exports.	Ship.	Tons.	Destination.	Cargoes.
C. Bk. 38, pp. 220–21	Herne	150	Bombay	Not given
,, ,, 202	Loyal Bliss	350	Surat	,,
,, ,, 220, 225	Armenian Mert.	200	Bencoolen	5,000[2]
,, ,, 233, 241	Aurangzeb	450	China & Surat	—
,, ,, ,,	Chamber Frig.	350	China & Fort	—
,, ,, 347, 352	Fleet Frig.	270	China & Surat	30,000[2]
,, ,, 285, 348	Colchester	450	Fort	50,000
,, ,, ,,	Wentworth	350	Bay	60,000

New Company's Ships.

Ref. for Exports.	Ship.	Tons.	Destination.	Cargoes.
L. Bk. XI, p. 293	Rebou	150	Surat	13,947
,, ,, 297	Upton Gal.	180	Bay	29,551
,, ,, 373	Tankerville	600	,,	96,961
,, ,, 393	Norris	600	Bay & Coast	110,200
,, ,, 329	Arabia Mert.	300[1]	Mocha	6,491
,, ,, 388	Leghorn Frig.	170	Borneo	No stock
,, ,, 384	Panther	350	,,	16,397
,, ,, 399	Edward & Dudley	300	,,	4,982
,, ,, 401	Herne Frig.	200	,,	4,939
,, ,, 317	Macclesfield Frig.	310	China	4,366
,, ,, 342	Halifax	350	,,	40,889
,, ,, 358	Macclesfield Gal.	250	,,	35,936
,, ,, 335	Canterbury	333	,,	34,423
,, ,, 353	Robert & Nathaniel	230	,,	35,640
,, ,, 353	Union	140	,,	29,743

[1] Tonnage is assumed. [2] Money.

1702–1703.

New Company's Ships.

Ref. for Exports.	Ship.	Tons.	Destination.	Cargoes.
L. Bk. XI, p. 415	Katherine	495	Surat	£41,190
,, ,, 417	Mary	468	,,	35,298
,, ,, 407	Samuel & Anna	300	Borneo	2,500

United Company's Ships.

Ref. for Exports.	Ship.	Tons.	Destination.	Cargoes.
C. Bk. 38, p. 323	Howland	400	Surat	60,000
,, ,, pp. 369, 418	Regard	230	,,	10,000
L. Bk. XII, p. 112	Mary	300	Borneo	4,184
,, ,, 119	Seaford	240	,,	3,129
,, ,, 89	Queen	320 }	Bencoolen	16,016
,, ,, 89	Anna	350 }	,,	,,
Marine, 765A	Rapier	—	,,	
C. Bk. 39, p. 12	Gloucester Frig.	350	,,	6,000
L. Bk. XII, p. 6	Northumberland	250	China & Bay	16,345
,, ,, 16	Sidney	400	China & Fort	20,195
,, ,, 25	Montague	400	China & Surat	16,504
,, ,, 36	Streathem	350	China & Mocha	10,097
,, ,, 49	Dutchess	450 }	Bay	30,000
Marine, 593A	Tavistock	750 }	Fort	

1703–1704.

Ref. for Exports.	Ship.	Tons.	Destination.	Cargoes.
L. Bk. XII, p. 128	Josiah	500	Surat	40,103
,, ,, 154	Abingdon	400	,,	30,966[1]
,, ,, 258	Westmoreland	340	,,	46,507
,, ,, 227	Martha	550	Coast & Bay	73,768
,, ,, 237	Scipio	350	,, ,,	61,548
,, ,, 222	Neptune	275	,, ,,	47,139
,, ,, 202	Eaton Frig.	350	China & Surat	29,797
,, ,, 184	Loyal Cooke	330	China & Fort	30,061
,, ,, 193	Herne	350	China & Bay	30,043
,, ,, 247	Featherstone	180 }	St. Helena &	4,175
,, ,, 271–73	Cæsar	380 }	Borneo	12,281
,, ,, 267	Loyal Mert.	420	Bencoolen	11,842
,, ,, 279	Dover	180	,,	5,447
,, ,, 213	Donegal	240	Mocha	11,935
,, ,, 166	Kent	350	China	41,449

1704–1705.

Ref. for Exports.	Ship.	Tons.	Destination.	Cargoes.
L. Bk. XII, p. 456	Hampshire	370	Surat & Bencoolen	406[2]
,, ,, 415	Frederick	350	Surat	15,932[2]
,, XIII, p. 347	Europe	300	Surat & Persia	25,938
,, XII, p. 397	Wentworth	350	Bengal	39,573
,, ,, 449	Loy. Hester	350	Bengal & Bencoolen	38,169
,, ,, 387	Somers	480	Fort & Bencoolen	60,727

[1] L. Bk. XIII, p. 347, states the sum to be £39,989.

[2] L. Bk. XIII, p. 347, mentions £57,658 on these two ships.

Ref. for Exports.	Ship.	Tons.	Destination.	Cargoes.
L. Bk. XII, p. 286	Arabia Mert.	150	Mocha	£8,093
,, ,, 357	Catherine	200	Borneo	5,886
,, ,, 328	Loyal Bliss	350	China & England	36,597
,, ,, 300	Todingdon	350	Batavia & China	11,815
,, ,, 439	Phœnix	350	Persia & Bencoolen	26,476
,, ,, 311	Panther	350	Borneo	10,116
,, ,, 314	Nathaniel	250	Bencoolen	2,566
,, ,, 357	Jane Frig.	240	Banjar	4,026
,, ,, 357	Blenheim	280	,,	10,097
	1705–1706.			
L. Bk. XII, p. 557	Indian Frig.	100[1]	Bombay	149
,, ,, 544	Aurangzeb	450	,,	47,215
,, ,, 507	Tankerville	425	Fort	80,819
,, ,, 535	Halifax	350	Bay	55,021
,, ,, 481	Liampo	130	Mocha	8,392
,, ,, 468	Oley Frig.	180	China	28,126
,, ,, 576	Carlton Frig.	275	Borneo	10,855
,, ,, 554	Little London	130	Private ship	3,000
,, ,, 554	Greater London	620	,, ,,	4,000
	1706–1707.			
L. Bk. XII, p. 601	Edward & Dudley	300	Bencoolen	8,941
,, XIII, pp. 48, 54	Rochester	350	,, & Helena	13,158
,, ,, p. 11	Stringer Gal.	220	China & England	23,781
,, ,, 118	Northumberland	250	Borneo	6,926
,, ,, 94	Bombay Frig.	300	Mocha & Bombay	9,119
,, ,, 22	Kent	350	China & Fort	45,680
,, ,, 109	St. George	420	Bay & Fort	73,256
,, ,, 74	Howland	400	,, ,,	73,323
,, ,, 70	Dutchess	430	,, ,,	73,909
	1707–1708.			
L. Bk. XIII, p. 250	Streathem	350	Fort	55,068
,, ,, 251	Litchfield	420	,,	62,499
,, ,, 244	Somers	480	,,	73,193
,, ,, 337	Despatch	110	,,	Advice vessel
,, ,, 284	Herne	350	Bay	55,645
,, ,, 284	Montague	400	,,	59,804
,, ,, 369	Tavistock	650	Bombay	62,689
,, ,, 370	Abingdon	400	,,	32,435
,, ,, 371	Wentworth	350	,,	8,480
,, ,, 373	Westmoreland	320	,,	12,155
,, ,, 136	Scipio	350	Borneo	11,210
,, ,, 159	Anna	350	,,	12,644
,, ,, 185	Donegall	240	China & Mocha	13,610
,, ,, 203	Toddington	230	China & England	36,290
,, ,, 287	Recovery	330	Banjar	11,266
,, ,, 372	Fleet Frig.	320	,,	9,083
,, ,, 171	Herbert Gal.	210	Mocha	10,951

[1] Tonnage is assumed.

The List of the Company's ships which returned home from the Indies as far as the same could be traced from the Records:—

Year.

1601 to 1614. All the ships despatched during these years by the Adventurers of the Separate Voyages, with the exception of the Susan, Ascension, Union and the Trade's Increase, safely returned home.

1615. Hope.

1616. Gift, Lion.

1617. Dragon, Peppercorn, Expedition, Clove, Globe.

1618. Charles, Hope.

1619. Little James, Bull, Anne.

1620. Rose, Lioness, Francis, Supply. (C. Bk. 4, p. 507.)

1621. Royal James, Unicorn. (C. Bk. 5, pp. 94, 97.)

1622. Hart, Roebuck, Charles, Eagle, Star, Palsgrave. (C. Bk. 5, pp. 447, 464.

1623. Lesser James, London, Jonas, Lion. (C. Bk. 6, pp. 1, 22, 93.)

1624. Elizabeth, Dolphin, Exchange. (C. Bk. 7, pp. 42, 85.)

1625. William, Blessing, Ruby, Discovery, Moon. (C. Bk. 7, p. 117.)

1626. Charles, Hart, James Royal, Jonas, Mary, Star, Scout.

1627. Expedition, London, Reformation.

1628. Discovery, Dolphin, Eagle, Morris, Christopher, Palsgrave, William.

1629. Blessing, Exchange, Expedition, Hopewell, Hart, Jonas, Mary, Speedwell, Star.

1630. London.

1631. Charles, Discovery, Jonas, Reformation, Swallow.

1632. London, Palsgrave.

1633. Blessing, Hopewell, James, Jewell, Star, William.

1634. Dolphin, Exchange, Mary.

1635. Jonah, Hart, Swan.

1636. Palsgrave, Reformation, Discovery.

1637. London, William, Jewell.

1638. None.

1639. Swan, Advice, Mary.

1640. Discovery, London, William, Reformation.

1641. Cæsar, Crispian, Jonas, Swan, Hopewell.

1642. Mary, William, London.

1643. Crispian, Aleppo M., Reformation, Ulysses, Blessing.

1644. Mary.

1645. Crispian, Dolphin, William, Blessing.

1646. Eagle, Mary.

1647. William, Ulysses, Dolphin, Endymion.

1648. Mary, Eagle, Greyhound, Antelope.

1649. Golden Fleece, Aleppo M., William, Dolphin, Bonito, Advice, Supply.

1650. Endymion, Blessing, Eagle, Ruth, Greyhound, Farewell, Anne.

1651. Love, William, G. Fleece, Lioness, E.I. Merchant.

1652. Eagle, Aleppo M., Anne, Welcome.

1653. Smyrna Merchant, E.I. Merchant, Love.

1654. None.

1655. Welcome, Katherine, Eagle.

1656. E.I. Merchant, Constant. Mert., Merchant's Adventure.

1657. Three Brothers, Endymion, Mayflower, Eagle.

1658. Constantinople Merchant from Surat; Katherine and Jonathan from the Coast; Coast Frigate, Greyhound, Vine, Peter and Jane from the Coast; Merchant Adventure, Reformation, Two Sisters, William and John, Little Eagle from Surat; and King Fernandez, Dove and Friendship were on their way home. (L. Bk. II, pp. 143, 184; Eng. Fac., pp. 139, 173.)

1659. Blackmore, Eagle, Smyrna Merchant. (L. Bk. II, p. 235.)

INDEX